questions. Society, he wrote, lives exclusively in the minds of its members. Which suggests that it is also democracy and the recognition of justice and freedom that exist in the minds of society's members; the psychoanalyst Erich Fromm alleged these powers to be innate. At times there are failures of democracy, too often in America for my taste, and too often as well in Durkheim's France and Fromm's Germany. But while I understand the Simpson verdict, I am not completely convinced that society, and more precisely justice and democracy, has failed. The treatment of people irrespective of sociological status like class, age, religion, race, sex, and sexual preference is one barometer of democracy. The behavior of people like Mr. Goldman is another.

INTIMATE APPRAISALS

something, quite frankly, my wife and I can't determine. The better she gets has nothing to do with what she earns. Then again, nobody really could quantify what she does. Some ball players performed worse this year than in past years and hence received salary increases. The only connection between this and my wife is that she has to explain the logic of this decision to her students.

There's another similarity, sort of. Baseball players are asked to do commercials and endorsements that pay them additional revenues. My wife is asked to serve on committees, make food for school bake sales and fund raisers, and attend athletic events, concerts, dances, and plays, some of which cost her entry fees. Many of the ball players are proud and stubborn. They refuse to be treated like horse flesh by the media and the public. My wife also is proud and stubborn: She adamantly refuses my suggestion that she charge students for autographing their report cards. She also doesn't spit a lot.

By writing their names, ball players may receive a financial bonus. My wife teaches children how to write their names. Ball players may receive money on top of their salaries in the form of incentive clauses. When my wife teaches children that money isn't everything, some of them look down at their sneakers and giggle. Ball players are protected by unions and agents and every day face the cameras and reporters. My wife is protected by a union and every day faces superiors, parents, and children (her own and other people's). Ball players have unlisted telephone numbers. They have to, otherwise people would pester them and they wouldn't get enough sleep. The public has to learn that they only watch Langston, McGuire, and Jeter, but they don't own them. My wife has to have a listed telephone number because she would get into trouble if people couldn't reach her. And she has to learn that the public not only observes her, but, in some ways, owns her.

While ball players are invited to hundreds of parties a year where they are held in reverence if not awe, my wife gets invitations to school functions where there is little reverence and even less awe, but much discussion of teachers' roles in society, their status, and salary levels. There's also a great deal of talk about baseball players' salaries, which is something else my wife has in common with Todd Zeile, Juan Gonzales, and Scott Brosius.

Actually, my wife has something significant in common with someone named Kent Hrbek who once rejected an offer of $16 million and settled for only $15 million to remain in Minneapolis. Hrbek was honored for his modesty and loyalty. My wife also has been honored for her

Sporting Assets

⌒

THE TALK AROUND BASEBALL these days is that Derek Jeter has signed a contract to play for more than $12 million a year. This means he has something in common with my wife, a public school teacher: He will earn in half a day what she earns in nine and a half months. She already shares something with Mark McGuire and Mark Langston: She earns in nine and a half months what they earn in two days. Some would say this isn't fair, but she doesn't have to change clothes when she goes to work.

I rather like the comparison to Langston. As a pitcher, he has to perform some forty days a year for about one and half hours each time, or sixty hours a year. That's the same number of hours my wife works in seven days. With Barry Bonds my wife shares two things: First, he will earn in one year twice what she will earn in forty years. Second, they both stand less than six feet, two inches.

My wife has other things in common with ball players. Like them, she has a God-given talent that she nurtured through training, discipline, and a great deal of coaching and preparation. Like them, she had to develop her techniques over a period of time when the salary wasn't handsome and the crowds rather small. Like them, she has to face the people who oversee her, judge her, and those who have gripes about her as well as concerns to share with her. Like them, she carries a weight of responsibility on her shoulders. Like them, she has her own locker and a host of children who watch her and wonder how good she's going to be that day. She is lucky in one way, though: She doesn't have to wear knickers.

I suppose a dissimilarity between my wife and people like Cal Ripkin is that what she earns next year is determined by a formula that applies to all her colleagues in the state, whereas what he earns is determined by

INTIMATE APPRAISALS

The Social Writings of Thomas J. Cottle

Thomas J. Cottle

UNIVERSITY PRESS OF NEW ENGLAND

HANOVER AND LONDON

University Press of New England, Hanover, NH 03755

© 2002 by Thomas J. Cottle

All rights reserved

Printed in the United States of America

5 4 3 2 1

Library of Congress Cataloging-in-Publication Data

Cottle, Thomas J.
  The social writings of Thomas J. Cottle / foreword by Robert Coles.
    p. cm.
Includes bibliographical references.
    ISBN 1–58465–141–5 (cloth : alk. paper)—ISBN 1–58465–142–3 (pbk. :
alk. paper)
    1. Psychology. 2. Social psychology 3. Child psychology. I. Title.
BF109.c68 A25 2002
302—dc21   2001007168

For Dr. Robert Coles

CONTENTS

IV. SOCIAL ISSUES

FOREWORD

Robert Coles

Many of us who work in schools and colleges, or who work with patients, have come to admire Tom Cottle's writing, and to appreciate
greatly his wide-eyed interest in people, in their stories, and, as well,
his compelling response to those individuals who have come his way,
and, through him, come our way as well—we who are his lucky readers, for whom he has become an instructive, even inspiring teacher. I
know of no social scientist who has Cottle's range of explorative and
responsive energy: his extraordinary willingness to engage with people, seek from them their experiences, their memories, their hopes and
worries—and then connect all that he has noticed, heard spoken, to
those who read books, and so doing, meet their fellow citizens. In a
sense, then, Cottle is a psychologist who carries his clinical training
and knowledge into the streets of ordinary folks—their homes and
places of work, their children and the schools they attend. He is also a
lively and often lyrical writer who wants to reach us—heart, mind, and
soul—so that we are given pause, second thoughts. Not least, he is, as
he tells us in his helpful and appealing Introduction, a storyteller who
learned as a child the healing and suggestive power to which a story
can be privy. He knows to mention and revere Erik H. Erikson, the
guardian spirit for so many of us—the intellectual pioneer who dared
take psychoanalysis into neighborhoods otherwise beyond its interest
or ken; and I think what Erikson said about psychological and sociological storytelling applies very much to Tom Cottle personally, and
to the clinical research he has done so carefully and earnestly these
past years.

One day, recalling his own attempts to link the lives of children to
the world, and to events that happen in their young minds, their
emerging sensibilities (as in *Childhood and Society,* whose very title

made an urgent, demanding statement), Erikson arched back in his office chair, looked at his bookcase, with its many volumes by Freud, and then talked not of the past, often his wont, but of the years ahead:

I hope that in the future we have many young psychologists and psychiatrists who are interested in going a little beyond the "psychopathology of everyday life" [the title of one of Freud's first books]—who are interested in everyday life as it can shape psychopathology. I'm being a little murky here, or ironic, but I'm trying to remind myself constantly that we inherit our problems from our family life, yes, but we do go from day to day, in the neighborhood whose distinctive life is its own—so, the issue is not only the passage of time and of events that happen, but also the specific events that take place here, rather than there, and for this reason or that reason. The long and short of it—of what I'm trying to get at—is that all of us live our own everyday lives, depending upon the country that is ours, and our place or situation in that country, and (I keep reminding myself) depending upon the time that is ours, the moment of history we call our very own.

Such words well deserve to be linked with those of Tom Cottle's, he who gave us *Time's Children,* and he who has made sure that he converses continually with a broad range of individuals in such a way that their human particularity is affirmed, is given its necessary and confirmed chronicle. In the pages that follow, we keep meeting, it can be said, Cottle's various informants—those whose stories he chooses to render, to tell in their various details. Those informants become ours, to the point that a book such as this ends up being a round-up, a lineup, of vivid, knowing, fellow individuals, who in their sum turn into a group of teaching companions, each one of them able to carry us forth, hand us along, through the assistance of the attentive observer, the persuasively arresting writer, Tom Cottle (his words energized by their words). To return to Erik H. Erikson, now speaking as he was working on his last major psychoanalytic study, *Gandhi's Truth:*

Sure, it's helpful to learn from the great figures of history, but we shouldn't forget those who looked up to them—we should know why [they did] and we should know what *they* taught their great leaders, who, after all, have to take the measure of those who follow them. By "take the measure" I don't mean take a poll, or a survey; I mean the human measure—which we do through listening to one another. That is, needless to say, the heart of psychoanalysis: speakers and listeners embracing a mutual path of discovery (of one another, of themselves), and that can be the heart of good writing, also—authors' helping us to know ourselves.

In that spirit, Tom Cottle's latest book invites us on a journey of inwardness, of recognition and self-recognition—his descriptive and evocative writing, always vigorous and summoning, claims us, prods us to take heed and care—so that, finally, we readers become the grateful recipients of the engaging thoughtfulness, the heartfelt social wisdom, which the pages ahead abundantly offer.

ACKNOWLEDGMENTS

There is no way to properly thank all of the people who have helped and guided me, not to mention worked to improve my thinking and writing over the course of several decades. Mere mention of their names hardly captures my appreciation and gratitude.

In the beginning were my teachers at the Francis W. Parker School in Chicago, Harvard University, the University of Chicago, The Tavistock Clinic, Children's Hospital in Boston, and the Hampstead Child Therapy Clinic in London. In addition, let me single out David Riesman, Erik H. Erikson, Anna Freud, Marian Wright Edelman, George Gardner, John Bowlby, Edward Shils, Fred Strodtbeck, David C. McClelland, Jacob W. Getzels, Merton Kahne, Benson R. Snyder, and Thomas F. Pettigrew.

Then there are my extraordinary colleagues and friends: Sara Lawrence-Lightfoot, Jerome Kagan, Peter Schrag, Philip E. Slater, Gerald M. Platt, Barry O'Connell, Daniel Frank, Craig R. Eisendrath, Oliver W. Holmes, Robert Weiss, Robert and Gail Melson, Michael I. Kessler, Eliot Liebow, David Gottlieb, Joseph Pleck, Jerrold Zacharias, Judah Schwartz, Leslie Dunbar, Joseph Featherstone, Gary Marx, Peter Manning, Stephen L. Klineberg, and Lincoln Caplan.

My newer colleagues and friends at Boston University include Professors Gerald Fain, David Steiner, Victor Kestenbaum, Alan Gaynor, Roselmina Indrisano, Rose Ray, Arthur Beane, Donna Lehr, Leroy Clinton, Kathleen Vaughan, Bruce Fraser, Robert Sperber, Joan Dee, Boyd Dewey, and our former Dean, Edwin J. Delattre.

Over the years I have worked with wonderful editors, among them Alfred Browne, William Phillips, Nelson Aldrich Jr., Eugene Lichtenstein, Theodore Solotaroff, Mariana Fitzpatrick, Leonard Fein, Stephen R. Graubard, Cynthia Merman, Ray Bentley, Paul Houts, and, most recently, Suzanne Stazak-Silva, Clark Dougan, and Christopher Myers.

And always there are our friends, Ruth and Richard Rogers, Patricia and Salvador Minuchin, Anne and Martin Peretz, Anne and Richard Rosenfeld, Paul M. Strudler, Florence Ladd, Richard and Clare Ryan, Brigitte Cazalis and Joseph Collins, and Joan and Robert Weiss.

Then there is our family, Kay M. Cottle, its proper head, Claudia Hinz, Jason E. Cottle, and Sonya R. Cottle, number two son, Dr. Anthony Hinz, our grandchildren Luke Thomas Hinz, Nicolle Kate Hinz, and Anna Carey Hinz, Judy and David Lahm, and, in blessed memory, Eloise and Edwin C. Mikkelsen, Gitta and Maurice H. Cottle, and Leah Weinstock.

This book came about because of the creativity and efforts of my editor, Philip Pochoda. I cannot adequately thank him or his staff, notably Ellen Wicklum and Lisa Sacks for their extraordinary efforts. Writing a book has never been easier, or more flattering.

Finally, the book is dedicated to Dr. Robert Coles who not only showed me the way, but has supported my work again and again as I continue to make requests of him and tax his generosity. I have always told him I will pay him back, but we both know it will never happen. Bob Coles seems to live by the sense of justice proffered by the late Emmanuel Levinas. Constantly he is called, summoned really, to give absolutely. Never does he refuse, and in this manner he emerges as just. How does one ever thank such a person!

Boston, Massachusetts
2001   T. J. C.

INTIMATE APPRAISALS

Introduction

Every great philosophy which, taken as a whole, always says in effect: this is a picture of life as a whole, and learn from it the meaning of your life. And conversely: read only your life, and understand from it the hierogylphs of life in general.

—FREDERICH NIETZSCHE[1]

IT WOULD BE UTTERLY foolish to suggest that I knew from the time I was a child that someday I would become a social scientist. The fact is that from the moment I was able to play baseball I always assumed I would pitch for my beloved Chicago Cubs, Alas, it didn't work out that way. During my adolescence, I did discover the world of psychiatry, but although I found much of the material to be fascinating, I employed my primitive understanding of psychology and psychiatry as a way of maneuvering in my family; psychology provided me with as much armor as insight. To say the least, ours was a complex family; negotiating with terribly sophisticated and powerful parents who believed that readily discernible motives and impulses lay beneath the surface of just about every human action caused me to become a miniature family therapist well before I had earned the slightest credentials.

Several other experiences probably formed my interest in a type of research that ultimately would strike me as intellectually and emotionally congenial. First, essentially because of my mother's rare verbal gifts and theatrical temperament, I grew to love listening to people recount stories, especially her. Almost nothing fascinated me as much as listening to guests sit on my mother's couch and relate all that had happened to them since their last visit to our Chicago home. Granted, many of these people were rather prominent in their respective fields so their stories contained more than intriguing tidbits. Still, whatever their status, when the great storytellers arrived, I found myself sitting in my special chair prepared to listen for hours.

I am certain that these stories resonated with me as well because I was always read to as a child, and although I have only the barest recollection of my mother reading to me—I have no recollections of my father ever engaging in this nightly ritual—I can only guess how marvelous her renditions must have been, for nothing for her was ever life-sized; everything had to be dramatic and exciting. So between the books and the great readers and narrators, my very conception of the world was formed by stories, and their authors.[2] In fact, stories and storytellers became in my mind inseparable; they were the foundation of culture.

Now, although the themes of these stories might involve most any human action that could be shared with others while a child was present and obviously interested in the proceedings, two themes emerged as especially salient. Not surprisingly, they most likely evoked feelings I barely could articulate as a child. The first was sadness. Granted, not many stories told in our family's living room were dominated by this emotion, but there were some. I did hear stories of illness and death— that my father was a physician meant that such stories would be recounted from time to time. Moreover, given my parents' interest in psychoanalysis, a great many people spoke of emotional matters as they came to be played out in the lives of individuals as well as families. As I say, for one reason or another, these certain stories seemed to stay with me, or at least the tone of them did.

The second theme was that of justice. Naturally, as a boy I doubt if I even knew the word, but I surely recognized when things inside and outside my family seemed unfair, particularly if they involved me. My capacity to reason moral matters was probably developing more or less on time, just as Jean Piaget described,[3] but for some reason I kept an eye out for the way the world treated people and gradually found myself feeling a conflation of sadness and anger when I felt that someone had not been treated as I thought he or she should have been.

One thing more seemed to be forming in those childhood days now so long past they seem trapped behind a veil: It was the matter of people judging me, speaking for me, attempting to express my feelings, sentiments, ideas. I remember experiences when this happened, when people assumed they knew what I must have been thinking, or how, presumably, I perceived some event or experience. I hated it, even when they were absolutely right on target. I would have denied anything had I not been the authentic author of it. "Don't tell me I want more apple pie. If I want more apple pie *I'll* tell *you!*"

Decades later, as I look back over research notes, transcriptions with people, young and old, and reread the pieces that appear in this volume, some of which, actually, I haven't examined in years, I tend to see, and hear, some of these same themes, now a trifle more sophisticated in their forms. I see, and hear, my childhood concerns and passions in the words of other people, in the stories that I have collected or, more precisely, been attracted to, and the ways these other people have encouraged me to perceive the world. Said differently, whatever any child's or adult's reading of or take on the world may be, how they perceive and experience truth and then describe this perception or experience, I at least try to honor the notion that their narrative (my childhood narrative) is as valid as anyone else's. Their slant, their data, in other words, no matter how significant or insignificant the world may judge them, or whatever criteria anyone employs to render these judgments and opinions, is as valid as the slant of the powerful figures who tend to construct the myriad definitions of the society in which we all find our selves.

So there it is, I tell myself, as best as I can construct it, the psychological foundation for my work in life studies, individual portraits of people in which I encourage them to tell the stories constituting their best rendering, at least at this point in time, of their internal dramas, their being in the world. Accordingly, I have been struck by researchers who suggest that for all we know, we are little more than the stories we tell. I am struck, too, by Elie Wiesel's notion that we are, perhaps, little more than our memories, many of which, this wise teller of stories suggests, are rather sad. I am struck by the theory undergirding that branch of philosophy known as phenomenology, what psychologists call "perceptual reality,"[4] just as I am by the description of portraiture proffered by Sara Lawrence-Lightfoot and Jessica Hoffmann Davis.[5] And, finally, I am attracted to Robert Kegan's[6] notion that a fundamental purpose, really a defining enterprise of human beings, is that we constantly attempt to make meaning of just about every event that captures any one of our senses.

Funnily enough, with all my training in psychology and psychoanalysis, my work with quite a few people now has convinced me that the social world, the sociological realm, may be as powerful an agent in determining individual personality and behavior as anything the mind will encounter. It is almost as though society exists not only to define the individual self, but serves as well almost as a second skin meant, perhaps, to protect the emerging self and provide the structure for its ultimate integrity. In the same manner, essentially like a second family, society has the power to affirm and provide just as it maintains the power to shame and withhold. We can be uplifted by the social world just as we can be openly neglected, betrayed, and humiliated by it. I suspect that any of these outcomes are felt as keenly by individual selves as the actions of any of their family members.

More generally, the mental representations that we maintain of ourselves and the social world are themselves affected by structures, constant and transitory, in the social world. Salvador Minuchin[7] was wise indeed when he noted that among the individual subsystems constituting the family was the extrafamilial system that defines the family's relationship with the world outside the family. Similarly, in outlining an ecological scheme of human development, Urie Bronfenbrenner[8] imagined the various layers of society—he portrayed them as concentric circles—all contributing to the identity of the emerging self, even those societal layers that the individual rarely if ever contemplated.[9]

All of my inquiries, if this doesn't appear to be circular, turn out to be inquiries of the self and the society by the self that has been influenced by the society. The two constructs, in other words, are practically inseparable; lifelong partners, they constantly redefine one another. In telling a story, therefore, it is the teller who emerges in all of his or her personal *and* social complexity and richness. If the event being described is one of multiple realities, which by definition it inevitably is—for there are always stories within stories and hence truths within truths[10]—if the reading of or "the slant" on self or society changes day by day, or even minute by minute, then so too does the individual self that each of us casts out into the world awaiting a reaction, as well as, perhaps, an intimate appraisal.[11]

Human narratives, alas, are hardly expected to reveal consistency. In fact, if Nietzsche's skepticism is to be accepted, consistency becomes an anthema: "People are nowadays so complex and many sided," Nietzsche wrote, "that they are inevitably insincere whenever they talk, make assertions and try to act accordingly."[12] Every interview, therefore, whether it be conducted over a kitchen table, in a homeless shelter, on a basketball court, in a school bus, or hospital emergency room, is nothing more, nothing less, than the encountering of two selves, or at least the witnessing of one self by another—and is it not the case that as individual selves we often work hard not to be seen?—one of them telling the story (of the self and the society) the other hearing this story of another's self through the lens of one's own ever changing self and conception of society. Thus every interview has at least two stories going on simultaneously, and two gigantic constructs constantly being defined and described. And all of this transpires in both rational and emotional tones. The result is a rather complex symphony, although, because my father was an amateur violinist, I tend to hear it as chamber music, the individual parts clearly distinct if only one can focus on them long enough.

This notion of the emergence of the self and the society simultaneously being explored through the story, calls to mind the idea that early on Aristotle chose to advance as a self-evident truth. Knowledge, Aristotle[13] alleged, is "called up" in us as though it were something that has to be remembered, or, even better, to play on a word, "re-cognized." When, finally, we understand or appreciate something, it is because we have conjoined the new data now being inputted with the old data that have been planted and harvested throughout our lives. Whether it is so-called intellectual, emotional, or sensate knowledge that we appreciate or comprehend, the act of learning something—which surely we do when we tell and listen to stories—means at some level that we are making connections between our interior world and the world of others, what Martin Heidegger[14] called the "with world," the *Mitwelt*. Importantly, it is this *Mitwelt* that shapes our self or sense of self as much as the world Heidegger defined as our purely interior world, the world of the self thrown against itself—he called this realm the *Eigenwelt*—ultimately the realm of our contemplation of consciousness and personal identity.

For both Heidegger and Rollo May, one doesn't *have* relationships as much as one *is* relationships.[15] Which means that in every storytelling session—what I have come to call life studies—in every interview context wherein we attempt to capture the visions and metaphors of the storyteller, in the pursuit of children's or adults' accounts of the way they see the world or feel themselves to be in the world, my own private self is being transformed and ultimately defined in this new "with world." Both of us, teller and witness, in other words, are exercising our voices. The storyteller and I might well disagree on a particular matter, yet irrespective of the content, the very premise of our conversation, our storytelling session is altering each of us and, hence, the world in which we live if only because my life is deeply changed when I offer my self to another who in some way makes an intimate appraisal of it and then offers it, my self now conjoined with the appraisal, back to me for my further appraisal. This is what Lawrence-Lightfoot and Hoffmann Davis appear to be speaking about when they refer to the "verbal canvas" in portraiture work.[16]

Similarly, when I listen and accept even a morsel of the multiple realities constituting the single story—for I know full well the story is far more complex than I shall ever understand or be able to recount, and it will be told differently tomorrow, especially if it is told to another person—my very identity has been affected, as has been that of the storyteller's. For even in quiet listening, really in attending to other persons, we are affirming in that moment their self, and they ours, that is, if we each allow the other to enter those private realms of our own being, what we call the realms of intimacy, where privately but ineluctably we make our own intimate appraisals of self and society.

This then is the basis of the sort of research I suspect a host of people presently are undertaking as they are very often in the world of journalism, where one human being asks another, and often the wording is just about this shadowy, to tell us something of the life they lead, and the ways they view family, society, and culture. The pieces collected in this volume make plain that the foundation of this brand of research rests on my old childlike attraction to good stories, strong emotions, or at least evocations of powerful sentiments. They reveal as well themes of fairness or justice, and people's readings or intimate appraisals of the forces that shape them, or more precisely are called up in them, recognized, as they, like I, attempt to forage about in our minds for pieces of our very selves, or at least bits of information that give meaning to that which we call the self and society.

The fact that these versions necessarily will shift, only naturally brings charges that by definition the research cannot be considered valid. To this I say: Then the notions or constructs of the self and society cannot be considered valid. As they too will change as a function of the realms of the biological—what Heidegger called the *Umwelt*—for surely our brains and bodies are changing. The world with others, Heidegger's *Mitwelt*, is changing. For with each encounter our self undergoes still newer appraisals and thus takes on newer forms, as is the realm of the *Eigenwelt*, the world Heidegger and May designated as the world of the self encountering itself, or what John Dewey[17] might have called the realm of self-reflection, which is always in motion.

In a word, each of the chapters in this book represents an extended moment of self-reflection, a reflection literally about self and those contexts, exterior and interior, that inform and ultimately yield this one moment's appraisal and assessment of self and society. In a sense, as Eliot Liebow observed, the self, really the two selves involved, become the research instruments, the media of the inquiry.[18] By very definition of the enterprise, the chapters are founded on the tenets of subjective inquiry, or more precisely what Jerome Bruner[19] and Donald Polkinghorn[20] have called narrative reasoning, in which the final renderings of thought and description—the story, in other words—is meant only to be lifelike. Verisimilitude is the ultimate calling of the life study; the convincing argument, more likely the product of what Bruner calls paradigmatic thinking, is often not to be found in exercises of narrative reasoning. Its fundamental purpose, its appraisal really, is captured in those phrases I have heard again and again from the storytellers who have offered nothing less than a portion of their selves to me: "Is this really what you want?" "Surely you can't find this interesting?" "What kind of a book are you writing, anyway, where there would be room for this?"

The first section of the book is given over to an examination of life-study research. Just what is it the researcher is doing? What is the purpose of the work, and what are some of the technical problems one encounters? And, finally, how does one justify this form of qualitative inquiry, what Christopher Jencks once described—he was speaking about sociology generally—as slow journalism?

Kegan is probably right: Each of us is seeking to find the meaning of this event or that one, this portion of the culture or that one, this life or that one. We formulate our impressions and observations, just as we attempt to make sense of the emotional evocations arising from some inner caves, often when we least expect them. We typically say that we work hard to keep our emotions in check; we promise ourselves that we won't cry over a particular experience or sensation, just as we once promised our teachers that we would never again laugh at something. But we know we are kidding ourselves. We are going to cry, and we are going to laugh, and we are going to learn that quite often it is in these moments of intense learning and emoting that, for an instant, we have a sense of what those vague, amorphous constructs or metaphors known as the self and the society are all about.[21] It is as though in our telling of a story, we come face-to-face with ourselves, just as the common expression has it. Face-to-face with ourselves, although the experience lasts but an instant, just long enough that we perceive some interior face, just long enough that we are able to render some intimate appraisal, sometimes one that we dare offer to another person. It is partly for this reason that in reflecting on the nature of the interaction between researcher and storyteller, I often fall back on a mispronunciation our youngest daughter once offered: Wishing to say the word, interview, she called it "innerview."

Truthfully, I sometimes cannot discern where the most private moment of the self and the most public moment of the society or culture reveal their boundaries. The marriage of the public and private, the social and the individual, is so intimate one is only fooling oneself to believe that I am really "in here" and the society is really "out there," even though it feels that way. The sociologist Émile Durkheim said it best: Society exists solely in the minds of its members. And, we might add, even when those members are momentarily oblivious to its majesty and power. In fact, we sometimes only feel it when we imagine, somehow, that it is beginning to unravel, or is it our selves that seem to be unraveling? What really is the sensation of injustice? What is it that my self endures upon experiencing something that at some primitive, almost childlike level, I "know" to be unfair. What truly is happening in the world "out there" when those special feelings of sadness, hopelessness and despair overtake me? For I am able to distinguish between dips in moods, even something I may label depression, and something occurring in the public realm that has dragged me down, depressed me, threatened me, assaulted my self and my freedom.

Erich Fromm[22] alleged that a sense of fairness or justice is innate.[23] We are born, in other words, with some template of fair play, the moral way, the ethical pursuit. I am not certain this is so, although no child could possibly escape the experience of injustice, even a child with the most saintly of parents, for at some point, alas, the child will experience his or her first tastes of the "real world." In my own research, I have been drawn to those families where, by dint of social and cultural circumstances, I imagine some form of injustice has been experienced.[24] I confess to being drawn to what Toni Morrison has referred to as "that recipe of American pie in which a society made up of an increasingly toughened crust of rich continues to rest upon and contain the seething, smarting poor . . ."[25] The first obvious place to hunt for such storytellers is in communities of poverty, although the researcher must be careful not to bring too many of his or her own preconceptions and ideologies to these neighborhoods.[26] He or she, in other words, must be mindful not to recount only those stories that document preselected issues and ideologies, predetermined readings and narratives. In the past, I have encountered, been drawn to, really, storytellers of poverty, homelessness, unemployment, conditions of untenantable housing, and woeful medical care. Most, though not all of these stories, contain their elements of injustice, just as they frequently contain elements of humor, good spirit, acceptance, and reconciliation. People everywhere know the wounds of alienation just as they recognize the comforting embrace of belonging.[27]

Early on I was drawn to the stories of children, not because children are, somehow, better storytellers than their elders; they are not. It was only because of their obvious innocence, the fact that circumstances over which they had neither control nor understanding were playing exquisite roles in their emerging destinies. What Nietzsche wrote about animals may well apply to children: "Deeper people at all times have felt sympathy for animals since animals suffer from life and yet do not possess the strength to turn the sting of suffering against themselves or understand their existence metaphysically."[28] I suspect a part of my own long-ago childhood was listening to these children as well, and feeling, perhaps, that same sting.

One cannot hear the story of a child, however, without wanting to track down that child's family. What has his mother to say on this matter, or his father, or grandmother? For that matter, who in his mind constitutes his family? And what are these individuals about to offer up about America? What are their readings and appraisals of a society that allow them to live as they do, or prevent them and their children from living in a manner they insist would suit them better? What are their appraisals of their children, their relatives, and friends, their work, their pasts and futures, their country? What self might they offer up today? And what self might they offer me if I show myself to be a loyal friend who returns to their home again and again, hunting for heaven only knows what beyond a "good story"?

Accordingly, the book's second section is devoted to the children and their families. Quite honestly, I had been undertaking life study research for years before I found myself able to articulate what it was I was actually doing. The work more or less commenced decades ago in a conversation with a boy on Prospect Street in Cambridge, Massachusetts, one hot autumn afternoon. I had recently arrived in Boston following graduate work steeped in quantitative research methods and fascinated with the way computers could generate results that had to impress, not that I ever fully understood what, mathematically, correlations, analyses of variance and covariance actually meant. But I didn't care because my heuristic inquiries were being transliterated into glorious numbers that the computer further transformed into significantly statistical findings. And that, after all, was the goal of the entire enterprise: Statististically significant findings.

Then I encountered Robert Coles. I had read the works of Erik Erikson, Oscar Lewis, Eudora Welty, James Agee, Jules Henry, Walker Percy, and a host of others, but there was something about this man Coles. First off, he was letting people speak for themselves in his books, and not judging them. Nor was he putting the final word, the final interpretation or "spin" on their messages and narratives. His refusal, furthermore, to instruct the reader what a particular child was "really" saying, indicated his awareness of the asymmetries of the relationships he was establishing with his storytellers, as well as his attempt to abjure control over the outcome of his conversations and the interpretations readers might make of them. After all, as Fenwick English asks, who truly is the final arbiter of a storytelling session or life study?[29] Must it always be the witness?

Second, Coles was letting even children speak for themselves. Not only that, he was allowing their parents to go against politically correct and ideologically laden positions and speak their minds. Then, finally, in the way he wrote about these people, he let the reader see bits and pieces of his own self, pieces that he almost invited us to appraise, and in so doing, caused us to undertake a reappraisal of ourselves. What could be farther from a computer-generated statistic than a woman somewhere in the South patting Robert Coles's leg and saying something like, "You know, Dr. Coles, sometimes I think you don't know what you want to ask me?"

Let me not sound melodramatic, but the early encounters with Robert Coles who, at the time, was one of a group of teaching assistants for Erik Erikson's course at Harvard University on the life cycle, caused a reappraisal of my own forms of sociological inquiry. I see now that his work, like that of Erikson's, Agee's, and then, later on, Kozol, Liebow, Lawrence-Lightfoot, and others, offered permission to fetch those intimate, albeit primitive, elements that defined my boyhood definition of my self. I could be heard in the same way and at the same time that I permitted others to be heard, others, significantly, whose voices were not heard all that often. All I had to do, if Coles's "call to stories," stood as a beacon, was find my special chair and allow the storytellers to speak as long as they wished.

It was not too long after my first encounters with Dr. Coles, called recently by James Carroll, a "compassionate prophet,"[30] that I walked around Cambridge looking for storytellers and met that boy on Prospect Street, not too far from his local basketball court and school. And as if God Himself were trying to confirm that I had made the right move, this fourteen-year-old youth, who was barely understandable, actually, given the adenoidal quality of his speech, began telling me of the most complicated family constellation I had ever heard. His father was long gone, his mother was desperate, his grandparents were confused, his siblings were all over the place. Then, before I could even ask the question, Of all the people in the world, why are you telling *me* all of this? he punctuates his oration with these words: "I guess I got one of those Oedipal things, huh, doc?"

There would be no going back to correlations and analyses of variance. Mere conversations and storytelling sessions were all that I would ever again require. Contrary to a good friend who suggested that this brand of inquiry cannot be considered genuinely qualitative research because I don't always know precisely what I am searching for—something, incidentally, with which I do not agree—I must confess, nonetheless, not always knowing what it is I hunt for, what story I genuinely anticipate hearing.[31] Quite to the contrary. When I know what I wish to hear—as when I purposely play a particular CD rather than take my chances with a radio station—I imagine that the best stuff is that for which I am not prepared, nor, more likely, defended against.

The self loves surprise—Fromm knew this as well. Science allows us to predict outcomes, or at least make logical guesses as to the likelihood of certain results. But Bruner warned that narrative thinking, the form in which we attempt to provide meaning for experiences, permits merely verisimilitude. The great story, the great account reminds us of the humanity rather than the predictability of the self. I never pretend to be making science, and if challenged would probably agree with Michel Foucault's assertion that social science can never really be science;[32] I can replicate nothing, nor make well-founded universal claims. I am never certain whether a period of storytelling concludes with either the teller or the witness feeling that something, or someone, using Foucault's term, has been de-mystified, or further mystified. I cannot be certain that what a person has told me in the morning will be repeated that same evening. My second visit with a child or his or her parent cannot be a reproduction of the first; if it were, the enterprise would be dead. Similarly, I have come to learn that no two children have the same parents. Whatever else takes place, no matter how many pages of dialogue and description one offers, only a minuscule amount of the actual storytelling session has been accounted for, and thus open for careful reflection and intimate appraisal. What could be less universal and mystifying than that!

To elaborate my hunt for the stories of children I travel to their schools, the allegedly good and bad ones, at least as the children and their parents adjudge them.[33] I speak with students, teachers, and administrators, guidance counselors, coaches and custodial staffs. Most recently, I have been tracking down storytellers by asking students to tell me the names of teachers who have mattered to them, hardly a scientific procedure. Then, upon gathering together some of the names that keep cropping up, I speak with these exceptional educators only to learn from them the names of students who have mattered to *them*. Thus the list of storytellers continues to grow.

Not surprising, therefore, the book's third section is devoted to education, observations of schools, and the people who inhabit them. Schools surely are the place where for the first time a child may experience ringing public success or utterly shameful failure.[34] Hubie Jones, at the time head of the Social Work Program at Boston University, once remarked that schools are lifesaving—he used the word redemptive—in the histories of many children. They are indeed, just as they can be destructive. Educators know this; America knows this. The children, too, know this, and speak of it. In Jonathan Kozol's[35] words, because of some schools, and the uncaring, unjust societies in which they conduct their business, there can well be death at an early age.

The book's final section is directed to observations of the society, that second skin or second family of which I have spoken. Throughout the course of my research inquiries, as much as I look forward to meeting with someone with the hope that they may have precious stories for me, precious bits of the self, I dread what comes at the end, or is meant to come at the end of the writing: the interpretation of the data. Irrespective of the sort of exegesis established by Coles and others, there is always the sense that upon completion of the story there must be my final take on it, my interpretation of the narrative or the account, my rendering of verisimilitude conjoined with theirs. What really do these narratives mean, critics have inquired? Surely you aren't going to leave us hanging with the words of someone; there must be an underlying principle or construct you wish to highlight.

For years I harkened back to the idea that an account contains an accounting within it. That is, within one's story is found one's interpretation of its meaning and import. Subjective to be sure, the various narrative components must at least attain a certain (subjective) coherence[36] and possibly, too, a certain esthetic completeness before the teller is sufficiently satisfied. It is not that the storyteller necessarily introduces or concludes the story with his or her program notes or some ingenious explication of the text. Rather, it is my belief that the story's final version in fact represents an accounting as much as it does an account. The meanings, in other words, are captured in the narrative; there is little else for the witness to tell. The final interview—that is, innerview—represents my research notes, my own personal rendering of the account within the account. Besides, might it also be the case that reinterpretation of the narrative only distances the teller from the witness and serves, therefore, not merely as explication but as an act of managing the story as well as the relationship of teller and witness?

In this volume, however, it is my accounting, my take on various subjects that constitutes the individual chapters, the last section of the book being devoted to society at large, or at least those portions that seem relevant to the sorts of matters considered in the earlier sections. Given the work that has occupied me over several decades, it is evident that social stresses and stressors that do anything but safeguard human beings, stressors like poverty, woeful housing, homelessness, mental illness, the lack of medical insurance and adequate medical and dental care, unemployment, domestic violence, and the world of crime, have come to dominate most of the stories I choose to collect.[37] In point of fact, some of the stressors may appear relatively benign: a local school closes; a group of neighborhood children are obliged to ride school buses; a man hunts for a job; a child waits in an emergency room; a woman seeks her birth parents; a family awaits a ruling in the state legislature; a girl is embarrassed by her weight; a boy is confused by the idea of attending his mother's wedding. In all of these instances, society comes forth in the minds and stories of individual people as a complex host for the emerging self. No longer a good custodian of the self, society appears to take a position antithetical to a person or a family, a community or an entire social group.

The theme of society as a second skin or second family lingers with me. One thinks in this context of an essay by Felton Earls and Mary Carlson[38] who, in attempting to define a family, put forth a rather startling definition. For these two authors, a family represents the sum of strategies parents and children together employ to work out matters of security, nurturance, and intimacy. At first blush I was astonished that such thoughtful people had failed to mention love, but then I noted that, combined, the three elements to which they point actually provide a rather lovely definition of love.

Similarly, although I am surely guilty of anthropomorphizing, I tend to think that the good and just society contributes to these very same three strategies. The just society does make people feel secure and nurtured, just as it aids in the self's adventures in revealing itself to others, which is, after all, the essential feature of authentic intimacy: I'll show you mine if you show me yours. It is the society, just as Fromm alleged,[39] that makes opportunities possible for fundamental human needs like relatedness, novelty, rootedness, transcendence, the search for one's identity, and a frame of orientation or object of devotion in which we discover personal meanings to be met. As glorious as the single self may be, we have learned from many stories, it can never "do it" on its own. It requires others to help define it, nurture it, make it feel free, worthy, not defective, and for that one turns, consciously or not, to the human environment constructed, not ironically, by each one of us through our actions, self-reflections and ideologies,[40] laws and policies, and ultimately our conceptions of morality. "If the child receives guidance from the adults whose lives are diminished by circumstance," Ralph Barocas and his colleagues wrote, "then that child may suffer a corresponding loss of opportunity to internalize growth enhancing experiences."[41]

In Fromm's words, the individual self seeking to satisfy its needs ineluctably makes compromises with the finite opportunities provided by the social environment. Indeed these compromises, eventually leading to our private and public narratives of ourselves and the social world, constitute our personalities. With each step we take into this social environment, with each reading and intimate appraisal we make of it, and simultaneously of ourselves, we move closer to or farther away from a lasting sense of security and acceptance, closer to or further away from an enduring sense of loneliness.[42] "Who does not want to have free choice," Scott Horton has written, "to have a voice, to grow, to have a place to be, to venture out? What person does not identify with and champion someone laboring to overcome great odds in the course of pursuing these most visceral and sustaining aims?"[43]

The truth, Fred Weinstein[44] has recently remarked, is that we don't know the truth. "There is no one story," Robin Usher and Richard Edwards wrote, "although there is a story, a very powerful story, that says there is."[45] Surely Nietzsche believed we will never understand the ultimate nature of self, no matter how diligent our studies.[46] Perhaps it is true that life is but an illusion, and that the worlds of the self and the society are mere constructs, able to vanish as quickly as they are formulated. If that is the case, then everything about our selves rests on our perceptions, our take of the society, our experiencing that which we tell ourselves, and occasionally our witnesses, what we consider to be truth, our intimate appraisals, in other words. Hence a soul that thrives or perishes within the society also is formed by our perceptions, constructs, and appraisals.

Here, then, are a few of my own readings of this social realm, predicated, it must be recalled, not precisely on years of study, but more likely on years of listening to exquisite storytellers and social observers, as well as the voice of a little child that never seems to go totally silent.

Notes

1. Frederich Nietzsche, *Schopenhauer as Educator*, translation by James W. Hillesheim and Malcolm R. Simpson. South Bend: Gateway Edition, p. 26

2. See John Maguire, *The Power of Personal Storytelling: Spinning Tales to Connect with Others*. New York: Jeremy P. Tarcher/Putnam, 1998; M. Mair, "Psychology as Storytelling." *International Journal of Construct Psychology*, 1, 1988: pp. 125–137; A. Parry, "Universe of Stories." *Family Process*, 30, 1991: pp. 37–54; and Bert O. States, *Dreaming and Storytelling*. Ithaca: Cornell University Press, 1993.

3. Jean Piaget, *Six Psychological Studies*. New York: Random House, 1967.

4. See Milton Seligman and Rosalyn Benjamin Darling, *Ordinary Families, Special Children: A Systems Approach to Childhood Disability*. New York: Guilford Press, 1997.

5. Sara Lawrence-Lightfoot and Jessica Hoffman Davis, *The Art and Science of Portraiture*. San Francisco: Jossey-Bass, 1997.

6. Robert Kegan, *The Evolving Self*. Cambridge: Harvard University Press, 1982.

7. Salvador Minuchin, *Families and Family Therapy*. Cambridge: Harvard University Press, 1974.

8. Urie Bronfenbrenner, *The Ecology of Human Development*. Cambridge: Harvard University Press, 1979.

9. See Erik H. Erikson, *Identity Youth and Crisis*. New York: Norton, 1968.

10. On this point see Fenwick W. English, "A Critical Appraisal of Sara Lawrence-Lightfoot's *Portraiture* as a Method of Educational Research." *Educational Researcher*, Vol. 29, No. 7, October 2000: pp. 21–26.

11. See Heinz Kohut, *The Kohut Seminars: On Self Psychology and Psychotherapy with Adolescents and Young Adults*. New York: Norton, 1987.

12. Frederich Nietzsche, op. cit., p. 12.

13. On this point see Stephen Tigner, 1993. "Homer, Teacher of Teachers." *Journal of Education*, vol. 175: pp. 43–64; and Tigner, 1994. "A New Bond: Humanities and Teacher Education." *Liberal Education*, vol. 80, Winter: pp. 4–7.

14. Martin Heidegger, *Being and Time*, translated by Joan Stambaugh. Albany: State University of New York Press, 1966.

15. Rollo May, *The Discovery of Being*. New York: Norton, 1983.

16. Sara Lawrence-Lightfoot and Jessica Hoffman Davis, *The Art and Science of Portraiture*, op. cit.

17. John Dewey, *How We Know*. Amherst, New York: Prometheus, 1991.

18. Eliot Liebow, *Tell Them Who I Am: The Lives of Homeless Women*. New York, The Free Press, 1993. I am grateful to Arthur Beane for this reference.

19. Jerome Bruner, *Actual Minds, Possible Worlds*. Cambridge: Harvard University Press, 1986.

20. Donald Polkinghorn, *Narrative Knowing and the Human Sciences*. Albany: State University of New York Press, 1988.

21. See George Lakoff and Mark Johnson, *Metaphors We Live By*. Chicago: University of Chicago Press, 1980.

22. Erich Fromm, *Escape from Freedom*. New York: Farrar and Rinehart, 1941; see also Mia L. Pringle, *The Needs of Children*. New York: Schocken Books, 1974.

23. On this point see Stephen Nathanson, *Economic Justice*. Upper Saddle River, N.J.: Prentice-Hall, 1998.

24. Thomas J. Cottle, *At Peril: Stories of Injustice*. Amherst: University of Massachusetts Press, 2001.

25. Toni Morrison, "How Can Values be Taught in the University." *Michigan Quarterly Review*, Vol. XL, 2001: pp. 273–278.

26. See S. Roberts, and S. McGinty, 1995. Awareness of Presence: Developing the Researcher Self. *Anthropology and Education Quarterly*, 26 (1), 1995: pp. 112–122.

27. See Urie Bronfenbrenner, "Alienation and the Four Worlds of Childhood." *Phi Delta Kappan*, February 1985: pp. 430–436.

28. Frederich Nietzsche, op. cit., p. 51.

29. Fenwick English, op. cit.

30. James Carroll, review of *Lives of Moral Leadership* by Robert Coles. *New York Times Book Review*, November 19, 2000: p. 76.

31. See Joseph A. Maxwell, *Qualitative Research Design: An Interactive Approach*. Thousand Oaks, Calif.: Sage Publishing, 1996.

32. Michel Foucault, *The Origin of Things: An Archeology of the Human Sciences*. New York: Random House, 1973. See also, W. W. Waller, "Insight and Scientific Method," in *On the Family, Education and War, Selected Writings*. Chicago: University of Chicago Press, 1970.

33. Peter Woods, *Inside Schools: Ethnography in Educational Research*. New York: Routledge and Kegan Paul, 1986; see also Daniel B. Frank, "The Live Creature: Understanding the School and Its Passions." *Child and Adolescent Social Work Journal*, Vol. 15, No, 6, December 1998: pp. 419–438.

34. See C. Flake, "Academic Failure, Alienation, the Threat of Extinction: A Global Perspective on Children at Risk." *Journal of Humanistic Education and Development*. Vol. 29, 1990: pp. 51–60.

35. Jonathan Kozol, *Death at an Early Age: The Destruction of the Hearts and Minds of Negro Children in the Boston Public Schools*. Boston: Houghton Mifflin, 1967.

36. See W. W. Waller, op. cit.

37. See Roberta Wollons (editor), *Children at Risk in America*. Albany: State University of New York Press, 1993.

38. Felton Earls and Mary Carlson, "Towards Sustainable Development for American Families." *Daedalus*, Winter, 1, 122, 1993: pp. 93–122.

39. Erich Fromm, op. cit.

40. See Stephen Kemmis, "Action Research and the Politics of Reflection." In D. Boud, R. Keough & D. Walker (editors), *Reflection: Turning Experience into Learning*. London: Kogan Page, 1985: pp. 139–163.

41. R. Barocas, R. Seifer, A. Sameroff, T. Andrews, R. Croft & E. Ostrow, "Social and Interpersonal Determinants of Developmental Risk." *Developmental Psychology*, Vol. 27, No. 3, 1991: pp. 479–488.

42. Anthony Storr, *Solitude: A Return to the Self*. New York: Balantine Books, 1988.

43. Scott Horton, "Making Gold of Our Lives: The Role of Metaphor in Describing the Experience of Change at Mid-life." Doctoral dissertation, Boston University, School of Education, 2000, ch. 5, p. 18.

44. Fred Weinstein, *Freud, Psychoanalysis, Social Theory: The Unredeemed Promise*. Albany: State University of New York Press, 2001.

45. Robin Usher and Richard Edwards, *Postmodernism and Education*. London: Routledge, 1996, p. 147.

46. Frederich Neitzsche, op. cit. I am grateful to Victor Kestenbaum and David Steiner for this reference.

I
METHODOLOGY
AND PERSPECTIVES

I confess, often, to smiling at the thought that the social science work I have undertaken over the last thirty years involves what is properly deemed a true methodology. Surely it constitutes a methodology of one sort—I have called it life study research—and must be thoughtfully scrutinized and critiqued. But a part of me thinks all I really do is speak with people hopefully about things that genuinely matter to them and relate, somehow, to their appreciation of their being in the world. As I said in the Introduction, I have never believed that the actual research part of the enterprise is anything more than collecting stories, stories in which people are enmeshed, as the philosopher Wilhelm Schapp suggested.

In and through the stories come the definitions, explanations, and interpretations of self and society, along with the outlines of my relationships with the storytellers. If the people who have spoken with me attempt to describe their relationships, their intimacies, their capacity to fuse with certain others or delineate boundaries with others, then to some extent they are doing the same thing with me, and hence their stories necessarily construct a piece of my own self-definitions. The stories, in other words, begin to construct the nature of the storytellers' definitions of and appraisals of kinship, a kinship that normally includes and implicates the witnesses to their stories.

What ingredients may enter a particular story, or, more likely, web of stories is anyone's guess. But few stories are told in which one doesn't hear the tellers' attempt to comprehend something, interpret or analyze something, or ultimately find the meaning of some experience or piece of themselves. It is in this attempt to discover meaning that storytellers and witnesses alike reveal their proclivity to proffer intimate appraisals. Inevitably, the definitions of self heard in the stories involve definitions of culture, society, community, neighborhood, extended family, that special group. Which means that the examination of the single story, or, again, the single web of stories, becomes an investigation of the human condition. The tiniest of villages to some extent bespeaks a piece of the greater culture.

In the end, all I am left with is words, the very words I have attempted to report over these last decades. For me, it is all in the words, all in the stories: the expressions of intimacy and ambition, the need for family and solitude, the search for individual uniqueness and the most mundane sorts of security and comfort, the joys of daily living, the extreme hurts endured, alas, by all of us. I choose to believe that I find these in the stories of men and women and most definitely children as well, and thus I cannot always differentiate methodology from perspective, a vexing matter for social scientists, to be sure, just as it is for the people with whom I continue to speak and who continue to inquire of me, as the one woman did of Robert Coles, "Is this really what you want?" "Are you really interested in this?" "Does any of this really matter to anyone?"

Private Lives and Public Accounts

⟡

ONE HAS TO KNOW Paulo Marcucci to know the way he speaks. One can recapture his words, even transcribe them accurately enough, and still not sense the richness of his language, his presentation in conversation. Paulo himself claims there is nothing special about the way he talks, but he knows he has a wondrous quality in his speech, an aliveness that is often so theatrical people sitting with him spontaneously break into applause. "Man's fantastic, isn't he?" they'll mutter aloud. "You should be on television, Paulo. How many times you been told that?

"I used to dance on television," Paulo Marcucci will respond.

"Oh yeah?" The men in the cafeteria are more than a little impressed, but distrustful at the same time.

"Yeah, it's true," Paulo Marcucci shouts at them, with the same serious face he wears coming out of church every morning. "I danced on the television until my father told me to get the hell off before I broke it."

The men laugh and applaud and whistle. Paulo Marcucci is delighted with himself. He is the hit of the moment.

Sitting next to him drinking a capucino that in this one Boston cafeteria is so sweet Gino has warned me it will rot my tongue along with my teeth, I said to my friend of several years: "And you say you speak just like all the rest of us. You're the poor man's Milton Berle."

He put one of his hands on my hand and gestured as if he were about the clamp his other hand over my mouth. "Please," he whispered loudly enough so that his audience could hear. "Tony Bennett. Antonio Benedetto, huh? Not Milton Berle. And where do you come off calling me a poor man?"

"I didn't mean that you were poor," I responded sheepishly, realizing how my remark could have been misinterpreted.

"What, you think *they're* poor?" Paulo gestured toward the men who, amused, were watching and listening to our conversation, and waiting for Paulo to nail me to the wall.

"No. I didn't mean. All I meant . . ."

"Please," he said with a smile starting to form. "We're working class, with an emphasis on the class, not poor. We're not poor because we don't pass the Marcucci Poor Man's Test."

Now it was I who sat straight-faced, determined not to ask about the Marcucci Poor Man's Test.

"You don't want to know?" he blurted out, seeing his straight man had quit.

"Go ahead," I mumbled.

"Poor man don't eat, poor man don't laugh."

"That true?"

"How do I know what I'm saying? Am I a psychologist? I make things up. I keep my eyes open and I make things up about people, things that make me feel good about myself. If they're true, they're true; if they aren't, what do I care? I still feel better about myself."

As the conversation appeared to be growing serious, the others began losing interest in what Paulo had to say, and I had all to myself this gentleman of fifty-five, a father of three children, a man who has fought the battle of unemployment for more than ten years.

"How long have I known you?" he asked, with a peculiar sternness in his voice.

"Five years. More than that." My answer sounded like a school boy's response to his teacher.

"Five years and I still don't see what the hell you get out of talking with people like us. Who gives a damn about us? Who do you know, honest to God now, you have one friend in the world who wants to know about people like me, people who haven't done a damn thing in their lives that would make news? You know what Italians are supposed to be? We're singers or we're mafioso. Right? So who wants to hear about Paulo Marcucci or any of the other guys here, some of which don't even speak English. Even if you wrote in Italian, nobody around here would give you a nickel to hear about them. So who cares? You make a few friends, but what does it lead to? What's the point?

"Look, if you got a man, like he's working in an office on Tremont Street, okay? He's got a wife and a couple of kids. He gets good money for what he does. Guy has a nice home out in the suburbs somewhere. What's he want to know about Marcucci and his cafeteria dropouts for?

He couldn't give you a reason in the world. You write books, right? He doesn't want your books. You know what he wants? He wants Mario Puzo. You know Mario Puzo?"

"Not personally."

"You know who I mean though. He wants action, mystery, love, killing, gangsters. You take and level this whole part of the city, push the people into the ocean, you think he gives a damn! He couldn't care less what you do to us. Give us jobs, take jobs away from us. He doesn't care. He eats, we eat. He laughs, we laugh. Doesn't phase him in the slightest. I've told you things so private and personal, gossip, you could write it out for him and draw pictures on top, and photographs on top of that, and he wouldn't look twice at it. Not twice. I'll tell you something. If I was him, if I had that nice steady job with the big home in the suburbs and the two-car garage and everything else that goes with that life, I wouldn't look twice at that stuff myself. Even if it was *me* you were writing about. Maybe I'd look once before I die, like I look at some of the old photographs we got once in a while, but if I never saw them again, what the hell, I'd say. What the hell."

"You wouldn't miss it," I said in a flat tone.

"I wouldn't miss nothing. I'm interested in my life 'cause it's *my* life. Somebody else's life living like me, what do I need it for? You want another capucino? Maybe it could rot out your whole mouth."

"I'll take the capucino and I'll tell you something, Tony Bennett. I don't believe you. You have a great sensitivity about what you see and hear. Your life matters plenty, and so do the lives of these people in here. You're furious with that guy in his office for not being interested in you, the same way I am. Nobody likes people not taking interest in us. You're right that outrageous types get in the news, but your life isn't a bunch of old photographs. Not in the least, and you damn well know it isn't. What about that time you and I went through the photographs in that Havana cigar box and you gave me a lecture on each one? That Uncle Guilliamo of yours? You wouldn't care if you never saw a picture of him again?"

"You remember Guilliamo?"

"I don't remember half of what you remember. You do a great act, Marcucci, but I still take everything you say with a grain of you-know-what. The crime is that no one does pay attention to human problems unless he's experiencing them himself. Guys like you, other families I see, everybody has a way of not having to look at them or hear about them. You know as well as I do that the guy you want to have listen to you is that guy in the office. The government couldn't care less, so it's that guy you want to educate."

"What do you mean educate?" Now Paulo was the school boy, I the teacher.

"You know exactly what I mean. Private things you keep for yourself. The conditions of your life that are caused by society, by all the life styles and laws and policies and institutions all the rest of us practice and uphold. Those conditions are what you want the world to know about. All right, my sermon's over. Now my mouth can rot with your lousy capucino."

Paulo Marcucci was sitting up straight in his chair. His deep brown eyes were flashing as though he wanted to tell me ten million things simultaneously. But in that instant he didn't speak, which even *he* recognized as being rather uncharacteristic.

"Look at me not saying nothing." His fingers touched gently on his chest. "You're *sure* you ain't Italian? Maybe you got a great uncle somewhere." He was teasing, of course, as we had been through all the differences in our backgrounds many times before. But there was also an edge of seriousness.

"I got uncles, Paulo"—I grinned at him—"but they're all named Weinstock and LeVine and Hornstein."

"You going to write about me some day?"

"You sound like you'd like it." We both had heard the plaintiveness in his tone.

"You want to know what I was thinking just now?" Paulo leaned forward and cradled his forehead between his thumb and index finger. It had been eight months since that hand had been engaged in work. "I was thinking sometimes when you come and talk to me, it makes me feel like I'm living in some peasant village in Italy, not that I remember any peasant village. It just seems that way. You come, like you were some tourist, looking at the buildings and the churches, studying the faces of the people, you know what I mean. Then it's like you want to take a picture of me, like for a souvenir, although I know that's not what you do this for. I think, the guy wants to be my friend even though he's just passing through. I suppose I think that 'cause you don't live here. I think of all the ways we're different and why it is we're so different. Money isn't the only thing. Then I think, he wants a picture, why not give it to him. Okay, I say, you can take my picture. You can even have somebody else take a picture of the two of us together, if that's what you want. Maybe you'll remember me better that way. After all, it isn't your fault I have to live like this and you get to move in and out of this peasant town. Besides, *you* want a picture of *me,* and that's got to mean something, don't it? What the hell, if you give me a copy, I'll have a souvenir of you, a reminder of what I looked like, too, when I was with you that time. Like I say, all the problems we face ain't your fault. Maybe they're nobody's fault—"

"And if I want to show the picture to other people?" I interrupted him.

"That's *your* business. If you think they might be interested, you can even sell them for all I care. I'm satisfied with a picture. It makes me know I'm alive. Tourist or not, you wanted a picture and you picked me. You'll forget me two days later, remember me for two days when you get the film back, then forget me again."

"You think it goes like that, Paulo?"

"I think it goes like that for millions of years. Millions of people have lived their lives with no one paying a bit of attention to them. Some of them like it that way. Some of them probably don't even think about people in other villages, not to mention tourists. But people like me, we're overlooked by the people who live ten feet away. Settle for a photograph? I'll settle for a wink if it means I might get the slightest break. Drink your coffee. Wait too long and it loses its poison."

In many respects, this conversation with Paulo Marcucci touches upon the concerns of this essay. For the last years I have been speaking with people who are mainly from the poorer reaches of American society. My research consists of nothing more than these conversations. There is no telling how any one morning, afternoon, or evening might go, for I bring no prearranged questions, no structured form of interview schedule. It is a conversation in which I am engaged, or an event in which, in one form or another, I participate. I enter these conversations and events knowing that I will be observing others as well as observing myself observing them in a manner I normally do not assume. Thus, there is something unusual for me about these so-called observant participations, in that I anticipate doing more with the experience than merely letting it pass into time. In a sense I am a photographer prepared to take photographs, aware that each photograph will be a subjective response to what I am seeing and hearing. I *could* claim that I render authentic, objective portraits of people like Paulo Marcucci, but I recognize that I am presenting nothing more, nothing less, than my impression, my slant, ineluctably my bias. In these portraits and studies, I, along with the other participants, provide our own reading of the social and personal situations in which we find ourselves.

In the past, the phrase that best characterized this type of work was observant participation. This is not merely a play on words of the well-known participant observation technique; by transposing the words, the stress falls on participation rather than observation. A better phrase might be observant implication, for the interviewer cannot help but become immersed in the lives of those people whom he or she is interviewing. These studies convey small pieces of life as it is led and described by people with whom I have spoken. More generally, they focus on the ways in which people read the historical and contemporary situations of their lives, and what they perceive as their fate.

No one who listens to people recounting these situations can possibly remain aloof, indifferent, and still communicate his or her interest to the storytellers. We are not engaged here in classical psychoanalytic psychotherapy in which analysts purposely arrange for their patients not to see their faces. These are conversations, like the one with Paulo Marcucci in a noisy coffee shop, a conversation with a friend, albeit a special friend, who looks at me with myriad expressions, one of which clearly evinces a concern that I may be losing interest in him.

Paulo Marcucci is not unique in his attitude toward the hypothetical man in the downtown office who cares little for the Paulo Marcuccis of the world. Paulo's observation no doubt is correct. The hypothetical man aside, few countries pay much attention to their poor families. Governments proceed with their master plans or, more likely, their bureaucratic inefficiencies and minor reform programs, relying on the fact that the poor will start no uprisings. As Paulo said, most people believe that the lives of the poor and working class are dull, that their minds are vague, their outlooks and problems uninteresting, unoriginal. In my conversations with people like Paulo, again and again I have heard the sentiment, "I don't know what anyone would find so interesting about us." But their concern in these moments is with me, the interviewer, the somewhat irreal friend. It is me they doubt, for I represent the society that holds them back, the society that finds them of minimal interest and value. They wish to talk about certain matters, but they are always alert to any clues that might suggest disinterest on my part.

Strangely, as the years of these special conversations accumulate, I discover this sentiment in a great many people, not merely those from the so-called lower reaches of society. Celebrities aside, many people doubt that someone else could be interested in them. Admittedly, there are good and obvious reasons for people living in poor circumstances to doubt the intentions of someone like myself who claims to be interested in them. A history of political and economic realities stands between us. As best as it can, society segregates the poor and leaves them to survive with one another. But there is no comparable history standing between me and others from higher social strata with whom I speak. So with all people, one must resolve the issue of mutual trust.

There is also the matter of examining the currencies that each of us is putting in and taking out of these conversations and friendships. What do I want from them? What is it they want and do not want from me? Although for different reasons, sociologists and the people with whom I speak share one fundamental concern about this form of inquiry: They wonder how my work can consist of little more than conversing and writing up these conversations. While some professionals argue that further analysis of the material must be undertaken, the people with whom I converse are convinced that I must have some greater purpose in mind, one that transcends the writing of a book. Surely, they say, it is not merely an interest in them that could dominate the work; I must be using them as illustrations of something.

There is another issue about these conversations that assumes significance. It regards the protection of personal privacy. The matter of simultaneously wanting to write about the lives of those with whom one speaks while preserving their dignity and privacy is a delicate one. At all stages of one's work, it poses a dilemma for the researcher. On the one hand, I strongly believe that it is essential to record the lives of human beings as accurately and systematically as possible, and that when one's so-called recording devices are subjective, they be labeled as such. On the other hand, recording the life of another person—which means recording only the smallest fraction of that person's experiences and recollections of those experiences—may well violate the sense of privacy a researcher wishes to preserve. The dilemma is intensified by the fact that in American society, there is tremendous pressure to have people expose their private lives; the more outrageous the divulgence, the more we encourage and accept it. Divulgence even becomes a part of political ideology. People wish to make public confessions or have others confess to one thing or another. Under the banners of freedom of speech, liberation, and psychological health, come all sorts of pleas to have people open up and lay themselves bare.

For the most part, the large majority of sociological research does not do this. Indeed, the criticism often leveled at such work is that it hardly seems to touch on the private, and therefore meaningful—that ubiquitous word—parts of people's lives. The temptation to encourage disclosure of all varieties of private issues is always alive in the sort of work exemplified by the life study. Many intimate questions might be asked, given the closeness of one's friendships with people. Many issues are talked about and could be publicly recorded.

It was with this dilemma in mind that the concept of life studies was formulated. I had participated in a series of conversations and events that actually had to do with the matter of privacy and personal revelations. Part of the dilemma was resolved by making certain that the confidentiality of the participants was maintained. Thus I changed names and a few places, except of course when participants agreed that it was important to publicize their true identities. But in the main, the dilemma is never satisfactorily settled. For me, this remains one of the crucial ethical issues of this work, although obviously my decision about how to proceed has been reached. I have chosen to make public the lives of those willing to speak with me, people who agreed to have our conversations published. It should also be noted in this context that, whenever possible, the participants read what I have written and are free to suggest deletions and changes in fact and tone.

One can argue indefinitely about the issues of public reporting and the preservation of privacy. One can assert, for example, that using only anecdotes from people's experiences preserves the dignity of these people more than would an extensive life study. Some would say it is better to present responses to attitude questionnaires or public opinion polls, for these measures generate all the information one needs, and in the process of collecting information one pays greatest respect to those providing the information. My own argument is that the so-called observant-participation life study provides its own form of information that is no less valuable than the information accumulated through attitude questionnaires and polling. The information obtained in both sorts of inquiry is potentially valuable both in the formation of a social science and for the people participating in these studies.

Conversely, both objective and subjective studies may be of negligible value in the development of a science, and even harmful to the participants. Any piece of conversation that one reports, no matter how extensive and elaborate, is open to interpretation. For example, a life study is produced in which I attempt to portray an articulate, thoughtful, and intelligent, young black man who has been bused to a predominantly white suburban high school. I make no claims that other black children share the views of this one young man; indeed I make every effort to point out that the young man speaks only for himself. Nonetheless, a panoply of responses to the study comes forth. The young man is seen by some as typical, by others as perfectly atypical. Some believe that I have created the young man out of my imagination. Some say that I have derogated him by not portraying him as intelligent. Some wish to use the boy as a justification for busing school children; others use "the case" as a justification for their opposition to busing. Some claim it noble for a rich researcher to work with poor children; others claim the life study contributes to the oppression of the young man and others like him, and that writers grow rich on the backs of the poor. Some claim that rendering portraits of poor people in even a slightly artistic fashion automatically turns them into the proverbial "noble savage," thereby convincing one's readers that these people, as attested to by the beauty and majesty of their words, require no special political or economic support. Finally, some contend that the truth must come from systematic studies and observations no matter how they are carried out; others contend that only artists record the truth.

All of these extremes, naturally, are dangerous and to a certain extent are expressed with little thought given to their meaning and implications. Still, the dilemma of preserving privacy while publicly recording the way lives are led is unresolved and will remain unresolved, although my own bias on the matter is clear. The issue, furthermore, raised one of the central ethical questions inherent in such work: What is involved in participating in conversations when, through the definition of the situation, one is distinct from the other person in very real ways? (Paulo Marcucci will not write a book about his conversations with me.) Facing this question forces one to totally reassess the nature of one's work. Should the researcher continue the enterprise when maintenance of genuinely ethical relationships is so difficult, particularly when the substance of these conversations is personal and meaningful for all participants? My own answer, again, is clear, for I have chosen to continue the work believing that the alternative, namely to turn away from the people with whom I have been speaking, is unthinkable.

Now, why unthinkable? Several reasons may be offered that hopefully will add to our understanding of the purpose of these studies. Let me begin to answer the question by proclaiming a philosophy of living I strongly support but cannot seem to follow: Live life every day, as if that day were the last day of your life; take in as much as you can, for there is so much to be gained, so much to be lost. The spirit of this philosophy appeals to me, but a laziness intervenes. I do lose too much each day, and confess to existing as if an endless stretch of time lay before me. But there is also a political side to the philosophy, for it assumes that each of us, no matter what his or her station in life, may live each day with a spirit of insatiable adventure and a delight in simply being alive. Looking for scraps to eat, or waiting in line at a welfare or unemployment office would seem to make it difficult to adhere to the spirit of the philosophy. Still, there is something significant about the idea of not losing human experiences. This is what strikes most intensely at my participation with others. I visit a city and want to walk down every street; I meet a person and want to know everything about him or her. The restraints on satisfying these needs are obvious, and as much as anything I feel the rush of time. How much longer will I stay with Paulo Marcucci while he is in this special mood? How much longer will he allow me to remain friends with him?

The result of this feeling is a desire to record conversations and ensure that our agreements, our contracts, really, regarding our work together will not be violated; that I will not reveal what someone has asked me to hold in confidence, but that I will also not allow those rare moments of our involvement to pass unrecorded. In other words, I feel that these conversations are as important as the daily events one reads about in newspapers. For a constant source of information about and awareness of the men and women in our society is better than a communication system that will dehumanize, categorize, generalize, and make pronouncements about us that reveal neither the truth nor the substance of our lives. I despise the fact that our society encourages people to dwell on the sexual habits of famous men and women and then turns this encouragement into big business. Similarly, I reject the belief that the worlds of quiet men and women must go unnoticed or be treated strictly as actuarial or statistical concerns. Lives are recorded because there is inherent value in preserving human experiences, especially those experiences that, for political and economic reasons, are deemed "less significant" and "less profitable." Let us not forget, as Paulo Marcucci suggested, that economic criteria of success and failure too often influence the assessment we make of our own and other people's fundamental worth.

There is a second reason for recording these conversations: Like it or not, American society thrives on the dehumanizing marriage between technological genius and a driving materialism demanding continuous acquisition. We want more homes and cars; we demand more and more information of any variety, no matter how seriously we violate our moral precepts. Little we do seems to affect this current. Some of us also formulate policy that dictates the ways people should lead their lives. We put into operation programs that directly or indirectly affect the lives of all human beings. All societies and governments do this; rules and laws are inevitable components of social order.

Thus, underlying the acquisition of material goods and knowledge and the surge to design programs and policies, is a dehumanization that already has taken hold in Western culture. It is a dehumanization that we now accept, expect, *and* justify. In our press for information in the form of tangible certainties and in our fear of tentativeness and doubt, we actually believe we know what other people need and want, the ways in which they should seek gratification, and the scientific reasons supporting all of this. Social scientists actually claim to understand the mysteries of child development and the emergence of personal capacities, both cognitive and emotional. We claim to understand the workings of the human mind and spirit; hence we believe that we can write our policy statements and support them with knowledge about men and women whose lives we never encounter. Indeed our information and the theories generated from it are so sophisticated we decide it is actually better to make claims about people we know little about, for in this way our decisions "prove" less biased. We claim to know about children because we have them, the elderly because we have a few older relatives still alive, minority people because we are minority people ourselves, or have spoken to some minority people, or because some of our best friends . . . So it comes to pass that some of us have earned the right to speak for other people and to claim that we know what it is they want.

The truth is, however, that no one literally speaks for anyone else. One may have earned the right to create policy, or politically represent a constituency. But speaking for someone else is at best a compromise and a convenience, if not an outright presumption, no matter how legitimate a political act it may be. Because isolation breeds dogmatism and righteousness, the best way to know that one's notions, theories, and suppositions are right may be to take them to the people about whom they were originally conceived. Well, goes one argument against this position, most people don't really know *what* they want. Moreover, says another argument, it is difficult to look someone in the eye when writing a policy that one knows is barely a stopgap measure. It is far more difficult to make claims about people you choose to be with every day of your life than it is to isolate yourself and make your claims, almost hoping that those whose lives you are addressing will never hear your remarks.

A literary critic once wrote that we don't need to know any more about people; we need policy. It is a familiar refrain. One can argue this position by saying that certain policies have hurt people far more than research projects purporting to study them. What we need, the argument would continue, is a world free of policies, one that truly honors and protects people.

But there is a more subtle argument to the critic's pronouncements. We focus on the word "know" because, in this context, it implies that we already possess all the necessary information on a particular subject of human behavior. That is quite an accomplishment for the social sciences! The word "know" implies something else as well. To know something is not merely to acquire still another material possession. Knowing how to speak a second language is not equivalent to purchasing a second house. To know something and to retain and elaborate on the original experience of the knowledge is a timeless adventure and ordeal. We do not know about poor children and working-class children merely from brief accounts. From these accounts we will learn a bit, in a material sense, for we will become "acquainted" with the lives of a few more people. That is, we will elaborate on our existing knowledge. We also will *feel* this new knowledge, since the lives of these boys and girls will evoke in us unpredictable reflections and emotions. Said differently, knowledge may represent, in a shorthand sense, the accumulation of wholly impersonal information. More likely, it is itself an experience, containing its attendant emotional lights and shadows. That the emotional aspects, the feeling part of knowledge, may not be conscious to us—using one terminology—or cognitively salient to us—using another terminology—does not mean that this part is absent.

We said earlier that no one can listen to the accounts of another person's life and remain indifferent or objective, particularly when one is a part of the situation or friendship that has created and perpetuated the conversation. Inevitably, something is evoked in us: Our mind is turned to other subjects; or we feel moved; or a particular emotion comes over us that we either cannot identify or choose to ignore. All of this is part of routine conversation, the act of preparing a life study, and accumulating new knowledge. Thus, we may turn the critic's words around slightly with the following statement: While politically it may seem that policy is more beneficial than the enlightenment or evocation derived from still one more life study, the fact is that, in the end, policies may not be better. Yet, productive or destructive policies do make it easier for us to deal with people when we do not wish to be touched by their lives. Writing policy is much easier than looking into someone's eyes as he or she reveals even the smallest morsel of himself or herself. No doubt there are times when preventing participants in psychoanalysis from seeing one another allows them to speak freely. But this method helps the analyst as well for there are moments when he or she winces or weeps while listening to patients, and does not wish to burden the patient with such responses; or perhaps the analyst does not want to admit to having been so moved, and to having felt so helpless.

The word helpless brings us to another aspect of the response of many people to the life study. Reading the words of another person or the accounts of some events creates a burden of which psychologists are well aware. What are we to do with this morass of words, this conversation just "overheard"? Are we to analyze it, place its words into some tradition of understanding that we find congenial? Are we to use these words, these lives, these events to shape political programs? Or are we to be merely entertained or informed?

Everyone responds differently to the words of another person. As the life study makes plain, what we know about another person, what he or she gives to us in conversation and friendship, is in great measure that person's response to *us*. We ourselves are the agents of information; people give us what they believe we want or assume we are willing to accept. Thus, our claims about another person may be unjustifiable, because we know only what that person has communicated to *us*; we do not know how this person would be heard and perceived by anyone else. Nor do we know what this person would tell anyone else. We may say that our work is phenomenological in nature, that people are offering to us freely their recounting of their private world or some public event. But just as thought and language have their social components, so too is the fundamental nature of the account and the art of recounting a sociological event based on ritual and the laws governing simple routines. We, the listeners, are part of these rituals and routines. To say, therefore, that during our conversation Mr. X was putting on an act is to say only that the normal and expected act of conversation and recounting was accentuated beyond normal, expected limits. But all social engagements imply actors acting, in a literal sense, a factor that in no way automatically renders disingenuous the act of recounting conversation.

The point has been belabored, perhaps, but it must be underscored. The richness, the depth of recounting conversation is lost if we say, simply, that there are environmental factors to consider. There are always environmental factors, but part of the environment is the invisible sociological realm of habit, routine, order, ritual, sharing, and everything else that constitutes the context of conversation. Variations in the rituals always exist, but the listener also creates some of these variations. To a degree that can never be accurately calculated, I, the researcher, determine the phenomenology and expressions, and, hence, the personal accounts of those people I "study." Even when I claim that I have done little, said little, allowed the other person to speak freely about whatever it is he or she wanted to speak about, my presence can be detected in the utterances of that person, just as their utterances will be found in my writing.

This last point may be developed further. First, the degree to which I, as researcher, choose to analyze the accounts of another person, literally his or her words, indicates not only something about the form of science or type of inquiry I am undertaking, but also something about my attitude toward those I study. I choose how much of the other person's presence I want to make public in my own accounting of his or her accounts. There is a great difference, after all, between merely saying that someone was talking to me about politics, and actually presenting the words of that person. Each way of recounting has its greater and lesser degrees of validity, its greater and lesser likelihood of recording the truth, subjective as it is, of a particular account. In the end, how many words of another person I include in my account suggest the value of those words in the act of performing my research. The words and the presence in the environment of both participants, the mutuality of the conversation—no matter how asymmetric the relationship of the participants—is part of the truth one consciously is choosing to present.

To repeat, we are always recounting life experiences *in process*. We are involved with private lives and public accounts; nothing and no one will hold still long enough for us to describe them perfectly and accurately. The world changes and changes us, even as we make our observations and recordings. Beyond this inevitable limitation of our science, our observations and perceptions necessarily are personal and subjective, if we are making accounts or listening to accounts of life as it unfolds. But note again the stress on the word accounts. People are telling us what happened, what crossed their minds, what they recall. What we are hearing is a tertiary elaboration of the original experience. Paulo Marcucci's *remembrance* of an event is one step away from living the event itself, as the event originally was experienced. Another elaboration is my hearing him tell of the event. My writing of the event yields still another elaboration. And all of these complicating matters belong to what we call the environment of a conversation.

Another point about the environment of the conversation involves the question of whether or not the presence of the researcher should be recorded in the final account. Is there a legitimate place in the recounting of speech for dialogue of the type, presented at the beginning of this essay? On the one hand, this matter raises serious methodological issues. On the other hand, the answer one chooses comes down to a matter of taste. Some people want to know what the researcher said and did, and particularly what was going through his or her mind during the conversation. Others argue that the researcher's utterances and reflections only get in the way and keep us from hearing what the person under study is saying.

Whether it is explicitly or implicitly drawn, the presence of the researcher is in the conversation, in the environment, and in the final accounting of the conversation. There is no escaping this fact, other than to disregard the conversation and conceptualize about human behavior as if one could not remember the source of one's insights. Aesthetically, it may trouble some readers to "hear" the researcher's insights, reflections, even words said in the course of conversation. But these insights and reflections, these words assuredly will influence the recounting, whether they are reported or not.

Reporting one's own contributions to conversations also affects that evocative aspect of knowledge acquisition mentioned earlier, although its effect on the reader is unpredictable. For some people, that which is evoked is enhanced by the researcher's participation. For other people, the obverse is true. Either way, the reader's reactions are formed partly in response to whether or not he or she wishes to identify with the presence of the researcher, or the so-called subject of the conversation. Upon reading a fictional account, the reader may say that it was like actually being there. In the social sciences, the feeling of "being there" is often taken as a sign that true science has not been made; it reads too personally to be "pure science." More importantly, one wonders whether the reader of the account does not share something of the qualities of the researcher; both, in a sense, are part of the environment that has shaped the conversation.

A word now about the limiting nature of the environment in which the private life and public account unfold. I administer a test of intelligence to a child. I score the test, and the child's result is 90. I contend that on the basis of this measure, the child is not intelligent. Someone else administers an intelligence test to the same child, who now scores 120. The other examiner claims that the child is highly intelligent. The difference in the scores is not accounted for merely by the fact that it was the child's second testing. The difference is in part due to the environment and the examiner. The range of people's behavior, capacities, and propensities is enormous, far more expansive than we normally acknowledge. Yet these ranges are finite. People cannot become totally different organisms or personalities as they pass from one relationship or situation to another; they must maintain some semblance of self-consistency to retain their health and sense of identity. Thus, we offer different parts of ourselves, with greater or lesser intensity, to different friends and associates.

How then do we make science from all this? How can we claim to know about people? How do we even know that the parts of one's personality that one exposes, or the experiences that one relates, are the most important parts? At times, the stranger, the interviewer, or psychotherapist, becomes the recipient of some of the most tender, raw, and intimate material. After making some revelation, the teller claims surprise, disbelief over what has been revealed, and may hope that he or she will not have to see the interviewer again. In psychotherapy, the patient's demand for intimacy before revelation is frequently transformed into a demand for a guarantee of no intimacy before divulging intimate material.

This point too must be underscored, for it touches upon yet another question of the life study—namely, who ultimately, is best qualified to do this work? Who, in the end, is entitled to participate in these special conversations? Can men interview women, whites interview blacks, older people interview younger people? The question is crucial, for it raises political and methodological issues, as well as issues of how we respond in terms of action to hearing accounts of other people's lives. It also raises the issue of whether or not the life study should include the reactions and responses of the interviewer during the original conversation.

A discussion of these issues must start with acknowledging the fact that any personal expression, even one that occurs symbolically, as in a dream, reflects more than the personality or the phenomenological apparatus of a person. We may wish to believe that each utterance, or at least some of our utterances, are purely our own, conceived by us in the twinkling of a moment. The fact is, however, that deeply rooted cultural and social structural forces influence these expressions and utterances, even the symbolic expressions associated with daydreams and fantasies. Paulo Marcucci's likening of our conversations to my taking his photograph in a peasant village neither one of us has ever visited demonstrates this point. A sudden notion comes into his head, an image that not only depicts the predominating quality in our relationship, but also reveals the arrangements of power, economic realities, and the circumstances of our respective lives. While we may choose to overlook the forces of our culture and society—as we typically forget the effect of the structure of our language on our thoughts—these forces emerge in our daily expressions, particularly when our expressions are made to someone who comes to us wanting to hear about the circumstances of our lives.

When, as researchers, our intention is to record the way life is led by anyone, not merely representatives of special portions of society, we necessarily will hear about and experience the affect of the social structure on the most innocuous or the most intimate details of that life. This is a fact of life. For we are not only bound by propensities that are biologically determined. We are also social animals in the sense that our public and private behaviors, as well as our accounting for these behaviors, are influenced by the values, norms, rituals, and structures of the world in which we survive. A personal diary, recording, novel, poem, in which a person divulges the most intimate and sensitive material, will necessarily reveal social structural qualities. Art is never free of them; it doesn't need to be in order to be considered art. The inner world may be distinct from the outer world, that which we call the unconscious distinct from the conscious. But interior worlds relate to exterior worlds, the unconscious touches on the conscious, and all realms of the mind along with public behavior "know" and "feel" the impress of the culture in which these realms evolve.

Many people demand that the life study include the influence of social and cultural forces when recording even the most idiosyncratic experience. A legitimate criticism of the life study is that it often may not make explicit what is implicit. It must be remembered that not only will oral history reflect social structural forces, but that these forces are at work in every conversation in which the oral history is born and matures. Merely to converse is to be involved in a process governed by social structural as well as psychological factors. All oral history necessarily reflects the relationship among political, economic, religious, educational institutions and patterns describing the way a single life is led. We may allege that our work is little more than a monologue or dialogue, the recording of one man or woman speaking about his or her life. But this so-called free monologue is colored by exterior influences that transcend even the patterns of thought and behavior laid down by the language one is speaking. To make the monologue a dialogue, as all interview situations are, is to make more complex the social reality and accounting of the dialogue by both participants, and to set the conversation even more securely within the province of the sociological enterprise.

Any conversation, any accumulation of information through interviewing, will have political overtones or undertones. Again, Paulo Marcucci's reference to photographs is apt. The subjective recording of a conversation is a series of still photographs, in contrast to a recording on film or tape of that same conversation. Each segment of the conversation, each photograph, lives in the memory of each participant. The memory, however, is the negative, not the photograph. Presumably, all of the conversation has been retained, but not all the potential photographs will be developed or publicly displayed. Moreover, each photograph, each segment of recollection, the souvenir, in Paulo's words, must then be developed individually. It is in the developing process that the personal, social, and political elements of the photographer-recorder will begin to emerge.

Let us recall, although the metaphor is not wholly justifiable, that just as two people will photograph the same event or person differently, so too will two people develop and print the same photographic negative differently. One person will emphasize one quality of the photograph, the other will emphasize something else. In this personal emphasis, in this final artistic rendering—the period when editorial and substantive changes are made—lies the heart of the subjective inquiry, which is what the life study and the accounting of public and private experience is ultimately about. We choose only certain photographs, select only certain portions of a particular conversation, remember only certain fragments of conversation. It has to be this way, even with mechanical recording devices. Data, no matter in what form, are reduced. The reduction process is a linear one, and it is an inevitable one. We cannot remember everything; we can only report what happened in linear fashion. Photograph follows photograph, one by one, in the same way that words follow each other, one by one. In this linear process of memory, in choosing what to tell of our experiences—which is what both participants in a conversation must do—political, social, psychological influences again have an impact. In the final product, we may choose either to present these influences in an explicit manner, or to mask them. Thus, our product, the life study, may be so subtle in its political message that we, the creators of the message, may not recognize the politics of our work until others point it out. Conversely, our political message may be explicit to the point of our product becoming polemical. Either way, to some extent the life study remains ideological, never value-free. Indeed, some who practice the method of observant participation depend on the ideological basis of the work, and rejoice in the work's explicit political content.

Now then, can a member of one distinct social group, one sex, engage in the sort of relationship required in the life study with members of other groups, or people of the other sex? Obviously they can, and they do. Typically, we rarely question the premise that a man may tell another man things he would never tell a woman, or that a woman would reveal things to another woman that she would never tell a man. Yet, research indicates that, in truth, male patients tell female therapists many things they have told no other person, and female patients reveal to male therapists the most private chapters of their lives. To be sure, a person may prefer to speak to an older man, or a younger woman, or a white man, or a black woman, or a professional person, or a distinctly nonprofessional person. But what ultimately emerges in the conversation is the expression of the participant in the context of political and social factors prevailing at the moment of the conversation *and* at the moment of the final recording of that conversation.

To understand human behavior and to enhance human life—which are the goals of the type of inquiry we are considering here—we must know the full range of human interactions. There are sound intellectual and political reasons why members of a particular group or sex prefer to remain with their own kind and speak of their private worlds only to one another. One reason is due to the oppression and exclusion certain groups of people experience daily. This experience testifies to the fact that we have not made much progress in dealing with people who, on the most superficial level, appear different from us. Apart from, or perhaps because of political inequalities, some men are edgy with women, some whites are edgy with blacks. Even a six-year-old child may appear diffident in the presence of a toddler. As Erik Erikson wrote, we often look at one another as if we were representatives of various species or subspecies, not sure whether our perceived—not to mention imagined—differences affirm the greatness of life, or antici-pate our demise in a battle among the species. The differences between us evoke a need to articulate what it is that constitutes the boundaries and substances of our private and public selves. What we decide about these boundaries and substances is found in our accounts, private and publicly recorded.

When people of similar backgrounds, so-called similar human cate-gories, participate in the life study, the political and social contexts shift. To say, however, that these sorts of interactions are more genuine, more likely to reveal the truth than are interactions between people of differ-ent backgrounds, is a perplexing matter. It is merely that at certain points in history, our intellectual, political, and psychological needs make demands upon us and teach us to value one form of research, one life study, more than another. The oppressive elements existing in a so-ciety will necessarily influence the science practiced by members of that society. These same elements will appear as well in our conversations and observant participations.

By the same token, blind spots also will appear in our conversations, sometimes because we are victimized by the political and social realities of our culture, sometimes because we believe that we are immune to the pressures of these realities. This is particularly true when we do nothing more than speak with another person and record bits of this experiential history. Political ideology supports us, drives our work, lingers in the air above us, settles in the ground beneath us. It also blinds us from time to time. We begin to make claims about people and speak for them in ways that conceal the truths of their existence and corrupt the images and re-membrances we have of these people and their circumstances. Thus, in our observant participations, we face the dangers of romanticizing peo-ple. We can be condescending, personally self-indulgent, irresponsible, patronizing. We also can be ideological to the extent that we convince ourselves and those with whom we participate that we are doing the "right thing," acting in the "right way."

The so-called raising of conscious awareness of human circum-stances is one of the main intellectual goals of the life study. We must learn about people, and feel through their words, or their words married to our words, the substance of their lives. Making policy, as we noted earlier, is a different enterprise altogether. But by engaging in conscious and explicit polemics, we often end up in the same position as those who write policy. The danger exists if we ignore certain facts of another person's existence and merely employ that person's words as grist for our mills of ideology and power. Like policy formation, the preoccupation with ideology may prevent us from feeling what another person has told us or, better, wishes to tell us. We may believe we are being our "most human selves" when we grab on to others who seem similar to us, and urge them to express what is on their minds. But in these instances we run the risk of merely offering different sets of constraints, different definitions of freedom.

In the end, one is left believing that there are good life studies and not such good life studies. Some studies genuinely honor human life, the circumstances that govern and provide contexts for that life, as well as the recounting of it. Some work also enhances the lives of the participants. How one evaluates the type of work we have been describing will not be addressed here. We can say, however, in light of our previous discussion, that these evaluations will be as subjectively rendered as the life study itself, and influenced by the same political and social structural realities. On the matter of enhancing human life through the type of work one does, a brief remark may be offered.

No one can say authoritatively what sort of social scientific inquiry ultimately will enhance human life. Hundreds, perhaps thousands of now faceless men and woman spent millions of hours cultivating molds in petrie dishes. The results of their individual efforts may seem small, but the methodological tradition of the inquiry led to Fleming's discovery of penicillin. There is, of course, the serendipitous discovery, but it always is grounded in a well-established, often effete-appearing tradition.

One cannot predict what people will do with the accumulation of words that constitute the accounts of private lives and public experiences. As we remarked earlier, the same data can be used to justify wholly antithetical intellectual and political perspectives. Regarding the life study, there is no guarantee that the information one collects is of greater or lesser value, as judged by any set of criteria, than the information accumulated through other equally tentative and imperfect methods.

Clearly, no one method alone will ever constitute a science. On a personal note, however, the method we call observant participation, the rendering of a life study, seems to be congenial to those researchers who prefer to "photograph" people and situations in more natural settings. Such researchers do not fit into the social-psychological harness required to perform other sorts of interpersonal inquiries. They are unlike those researchers who make their inquiries into human behavior by staying as far away from people as they can, or at least by ensuring that the social situations in which they make their inquiries are free of genuinely personal exchanges and sharing. Right or wrong, these investigators claim that the sort of mutual recognition and the friendship upon which the life study is predicated would contaminate their investigation and distort their results. Their contention well may be true. For scientific, psychological, and political reasons, there are times when human beings label and treat other human beings as research subjects, guinea pigs. Their involvement with their subjects is highly circumscribed and, in many instances, presumably justifiable. But in undertaking the life study, many of the principles and ethics of the so-called laboratory experiment are irrelevant and inappropriate.

Our work is not a collection of manipulations with experimental subjects. However, no research can totally avoid human manipulations of one sort or another. In simplest terms, the researcher possesses a special power; he or she maintains ultimate control, although manipulations work both ways. Nonetheless, I prefer to regard the research as a series of conversations with friends. These conversations, as I have stated, are never free of the influence of political and social realities. Whether or not my own words from the conversation are included, my sentiments, feelings, and politics could not be more in evidence.

As for whether or not these studies enhance life, one cannot say. Partly, it is too soon to tell which one of the petrie dishes with which we presently work in the social sciences may lead to some valuable method, insight, or theory. Partly, too, what one does with and for one's friends is not necessarily relevant to the recording of the accounts of lives. It is appropriate to suggest, however, that the researcher's attitude toward someone he or she calls a friend is likely to be different from the researcher's attitude toward someone he or she calls an "experimental subject"; again those social structural realities that so strongly influence our private beliefs and tastes. Different sets of ethics develop from these two styles of research, along with characteristic perceptions, emotional responses, and definitions of the relationships and situations in which participants find themselves. An experiment has a finite stopping point, a logical, possibly even predetermined instant of conclusion. A life study has no such ending point, except for death. The conclusion of a particular experience or event does not imply the termination of a relationship.

There is another difference between these two types of research, one which Paulo Marcucci also perceived: The life study thrives on the dynamics of memory, recollection, remembrance. In an almost sentimental mood, as in the example of the tourist snapping photographs in an Italian peasant village, the entire enterprise rests on the concept of the souvenir, the tangible present holding tightly to an intangible past. Memory calls for the material that is then processed and presented. The researcher then goes away, and in his or her ideological, psychological, intellectual contexts, creates a final statement, a piece of work. Here memory acts again, as recollections of recollections take form and come together as a subjective recording of private lives and public accounts. The tangible product in this instance may be a book, a souvenir for the participants, a testimony, a statement of belief in the value of preserving human life through daily encounters and friendships.

Reflections and Observations

IN EVERY POOR COMMUNITY in which I have worked, be it in Appalachia, the Midwest, the Southeast, or Northeast, I have heard the theme of genocide. In one form or another, the idea is promulgated by certain groups of people that their unlivable conditions must bespeak a desire for the collective death of the entire human group. Slavery, the death camps, and the Armenian tragedy are constantly cited as proof of the viability and utter seriousness of this ghastly concept. As Menachem Kanter once told me, "How far-fetched can it be? Look at what happened, look at what's happening. What does one need for proof!" In response to the specter of mass extermination, the young ones claim they will fight it out, or make trouble, or seek adventure, public or private, in whatever ways they can. Those in their middle years struggle on, survive, and tell me that it hasn't yet reached the breaking point; at least the government doesn't own them completely yet. With the elderly, however, the death camp sentiment, where it exists, is not so easy to extinguish. Life is reaching its final moments, and the culture seems to be doing everything in its power to hurry the passage. One cannot fight like the young ones; one does not turn so naturally to sexual powers and sexual freedom for release, as one did or might have done a few decades before. Given these conditions, what do elderly persons do or think about to maintain their equanimity and make themselves believe that, in all meanings of the phrase, they are still "holding on"?

In part the answer to these questions is found by rereading the very precious utterances of the people heard in all the books where investigators have encouraged the so-called forgotten ones to be heard. It is through personal experience that people hold on and thereby remain alive. It is in their need to tell their experiences that people hold on to these experiences, to the people who would listen to these experiences, and ultimately to life itself. For a story, a little vignette, "a little nothing," as Leah Cramer would forever call her lovely accounts, may very well be all that a person has, all that a person can reveal of himself or herself.

The point has a certain validity. Indeed, in the end it may be the quintessential point about the life study, especially if one considers the words of the German philosopher Wilhelm Schapp . . . : "We mean not only that we are at all times enmeshed in certain present stories, but that we are at all times enmeshed in many stories, and this being enmeshed, or perhaps having been enmeshed, constitutes our existence."[1]

If we take seriously Schapp's rather dramatic point, then perhaps the act of collecting stories is all that the life study researcher can do, all that anyone can do who cares to hear about another life. Surely the stories told by elderly ones represent or perhaps constitute their attachment to people and to life.

Overhearing conversations with elderly Jews reminds us of the peculiar and not wholly comprehensible status elderly minority people occupy in this country. It would seem in a land that consciously opened its doors to peoples of variegated origins and cultures, America has yet to resolve, in political, social, and psychological terms, its investment in the reality of immigration generally, and its immigrant cultures in particular. This is not to say, of course, that a culture predicated on homogeneous families evolving in the same land for generation after generation is by definition bland or free of profound human differences. Yet a culture like that advanced by America continues to feel the repercussions of decades of immigration. The so-called majority and nonimmigrant families feel these repercussions; so do those people who sense a peculiar closeness to their native lands, or the native lands of relatives they knew only too well. There continues to be in this culture a special status designated for individuals who are perceived as being different, and while a form of situational relevance constantly dictates the terms of how one group is different from another, we nonetheless have set for ourselves standards that all people are meant to attain if properly they may be called Americans.

Putting these various strands together, we behold the picture of poor, elderly Jews sequestered not only by their culture but in some cases by their own families. They become a subspecies, a species of humanity characterized by their differentness and their wholly unstable, even probationary status. Extending the metaphor, the poor and the elderly tend to become in our minds immigrants of a sort. Surely many readers would imagine that all the people with whom I spoke in conducting research on poor Jews in America were born outside the United States. In fact, only a small number were. But their economic, family, religious, and significantly chronological status renders them different; hence we sequester them if only to build up in our attitudinal repertoire a dazzling number of misconceptions about these people. In addition, their sequestered status suggests our own complicated anxieties about aging and our most pitiable standards of relationships, often, with our ancestors. The elderly, one might suggest, do indeed live on a probationary status: Biology gives them but a limited time. But a culture remains free to choose the manner of dealing with this biological given. It may opt for one of the two antipodal extremes: namely, honor the elderly to the extent that they become almost cartoon figures, or put them away where they need never be seen or heard (of) again. Somewhere in between lies the average, expectable treatment of the elderly, which, in America, clearly needs major readjustment. As others have argued, we pay an enormous social and psychological cost by easing the elderly out of *our* normal and daily life. In social, economic, and psychological terms, divorcing ourselves first from our grandparents and then from our parents may be more destructive than the separation and eventual divorcing of marriage partners!

There is another important theme here as well: If the culture in some sense grants, though hardly in magnanimous terms, a probationary immigrantlike status to a number of its human groups, then it must have some feeling that the culture's very life has some probationary status. The culture, in other words, like its members whom it teaches, has decided that human life must be made or broken, proven or disproven, avowed or disconfirmed, within a short period of time. Like the culture, therefore, Americans may tend to see their own lifetimes as experiments, and always with personal time running out. Time must not be wasted, lengthy games are hazardous to our health, for time is running out; if you haven't "made it" by a young age, you'll never make it at all. Ultimately maturation comes to be defined not in terms of its etymological origins as ripening, but as aging, atrophy, and disintegration. To be mature is a deadly prescription; immaturity, while difficult to control, at least means one is still alive. To settle down and lead the so-called mature life means that one already has a foot in the grave. And if this sounds excessive, then let us suggest that even after the years of our short history, we still believe normal life cannot tolerate or accommodate the elderly. Notice we say the elderly, not the weak, the infirm, the sick, the dying. My own research on the elderly was not about sick and infirm, weak and dying people. Indeed, from the outset, I was continually struck with the life of these people, as well as their health and vitality. As Ella Crown once remarked, "An Olympic race I'm not about to enter, but an old ladies' home where you go to die, that I'm also not about to enter!"

Several of the stories are easily identified as pertaining to income, housing, employment, and other specific issues. One theme that recurs in almost every account is that of family and kinship. Much has been said of the Jews' attachment to the concept and reality of the family. Doubtless, some have attempted to prove that the Jew is more involved with his or her family than other religious or ethnic groups are attached to theirs. I would find such attempts foolish and superfluous. The point worth noting is only that I found family attachments to be of the greatest significance to the people with whom I spoke, and hence the natural or forced detachments or uncouplings to be of the most profound significance. Clearly, many people, irrespective of age, wish to live alone. The person who chooses not to marry, not to have children, to live in solitude, is hardly a psychopath or incipient criminal. This is not to say that many elderly people desire to live alone. Yet many, wishing not to be burdens, choose this path only to have those close to them believe this is the way they actually prefer it. If pressed to make a comparative observation on the matter—and it is really little more than an impression—I would say that of all the ethnic and religious groups living in poverty that I have studied, the elderly Jews expressed the greatest amount of criticism, not of the society that bears responsibility for their inadequate circumstances, but of their immediate and sufficiently close family members of higher social standing for simply not taking better care of them.

To make this last point raises the very specter some of the people warned me not to raise: The Jews mustn't reveal their dirty laundry in public. Hardly liked or fully accepted by the majority of the population, the best thing Jews can do, Menachem, Ella, Willy Goldman, and Sonny Blitstein all told me in one way or another, is to keep the proverbial low profile. Lead a good life, a pure life, accomplish, make money, and stay invisible. Then *they* can say, as Sonny once told me, "Sonny Blitstein? He's Jewish? Such a handsome, nice, rich, famous guy? He's Jewish? I never knew it. Is Blitstein a common Jewish name?" Or perhaps the best sort of story is that told by Johnny Murphy, whose first and simple encounter with a Jew was touchingly memorable. Acknowledging all of these people's experiences, one can concur with their attitude and not raise the matter of those instances—and they are hardly typical—of the personal mistreatment of the elderly Jew by his or her younger and quite likely more affluent relative. Perhaps one should never publicly raise the matter of human mistreatment within groups of people still not fully accepted into the mainstream culture, as it only feeds those who would hunt for ammunition to justify their own acts of arrogance and exclusion. To pick on the Jews, moreover, is particularly precarious as in fact the Jews may have, as they say in political circles, one of the better records in the handling and care of their elderly. But there is a significant point to be made here.

The poor, elderly Jews suffer in this country precisely because they are poor, elderly, *and* Jewish. The many strange, hurtful, and utterly inaccurate slogans and assaults heard by Leah Cramer's parents in a small southern town almost a hundred years ago have not wholly vanished from the language and consciousness of America's citizens. Sadly, many people insult the Jews or perpetuate dangerous stereotypes unwittingly. I write these pages in the year 1980. Several months ago I overheard a young girl, thirteen years old, tell three friends how she had tried to "Jew" a guy down but he didn't budge. I admitted to overhearing that infamous "verb," and inquired of her whether she knew what it meant, or what its origin might be. She knew nothing of the word. Did her parents use it? I asked. No, they did not. Did her school friends use it? Sure. All the time. Did it have anything to do with the group of people known as Jews? No, there was no connection; she and her friends were quite certain of this. Finally, had she or her friends ever met a Jew? No. Well, one of them thought she might have once, but then again, she wasn't sure. The scene was a McDonald's restaurant, downtown Boston, across the street from the old Boston Garden, where the Bruins and Celtics played their home games. I told this story one night to Leah Cramer. She nodded, then remarked so softly I barely heard: "You'd like to think things have changed. But no, they haven't. Still, they *must* have changed in all these years. Life can't be led without reason. All of us *have* to make a difference."

Things *have* changed; there can be little doubt of this. But within the Jewish and other ethnic communities a strain of prejudice is still felt, by all members, whether or not they choose to acknowledge it. When the Jews immigrated to America in increasingly larger waves, they received open attack. Not only varying from their European ancestors, which became still another reason to dislike or distrust them, their incorporation and presentment of so-called American values and ideals became grounds for abuse. Howard Morley Sacher writes: "They were criticized by newcomers, and some acerbic native critics, for being shallow, materialistic, secular, nonintellectual."[2] But notice Sacher's next point and its relationship to a point made earlier: "This was the criticism that was leveled *at America itself* by many Europeans and some of it not without validity."[3] . . . Unfortunately, if the Jews in general were made to feel only barely welcome, if they were, as we suggested, placed on a probationary status not unlike, in symbolic terms, the Ellis Island status of newcomers, then elderly poor Jews receive the abuse felt by other members of their own community. The family living on probationary status, the family feeling a not at all imagined sense of distrust or disapproval from the greater society, in the absence of genuine power and status offered only to those members and descendants of the main culture, will inevitably turn their reaction to this probationary immigrant-like status into self-deprecation and shame. Being the objects onto which destructive and negative attitudes are *displaced*, the minority group member is bound to displace his or her own sense of discomfort, shame, or hurt on to the next one in line. This may be another minority group person or, more likely, members of his or her own family who seemingly represent the very qualities the main culture attributes to the Jews, or the very qualities, as Sacher observed, that Europeans attributed to America itself.

What better target of shame, self-consciousness, displeasure, embarrassment, than the elderly poor Jew who perhaps speaks only Yiddish, or English with what is still called a "broken accent," who likes the food from the *old* country (which may say something about the food in the *new* country), and who in many ways represents everything the Jew should not be if the main culture is first to accept him or her, and second, accept its own value structures and cultural ideals. Said simply, despite the existence of a widespread Jewish philanthropy, there remain the Jewish poor, some of them possibly mistreated by their own family, not primarily because of personal hostility and malfeasance, but because, in a much greater historical and sociological context, the Jews have not yet been accepted in the world or in the countries they chose to adopt as their own. Thus, the weakest of their members, the most vulnerable of their group, become objects of supreme ambivalence and painful guilt to their own families. Elderly poor Jews may symbolize one's own feelings, but even more, they symbolize the failing of a country to deal honorably and decently with all of its populations.

Some people, inspecting their own relatives, may just think, if *they* ever saw my old relatives, what would they think of *me*? Will I be brought down by my old mother's or father's condition, lifestyle, personality, accent, breeding? Will I be punished, mistreated, or demoted by dint of the presence of these elderly people? It seems an utterly selfish and unforgivable sentiment, but if it exists it does so because full human inclusion of the Jew has not yet been attained.

Perhaps the underlying theme of this entire study may be summarized in terms of a separation of groups of people, groups who under more noble circumstances would be living, if not together, then at least connected by a viable social tissue. Approximately 100,000 Jews entered the United States each year from 1900 to 1913. About that same number of Jews left their homelands to enter other countries during those same years. Literacy tests as forms of immigration obstacles were voted by the Congress of the United States in 1896, 1913, 1915, 1917, but presidential vetoes kept the immigration flow active. Still, in quantitative terms the numbers are small. "The numbers are always small," Menachem Kanter once advised me, "when it comes to the Jews, except when you count the suffering and the dead." In qualitative terms, the enormous separation and disconnection in social, psychological, and philosophical dynamics, which in some measure is what the diaspora is all about, is so great no single culture will ever fully comprehend it. Surely the Americans, Jews and non-Jews alike, have barely begun to articulate and integrate this continuing immigration experience, seemingly, of an entire people.

For the Jew, who feels or chooses to ignore the intellectual as well as personal ramifications of these broad and intensely complex social, historical events, something in the nature of an everyday experience must be played out. Partly this is done in reaction to the constant need to resettle oneself and one's people, partly as a way to solve the burdens, anxieties, and guilt associated with the constant reshuffling and uncoupling of people who by human right ought by now to have their homelands. The arena for this trying psychological drama, naturally, is the family, and most particularly the characters who stand for the various generations, and the experiences of these respective generations, not to mention the tensions between them. One's social class, lifestyle, age, or even name necessarily will carry a special added weight because of the social history of that particular human group. It goes with the territory, as the saying has it. It's an ironic expression in this one instance, since the people in question, in this country anyway, don't seem to possess much of a genuine territory. What they do possess is the territory constituted by their unique social and personal histories, a territory we have sampled through a research method called the life study.

Human experience, personal as well as collective, contemporary as well as historical, comes down to a single story, the biographical or autobiographical rendering: this remains the sacred territory, no matter how profane may have been the treatment shown the teller of the story by his or her present culture or prior cultures. In the end, what makes us all great is not the particular story we might tell, but the fact that we all have a story; and the story connects us to history and to one another, even those people significantly older or younger than ourselves. The point of the story, finally, need not be that we learn about ourselves and our own particular histories when we listen to the story of another person. The point is simply that we may learn about that other person and his or her history, and that lesson may well suffice. As the Jews might say, *Dayenu:* It would be enough.

Notes

1. Wilhelm Schapp, *Philosophical Stories,* 1959.
2. Howard Morley Sacher, *The Course of Modern Jewish History.* New York: Dell, 1987, p. 540.
3. Howard Morley Sacher, op. cit. (emphasis mine).

Observations by Way of Conclusion

⌒

AS AN AMERICAN WELL aware of racial violence, it is logical that I would speak to West Indians about the possibility of violent action in England. Their views, as always, vary, although many young people seem to believe, as I do, that increased violence is likely. Their assessments of the situation are made carefully, and with sophistication. The young people with whom I spoke are informed on English racial matters, as well as on the situations in South Africa, America, Rhodesia. To be sure, the social and political developments of these countries are not identical to the developments in Great Britain. Still, people learn from these developments, and young people are learning their role in the liberation movement of these various countries. Moreover, it is misguided to say that on racial matters England is America, 1950. England lives in the 1970s. Its West Indian families know all about American race riots, civil rights protests, and the S.S.R.C. movement in South Africa. On the surface, certain aspects of the British civil rights scene look to be vintage 1950s, but to the West Indians they are most definitely vintage 1970s. The families spoke to me of increased dangers in day-to-day living. Some observed that England's politicians were walking the same path to tragedy that American politicians had walked. And in almost every home I heard the statistics regarding rising violent crime rates in London.

It should be said that my conversations about violence, especially with West Indian parents, were not conducted in vengeful or defiant atmospheres. Typically, the conversations were thoughtful and calm; words were spoken with a resoluteness and an acute poignancy. Many West Indians spoke in characteristically calm, unfretting, unaggressive tones about white English people. They saw England as a nonviolent nation, a culture safeguarding a stronghold of civility. They also felt white English people concealed their anger, impetuosity, even joy. They agreed that the notion of keeping a stiff upper lip, which I've always imagined means keeping oneself from screaming or crying, is a difficult posture to maintain. White English, several West Indians suggested, keep a tight watch on themselves, and expect everyone else to do the same, except, they said, when it comes to immigrants. "When it's us," Georgina Pointer told me, "they think they're back running their colonies. Look around, and you'll see all the signs of privilege you'll ever want to see. To those people, we're just animals."

I responded by telling Georgina it was my impression that when black people in England break forth in a concerted angry demand for social change, we may see a cracking in that English civility. "Well," she said, "we'll just have to see, won't we? But right now, from where I sit, it's all pretty quiet still."

What scares many of the parents is what scares me as well: Too much of English culture seems to be receptive to violence and violent imagery. Like me, the West Indians were intrigued by how England despaired of America's violent ways while importing as many violent products from the United States as they could afford. We spoke often of how British television was riddled with America's violent programs, and its movie houses jammed with people revelling in America's portrayals of violence. I told Eleanor Cressy once that while I believed certain personalities may hunger for violence, it was more important in the long run that a culture allows it. "People are like animals," she replied. "They can be domesticated. Treat people like animals, and they'll act wild. Seems so sad that we know so much and have come so far, but in many ways we're not that much advanced over our animal ancestors."

As a teacher, Eleanor has observed closely some young people's fascination with violence. They see it as a thrill, a challenge, what many call a rush, because one feels a rush of excitement when one engages in it. "It may make some of us feel safe," she said, "believing that violence is purely an imported product, but it's here now; some people even produce it here. And because it's here, it doesn't do too much good analyzing it. You have to stop it, or the source of it. Violence is like a bacterium, it has to have a host. Then the disease takes over."

Irrespective of whether or not aggression is inborn, people are taught through a process of socialization how to control it, how best to express it. A parent forbids a child to hit his sister, and remarks, "We don't hit people." In time, the boy's hitting of his sister ceases; he has learned his lesson. Somewhere else a child learns how to steal a woman's purse on a street, even hit her if he has to. He may even practice his action and add a few of his own personal twists. But the action, and the necessity for it, are embedded in the structure of the culture in the same way that the culture along with the individual parent cannot tolerate that other child hitting his sister. This is the point Eleanor Cressy drove home to me one afternoon: Violent behavior is learned and expressed as a *reaction* to something real in the environment. People hardly rebel for no reason. "When a person acts violently," she said, "there must be a source, a something against which the person is reacting." She didn't need to finish the point.

Racism, poverty, powerlessness, teach children to be violent. Deprivation teaches violence. Living in untenantable housing, attending unworkable schools where one is psychologically if not physically assaulted, having insufficient food, and being unemployed, teach one violent behavior precisely because they are themselves forms of violence. To be cold in one's own home, day in and day out, is a violent act. These are not empty metaphors. The words of Dionne Stapleton, Polly Davies, Warren Oster, Chloré Donane, and Frank Delano confirm it as fact. "But see, the problem is," Oliver Cole once remarked, and with an uncharacteristic eagerness,

all *you* people ever see is *us* being violent, because you all are too busy wanting to punish anybody who looks like he's about to get into a fight. But you're always too late for the fight. You miss the person who threw the first punch. You always end up blaming us, and go locking us away somewhere. But some of the time, you know, not all of the time, just some of the time, *you're* the ones who throw the first punch. You throw it, then you look the other way 'til we're ready to throw *our* first punch. And you don't do nothing to make sure there won't be another fight. You get what I'm telling you?

I have commented on violence since it was such a frequent topic in my conversations with West Indians. Naturally, it concerns these people enormously, particularly now as they observe an increasing opposition to their presence in England. Granted, they know about agencies working to enhance their rights, but the opposition to these rights seems stronger and more vociferous. Watching the National Front Organisation closely, they remarked on how resistance to immigration seemed to unite people of so many political orientations. "The people are saying," Charles Dooney said, "we don't have enough for ourselves, so how can the government go ahead and let more of *them* in?" A fifty-year-old dairy worker from a town just north of Coventry made exactly this point. His words and attitude made me feel that he had been burned by the touch, the presence of the West Indians, Pakistanis, all immigrants:

It is a crime, all of it. First they come here where they don't belong, and they know it. Then they want their relatives and their relative's relatives. And would you believe, the government lets them have anything they wish, at any time they wish. But help those of us already here? No, they haven't an ear for that. I suppose the next step will be the government telling us *we* don't belong here any more because we're sixth generation, or tenth generation. All you have to do is look at a map and you can see how small the country is. There isn't room for these people. The laws on immigration are so confused the M.P.s themselves haven't a clue to what they mean. But they turn their back on it. They just turn their back on it. But help the people who've been here these hundreds of years? Oh, no. We're the new immigrants. I see what happens in countries where all of this has taken place. This isn't new to the world, you know. But can we learn from it, do you suppose? I should have thought so, but I'm pessimistic about it now. I don't see but that they've let it go on too long. They should never have let in those people, people who make all these demands, and complain about their circumstances. There are no jobs for them, no money, all the schools are crowded where their children go. It's no good at all.

Now he began pointing at me in a strangely accusative way, as though *I* had brought to him the menace he was describing.

They're going to bring down this country if they're not careful. They'll topple it. The rich will leave and the rest of us will go along with them. It will come down. You remember what I tell you. But there will be blood before it happens because people here won't take it. We've asked for nothing special, but we'll start asking now. That's the only way to stand up to this. You know, I talk about this and I feel my body reacting to those people. It's not just my mind. It's my whole person. Oh, you'll see changes now. They've already started.

If the West Indian families feared the National Front, or the import of its movement, they feared equally much those people who maintain utter misconceptions of immigrant families and outdated and pernicious plans for the way these families should be treated. "What gets me most of all," Charles Dooney said,

is that these people's attitudes have never changed, and never will change, and they aren't going to come into contact with people like us if they live a thousand years. But what's worse than them are the people who think like that, and sit in their little offices all day long writing reports about us, and telling the government what the *policy* about us should be. That may be even worse than any National Front!

Charles Dooney's words may have been meant for any number of people, but they were essentially meant for me. His message could not have been clearer: Write a book about us if you must, but don't write policies for us. I chose to read something else into his statement: Instead of analyzing our lives, why not try to analyze why white people hold such grotesque attitudes toward us, as immigrants, and as blacks?

I say "chose" to read this into his statement because it is always difficult to reconcile racist attitudes and outright misperceptions of people, with one's knowledge of and involvement with these people. The conversations I had with black and white families throughout England gave me a clearer picture of attitudes toward immigrants. They let me learn firsthand how teachers felt about the enormous unemployment in their own professions (15,000 of 40,000 teachers unemployed in 1976). I heard various reactions to programs like Job Creation, instituted to get people under twenty-five and over fifty working. Some of the families saw it merely as a stopgap measure. Others described situations in which certain London borough councils had money offered to them by the government for job programs but could not find ways to spend it. And of course there were words about the inevitable budget cuts. With vagueness and confusion about the daily running of government, people could justify to me any and all attitudes toward unemployment and race. Some people claimed that the country's few available jobs always went to immigrants. The West Indians assured me they never saw an extra job or pound. "Let those white people snicker over the twenty-four thousand jobs in that [Job Creation] program," Dionne Stapleton said. "I got lots of friends over here ready to snatch them up." Ironically, the morning after she had uttered this sentiment, I read a report published originally in 1951 by the London *Times*. Children in Czechoslovakia, a correspondent had written, could be legally assigned to whatever agricultural or technological jobs the government chose for them. A child's entire career was determined at this early age by the state. Children could select their own destiny if they chose to work in the mines or heavy industry. A small number of students, usually the children of Communist Party members, were allowed to finish their education.

Along with jobs, and the lack of them, problems related to school and school-leaving always emerged in my conversations. I heard husbands, wives, children arguing among themselves over the issue of whether the government should subsidize school-children's meals. Feeding children was a family's responsibility, many insisted. Then they recited for me the statistics that whereas the average yearly expenditure for subsidising a student's meals is £32, the average subsidy for text-books, pens, and papers for the primary pupil is £7. "They want to clothe them and feed them and treat them like royalty," the dairyman told me. "Feed them, mind you. I suppose that means dipping the fork into the food and lifting it into their mouths as well.

"I can't see what's bothering all these people," Oliver Cole once remarked.

The rich are going to get food subsidies, so what's their complaint? We aren't getting anything they aren't. If they're saying that what they really want is for the government to make *all* of us, rich and poor, pay for our children's lunches, then the writing on the wall is pure and simple: They want to starve us!

If job creation and food-subsidy programs lead to discussions of im-migration and racial tension, then the topic of comprehensive schools practically invited such discussion. Unlike job and food-subsidy pro-grams where family members often disagreed with one another, the comprehensive-school topic usually revealed family members in total agreement. I heard every side of the argument: Education should be open to all; only children with a demonstrated aptitude for learning should be given the best places; schools, like all institutions, necessarily involve exclusionary practices; it's a moral responsibility to move toward the comprehensive; the child is enriched by comprehensive education; society must be opened up; if everyone is entitled to the best, then how can the best remain the best! Then would come the outpouring of atti-tudes toward immigration, those certain recent changes in the United Kingdom, those certain people.

The conversations hardly dispelled my suspicions that a certain de-gree of opposition to immigration was related to attitudes and belief-systems one associated with racism. I naturally spent a great deal of time thinking about the West Indian families and their problems, and increasingly more time wondering about families like my own, and *our* problems about immigrants. How is it, I continually ask myself, that racist attitudes and behavior appear so early in a person's life, and re-main almost unchanged throughout that life? How is it that these atti-tudes, as demonstrated by the intensity with which they are held, could lie so deeply embedded in the core of the personality? As I have just suggested, large-scale social, economic, and historical developments affect people's attitudes toward jobs, schools, housing, immigration, even the future. But there must be a psychological aspect of racial prej-udice as well. After all, we recognize intense feelings in ourselves about certain groups of people, and we observe distortions in our perceptions of certain groups of people. That is, we recognize and observe these feelings and distortions in perceptions, when, after becoming implicated in the lives of these people, we notice our feelings and perceptions changing. Our consciousness, as the contemporary expression goes, has been raised.

In undertaking the type of research I have described, which means walking into new neighborhoods, visiting in homes where I have never been before, with people I have only just met, I invariably think of the human boundary lines the enterprise requires. Always I must work through in my own mind the relationships I have established with people who have consented to speak with me. I have to align and ally myself with the families, and arrive at some fundamental definitions of what sort of friendship is possible at this moment in history. How close would the West Indians let me be with them? How close was I capable of being with them? Where, really, did the boundary lines of friendship and work relations lie? For personal reasons, then, I am fascinated with the following type of psychological theory relating to prejudicial attitudes and feelings, and the tensions inherent when human beings readjust the social and psychological boundary lines between themselves, or do away with these lines altogether.

According to some psychologists, the normal development of the self, and the concept of the self, as being differentiated from other people, other selves, and objects requires that a person construct human boundary lines. A boundary, according to Dr. Sidney Blatt, represents the juxtaposition of supposedly diametrically opposed objects, events, or people. From this juxtaposition, one derives a sense of being differentiated from people and objects: I am me and not my mother. Other juxtapositions common to all of us would be hunger and satiety, exertion and rest, wakefulness and sleep, me and non-me. Still other boundaries aid in differentiating feelings and attitudes from the experiences and people who may have stimulated these feelings and attitudes.

To repeat, boundaries contribute to our sense of what we are, and what we are not, which in turn contributes to our sense of ourselves, our identity. The child, for example, learns that he is a boy, which means not a girl; young, which means not old; short, which means not tall, white-skinned, which means not yellow, brown, black, or red-skinned. In learning about and establishing these boundaries, moreover, children gain practice in letting certain images, perceptions, and feelings be part of themselves, while rejecting other images, perceptions, and feelings.

Thus they are experiencing their first taste of inclusion and exclusion. Equally important, we begin to see that the boundaries have cultural as well as psychological meaning. I am short, but it is not good to be short. I am young; it is good to be young.

Theoretically, children live in a state of tension with the objects or persons from which they differentiate themselves. More precisely, they simultaneously experience a desire to fuse with the object or person on the "other side of the boundary" and a fear that they might fuse with the object or person on the "other side of the boundary." According to some psychologists, moreover, the fear of fusing may represent the wish to fuse with the person or object. The child, after all, wants to be close to its parents, but fears that it may be devoured by them, since devouring represents the most primitive sensation of inclusion, as for example, eating and drinking. In the uterus, moreover, the child in fact is fused with its mother, and possibly continues to represent itself in this fused form during the first days or weeks after birth. In psychoanalytic theory, the baby's mouth and the mother's breast become one, indistinguishable. Self-consciousness is born when one can imagine oneself separated or split off from the other, which in turn allows one to conceptualize a relationship between oneself and one's mother. I cry and my mother comes. My action (crying) brings my mother to me. I am not my mother.

The desire for and fear of fusing remain part of the most primitive sense of self and knowledge about the self. Boundaries, theoretically, represent protections against fusing. Society contributes to the shape of certain boundaries; it sanctions some thoughts and behavior while proclaiming other thoughts and behavior illegitimate. To keep one's boundaries intact, which means remaining differentiated from potentially dangerous objects and people, we employ at least three distinct forms of behavior. They are called by psychologists assaultive, negative, and aggressive. That is, we attack these objects, derogate them, and oppress them. Through these behaviors we ward off the objects and people we fear will fuse with us, devour us, or otherwise destroy our sense of our identity. But fusing itself, we remember, is terrifying because it is a psychological process characteristic of a primitive period in our lives when we were unable to differentiate ourselves from objects and people. So we seek to keep threatening objects and people in their proper place, and apart from us. We do it psychologically, cognitively, politically, culturally. In establishing housing projects and neighborhoods, we reveal the interpersonal boundaries and differentiations we feel we must maintain.

The notion of boundaries differentiating one from objects and people often involves the concept of competition. In assessing ourselves, we run the risk of comparing ourselves with others: I am short, he is taller; I am intelligent, she is more intelligent. Comparison and competition inevitably emerge in differentiations between sexes, generations, nations, and races. At times, the competition results in little more than joking behavior; at other times, it results in an urge to destroy the people with whom we are in competition. But now, if the theory of fusing and boundaries is valid, it is precisely the people with whom we compete most intensely who threaten most profoundly our boundaries, and our sense of self. It is their presence that endangers our own presence, their identity that threatens our own. Manifestly we protect our personal boundaries by derogating or destroying these threatening objects, but latently we fight the primitive impulse to fuse with them and become one with them. It must be this way; why else would white culture continue to perpetuate such unjust practices in housing, employment, education? Why else would physical sequestering and psychological death dominate our policies for poor and minority families? Why else would people retreat to and be obsessed with such primitive forms of assessment of minority families, then treat these families as if they were things, doubt their native intelligence, and distort the facts regarding their everyday life?

In our conversations, many white people insisted that blacks cannot hold their families together. It may not be the fault of black families, they allowed, but it's true. But it's not true, as sociological studies demonstrate. These same people seem to have forgotten, moreover, that the major reason West Indians continued to immigrate to England was to be with family members already residing in England. In listening to these unfounded, psychologically driven arguments, I couldn't help but wonder how I would react to having such primitive and dangerous perceptions publicized about me, and my people. Nonetheless, the important point here is the degree to which distortion of fact is necessary for the maintenance of psychological and institutional racism.

To belong to a racist society, to be part of racist institutions, is to assume racist attitudes even when one is unconscious of these attitudes. More generally, a society's institutions shape one's knowledge of oneself, other people, and objects. Racism requires a set of perceptual distortions, misreadings of reality that are employed in the maintaining of personal boundaries, the juxtapositions of diametrically opposed objects, events, and people. In performing psychological tests, the so-called paranoid person overestimates the size and stimulus intensity of various test objects, and focuses on them to the point of seemingly being obsessed with them. The racist mind seems to work in similar fashion, suggesting that racist institutions teach people to act and perceive in the manner of paranoids. Also like paranoid persons, racists appear unwilling to let information come into them if it conflicts with their present belief systems. Again, in order to maintain their sense of being differentiated from the stimulus object, they seek to control, neutralize, or even annihilate it.

To break this pattern of needing to control people and maintain distorted perceptions about them may be the most difficult problem faced by those in the business we call race relations. The word "relations," not incidentally, is relevant to this discussion of boundaries and human differentiation. It implies reassessments of one's interactions, and one's identity, the very assessments we make when beginning friendships with people about whom we hold such complicated and often dogmatic beliefs. The new assessments of ourselves and our boundaries begin the instant we find ourselves listening to someone, letting their words and experiences pass across the boundary markers we have constructed. It goes without saying that my sense of self and understanding of human differentiations, not necessarily differences, have been influenced by my West Indian friends. In their presence I feel obliged to contemplate human boundaries and the origins of the differentiation of self from other objects and people. When I ask them, "Where did you come from?" it is not only to build up a picture of their migration. The question reflects fascination in origins, sexuality, biography, history. I hear them speak of ancestors and wonder, as a child might, whether long ago we were related, fused. What remains of our phylogenetic associations? Was there ever a time when there were no boundaries, no divisions of people into subspecies, no grotesque nationalism, or distortions in human differentiations? A haunting as well as terrifying directive: "Why don't you go back where you came from!"

While the notion of boundaries remains metaphorical, there is nothing metaphorical about the boundaries established by neighborhoods, council houses, living conditions generally. As I noted earlier, the setting of a conversation affects the topic and feeling of that conversation. I cannot forget Warren Oster's abject dissatisfaction with his home, and his way of always getting me to take a walk. Doreen Grainger was almost two different people: one in her home, one outside of it. All of us know the importance of our neighborhood and home. Neighborhoods and homes have symbolic as well as very real meaning. They represent, often, our beginning; we employ them as standards against which to judge our growth and evolution. As many writers have suggested, the environment, and especially the home, become an extension of oneself. We put life into the objects of our homes and neighborhoods by investing our feelings in them. Part of our self-knowledge is born in the awareness and understanding of our environment. Like the West Indian families, I too have had intense reactions to my own environment as well as theirs. I walk into a room that is dark, barren, uninviting. I tremble and feel cold. It is the room, I know, that has produced the same feelings in me as a scolding from my parents. I had these feelings often in the council flats I visited. Warren Oster, Doreen Grainger, Beatrice and Henry Waters experienced these feelings every day. I felt something else in my own home, however, which I rarely sensed in the council flats: I felt safe, protected, even a bit confident. My environment, moreover, seems to link with my future: When I feel good in my home, I know a sense of hope. Dionne Stapleton agreed with me on this point. She saw her environment running down, her sense of hope running out.

When Doreen Grainger was very small, she announced to her mother one morning, "I am a horrible girl." When her mother asked why she felt this way, Doreen replied, "Because I hate my room!" Mrs. Grainger embraced her daughter, but said nothing on the matter.

Scientists and artists have helped us to appreciate notions of inner and outer space, the realms of the interior and exterior. From these notions we begin to recognize the mutual arrangement between a person and his or her environment. If we are extensions of the environment, then *it* is an extension of us. Residues of the physical world are contained in our temperaments, attitudes, and perceptions. They remain in our approach to the world; they live in our unconscious. People may be reconciled to the inadequate or assaultive features of their environment, but they are never numb to these features. I wonder whether any of the children I have spoken to will ever fully get over the effect of growing up in dirty, smelly, crowded, unsafe rooms. If Doreen Grainger and the others are to be believed, they never will.

The issues are obvious: How can one feel good about growing, ageing, merely living day by day when everything about the physical environment is noxious to the point of causing death? We must want the same things for all children: a home where one is safe, free, healthy; a place where one can be alone as well as with others; a space that sings of home, not prison; a space that receives rather than rejects; a space that repels all the huffing and puffing of the world's big bad wolves. The children's words capture these sentiments and perceptions. Death lurks in too many of their neighborhoods and housing projects; the insidious structures that pass as homes shape their entire destiny. Houses, the children remind me, can kill dreams and aspirations. From the materials, floor plans, the partitions, architecture, too many of these children receive the message: Your whole life will be nothing but surviving; there will be no rewards.

If the weekly visitor to these homes feels this, what can the permanent residents possibly feel? How does a person tolerate toilets that have never worked, windows that have never opened or closed properly, hallways that have never been lit, stairs that cannot take an adult's weight, tiles that cannot contain water? How does one create glorious plans for oneself or one's children when one is beaten down by the environment, and tortured by the suspicion that somewhere people want this environment to be exactly as it is? I should think that it wouldn't be a difficult operation, really, to design adequate hope-giving homes for all people. But, then again, I'm neither a designer nor a politician, merely a dreamer certain of a safe place to sleep tonight.

It is said by some that we must understand that West Indians have no culture of their own, and therefore do not fit into any culture. In fact, West Indians, like all immigrant groups, acknowledge not one but two cultures. Their heritage is more complex than we imagine. The complexity is revealed, especially, in conversations with children, who exhibit a telling involvement in the historical tracings of their families and communities. I recall the words of Doreen Grainger: "Well," she began in response to a comment I had made after studying a photograph of her grandfather,

my family can be traced back hundreds and hundreds of years. We go back to different countries and then to Europe, and then to Holland, and then to France and then to Africa. I think my father said North Africa, but it might have been East Africa. I'm not sure. I should be sure because all of this is important now. But I'm not sure. There are many people whose blood is in my blood, my mother says that. Some of them are white, too, and maybe even there are Chinese people in our family, too. You can look at a map and see where all the people came from if you want to. Each one who is now alive was just a little step, if you see what I mean. History is like a puzzle. Sometimes you have to work backwards to get there, and sometimes you have to work frontwards to get there. I think it must be fun to be a person who studies history, because then you could tell why everything is like it is, and why it isn't different.

Sometimes I wish, instead of getting older, you could get, well, not really younger, but like the years could go the other way and you could end up knowing all your dead relatives, like your grandmother, then your great-grandmother, then your great-great-grandmother, and so on. That would be getting younger and older at the same time. At least I think it would be like that. I can't really decide how it would work. If you went back, would you still be getting older? Yes, that's it. I could die in a hundred years, only it wouldn't be a hundred years from now, it would be a hundred years ago. But that would mean my future already happened, which I'm not sure I like so much. Can you follow any of this?

As I have indicated, children develop a real sophistication about the future. It takes a while in coming, this knowledgeability about fate and destiny, but by eleven it is established. More specifically, I continually noted an appreciation of how the present will be played out in the future. It is said about poor children that they are old beyond their time. In some respects, the remark is valid, in other respects, not. Thankfully, children will always be children. Still, the colossal burdens of poverty, which do age people, are omnipresent. Very young children see precisely the way their life will be led in five, ten, twenty years. They see it because they see their family's and community's development over time. They are experts on this "over time" phenomenon. Projecting the future, and themselves, into it, becomes a special algebra for them, except that the supposed unknown, their destiny, is already known.

The mistake we too often have made in assessing the lives of poor and minority families, is believing that they live impulsively, strictly for the moment, and find planning, expecting, anticipating, unrealistic if not incongruous activities. This unforgivable misrepresentation stems from the fact that we oblige the poor to live in a way that makes them appear as if they live only for the present. We destroy the belief that one can improve one's lot through the housing projects we begrudgingly provide the poor. We crush incentive by denying them achievement, opportunity, mobility. Finally, we perpetrate a belief that poor people, like Margaret Jayner, cannot think in the context of the future, because they have no need for this context.

In my conversations with West Indian young people, I heard myriad images of the future described. Many children spoke of an idealized future in which they saw themselves living in safe, calm, lovely environments, caring for children, earning a decent living. Others drew these same images, then immediately derogated them with a ferocity that almost made me believe *I* had created the images in the first place. But in symbolic terms, I *had* created them. For it is *my* sector of the culture that erects the standards and styles that come to be called the "good life." And it is my sector of the culture that creates the styles and standards of their sector, then labels them "lower class." But this doesn't account fully for the tension I heard in these pictures and assessments of the future. The tension results, too, from the knowledge that experientially the present and future to a great extent are one. It is this belief that underwrites the sense of hopelessness that any rational human being knows if he or she grows up in poverty.

Periodically in my work with children, I have asked them, "How do you see yourself in ten years?" Their responses to this rather inane and unimaginative question have been rich and varied, but many children answered simply, "I'll be ten years older." Such concrete thinking, I remarked to myself, missing the poignancy of their answer. If the sense of competence, motivation, capacity to affect outcomes is denied, if one cannot build present plans into future action and accomplishments, then one is left with nothing but the mathematics of time: In ten years I will be ten years older.

Even knowing that we cannot speed up, slow down, or in any way disrupt time's natural flow, we nonetheless reveal our subjective attitudes about time, and utter statements like, "The future's coming too fast," "Next year's going to be terrific; I'm going to be a new man." The response, "In ten years I shall be ten years older" may well be a concrete answer for the clinician. It may even be a clue to psychopathology or brain damage. In my own conversations with children I believe to be in normal psychological and neurological health, the answer is not concrete. The emotions have been neutralized, perhaps for my benefit or for the sake of a congenial conversation, and the projections of oneself into the future have been made. The result is hard data—the child is going nowhere. Time will move, the world will age by ten years, but there will be no *noticeable* accomplishments, no social advancements, no feeling of change. The sensation must be terrifying, for what greater alienation and oppression can there be than the realization that one's entire life is little more than the ineluctable flow of sand through an hourglass?

The vitality of life is captured not only in the proverbial notion of living each moment as if it were one's last—as if all of us could afford to engage time in this manner—but challenging the unknown quality of the future. It is from this mystery that we derive much of the sense of life, and of living. A person may say, "What's the use of going on, I'm only going to die in the end?" To be sure, the *fact* is right, but the *attitude*, some would allege, is depressive, defeatist, cynical. Yet I have heard this attitude a thousand times in conversations with poor children. In this attitude, they reveal not their terror of the future, exactly, but their dread of it. The future they dread contains their real and imagined destinies. It appears as a closed future, empty, without life and possibility, a mere repetition of the present. Children's religious training will affect their sense of personal evolution and their perceptions of the future. Poverty is the grand teacher, but the type of growing political awareness, resoluteness, and commitment that young people like Jamie Pinkerton, Winston Forgus, Lanny Wheeler, and James Coster exhibit may well change not only some people's attitudes toward the future, but much of what exists in the present as well.

Inherent in the concept of the future is the concept of freedom. As the young West Indians know well, without freedom there is no genuine projection of the self into the future; there is only recapitulation, habit. The habitual response, learned or instinctive, is part of human inheritance. But what will children, who can be so wondrously alive, allow themselves to think about the future when habit above all describes the future a culture has sculpted for them? James Coster, I am convinced, intends to break a great many habits, his own and others. He knows that the very sound of his speech is enough to freeze him and his family in their present social position forever. His father knows this, too. Louis Coster told me once, "Immigrants are like transplanted roots. The only question is, which of the plants will make it, which of the plants will die?" As far as James Coster and Jamie Pinkerton are concerned, their parents' generation dedicated themselves to survival in a new land with the hope of producing a generation that would be able to accommodate itself to the physical and social conditions of this new land. But James, Jamie, and a host of others, I imagine, have a wholly different approach to living in England. They seem unwilling to accept the conditions, stated and unstated, that were imposed on their parents, and thereby meant for them as well.

While the definition of a worthy life may change over time, the young West Indians, like their parents, want to be seen as productive, contributive, worthy. To end their lives where they began is unthinkable, but improvement, they know only too well, requires opportunity. Louis Coster once told his son that if he, James, ever made a lot of money, he would be the most outspoken supporter of England and English traditions. James grumbled, "I doubt it." Louis came back, "You may doubt it, but it's true. The successful ones, even with an immigrant background, always end up loyal to their country. Don't get me wrong, it's good they do. That's the reward they get for ending up successful. It's a taste of the promised land." I saw James staring at his father. If there was an emotion in his expression, I could not discern it.

On Exposing Ourselves in Public

THERE ARE MANY PROBLEMS with capitalism, it has been argued again and again, problems that perpetuate the cruel treatment of the powerless and poor by the powerful and rich. Tax loopholes, the process of inherited wealth, and, above all, private property are among the problems, indeed evils, of capitalism. The question one must address is this: Can a democratic society emerge when people *own* the land, *own* the tools and industries, *own* those who labor for them?

In the 1960s, a decade some point to as a period of genuine social revolution, capitalism came under brutal attack. At the most moderate and sanguine professional meetings, one heard references to changing the economic system, fighting the laws of private ownership. America needs changing from top to bottom, these professionals said. Money is the root of all evil, and private ownership, the ground in which this root grows.

But this is only part of the so-called social revolution, the part that attracts the economically and politically minded. There is another part that involves the psychologically minded. This part too has as one of its founding principles an abhorrence of what one might call the ownership of psychological property or, more simply, privacy.

It is peculiar, this psychological part of America's social revolution. It seemed to surface quietly enough, but gradually, among a great hubbub about the importance of free expression, the release of the repressed, the necessity of being open to everyone and to every experience, came a new cry! Let it all hang out! To have private thoughts, private emotions, was deemed as pathological as owning land, a cotton factory, or company store while others went hungry, unclothed, unsheltered. Now at these professional meetings where everybody agreed on the evils of capitalism, they were speaking of the importance of spilling guts, baring souls, opening up fully to one another.

New businesses developed from all of this, and a new professional cadre was born, seemingly overnight, to help the rest of us uptight folks become downright loose. They were telling us, this new cadre, that even if it meant taking lessons or traveling long distances to special resorts and retreats, it was essential that we learned to get those inner feelings out of ourselves right there up front for everyone to see, and hear, and touch. First the clothes, then the easy feelings, then the tough feelings, the easy-to-tell secrets, then the hard-to-tell secrets, then the entire inner self. And when all this stuff had been exposed and we were just about psychologically everted, the reality of psychological private property would be obliterated and we would be free, or equal, or renewed— or something.

Almost any history of a small town contains references to gossips, informants, distributors of illicit news. These histories reveal both the need of people to have their private news broadcast on gossip circuits, and the need to receive some affirmation of their status by giving or hearing news in return.

In the United States, the advice to the lovelorn column and, most conspicuously, the gossip magazine, gradually turned the expression of private fears and wonderings into a multimillion dollar business. In the fifties, there was an exposé rage. Movie stars, the objects of our erotic and infantile fantasies, became the victims, along with athletes and political figures. If a person did anything public, there was no justifiable reason for that person to claim any right to privacy. The exposé magazines entered the bedrooms of these people; Hefner-like industries undressed them; television and newspapers probed whatever was left. Some of America's stars loved this sensuous trespassing on their private property, some of them fought the exposure hounds. What too many of the trespassers forgot was that even the most narcissistic of us occasionally needs to worship our own reflections in private.

Then, too, the 1940s and 1950s ushered in the paranoia about communism, that seemingly fuzzy body of political theory that in fact contained some rather trenchant notions about private ownership and free speech. So, while some dug around in the social lives of celebrities, others dug into files and private papers and eventually into the ideologies, psychologies, philosophies, indeed into the very minds of men and women. What had been covered was exposed; what had been silenced was made audible to the point of its being deafening; what had been discretely private was made outrageously public. At that point almost an entire culture was involved with erasing a significant boundary line between public and private domains, between collective and individual existence.

The issue of whether or not an individual has any right to privacy or even to value privacy was complicated not only by the actions of the media, but also by research findings and the dissemination of these findings. Countries have always spied on one another, as have competing industries. Keeping watch on next-door neighbors is no new business as Thorstein Veblen made clear, and as David Riesman articulated in his description of the other-directed person in *The Lonely Crowd*.[1] But in the last thirty years, research in the natural and social sciences also has been influenced by the desire to divulge the mysteries of the universe. An ethic of investigative reporting has grown up in the enterprises of many researchers. While some scientists work—as we imagine scientists have always worked—quietly, modestly, amidst their mysterious paraphernalia and idiosyncrasies, other scientists push for divulgence and recognition, seemingly unaffected by the personal hurt such divulgences may cause, or what ramifications might ensue from their hunt for recognition.

In its schools, this country has seen a revolutionary transformation in attitudes. Granted, since the turn of the century public schools enunciated personal development, discipline, and getting along with others as the major purposes of education. In the last decade, however, the classroom has fostered both the colossal rise of a business known as psychology, and the growth of an apparatus known as guidance counseling. In many grammar schools now, one finds compulsory sensitivity or human growth groups where children as young as six years old are obliged to reveal intimate feelings as well as attitudes toward one another. In some of these programs, children earn points for their team merely by talking. Thus, taciturn children run the risk of seeing themselves as "problematic," not to mention losing the game for their team. While the children sit in their little chairs feeling the assault on their little psyches, their parents—in after-school programs, most of which, thankfully, are voluntary—sit in their big chairs feeling the assault on their big psyches.

It all seems bizarre as one describes it, but the preoccupation with people revealing and divulging has gone far beyond what many of us imagined. In California schools, professionals are beginning to diagnose a new childhood illness called shyness, from the Middle English "schey," meaning, alas, timidity. It has been deemed pathological, dangerous for the child. In some cases, drugs are administered to these children in order to "open them up" and have at least some of "it" hang out.

In many schools, the value of individual study habits and working alone, encased in one's privacy, has been philosophically and architecturally precluded. Consider a simple question: On what surface should children write? A desk in which they can store their own belongings, or a table where space, by necessity, is shared with three or four other children? The mere presence of the desk or table bespeaks the value that a particular school places on individual learning or collective learning. While myriad factors obviously go into the decision of desks or tables, open classrooms or closed ones, rooms without walls or spaces with built-in cubbies, one might well discover that schools without desks are also schools with elaborate guidance personnel systems.

The major point one draws from the increased use of mental health facilities in schools is that certain educators believe that affective learning is as important to a child's development as is cognitive learning. Once, there seemed to be a distinct separation of these two approaches. One either advocated traditional pedagogic and traditional course work, or one argued for sensitivity training, psychological openness, and the *feeling* of learning.

The disparity between these two philosophies partly reflected the traditional distinction between the child-rearing role of the family on the one hand, and that of the church and school on the other. Historically, it was the family's responsibility to shape its children's emotional lives. Schools were meant for learning, the church for moral development. Now, with the influx of mental health workers and psychological researchers, schools are taking responsibility for cognitive, emotional, and moral development. In this regard, families have also been pried open and their once-private negotiations made public. Thus one finds traditional structures underwriting affective educational procedures, and, in consequence, sensitivity training is valued in the same way as language arts, social studies, and mathematics. One of the more distressing results of this human growth industry in schools and the more general popularization of psychology is that too many people have actually been trained to believe that only professionals can deal with their children.

In the practice of psychotherapy, a similar though frequently inadvertent attack on privacy has been lodged. Medicine and its allied fields of healing have always confronted the question of which patients receive special treatment and which ones can rightly be used as case studies. Once it was the rich, in their private rooms with private records, and as much anonymity as hospitals could muster who were allowed the greatest privacy. Public clinics meant public knowledge of patient, illness, treatment. The poor were used as specimens, displays, for experimentation. In mental health treatment, this same pattern held. The names of wealthier patients—those referred to as private patients—were withheld from practically everyone, while the names of clinic patients were bandied about hospital meetings and social gatherings.

Someone once wrote that studying the poor is called sociology, studying the rich, exposé. This distinction may no longer be valid, for now even the rich cannot be assured of privacy or immunity from being used as specimens for grand rounds. Similarly, one finds a great many psychotherapists revealing facts about their patients to the point where patients' identities can easily be inferred. While confidentiality may be promised by psychotherapists, it frequently is not delivered. One hears stories of videotapes of patients being played for audiences, some of them not even professional therapists, when patients are not aware of this practice. One hears the spouse of a psychotherapist speaking about patients, occasionally even by name. Indeed one hears many patients speaking about their therapists. Apparently these people assume that their own psychotherapy is an act necessarily open for public consumption. Someone recently likened the announcement that one is entering psychoanalysis to the announcement of a birth of a child. "With great pleasure and extreme humility, Thomas J. Cottle is proud to announce the birth of a 190-pound character disorder with underlying depressive traits." Can anyone anymore assume confidentiality? Can anyone guarantee it?

Research subjects, too, are often left unprotected by investigators. Having been promised confidentiality, their names, interview protocols, test results are discussed in the cafeterias, offices, and elevators of research institutions and universities in the same way and with the same irreverence with which one discusses professional athletes. There are always the careful therapists and researchers who abide by the covenants of confidentiality, but transgressors abound. Like adolescents experiencing sexuality for the first time, they must tell all.

If one recalls one's grammar school and high school days, images quickly return of students daring one another to try something, forcing one another to engage in some act. Peer pressure always has been around, but it is now being accentuated by the growing ethic to make the private public. Free speech has been turned on its head. Divulgence and revelation are the battle cries. Nothing human beings do must remain secret; no one is to be reclusive; nothing about the body must be mysterious. As the physiology and biochemistry of the brain are slowly, slowly understood, the contents of one's mind must be quickly, quickly reported. If it takes drugs, electric shock, psychosurgery, or some other form of artificial stimulation to open us up to new experiences, new levels of consciousness, new forms of public display, then we will not only embrace these stimuli, but we will develop astonishing rationales for their value and locate some grand historical moment when people contemplated similar ideals. It's becoming so hard nowadays to keep a secret, so hard to lose one's job or virginity, one's identity or sanity, one's health or loved ones, and not write a book about it. Holding things in is dirty, letting them out is cleansing. There can be no more fright when one's inner world is seen in the light of day, in the presence of other people. When we tell everything no one can control us.

One of the sad ironies of America's mania to expose everything and make privacy an impossible reality is that those who present themselves as anti-capitalists have in fact found a new commodity, the inner life, which becomes a marvelous source of profit. About the only book not yet written in that how-to-live-your-life category is how to survive in the face of the onslaught of how-to-live-your-life books. The sequel to Eric Berne's volume, *What to Say After You Say Hello,* might well be, *I'm Leaving Now; Hello Is All I Wanted to Say.* The new profit takers of revelation may be fighting the old warhorses of individualism, existential aloneness, and what David Bakan called the agentic quality of human endeavor.[2] Their hopes, presumably, are to replace these old spirits with a public effort at communalism, the sharing of all goods and services, and a society based on the collectivization of everything from family to industry to government to people's unconscious.

The danger lies, as it always has, in coercing people to reveal that which they prefer to hide. The problem, as educators and physicians well know, is how to keep everyone's records private when the police, employers, armed forces, and insurance companies insist on inspecting these records. The danger is that with an enormous amount of information being collected by hundreds of agencies on millions of people, there will come a movement to predict human behavior instead of just analyse it—which often seems bad enough—and to control behavior on the basis of what *might* evolve. Without valuing private behavior and in opening all records, we will begin to treat people as *potential* psychopaths, *potential* criminals, *potential* delinquents, *potential* assassins. In fact this movement has already begun. We are less than a decade away from 1984. The danger is that the FBI and CIA will continue to spy on citizens, and that reputable newspapers, themselves decrying yellow journalism, will print the findings that the CIA and FBI uncovered but had never before made public. Already there have been victims of this so-called legitimate revelatory reportage.

The purpose of any sane political ideology should be freedom for all human beings. In psychological terms, we want all people to experience the feeling of freedom and be affirmed in their desire to feel free. In many instances, divulgence, revelation, candor, yield a wondrous sensation of being free. Unquestionably, people must be able to free themselves of ideas and emotions that trouble them and upset their relationships with others, and that in many cases confuse and damage institutions. Children must be allowed to safely reveal their problems to school personnel, workers their inner worlds to one another and their employers, family members to one another. The quest for knowledge must never cease. One might even say, albeit reluctantly, that people have a need to confess or let others know bits and pieces of their private selves.

But if there is a need to reveal, there is also a need to protect and withhold. We may be making a grievous mistake in forcing people to believe that every secret, every sentiment, every inner inch of themselves must be exposed. Freedom of speech must not be confused with perpetual human openness. One is not attacking the concept of private ownership or safeguarding the First Amendment by supporting publicness at all costs. One is merely creating another artificial need, the need to cleanse by candor and exposure. Watergate administrations, foul dealings in industry, CIA interventions in foreign countries, the oppression of peoples, these must be exposed and expunged. But as the oppressed of the world well know, freedom demands restraints. How many thousands of times one hears in conversations with the poor of this land, "The government can make all the rules for living, but it will never tell me what to think, what to say, and when to say it."

Sometimes the poor reveal a quality and intensity of expressiveness and openness unmatched in our society. Their openness and seeming lack of privacy is so dazzling, one believes they have never known constraint. At other times, however, they reveal that posture, that way of surviving in the world they first called, and now we call, "cool." Suddenly the expressiveness and openness vanish, and we have no idea what plays in their heads. We have no sense of their attitudes toward us, no idea of their plans. The cool ones, like the silent and reclusive ones, frighten us. It is best to know where they stand, what they think, what they feel. When they reveal themselves, we have some hold on them.

The balance between personal and societal exposure on the one hand, and privacy on the other, is precarious, to say the least. Presently, a band of new profiteers is yanking us toward a world without personal protection, fences, shower curtains, clothes, a world of eternal lightness, without shadows, without night. Some of us prefer to hold on to a few secrets. We don't fear psychoanalysis stripping us of our meager bursts of creativity; we fear the ethic of publicness ripping away those private vessels in which the fluid of life is kept fresh, if not always pure. We fear a point in time when, after accommodating ourselves to seeing nakedness on television, and then sexual behavior on television, and then sexual behavior in the midst of family therapy sessions on television, and then videotape feedbacks of ourselves watching sexual behavior among and between several species in the midst of interphylogenic therapy sessions on television, the tube will suddenly glow white, and all the lights of our homes will glow light, and the light outside will blaze, and we will see nothing and feel nothing.

Notes

1. David Riesman, *The Lonely Crowd.* New Haven: Yale University Press, 1950.
2. David Baken, *The Duality of Human Existence.* Chicago: Rand MacNally, 1966.

A Family Album

IT HAPPENS THAT I have begun writing these pages at the end of a visit from my uncle, a man who served as a grandfather to me. Although he promised to stay longer, he spent only a day with us before driving south to join other relatives, some of whom, he said, he expected never to see again. He said, too, that he was eager to return to his daughter's home so that he could be with her on her wedding anniversary. He had plenty of time, it seemed to me, but he wanted to leave. He is eighty-three now and has been a widower for several months. He told me he had known his wife for almost sixty years. It was strange seeing him without her. When we were young we would see her and not him, for my uncle's work required him to travel a great deal. But now he was here, and she wasn't.

Our children understood when I said that my uncle was like a grandfather. Like Pappa I told them, using their word for their two grandfathers. Our daughter did not ask about his wife; she remembered we had told her about my aunt's death. By the time my uncle left, she was calling him "uncle." She knew the elderly gentleman who had stayed with us only one night was a special man. She knew, too, and she was only four, that by putting the word "uncle" before his name, she was pulling him closer to all of us. By tying herself to my uncle, she knitted us all together and, I suspect, felt comforted knowing that she was part of a family larger even than our present constellation of mother, father, daughter, son, and two cats.

In great measure my uncle's visit and my own and our daughter's responses to him is what this work is about. In all the lives represented here, I have heard this call for a family, a family not only of children, parents, and grandparents, but for one that cuts across more extended boundaries. In spite of talk about the decline of the family, my visits in the homes of people in poor and rich communities convince me that the idea is very much alive, that people want to be related to one another. Our age has ruled against sentimentality in favor of tough thinking and analytic discourse, but people's feelings do not always honor this ruling.

Something else that these visits and conversations have made clear is that the notion of a personality being formed in the first few years is only partly true. Sociological events like courtship, marriage, the accumulation through marriage of a new family, and most especially the birth of children yield a new foundation of personality on which the first years of life may find a successful resolution. And then there are separation, divorce, and death with which to contend. Sociological events refer to more comprehensive phenomena than ceremonies or momentary happenings. They refer to the features that describe one's age, one's point in the life cycle, and one's position in the culture. How casually we often take someone's age or social standing to be. We say, "He's eighteen," or, "She's a poor kid," and these simple words and numbers adjust our conceptual categories so that all sorts of issues are automatically "explained." But no outsider can ever know the meaning of being a particular age or growing up in a particular neighborhood in anything but the roughest ways. The precise experience of being poor or eighteen requires a closer look. Without this, one is, I think, in touch with one's own perceptions and categories but not with the substance of another person's life.

Here is the point: The marriage between professional analysts and the media has produced an increased need to know. In itself, there is nothing wrong with this, for analysis of something like the American family and hopefully the knowledge that comes with it enhances each of us, presumably, and our culture as well. But what frightens some of us is that the need to understand and analyze has frequently meant that individual life histories become minimized or treated in a fashion that eventually makes us distrust them. It is as if we are saying, "Tell me what it means, but don't burden me with the actual events of that person's or family's life." Analysis can get in the way, too, by interposing itself between the viewer and the viewed; and the experiences of the viewed are never felt by the viewer.

In studies of personality and family, this tension between feeling and analysis will inevitably be a brittle one. To counteract it and, in a way, to attack the culture's overriding technological rationality, we develop still another rhetoric, another medicine, another life style. Words like autonomy, liberation, and freedom pass among us as if they belong to a chain letter. From this rhetoric, which many people use as the basis of their developing life styles, comes a monsoon of slogans that may lead to constructive acts as well as destructive ones. Under the guise, for example, of "do your own thing," genuine autonomy may be bred. But crippling dependencies are also born from this philosophy and so, too, are some of the cruelest acts human beings can do to one another.

I discover, as I write this, an anger toward some object or person, as if I wished to blame someone for the hurtful events that have touched so many people. Paradoxically, I feel the desire to care for people, many of whom clearly don't need my interference in their lives. And this is my next point: The need to know leads in the social sciences, just as it does in medicine, to the search for cure. The medical model is an apt one, for there are those of us pushing cures for something we call an illness, when we're not even certain of the problem, or the cause, or whether the treatment is part of the problem. Each of us lives with the temptation to help someone according to our own conceptions of cure. Some of us do well; some of us push our medicine at others because it is the medicine we are committed to, but not the lives of these other persons. Today, the medicine people are everywhere.

It seems strange to be saying this, particularly as I believe in the necessity of psychotherapists and researchers participating with their patients, clients, friends. But what touches me again and again is the need to listen and to let other persons instruct us in the forms and interpretations of their lives. I am uneasy about the concept of empathy. I know I cannot feel what anyone else is feeling and that I have only the slightest sense of whether my feelings approximate the feelings of another person. I can tell, however, when I am genuinely listening, and my mind wandering is not the best clue that I have turned away from this other person.

The best clue for me is when, hearing the words of another, I begin to assemble some complex structure designed to explain not only the circumstances of this other person's life, but also the lives of those in "similar" circumstances. Then, invariably, I am reminded that no two people share a circumstance and that I had better listen to this one person. When my mind fishes for the "right" thing to say, I know that I am turning away again.

I feel self-conscious saying that the act of living is the most difficult of ordeals, and the creative maintenance of human relationships the most difficult of endeavors. Although surprised by my own triteness, I cannot tolerate an ethic that demands one live purely for oneself and says that if people are to be hurt in one's singular attempts at living, then so be it. Without selfishness and egoism there is no personal drive; no book is written. But the dance cannot be choreographed forever as private and selfish exercises. As frightening or delightful as it may seem, one must learn to dance with another and then another, at times to lead, at times to follow, at times to be merely side by side.

Speculatively, the child, through the stimulation first of the womb, then of touch, smell, and sound, and later of sight, begins to accumulate basic patterns of human relationships. It may be nothing more than seeing the same people together again and again. Too often we forget that children perceive relationships in which they are only indirectly involved.

This would seem to be a simple enough notion, but one must think, too, of those people who watch relationships disintegrate and of those whom society prevents from experiencing constant patterns of relationships. Still, no one should believe that the notions of family and kinship are absent from the minds of children raised in poor neighborhoods. Let no reports or documentaries convince us that such fundamental realities have vanished from their lives. I can understand that families in Appalachia might feel uncomfortable receiving a small gift from the children in Boston. I can appreciate that their sense of accomplishment might tell them to decline the Northern children's money. But I feel from the efforts of Kenny, Tyrone, Kim, Edwin, and the others that a desire to be connected in some greater kinship lives within the children growing up in poverty. Not only do they watch closely and safeguard relationships with blood relatives and friends whom they quickly absorb into their families, they seek to be related to children hundreds of miles away, whose fate somehow touches them. Just touches them, for I can vouch for no more. I have no evidence that these children perceived themselves in the descriptions of the Appalachian poor. I have evidence only that words connected them to these other children and that something of a personal as well as collective nature made them want to touch these other children. This is the kinship they sought to establish. It does not substitute or compensate for some lack of kinship at home. It adds to this other kinship and is made possible by a stable, if not momentous, sense of family integrity.

Arthur and Estelle Downey, Keith's parents, have spoken of kinship with me. Sometimes they refer to the kinship of those persons whom they feel destroy their own family. Like complex molecules, the strands of relationships they see interweave with one another, yielding patterns of social groupings, some of which attract one another and some of which remind the Downeys of the alienating and repellent features of our civilization. But as yet no statistics direct them to those places where family integrity is either easier or more difficult to maintain. They know only of the unadulterated work that the harmonics of family require and have not yet learned that one group is more successful at performing this work than another. Estelle Downey's words remind me that the term "working mother" is redundant.

I hope that no one will take these remarks to mean that I doubt the concept of autonomy. I merely hold that it grows out of experiences of kinship as well as more symbolic or spiritual relationships in which connections may be made with anyone or anything. The acquisition of language represents an early moment of acculturation, an early step in the association of a single life with a broader culture. In the midst of this association lies the development of the family, and within the family are those persons whose voices we continue to hear.

My problem at this point is how to honor the institution of family and the complex reality of kinship—both "actual" and "symbolic"—and still not detract from the life power of the few people whose words constitute my research. It is the issue of the life cycle, the movement of people from childhood to adulthood to parenthood to the hours when their children give birth to children and then beyond, that dominates this work. Intimacy, sexuality, morality, the constraints and freedoms associated with aging, the valuable but still questionable notion of maturity, the final instants of gratification, and the sight of death are also part of the life cycle markers that appear in the lives of these people. But always the private expressions and resolutions of individuality fall within the boundaries of groups and families. They touch, in other words, the lives of others and the institutions these others and their predecessors created, opposed, and eventually lived within.

Young adults struggle with these notions as much as anyone. The balance between individual freedom and institutional constraints represents a major concern for young people. In their efforts and show of will, they make us believe that life can be led at times purely alone, at times genuinely with others. Children feel these same issues, but the impact on them of older people seems especially significant. The reality of generational shifts seems less distinct among young adults, more tangible among children. But whatever the role of older people, their presence is a part of young persons' definitions of their identities. The role of family, in other words, and the sense of spiritual, intellectual, and emotional kinship commences very early indeed.

* * *

Even as a child, and certainly as a young man in my teens, I knew that much of what I thought I was turned out to be what others thought I was. Among my parents, relatives, friends, enemies, and heroes, I was constantly at work rearranging my definitions of self to satisfy others. There were parts of me that I felt to be totally mine and free from the influences of other people. But often, when I sought to proclaim just exactly who the real me was, I found that even these private spaces had been affected by my relationships.

All of this made for a rather confusing period of time. The years of adolescence seemed to be devoted to self-study and searching for the outlines of my identity. From every part of society, it seemed, came a press to know myself, to evaluate honestly and face up to my assets and liabilities, my talents and inadequacies. So there I was, attempting to locate the permanent features of myself on which I could rely, when every day I felt myself changing with each human contact I made and some spiritual ones as well.

How, then, could I possibly have been content with my definition of myself when I was continually changing? For that matter, how could others have believed that they knew me when I nurtured such conflicting, if not antithetical, qualities? I was serious and fanciful, independent and dependent, outrageously conceited and modest to the point of shyness, corrupt and ethical, noisily physical and quietly cerebral, ingenious and compliant. Even with my friends I would take on a new quality or let go an old one, all the while making everyone believe that nothing about me had changed.

Of the many ideas that I considered during adolescence, by far the most important was what I would become. Would my plans, however well formed they might have been, work out? Would I ever amount to anything? Was I a person of worth, and just how did one decide whether or not he or she was worthy of love, acceptance, and an opportunity to lead a rewarding life?

A second consideration was what, in fact, was the real me? This question I carry with me to this day; it is part of my inheritance. It is a question that while never satisfactorily answered, looms especially significant during one's youth. My own sense of independence, for example, was fairly secure, for I believed I could make it in the world on my own. But then came the moment of leaving home for the first time, and my independence was shattered and replaced by feelings of aloneness and a desire to be cared for. I wonder whether people ever get over the shock of leaving home. Like the trauma that is birth itself, the separation from parents must take some toll on one's psyche.

One thing that hasn't changed in the years since my own youth is the need of young people to seek intimate relationships not only for what these relationships provide, but because they compensate for the inevitable separation from loved ones. While comparisons between oneself and one's parents are natural products of maturation, they imply as well a bond between children and parents, one that symbolizes the integrity of the family. My concern, therefore, for what I would become was tied to my involvement with my parents, their values, ideals, and history. Even today, when enunciating my own values, I hear the voices of my parents coming from my mouth as though they lived inside me.

I cannot with any authority point to even one feeling that all young people everywhere know. I often think that the variations and paradoxes one sees within a culture, indeed within a single family or individual, are as profound as the variations among cultures. Still, something causes me to prescribe to the notion of universality; that is, characteristic features of young people spreading across all cultures.

One such universal feature, I imagine, is the need to differentiate between the space one calls one's own and the space belonging to a group, a family, or an institution in which one is a member. Through biological maturation and the process of socialization, young persons appreciate the boundaries between their single selves and those families, groups, and institutions that necessarily influence them. If small children work out problems of phenomenal causality (the door opens because I turn the knob), young adults examine issues of social psychological causality: I am what I am, in part because others affect my evolution.

Although I have used the word several times, I have never been comfortable with the concept of maturity. "He's immature," we used to grumble contemptuously about some kid, and "Wow, is she ever mature," we would swoon after a Saturday night date that proved conclusively how underdeveloped we boys were in comparison with the girls. Perhaps it was the use of standards and the relative development of human beings that troubled me. For, no matter what anyone said, it was good to be mature, bad to be immature. The standards of maturity and immaturity, moreover, were rarely questioned, even by those of us who were still young and immature.

Gradually, the medical and psychological uses of the concept crept into the admonitions of our teachers. "What you did out there in the hall, Tommy, was very immature. I certainly hope your parents don't allow that!" Later the same behavior was called childish or adolescent, but either way the notion of immaturity was implied. It had taken hold, so that even as children we went around labeling people mature or immature. We were students in a progressive school, our bodies in tip-top shape, our psyches rattled a bit by the psychological sophistication of our parents, but nevertheless going through the psychosexual stages the psychoanalysts described like passenger trains traveling from New York to Los Angeles and hitting each intervening stop right on schedule. Still, we found one another deliciously mature—ripe might be a better word—and incorrigibly immature. And, incidentally, this last designation meant undesirable, untouchable, unworthy of equal treatment.

The word "maturity" survives in the literature and language of young people. Where once it implied something or someone being at the point of development it should be, now its uses have spread into social, political, and moral rhetoric. We hear *groups* of people being described as immature. A presumed unwillingness to work, sexual license, and an ability to hold families together have emerged as criteria of immaturity. That social and political factors make it impossible for people to find work and that sexual license and family "breakdown" have never been demonstrated as characteristics of these groups appear to make little difference. The "fact" remains that some of us just seem to be more mature than others.

An important assumption underlies the application of criteria of maturity to personal and social behavior. If maturity is attributed to persons and groups who behave appropriately, not necessarily with style but as "proper" adults, then immaturity becomes associated with child-like behavior. Not only does immaturity connote a failure to live up to one's potential—the phrase we heard again and again as students—it also connotes acting like a child. It means vigorous protesting, talking out of turn, swearing, demonstrating intense outrage, making non-negotiable demands, not dressing as someone "that age" ought to, and not saying the right thing at the right time.

While having utility in scientific and medical areas, the term has become another ingredient in the attempt to neutralize certain lifestyles as well as social and political movements. By labeling someone or some group immature, we may well be addressing a proven psychological or medical condition, but we may also be derogating certain behavior. And because of the medical significance of the concept, the derogation is rendered legitimate and unequivocal.

Typically, the term "immaturity" is invoked when behavior is deemed excessive. It is fine to love, even to argue, but only up to a point, and nothing is more immature than sustained displays of anger. Mild protest in our culture is tolerated, but persistent protest is proclaimed childish. The mature person "ought" to be able to "handle" rejection, loss, deprivation, and frustration. "It's how you play the game," we were always told. "The most important thing is to be a gentleman or a lady."

An important aspect of the imputation of immaturity is situational. No one needs to be reminded that the limits of medical normality are wide indeed. But what are the limits of normal anguish, normal outrage, normal hurt? Do we not say that given one's impoverished circumstance, a certain degree of anguish, is expected, but that after a point the outcries are immature? We may do well, in other words, to diagnose the circumstances in which we oblige certain people to live in terms of maturity and immaturity. Is a housing project or the few staples that can be purchased if a person lives on welfare or the medical care people living in poverty receive capable of allowing human beings to reach their full development and achieve full vigor? Presently, the temptation is to honor only those who "rise out" of poverty and "make it" in more established ways and call those who remain "behind" less vigorous, less industrious, less mature.

As I look back to my childhood, I suddenly remember a phrase that came up in response to someone being called immature. It was a simple phrase, one that everybody recognizes as being a protection, a way of passing on the blame: "But it wasn't all my fault." Evidently, children recognize that their personal development and capacity for growth depends on institutional support. Little is anyone's *entire* fault. Even as I write this, I realize that passing on the blame can be construed as an immature response. Is not autonomy and personal responsibility the goal of the mature personality? I suppose it is, but autonomy is hardly possible in a sick body or in a diseased society, and so the ring of the word "maturity" continues to evoke that earlier uneasiness.

A second universal feature, my imagination says, is young people's growing appreciation of their parents' fortunes and misfortunes. Every young person learns of the constraints society puts on its members. With this understanding comes compassion, and, ironically, new perceptions of time. Notions of reality and fantasy are resolved in terms of their meaning for the present and future. What must people do now in order to become whatever they see themselves becoming? What is the nature of becoming, and how much does family, kinship, and history affect one's own possibilities? Young people conceive of time in ways they were unable to as children. The use of brothers and sisters or parents and grandparents as standards against which to judge their own development bespeaks new connections between the past, present, and future.

Young people's understanding of their parents' circumstances suggests a more general appreciation for periods of time that properly belong to history. Adolescents have reached the stage where they understand the conception of life having gone on before their births. They know, too, about time succeeding them and what destiny means. An impressive developmental step is taken when young persons comprehend the facts of their parents' and grandparents' childhood and adolescence, and, of course, old age. It may seem that the young are hopelessly self-centered and at best indifferent toward their elders. Yet I think it more accurate to say that in the development of the will it is imperative that young persons exercise self-interest and self-love. For like the heart, the will is too easily weakened later on without this early exercise.

Finally, whether they represent universals or not, young people must safely pass through the experiences of first loves and first separations, first encounters with failure and death, first commitments to work, learning, and career, and first thoughtful confrontations with their often paradoxical emotional and intellectual needs. To accomplish this passage requires strength and resiliency that only the young seem to possess in such boundless quantities.

As I say, these tentative universals are merely impressions, nothing built upon reliable evidence. Still, there was an afternoon not long ago spent with several young people, when I thought that perhaps my impressions were confirmed.

"Here's my problem," I began, when the group of fourteen-, fifteen-, and sixteen-year-old students had settled down on the front steps of the old high school. "Do you feel there are things about young people that are the same everywhere?"

"You mean *all* races?" a young man asked.

"How about both sexes?" someone questioned sharply.

"Sex!" another young man blurted out. "Everybody our age in every culture must have heard of sex, or done something, or seen something…"

"Or tried!" someone added laughingly.

"Boys and girls being together," he went on. "That's something everyone our age must have experienced."

I watched one young woman. She had not spoken, but her posture told of an eagerness to contribute.

"It's not sex, exactly," she said. "Oh, sure, lots of kids are having sex. Girls my age are mothers already."

"How old are you?" someone wanted to know.

"Fifteen," she answered. "So sex, well, you have to say sex, I suppose. But a better word is love." There was silence now as the others let the word settle in the air around them. But they weren't buying it.

"Babies and little children love," someone argued.

"Okay, I'll amend my position. Take back love and insert intimate." Just as before, they sat in silence.

"Intimate," someone whispered.

"Intimacy ties us together," the young woman continued. "Something different from love but close to it and related to sex, too, I guess."

"She's absolutely right," a young man broke the silence. He looked at his friend with admiration.

"What about career?" someone wondered. "I never took seriously before what I was going to do with my life. It's like it's only now that I'm old enough to know what decisions about a job or profession really mean. It's real now, for a change. I don't feel like I'm making up things."

"Intimacy and the end of pretending," a young woman suggested. "Knowing the difference between wishing and fantasy. Really understanding how society works, and how it makes you what it wants you to become."

One of the young men picked up her point. "First, you have to realize how much your parents do that makes you what you are. Then you have to realize that what they do to you is influenced by how society impinges itself on *them*."

"Yeah, it's a wonder that anything ever changes," someone muttered.

"You think things really do change?" I asked.

"We're not *all* that different from the way you must have been," a young man replied. His gentleness was comforting. "You must have thought about intimate things and what you'd be and what society was doing to you."

"I've got something." It was the young woman who had brought intimacy into the discussion. "Our age group goes through a special kind of learning. In the first place, we learn what the future's going to be like. No more fantasies about it, it's for real. Then, we have to rethink our past. This is the way our life really *was*. We're not just living day by day. We may *think* we are, but we aren't. Kids younger than us don't see the difference between feeling and knowing. But, like I said, intimacy ties it together. Boy-girl, parent-child, getting involved with one person and then another and then breaking off with someone, something you never do as a kid, I mean a real kid, that's what characterizes *adolescents*." She said the word derisively as she pushed her face up at me. "Right?"

"I don't know," I answered sheepishly.

"Kid hater," someone growled. It set us all laughing.

I keep thinking of that young woman's ideas about intimacy. Personal attachments, getting close to people and then having to move away from them are part of development; learning the grammar of intimacy is one colossal attainment for the young adult. The sense of a social order and the anthropology of human kinships is related to these aspects of intimacy. So is sexuality, vulnerability, the experience of having to give up something, or someone, and the realization that one possesses God-given limitations. Whereas I might have accepted her first suggestion that love, or the experiencing of intense feelings, is what characterizes this stretch of the life cycle, I now abide by her more subtle amendments. Intimacy does indeed tie them together. They know it, just as they know what transformations of the heart and mind they yet must undergo before adulthood settles in for good.

To belong to a period of great change is to have wholly new matrices pervade one's social structure, wholly new images imprinted on one's unconscious. It means that ethics must be invented and, paradoxically, older forms of religion retrieved. While certain groups of people will, by joining their lifestyles, effect alterations of values, other groups will be unable to make these same adjustments and commitments. They may feel personally attacked and unable to stand the ordeal of history taking such precarious turns. In times of revolution, after all, there are the dead and the wounded, the prisoners, the stragglers, and those who bolt from the action because they are unable to locate a principle that justifies their morality and purpose. There are temptations of new regimes and cultures and a primordial sense of allegiance, justice, conscience, and family. There are new involvements with authority and an extraordinary set of experiences in which intimacy and death are entwined.

But those remaining behind know pain. They know it like they know mystery and the darkness. They know it in their bodies, in the bodies of their comrades with whom they lie together; they know it in their psyches. So the young appear with their visions from the East, their blend of psychologies, their experiments with sound, sight, and language, their healing by faith, their image of families extended in ways that only God might understand, and their spirituality nurtured by movie stars, political revolutionaries, rock singers, writers, painters, and, now, again, a man called Christ.

We have spoken too infrequently of the conflicts and the ambivalence that lives within all persons as they make peace and war with Eros, Apollo, Dionysius, society. For many, the themes of love and sexual attractions existing among and between children and parents seems too confusing to sort out. These themes have always prevailed in art, just as they have always served as motives for human action. Still, the ambivalence attending intimacy and sexuality, the pain that drapes the ecstasy, the titillation that mixes with distaste, the inclusion that mixes with rejection, and the freedom that mixes with constraint are often omitted from our accounts. For, there are people everywhere feeling or hearing of the hurts attending the new and "revolutionary" ways of dealing with intimacy, who never speak or write, who never disclose or repeat. At times professional or situational ethics demand confidentiality, at times a sense of the poetic or private bids these people to preserve secrecy and uphold the mysteries of intimacy.

It is not stringent Victorian values, "latent adolescent anxiety," or skittish prudery that silences these would-be tellers. More likely, it is a sense of wonderment they hope to perpetuate and bequeath to their children. For this reason, they scrutinize the dangers and wisdom, the humanity and inhumanity of every document that speaks to intimacy and kinship. They would be called, ironically, the silent majority. With them, I share an uneasiness about reporting their words. What I fear, actually, is not the topics of intimacy, loss, and human suffering or even what has been evoked within me, but rather that I cannot transport the contexts of family and kinship, religion, love, school, and work in which these lives unfold. I constantly wonder whether I have dehumanized these people in the process of describing what is for them the quintessence of the human form and substance.

At one level, intimacy and the experiencing of kinship mean encounter—the encountering of others as well as oneself. Intimacy implies that the processes of maturation and socialization teach one the necessity of linking some restless inner feelings with contemporary and atavistic feelings born from the same inner restlessness of everyone who has ever lived. It means encountering one's inner spaces, just as it means the encountering of the private spaces of another. It means investigation, penetration, immersion into oneself and into another. It means trespassing on magical lands long enough to be certain that one has been there and that the mysteries of intimacy have been kept safe.

In a culture like ours, that simultaneously celebrates impulsive revelation and controlled technological rationality, a culture that tends to confuse, I think, the disclosure of social, political, and economic evils with the disclosure of personal feelings, inner longings, and profound human emotion, a new mystery is unraveled and called revolutionary. In some places, just as at some levels of consciousness, the encountering or the sexuality is collective and communal. Intimacy and not legislation challenges capitalism and the concept of family, and people begin to experience one another in ways that demand redefinitions of marriage, incest, and probably spirituality as well. And all the while others ask wistfully, "How far can 'they' go?"

In every society there lives an extended family or power. It is characterized by its visibility and capacity to affect human rights and feelings, justice and morality. It manipulates mood and action even as it asks for support and license to speak for others. Not unlike classical gods and goddesses, the members of this family watch over the forces of life and death, desiring to touch every person in the world and thereby become intimate with others. Finding themselves attracted to one another through the chemistry of power and fame, they rely on intimacy, if not sexuality, to secure their continuance and immortality. Peculiarly sensitive to finitude, they tend to counteract personal forfeiture and the impulses to destroy and overthrow through forms of intimacy. Ultimately, it is their imaginations that are revolutionary and their public changes and conflicts about style that become incorporated in our own private considerations of intimacy and kinship.

But if there are such things as a sexual revolution or a generation gap or a decline of the nuclear family, then many of us have not yet experienced them. Instead, we know the same old pleasures and ideas, the same old pains of rejection, competition, envy, and exclusion. We know the pain of people hurting one another and of feelings taking bitter tolls. We know the pains of loneliness or of someone—child, parent, or grandparent—being no more. We feel the glory and pain of our conceptions of ourselves and others, as well as the anguish of not knowing how to build these conceptions from scratch, from those we love, from those we thought we hated. We know the pleasures and pains of selfishness, self-interest, and narcissism, ours and the other person's. We know the pleasures and pains of giving, too, or the feelings that derive from responding to "the call" and getting prepared to give. And each of us, from some not so metaphysical inner depth, knows the pleasures and pains of being the sex and age we are and senses the pleasures and pains of the other sex and other ages.

Then, in the midst of acknowledging these pleasures and pains and sensing, too, that morality and the nature of the family are out there somewhere changing on us even as we adjust our lives to them, we abide by still more modern dictates of intimacy. We convince ourselves that existential problems are fundamentally problems of intimacy; the encounter, we prescribe, holds the cure. We beg to hear scientific analyses of our predicaments and feelings and expert generalizations built upon the utterances of some children, young adults, parents, and grandparents who, even as they spoke with me, knew that they represented only themselves and chose to refer only to circumstances they call their own.

It is not the dream of a child to say that our ultimate purpose in these inquiries is the application of all fields of knowledge to the reality of living and dying. It is the life cycle that becomes the crucial variable, the life cycle of a cell, a psychic experience of a human being, a family, a culture. Because of our need to make things endure, we are constantly on guard to assure full development, whether that be in organic or psychological terms. But, again, there is no full development without commensurate health and maturity in families, communities, and cultures. To be ripe, full grown, vigorous, and on the way to becoming due is precisely what the disenfranchised everywhere have never experienced.

It is not purely metaphoric to say that the observation of a single life is also an inspection of the human condition and its place in some evolutionary scheme. As observers and participants we look both within the single life and beyond it to our own and to other cultures. We look to political, economic, educational, and religious institutions as we become implicated in the life of another person. We look to the meaning of an age group, to the families in that age group, to those with families and without families, to those who have enough to eat, to those who have never felt satiation. And we never forget the relationships between culture, society, personality, and body, even though we may conveniently use the words "family" or "kinship" to encompass them all.

II
CHILDREN
AND FAMILIES

As naive as it may sound, I don't think it is possible to work with young people and families and not, from time to time, reconsider one's own youth and family history. Indeed, I am certain that much of my motivation to work with young people and families stems from my desire to go back in time and repair some of the unsettled matters of my own childhood. (For that matter, I may even unconsciously wish to settle some unfinished matters of my parents' childhoods.) Rarely in the sort of research I conduct do I fail to examine my relationships with families and my closeness with individual members—that issue again of boundaries. And always, as I leave these conversations, I remark to myself about the absolute impossibility of understanding a notion like maturity, or putting myself in a position where I could construct even the barest prediction about a young person's future.

In many respects, the concept of the autobiographical consciousness, the personal stories of various family members mixed with my own stories, help us all to redefine not merely our singular or familial identities, but delineate for us the continuities and sheer discontinuities in our own development, our own maturation, our own narratives. Thirty years ago I recognized that in speaking with the young I was exploring, in some minimal fashion, the meaning of time, my time, their time, family time. I was exploring, moreover, the notion of young people, and families, too, being frozen in time, as if a series of experiences or circumstances prevented them from going on as time would, well, properly determine. People were being held back, or perhaps asked to advance more quickly than they reasonably could.

It wasn't difficult to discern the role of social opportunities in the maturation of young people and families, just as it wasn't difficult to detect the degree to which I, as a researcher, often came to identify with various family members. The young have always struck me as being mirrors of my own past. In watching families play, in hearing them laugh, in observing (and appraising) the way family members cooperate and compete, or contend with their choices as well as the inevitable constraints on their lives, I believe that I am witnessing the most social and the most intimate human behavior. As Rollo May suggested, within our personal involvements, so many of them centered in the cauldron of the family, our most private of human deliberations come to be formed.

Never did this seem more true than when I began speaking with children and adolescents about their family's secrets. Here, amid the mountain of stories that children and parents would tell themselves as well as others, I thought I was beginning to detect the roots of myths and the very foundation of sanity. I know that I heard in the justifications of various behavior, the presentations of self in everyday life, as Erving Goffman titled it, and surely the attempts to conceal experiences and sentiments. I heard as well personal philosophies being developed, and perhaps, too, personal pathologies beginning to take root. Yet, whatever the topic, children playing in a park, children covering up the ignominious behavior of their parents, or simply children and parents "growing up," I find myself insinuated into the lives of these other people.

No, that is not perfectly correct: I *choose* to insinuate myself into the lives of these other people, even the small child happily playing in the sandbox whose name I shall never know, and whose voice I shall never hear.

Time's Children

On my last birthday I was ninety-three years old. That is not young of
course. In fact it is older than ninety! But age is a relative matter. If you
continue to work and to absorb the beauty in the world about you, you
find that age does not necessarily mean getting older.

—PABLO CASALS, *Joys and Sorrows*

I have nothing to do, but watch the days draw out,
Now that I sit in the house from October to June,
And the swallow comes too soon and the spring will be over
And the cuckoo will be gone before I am out again.
A sun, that was once warm, O light that was taken for granted
When I was young and strong, and sun and light unsought for
And the night unfeared and the day expected
And clocks could be trusted, tomorrow assured
And time would not stop in the dark!

—T. S. ELIOT, *The Family Reunion*

TO SPEAK OR WRITE about youth means, I think, confronting the
time of one's past, that is, one's prior self. Perhaps, too, it means examining one's priorities. Anyone who lives or works with young people
knows that to look out across at them must be to look back at them, in a
way, though not down at them. It is to look back at them across the
grain and purpose of time. Often it seems so right being with people
much younger; it "works," as the artist might say, since our times and
lifestyles seem to move together, cautiously but successfully. At other
hours, however, as for example during the first few days of school each

autumn, when we see the new crop and feel them to be so unjustly young, our respective times seem disjointed and the space between us seems unbridgeable. The feeling is like what parents feel when, in a moment of endless duration, they turn swiftly about only to discover that their children are no longer children, that they are no longer young and no longer wholly together as part of a family. The parents turn about and realize that their children have vanished, leaving as an afterimage a swirling glow in a suddenly sorrowful room. Parents and some of us who teach discover, too, that the children who depart take a chunk of time with them, an irretrievable chunk that makes us feel that we may never again get close to young people or, even worse, to the remnants of our own childhoods.

Sadly perhaps, gratefully perhaps, we find that the motion of young people everywhere is in a sense the motion of ourselves. It is a reminder of the passing of our own private and unshared years, as well as a conclusion to the public and social years we spend with children or as children. The motion of youth and the passage of years imprint time upon all of us, or at least upon those of us belonging to that generation now feeling its age. Children, certainly the very youngest people, it often seems to me, are time itself; not its embodiment, really, but its flame and reality. The future seems to them, or ought to seem, so open and endless, complicated, to be sure, but ultimately possible. And their past, I imagine, is unusually pure, even with all the errors and impertinences it contains. The hours of their past become friends with the present, and the present remains each second changed, barely altered by a culture and civilization that crash into the environments of the famous and disenfranchised, the young and the old.

Time in these years of youth moved, as I recall, at its appropriate and appointed tempo, a tempo marked somewhere at the head of a logically computed but still artistic score. The moments of speeding advance and trudging retreat were all part of a plan for youth, all part of a temporal mechanics for living. The moments constituted a tempo that gave direction and motion to us even though our actions and sentiments must have seemed and maybe still seem like random notes and random rests to those who observed us and cared for us. These were the people, of course, who taught us constraint and promulgated the values that ultimately held us and our culture barely together. And so we keep in our memory those special and particular experiences and those particular people who in their way tie us to a tradition, a convention, a family, and a name. And later on we reason that it must have been the constraints on psychic and social action that preserved the tonalities not just of ourselves but of entire generations.

Time and youth were once somehow together, the one being the other, both enduring for themselves, both enduring for the other and presenting to us spans of splashing aliveness and testimonies of achievement, excitement, and critical pain; presenting to us as well the fibers of expectation and inference and every taste that can be had of death. We grew up to learn that a measured flow of time had been bequeathed to us for as long as, well, for as long as our spidery tenure might last. A peculiar word, "last." It gives promise of endurance and pronouncement of finality. So do the words "youth" and "time."

We matured, changed, displayed before ourselves some bit of what was being transacted behind our own eyes. And we all believed, even truthfully reported, that a mutual understanding, a truce made in and of time, had been completed, and that we had resolved all that life and death and being young and old might mean. But of course no truce existed, for in our aging we were soon enough obliged to look again, not upward this time but backward to where we had been. Like time itself, youth was again appearing to engulf us.

Then, in maybe the single discovery we made apart from the younger ones, apart from our own youth that is, they became us and we them. Or so it seemed. The young surround us so naturally, their bodies and chants pushing, urging, punishing us; they lead and follow us. As though in battalions, they order us to march in the footsteps of their pride and diffidence or gallop amidst their sexuality and adventure. How is it possible that they arrive before us and after us, smaller and larger, more amusing and urbane, more naive and unexposed?

To examine youth, therefore, means either to walk in their tempo for those instants when the tempi of the generations may be contiguous, or to settle in among the years that accumulate for us, confront head-on the clashing of the present and the past, and hear the explosion of regrets and life plans made so long ago they hardly seem to carry our name anymore. But so much time has accumulated that our examination seems false and uncertain. We have passed into what we all call adolescence and early adulthood only to find that photographs of our childhood have become crusty through our own disbelief. They seem foreign and unfriendly. The space of the photograph is reminiscent of something: the high school room, the smell of lockers or hideaways, the feel of streets, beaches, and stony concrete. But the faces must be identified through an act of inference normally reserved for dealing with the future; hence it is hard to believe that we are recalling and not prophesying. Isn't this the case? We look at the picture and say, yes, I remember that schoolroom. I used to sit next to Bobby and Henry. And that teacher, Miss Marshall, and . . . and . . . is that what I looked like then? I guess so. It must be. That must be the past.

It seems ironic, though, that these self-conceptions linger this way in the past and that they must be guessed at or reasoned out. It seems impossible, even a trifle unjust. How can there be such displacements and discontinuities in time when at most all we can admit to feeling are the slight but delectable interruptions of sleep and dreams? If the days follow along in line, we argue, like children well behaved on their way to a fresh, green park, why is last year or five years ago, why is our youth so separated from us now, and at times so incongruous? Why is it that the children at the head of the line have already disappeared? Very small children have similar reactions when they in turn undertake their examinations of youth. We see the sentiment in a three-year-old's expression as he sees a photograph of himself of two years before: "Baby. See the baby! What's the baby's name? Who is that?"

2

Everyone, presumably, protects his own notions and treasures of the past and of youth, extending or limiting their boundaries and seasons. And everyone of a certain age, an age that institutions and cultures help to compute, eventually decides he is no longer young. When one becomes that age, whole measures of time seem to be dismissed, dropped from the repertoire of habits; the congeries of time undergo a preparation and are put into storage. But they are stored, these years of the past, in peculiar fashion, for often we feel that we have continued on in the identical modes and styles of our youth, in the ways, that is, of our parents, so that the past doesn't seem dead at all.

Yet, often, too, we find ourselves performing actions that bespeak what seem to us an historic urgency and dazzling spontaneity. Suddenly nothing has to do with yesterday's styles or childhood or our parents. Everything is new and totally recast as if our lives were made of clay hardening in society's molds and emerging finally in the forms of single days. These particular actions do not necessarily appear genuine or reasonable to us, but they come about, so we imagine, without preparation or rehearsal. Somehow we just do them. They just happen. We may even wonder where such actions and responses came from. Where was the action waiting? Was it pausing, perhaps, in some interior anteroom? Some of us wonder, too, where actions or reactions live after they have been sent from us, presumably to return to time. Are they retrievable or but quicksilver, showing us their face a mere once and no more?

Youth has this uncertain way about it, for in one sense we as young people did not contemplate time the same way we did only moments after our departure from the buildings and persons we associate with being young and hence come to define as our younger years. The flow of time is gradual, as the buildup of a conception of the past grows in proper and tolerable duration. But then miraculously, often violently, we recognize that while most assuredly we are with people our own age we are no longer with young people, no longer with people young as young meant before. We begin to think about age in a new way, especially on our birthdays, and in the beginning of this series of recognitions and required reconciliations it is first the past that closes itself off to us. Exhibiting an antipathy and haughtiness, the past turns a heavy shoulder toward us and bids us in unbending fashion to move ahead, although there remains a voice somewhere daring us to seek impossible replications of prior years.

Do we not know an uneasy feeling when we think of how the play and freedom of childhood (and for some of us college as well) have been altered by the constraints and opportunities of adulthood? The constraints are like iron edges pricking our personalities and somehow destroying the smooth and linear flow of sweet time. Time, too, so it seems, possesses these edges, angularity amidst its unequivocal forms. For we learn that no one returns to the past, no matter what.

Before we truly understood this, however, time seemed to have played a casual game with us, offering freedom and caprice. One might even say that time played jokes on us and on itself. For the long and magical moments of childhood the years meant so little, and maturation for the most part went unfelt. Life was adventure and defeat, trial and setback, but it was encased in a resiliency sanctioned by a usually stern but frequently mischievous sense of history. One could come back and try something again, repeat a day of fun or a whole year in school perhaps. One could pass as a young man or young woman, and a culture fragmented into chips from the cracking of social reordering on its surface let it all happen. At least some of the culture's chips, the richer ones probably, permitted these youthful gambles and lines of failures. Let them have their fun now, we used to hear, for soon they won't be able to get away with this kind of light foolishness and aimless leisure. Soon their interminable dance will be stilled.

Yet in other parts of our culture it seemed as though water had seeped in between the cracks of the years and had frozen to a thick, crusty shell. It seemed as though water had trapped those persons whose simple measured destinies precluded free and capricious movement and some final hopeful liberation. Large groups of young people and old people stayed right where they were, frozen in the houses where their parents and grandparents lived what some have felt to be lives deprived of a substance and a joy that come from sleight-of-hand tricks with time, like rearranging the flow of preordained histories or shocking everyone with absolutely audacious expectations. We don't always think of it this way, but not becoming what your father was, living better than he did, more enlightened and more dramatically, is, after all, reordering history and, hence, performing rather nifty sleight-of-hand magic with time's sense of direction.

We have names, however, for those unable to perform such magic, just as we have names for the cultures, states, and forgotten monochromatic towns where the children march to school and then, cerebrally, march among their day-by-day lessons, abiding by the social and educational currents, honoring the brittle habits of teachers and bosses, and then march home. We say about these towns, or about the poor parts of our own cities where the people stamped for avoidance were dumped and remain penned, that only the day matters, that only the single beat matters, presenting its force and slim royalty once every turn of the world. One by one, one by one. We say this and much more about the places we see from the trains entering or leaving the smoky, smelly stations of enormous cities where concrete platforms hold the very world upright and stand bracing the black iron beams, old and tired, sweating their rust and decay. The beams are themselves like the men who brought them there and lifted them into a position and posture so that others might be kept safe before their own departures for better times and better places.

We say about these rotting places that some of us study from time to time that they offer a special glory in their day-by-day, beat-by-beat theater. But we also say the children there lack a drive to become all that they might, that the years have frozen them solid, and that they actually prefer the meager tonalities of their own compositions, their own flamboyant street styles and the lugubrious architecture of their own craftsmen and fathers. We say these children do not speak aloud to themselves or dream too much or even wish. And we say that because of an evil accumulation of years discolored by the blackness of the mines, or the frazzled whiteness of cotton fields owned by the good but still the very richest, or by the coldness of the brown earth surrounding the falling fences, or the forests that literally upped and moved just to stay out of sight of their churches, stores, latrines, and grave sites, the genes that no man has yet begun to comprehend have been disabled or discredited and made malignant.

There is, then, something called our time, the time we inherit from our own and bequeath to our own, and something called their time, the time of *them,* and the time of their youth. The two times coexist, of course, which is to say little more than that they hack their rhythms, their periodicities all they like, just as long as nobody gets hurt. But does this mean that a truly universal youth exists, a youthfulness that everyone shares? Or is there instead a segregated youth, a time divided so that now youth has reassessed itself and chosen to open its time only to those of the same color or of the same demanded style. Does youth now stand begging to hold together its isolated strength and greatness, or are the disparities of culture so great that we continue to think first of our own youth and then of the youth belonging to all the others?

An anger has arisen in this land, a momentous rage with a force almost as great as life itself. Its smell is sweet, its heat is delicious, its voices are assuredly young. One result of this anger is that time has been made groggy by this youth force and has found itself scared so that it may just contemplate throwing off the capes of its own original laws and begin anew, as "they" do when buildings are razed on dusty lots where moments before people lived. Time has been urged by youth to contemplate starting fresh, from scratch, or pay a cataclysmic consequence. Thus we live in a time where there will be more and more thorny discontinuities and entire redefinitions of what it means to be young, what it means precisely to be twelve or eighteen.

3

It is a well-known fact that recent years have brought young people to a dominant position in our country. They have been stretched "upward" by capitalism, by wars and universities, and by their firmness if not sophistication in debate and protest. Perhaps also by their overeagerness and nerve. The styles and language that they advertise but that to a great extent we manufacture have reverberated in our own placid "adult culture" such that they now shock the persons who designed them in the first place. Many have written that young people, as another of

America's minority groups, have received some of the treatment accorded their minority group siblings. Sexual potency and wild eating habits, irresponsibility, street dirtying, animalism, ignorance, and positively incomprehensible language and music patterns supposedly characterize them as much as any other group that has come under the glowering eye of America's "middle" ways and "middle" people, the people, that is, who guard the "middle years."

There is, however, a curious turn about the young, or of any group that because of its peculiar nature the rest of us tend to sequester or grant a semicitizenship. It has to do with the fact that at some point in our relationships with other groups we project onto these groups the traits, drives, and maybe too the ambitions and animus we despise or at least find uncomfortable in ourselves and in our groups. The derogation of those who appear to us beneath our eyes, for example, helps us to stand a bit taller. We look down at some people and, intentionally or not, we appear like a man bending to crush a cigarette under his foot and then straightening out again to his full height. Our attack on someone of another category is most likely an attack on all of that category, and because it is it serves to integrate our own groups a bit more and enhance our own delineated categories. The attacks on disapproval imply that along with our publicly announced proposals for equality there lives a fear that inevitably all categories might actually come together, blurring our distinct personal edges as they do, thereby destroying our precarious sense of uniqueness.

The machinery behind these attitudes, however, is not so recently learned. The infant's early confusion with names and classification generally, mommy as baby, baby as daddy, or nonsense syllables serving for all three, reminds us that at some level in our actual or fantasy engagements we sometimes steer so closely to others that we not only fuse with them, we believe that we superimpose our tissue one on another. At times the child feels he has become a parent, then both of his parents. At times the parents fantasize totally incorporating the child unto themselves so that the family may truly be one organism. The parents wrap their arms and their coats and blankets so tightly around the child's tiny frame that in one instant he has disappeared and in the next he has been suffused among the mysterious creases and folds of adult bodies. Then there is only one again. Ring around the rosie, pocket full of posie, all join hands and become one again.

Some of us call this suffusion, identification. It resembles the "group grope," where we are instructed to hunt in the dark or, even better, in the most dazzling daylight with our eyes closed for the other people in that temporary family, the group. Using only our hands, we begin to build a filmy identity but a definite foundation nevertheless among their bodies, hair, and barely remembered first names. The suffusion of persons resembles, too, the ideas of communes, communality, and community. No longer do two people alone share a baby and take responsibility for introducing him to the earth. Now there are places where worlds upon worlds of a constantly changing mini-nation claim birthrights to all of these most fragrant arrivals. "Come on people, now, smile on your brother. Everybody get together, try to love one another right now."

This in part is what sits at the bottom of our involvements with other people. May we call it identification? In a way, we find ourselves becoming the other as well as becoming the image of the other. Not just during insanity but always, or from time to time, or once in a while. Or once. We force ourselves to wrench the instruments guiding our perceptions so that husbands and wives whom we know and whom we care for might actually look alike. We make them look so much alike that they too become one, a fusion or confusion of each other. Then, when we have rendered them one, they come to share the same soul or speech as well as the same name and much of the same time, but certainly the same portion of the nation. But really it is incredible, as we think of it, that over time, as the crooked line of lived societies has made its way to the present, we have devised means for assimilating the most disparate times: not the times of generations, but the times of young men and young women. From women, men learn periodicity and that special sense of ineluctable continuity. And from men, women apprehend and tolerate the military game males play with destiny and what we call "lady luck." Nonetheless, it happens that despite the anger, the derogation and the proverbial gap that might remain between the generations the sexes find ways of moving together and concocting the ceremonies we know to be marriage.

When a baby is born, the instruments of our perceptions are again coerced, at the moment of birth even, to see the likeness between it and its parents. At the very instant of birth, at which instant we as children wrongly believed all babies look exactly alike, we as parents or the friends of parents not only detect an unequivocal difference among babies, we imperiously proclaim that the newly awakened spirit resembles its mother. "It that unbelievable! It's the same face! Don't you see it?" We experience the same thing in families where the children are not the biological inheritors. "Uncanny," we say, the "real" parents having never been seen. "Look, look there how that baby is the image of its father. Uncanny. The spitting image. Unbelievable."

But the image of this new family that drapes our perceptual scheme is in large measure the primordial image of family, of unit, of the many made into the not at all artificial one. This is what we mean by categories coming together. At first, each family member, each role, is resurrected and preserved, and then with superhuman power the pieces of all families from the beginning of time, just about, are transformed into the mold of a single monument, a single unblemished family portrait. For in that perceptual likeness that we impose, in that similarity, even identity of form that we insist on seeing, the generations collide, age disappears, identification becomes identity, and the young and the old move together. And here begins our study of youth, or at least our interest in such a "subject."

In not dissimilar fashion, we experience the essence of simultaneity. For example, we know the experience of all events and all human beings flowing at once together. As we do with individual family members, we first make the separate and isolated ones come together as in a marriage of convenience. The bringing of these many objects together simultaneously reminds us of images seen through a camera that in focusing all come together. The hazy becomes the defined, multiplicity turns into single aloneness, and the many images are reduced to one image mechanically captured and made permanent. We become composers in a flight of extraordinary purpose, slinging our notes upon the page in patterns only saints might decipher but returning at last to an order, to a molecular symmetry we call a chord or resolution. Indeed, the very concept of a tonality rests upon this need to bring the many and the disparate together into a structure that no one in his wildest dreams would have thought could be arranged from such a frizzy string of ideas and experiments. Yet the wholeness evolves, all becomes simultaneous, and then everyone is compressed into a fitting shelter and given his single name and single remembrance: the family, the one, the all of them uniquely separate yet all servants to a single household. The young and the old, the men and the women are together. "Come on people now, smile on your brother. . . ."

4

Youth, in this same rhetoric, becomes both the mirror on which is recorded the images of our lives past and present and the field on which the residues of our own triumphs and incompletions lie weakly asleep.

The return of ebullient neighbor children each school afternoon triggers underground explosions of our own private attempts to return in time. Through youth's rhythms and tireless strength it feels as though we have surrounded the past and made a glorious reunion with the most personal of history. We edge back slightly toward the past, and the past, once again the generous partner it once was, moves quickly out of its own lane, racing ahead of itself, so it seems, and best of all reaching its years out to us all over again.

When in the morning the children leave, we wonder, all of us in the clean, dry fabrics of our familiar protections, what world it is that they might learn of that day. Are school and play our world scaled to their size and their units of comprehension? Do their schools constitute our world plus one something that makes them in this way genuine possessions of children? Do we in our regulations and conventions liberate or choke young people? Do we ever offer to young people an even exchange? Is even exchange a possibility? Can the young and the old really be together?

Just whose time is it that we consider in fabricating styles and courses for the young? Is it our time sealed and finalized? Is it some temporary time, some makeshift pier extending outward between the generations, an isthmus giving earth and gentle foundation to their half-serious, half-solemn experiences? Is the time of youth a real time, one that spreads its covering over the nation? Or is the time of youth subdivided among its tenants such that some are granted privacy and special rights, while others are left like the remains of a Christmas pie for certain ones among us to devour? Do we grant the young a space, a moment, anything at all that is really theirs; or, like the poor, do they receive our own tired residues and hand-me-downs?

Are the young sent away each morning to our schools, their schools, nonschools, or are some of them hovering about that half-eaten pie from which most but not all of us get to steal delectable tastes whenever we want? And when we look at youth, really check them out behind the ears and under the nails, whose vision do we trust? Our own, or the image the young reflect or transmit to us through our age and activity? In that exhilarating consciousness-of-consciousness happening that surely overtakes us in our examination of youth, are we not caught in the years of someone else, someone older, someone wiser maybe? Are we not perpetuating prior rituals and reawakening the temperaments of those persons who once—it seems so long ago—made their own inspections of us, then bundled us up, and sent us out to school and to play and, well, to life?

One probably cannot view the children scrambling on that scaffold forming the generation beneath ours without contemplating the mirrors of petulance and energy they unwittingly hold up to us. At times, the young seek to shatter our histories and our very sense of emotion. In one instant of unconscionable gall they attempt to forbid us our pasts, but then they reflect for us our own insides, perhaps, by skipping between their obsessions with monotonous compliance and audacious adventures. Where we have finally straightened the seams of previous trials and settled our anxious flurries with knowledge, sexuality, law, religion, and politics, they come along ripping open these seams and delighting uproariously in their attacks on the fragile institutional and human surfaces that hold back our secrets and keep our morality together. Where we have decided on natural silence, they create explosions that sweep away the ground on which we stand together and wreck the treasures we have worked lifetimes to procure.

Oh, that supreme of all supreme narcissism the young invariably sculpt and about which we invariably feel so ambivalent. That way they have of throwing their bodies at us like wanton spirits of mythological origin. And that unembarrassed irreverence and supposed openness of their plans, regrets, and their interminable bargains and resolutions. Every day for them seems to stand as the last day of the last year. Every night evokes celebrations and innovations that crowd their rooms much as the radios and televisions crowd their brains with language and a music not even the most patient would undertake to review. But in these sounds nestle a few of the treasures that youth, too, has worked to procure.

5

The sounds and language of their friends whom they surely love and surely despise with a single and collective strength bring young people "in touch" with all their scattered armies, with their international allies, as it were. The sounds recall as well their own private histories of momentous fear and diffidence. The radio sounds pouring into the dutiful listeners who march across the streets and fields replay the voices of parents. How easily we remember ourselves lying quietly, nervously in bed, frightened by the darkness and by the suddenly invisible status of objects we, like blind persons, had depended upon for our bearings. We remember, too, being frightened by the aloneness, the natural end product of a black stillness, the newborn of the night. Radio and television serve to draw us away from that darkness and that aloneness.

Earlier it had been myriad friendships and yet a persistent drive toward individuality and autonomy that sparked much of our childhood. Late into the night the midnight sign off would be heard, marking in those blackest hours the cessation of the noise that had just before guaranteed company and companionship, the very things preventing individuality and autonomy. We pulled the sheets up over our heads, and the radio was shoved down into the bed along with a dog or cat, or books or toys. Or maybe we recall lying nearer the radiance of heat, the brother or sister who shared the room and the bed, and hence the dreams they magically produced. Night continues to possess the hours of silent awareness that for some have meant the best time for doing homework but that for others have aroused a terror neither conquered nor comprehended.

Now radios and CDs endlessly blare reminders of the voices of a mother or father in the next room, or even of the old television or radio set that sat with them when they were babies and brought movement to a stale emptiness. They remain the identifying sounds, the call letters of infancy, childhood, and adolescence. Sounds like these mean being in touch, tuned in, as well as the assurance that desertion and rejection by the young and old alike exist only as fantasies, never as perceivable events. Sounds like those drive the presence of parents, family, neighbors, probably of all society, deeper and deeper inside the heads of young people, and yet, apparently, farther away from where the young might be able to build something special and significant from these sounds. With noises from the outside cramming their interiors, the few sounds generated by youth that might escape have been temporarily silenced, hence some of the demons of creativity alive within these young psychologies have been neutralized, such that many young persons have been rendered mere consumers.

There are also the sounds of time, sounds that do more than merely symbolize associations with external reality and those who inhabit it. Sounds become the corridors of receptivity and extrusion. Perception, after all, has more than a perfunctory social context. When we recognize our mother's voice or father's footstep, for example, we recognize not merely the distinct characteristics of those who live close, we begin to recognize our own interior processes capable of discerning between voices and footsteps. When we hear the unqualified outside, furthermore, we hear the vague inside as well. We hear, as it were, the apparatus of our interior or of our psychology, or, if that's not it, we hear the image of the interior. Then, through this introduction to the images of senses and perceptions, we commence imagining the shape of our "innerness," our cognitive talents and most especially our values and feelings. Eventually we learn that located within ourselves is an interior where memories doze and personal hurts line cracking walls, and where sorrow, anger, pride and a peculiar sense of loss safeguard a trouble darkness. And this, some believe, is what youth is all about and what we older ones keep of our own youth.

One thing school is all about, or maybe should be somewhat about, is putting us in touch with this interior and the experiences sunk in its depths. But well before school, each of us discovers wondrous people who possess an influence over us, leaving their mark as a handwritten language on these interior walls. Voices that practically speak to us from the inside come to be recognized as the voices of those who work or sleep alongside us, share our dinner table, or at least provide for us in all sorts of ways.

Amidst our private instincts and collected cultural residues (should they really turn out to "exist in our science" as they obviously do in our humanism) float the sounds of intelligible voices waiting to be labeled. On the diamond surfaces of our consciousness, their messages remain indelible, their directives decisive. Like charms on a bracelet, the voices and moods and the language and manner they softly imply continue to appear, untarnished even in our oldest age, purely cut as the day they were linked to the chain. In this way, our youth and their youth stay with us. Then, at some incalculable hour, the ways of the generations before us, the tricks or the ones on the scaffolding above us find their way into the architecture of our own privacy and into our hidden resources. Now we become genuinely linked to history, and yet somehow more separated than ever before from the generation immediately behind us. And this is only part of what many of us call the process of socialization.

Another part of socialization is the onset of the battle of battles, that war against oppression and imperialism fought out first in the hideaway tree houses and alleys of childhood. It is the battle against those by whose loins our existence owes its permanence. It is the battle that first dominates our drive toward the denial of our origins and sustenance and then urges us to believe that we may be immortal, the products of a virgin birth. Evidence of pure autonomy, after all, would be selfish independence or, better, discourteous abandonment and flight. This would be man totally in control of the stars! The proof of autonomy would be the demonstration of a parentless status, a familyless society. Part of socialization is found in the noises of the young that neatly drive away their families, their origins, the kingpins of the past. Part of it, too, is the rancor of their own interiors that soon produces its own sounds as well as visions and illusions enough to stimulate entire battalions of young frenzied soldiers.

The young have come loudly alive, redefining dependency and autonomy as they grow older. Family names may be dropped, personal names erased, and while some assume the names of peoples of different lands and different times (although many have been named for these in the first place), thereby extending connecting hands to a more comprehensive history, others take on names as apparel, as they see fit, according to some social size or political style. And by this many young persons would believe that a personal strength has been assured and that a steady independence has been made eternally real and genuinely worthwhile.

It is all so humanly complicated. When the child is small and his language appears to be "little more" than the effusion of sounds he has by some miracle internalized as the sounds of adults together, he holds his possessions so tightly to himself and to his land that no one could take them from him. Surely no one his size would dare bargain with him for the right even to share. So we urge him to let the others play with his toys and books, to take turns, give and receive. Here is a friend, we suggest, your first real friend.

But the child doesn't give an inch. For at the core of his refusal to share and what consequently we see as his lacking a sense of a social self, a sense, that is, that would permit our sense of self to coincide with his, are the objects of an extraordinary new world that offer to him the companionship of living sources and resources. The toys he now protects will soon be part of his cognitive processes; his animals and dolls the confederates, real and imagined, with whom he'll work; the corners and cupboards of his room will be the boundaries, regulations and mysterious but thankful rituals of a comprehensive social life; and his books the cornerstones of intellectual and fantasy adventures. To lend out his toys and his books is to part with the seeds of his imagination and the images of what will evolve into the notion of microcosm that someday he will incorporate as the father of sensation and reality. He cannot, therefore, relinquish even one possession without suffering a loss not merely to an inchoate pride or ill-defined contract of ownership but to the buds of yet undetermined assertiveness and maturation.

6

This, then, is a part of the battle for autonomy and freedom and the quest for an end to an expanding social psychological oppression. Endlessly, youth wishes to secure an agreement that the direction and placement of each step will be its own. One goes, the young invariably decide, exactly where one has to, even though so many of their (our) freely chosen steps are in fact made in obeyance of those wondrously powerful ones. But, just as an irreconcilable tension exists between the boundaries of the single purposeful self and a scorning, controlling society, so is there a pressure to determine which steps one takes on one's own and which steps one takes as acts of loyalty and obsessive learning. How, youth asks, do I know when I'm doing something for myself alone because I elect to do it? It is not just of symbolic value, therefore, that we find schools offering, apart from the "required" courses, what are called "electives," bits of the pie in a well-baked pan from which the young may choose a preoccupation, even a destiny. An elective is one of those self-created steps.

But even electives are nowhere near enough. For there needs to be among these steps, along with the required and the electives, personally initiated steps like a decision to quit school, steps coming from out of the blue, or, more accurately, from the interior's darkness. Here in personally initiated action and effort change is strapped to energy awaiting a discipline, and all are held together, presumably, by work. Here is creativity in a peculiarly intimate and loving form, yet here too is the potential for unordered and unpredictable propaganda and politics. Here is the basis, sometimes resolute, sometimes precarious, of an individual moving freely and cleverly, sometimes within, sometimes without the usual structure designed by and composed of everyone else in the world. Here is what they call an extracurricular activity in the raw. Most importantly, here is the origin of a new adulthood of genuine autonomy: "I don't want to be like everyone else," they say. "I mean, you know, like anyone else. I want to be me. Is that so hard to understand?"

It is not so hard to understand knowing even a bit of the genetic tracks that govern and offer human individuality. But at the same time it is impossible to understand or grant that individuality or autonomy knowing even a bit of human experience and knowing that unfathomable push in each of us to render homogeneous any groups of people we see as being different from us, even as we stumble among the roots of our own identity in which the goals of uniqueness, specialness, and personal worth loom so enormous. We saw before how, in making an environment sufficiently constant so that we may more easily trace our steps across it, we tend to collapse everyone and everything else in order that we may stand out, so to speak, in greater relief. We do this cognitively as well as with our social psychological snares in which older or younger people, teachers, the "establishment," men or women get slung together in a heap then crushed under our heel to the bottom of a bushel basket and disposed of. We do this with our families, this action of hording people then lumping them together for our selfish conveniences and esteem.

In school, the habit of hording and clumping people together is somewhat altered. We have our best friend whom we love the most, naturally, but from whom we also sustain antagonisms that, if enlarged to adult proportions, would with one stroke destroy whole empires and continents. But we stay with this one friend, learning more about what might be called the extended family of trust and fidelity. And in these hours with our best friend, how ghastly and earth-shaking is the threat of an intervention by a third person who could so easily cause us to dissolve the friendship. The mathematics and natural logic of cultures, we think, should take measures to forbid any sort of dissension and personal separation.

All of this has to do with the emergence of personal autonomy, self-regulation, and the resolution of that slim tension between the person existing solely by himself and having to be with the others on whom he mightily depends.

"I don't like Billy, do you? He always wants to hang around with us."

"Line up by twos," the teachers used to order, sanctifying the bonds that, without our teachers' insistence, we as little people had already erected. Then we would walk as partners, as junior parents, as single selves together. We were learning how to share as well as how to be alone and (by) ourselves. Gradually the architecture of these unions relaxed, and additions, carefully designed of course, were constructed. Soon we had four friends, then eight friends, then pals, gangs, clubs, fraternities. Then we spoke of our race and religion, our sex and our age group, our parts of a whole society enjoined. Brothers and sisters. Members of the family. Members of the tribe.

But in taking each of these significant evolutionary steps of social and psychological consequence, we have at one time or another combined all the others, the "residual people," clumped them into categories of convenience and homogenized them almost as a mound over which our own ascent into society's positions commences. We speak of climbing inclines where success and fame are involved along with many, many people. In what appears as the physics regulating our social psychology, we push off from these people in an effort to gain secure and success-oriented footing as well as proper momentum. Sometimes the others provide a resistance, sometimes a solidity meant to support our travels, our daring, even our biological growth and misdemeanors.

In the end, however, we come to recognize the well-delineated stress points of independence and dependence. For, despite our protestations, it *is* essential that we believe that our place of origin, our home base, will not budge one millimeter under the impact of our energies, our shoving off, or our first steps and later stampeding in space. It *is* essential that we maintain our ability to balance independence and dependence on one scale and perfect autonomy and trusted reliance on another.

Independence and dependence, slipping away and returning again, the slender animal moving each day a bit farther from its mother and from its group. Each day a bit farther until one day we felt ourselves to be far enough away. Then we were gone. We were the astronauts on the moon, our one small step preceded by touches and leaps on our own ladders. Down and up, down and up again. Then down for good, our commitments finally congealed. During all the school years we had waited our turn to be detached from the world of childhood and ushered into an entirely new world hung in an incomprehensible adult space, presumably out there somewhere. But for some of us, the two worlds continued to be as separated and foreign from one another as was, well, the eighth grade from the sixth, the senior high from the junior high.

"I'll never make it. God, they have all that homework. I don't want to go back to school in September. I don't want to grow up."

"But I thought you wanted to go. After all, you'll still be with Robert and Jeff and John and Ernest and Homer. You'll still be together. And someday you'll be as big and strong as Daddy."

7

To speak or write about youth, as is so fashionable today, is to wonder aloud whether or not siding with the young promises acceptance by them and therefore grants reentrance into a time we have forever lost. Such a notion would seem reasonable enough if its simplicity did not make it somehow weak and sterile. For one reason or another, writing about youth seems to have become the means by which some of us kick off from the young into an occult or transcendent life space all of our own. Then again, writing, with its sane aggressiveness, may just be a kicking at youth with such unequivocal force that the demons inside us, who prompt us to seek a return to childhood to see again our parents when they were young and so beautiful that we would fight with people bigger than ourselves just to preserve their image, might turn to stone and hence be silent forever.

Some of the statements recently made about youth, for example, at first glance seem naked of all truth. One author says that the political knowledge of any person twenty-five years old or younger is by definition superior to and more sophisticated than the political knowledge of any person over twenty-five. By definition, no less! Twenty-five, this writer has marked as the point in a real chronology as *the* time barrier, and here am I, barely reconciled to yesterday's announcement that the magic number, surely dripping death on its stems, was thirty. Barely as I age, the market of my youthfulness and adult illusions drops, and my stocks continue to sink.

Another writer has asserted that the anger mustered by "youth" and then directed toward the inequities of schools and societies not only is destructive from a political perspective, but represents little more than the "acting out" (that ungodly phrase) of infantile neuroses or adolescent antipathies. To this person, everything seems to be displacement or overidentification. And someone else said the other day: "All those political protests you see? They are little more than psychodramas. Psychodramas pure and simple."

What's so frightfully complicating about this youth business is that at the same split second all of these statements seem absolutely false and absolutely true. True, that is, as the existence of youth itself. To be sure, the sophistication of some young people is right out in front; it cannot be denied. But like the motives or capabilities that fill each human being and challenge him to action, the sophistication is a complex one, for it reflects all humanity in a single pot, its contents far from melted but far, too, from their original state. For some young people, sophistication has come easily, for they have captured and contained the language of their mother, which was poetic and rare. For others, the sophistication has come easily from what at first appears to be a contradiction of progress and passivity. Without invitation and, even worse, without exertion, television has plopped a new language world in the laps of a generation.

Its coming most certainly has raised the awareness of younger persons but, as John Aldrich has suggested in *In the Country of the Young*, lowered, maybe permanently, their sense of quality. Now, almost laughably, and partly because of television, teachers face the problem of making human biology of literature interesting, while television personnel themselves, as Daniel Boorstin has noted in *The Decline of Radicalism*, must market oppression, starvation, and war in a new and dramatically salable fashion. Whatever the consequences, and television exposure of inequities has many, technology seems to have conspired against the older generation to sculpt this "sophistication of ease" among the young. For now the young not only publicly dismiss the pasts of the old, as they always have (their private conversations often turn to these pasts), they have become the most acute perceivers and rightful inheritors, so some say, of a most expanded sense of the present.

"The times they are a-changing." In some ways, many young people have become sophisticated, knowledgeable, too, well beyond the real and imaginary levels set by those like myself who obsess over and compare the generations and argue by theory and observation that in most "battles" the young must triumph. But twenty-five, by definition! It is also the case that many of the young mirror in their intelligence much of the faulty sophistication of a world of utter escape and fantasy that technology has also offered to them. (We must not forget the almost immaculate and endless unreality that television heaps on us before and after its documentaries.) Their knowledge, in fact, is not comparable either in breadth or variety to the harder-earned knowledge of many of their compatriots and many of the adults with whom they study and work. Sadly enough, there are people under twenty-five whose interest in a world so enormous and problematic has, in some instances, become dulled. They have, these young people, restricted their engagements, ignored the realities that have literally undercut the lives of other children and turned to watching the classroom clock that ticks them and their families through school days, holidays, and ritualized ceremonies reifying a bland chronology and a vacuous calendar.

For these people, time itself drapes long expansions of drudgery and sleep between the prongs of celebrations that honor repetition and predictability. For so many, life remains little more than weekends, Christmases, Fourth of Julys, and summer vacations. And nothing, or very little, appears to arouse their sense of either indignation or joy. The threat of a holocaust, the existence of hunger, the presence of oppression seemingly cause barely a tremor in their linear routines and responsibilities.

They do exist, these people, and more than once in their lives they exasperate teachers whose task it is to make poetry or drama, psychology or politics, history, science, painting, drawing, or just plain reading palatable. Probably, too, they exasperate television bosses who are obliged to adjust films of war and poverty to these persons' fluctuations of taste and interest. Let's be fair about all this and recognize that many of us gracefully avoid our suspicion that much of society houses utterly boring, insensitive, and recalcitrant people.

Some of us might choose to assume that the majority of America's children have been murdered by schools or by those portions of society demanding compliance and conventionality. Maybe so. But a more pertinent issue than whether a spirit of humanity is so quickly extinguished by schools is that every year of growth provides its own magic and its own rational and irrational checkpoints. Eight-year-olds cry because they are not twelve; twelve-year-olds wish a taste of the free pleasures of eighteen, and many of us seem to be frightened and thrown backward by the notching of decades: nineteen to twenty, twenty-nine to thirty, 1969 to 1970, 1999 to 2000. So it isn't that any real integer like twenty-five marks the beginning or end to anything magical or profound. Certainly sophistication, with its valuable as well as ludicrous qualities, knows no birth or death date of twenty-five.

Now about youth's anger, an anger, one would think listening to some observers, that every day brings youth closer to philosophies of hatred and nihilism. Were we perhaps misled by a certain group of intellectuals who taught us that aggression was the most prominent activity of children and hence the cornerstone of life and death? To read some authors, we might think that youth bleeds and sweats its anger in a climate so hot that no negotiation or "radical confrontation" could ever soothe it. Dammit, we cry, why do they stomp so, their bitterness and pomposity sewn into their clothes and combed into their hair? Why do they scream obscenities, disloyalty, and malcontent without respite, without consideration, or apparent purpose? Why all of that stoked-up aggressiveness and crystalline anger? To touch angered youth, we fear, is to be wounded and, even worse, to have our blood mix with theirs. If we meet up with hostile, politicized youth on a rampage, we're liable to be contaminated by the scent of their culture, bowled over by their collective strength, or perhaps won over to what we perceive as their free-swinging, fault-finding parade.

But if we count the seconds of anger, rudeness, or aggression in a child's life, or tally up the moments of unadulterated hate and antipathy either exhibited or implied, if we count the instants of militant action and open attack, we will miss nothing less than the form and stuffing of everyday life. Anger just is not as dominant a life force as we might wish to believe. There is just too much to existence. So how can we destroy for good and always the image that a "delinquent" is delinquent every waking second and that even in his dreams he plots the desecration of societies that bounce him and his blood-brother "gangs" into the seedy corners and wrinkles of cities embarrassed by their own inadequacies and injustices? How can we destroy the image of a college student as a full-time political warrior, draft card burner, trasher, or whatever?

As in all acts of unmitigated anger and frustration, as in all confrontations with bitter denial, most delinquent acts and most student protests are but matches suddenly lit and as suddenly extinguished and thrown away. There are no flames burning down all that is good, no gutting of buildings yet; there is just the firing of nerves for good and understandable reason, probably explainable by some metabolic force and social science. No flames yet and no indication, either, that a young person's love and fear, mischievousness, fright, and style of testing the world are not parts of that aroused state. Only the body's witches know the concoction for anger, spite, and revenge. But it would seem, even now in our own slowly receding ignorance, that human anger erupts in the presence of many, many ingredients.

In truth, when the description and diagnosis of anger become a fixation, as for some they have, then to a certain extent the data recorded by these people are an admission of their own anger, in part stimulated by those they study but perpetrated too by social factors as well as real people, whom we long ago or just today believed we had successfully bypassed or psychologically transcended. When we diagnose or analyze we sometimes liberate an energy from those we examine, but too often diagnosis and analysis also mean a neutralization of badly needed political dissent and a doubtful invasion into the hearts of real human beings. But this is the chance we take in scientific inquiries involving human beings. If we only psychologize youth's anger, therefore, we may successfully avoid those very real situations that contribute to their anger and make ourselves believe that anger is the mold from which pure youth takes its shape.

Still, the anger is there, and it cannot be ignored. Its facets are complicated, for just as there are times when situations make certain young people incensed, so is there inevitably a group of people on the earth who by the anger they carry about within themselves seem to ignite situations, institutions and customs that previously seemed so "neutral," innocent, and calm.

The anger cannot be ignored, regardless of where it may appear. It is strange, for example, that during youth's sieges on the "establishment" or on their chosen objects of adult social order we rarely comment on the excruciating loss of purpose resulting from the inability of certain young people to temper the hostility they maintain towards one another. This is anger apart from well-recognized political disagreements and violent factionalism. But let no one call this anger "typical infantile self-indulgence," for the young own no monopoly here, and infantile self-indulgence knows no age barrier of twenty-five. The cruelty and hurt that the young can generate in a flash seems staggering to us, probably because we might like to believe that a period of years can be sustained, between childhood tantrums and the time when the children must go to war, in which the young actually live according to an ethic of uncorrupted love and gentle kindness. What happened to that sweet-smelling bundle I used to call my baby? we ask again and again.

When, but a few years ago, we saw the hate of adults, the lust for power, as they say, and the obsequious planning that launched human spaceships to unattainable heights of isolated strength and dominance, we said hurrah for those men, but heaven keep my children, now so clean and young, away from that power and that fire of self-aggrandizement and ambition. But as our wisdom grew, the truth emerged: If we are willing to forfeit our sensibilities of proportion, then adult power and hate and child power and hate look almost identical. The competitions, the thumping of others' heads, the smashing of others' dreams, and desecration of their simple place on the land are all there, as big as a child's life, as big as an adult's life, if not bigger.

Like assassins, the young and the old plot to undermine the routes of youthful as well as adult travel and poison the wells of seemingly anyone's sustenance and luxury. At times these plots seem justifiable, vengeful but vindicable in some primitive legal sense. But at other times they seem, even to understanding observers, as being nothing short of bizarre and heinous. There are actions that seem so utterly bizarre they make one think that only demons could choreograph such horrible movement and render such sickening pain.

How can it be, for example, that children with barely the strength or control to climb to the back of a happy stone whale built by someone who remembered the ways in which children give birth to make-believe, unembarrassed, in the midst of adult traffic would mercilessly fling a smaller child with practically no strength or control to a pave-ment of iron-hard cement? How can it be that so much damage of superhuman scale is meted out by children with brains incapable of fathoming the mysteries of addition and multiplication? How can it be explained? Sibling rivalry is not sufficient explanation. And instincts? Well, possibly so, if we knew exactly what instincts were.

8

In writing about radical students, many authors speak of the vilification of members of one political group by members of another. But the anger they observe is more than even vilification. For there is a burden in a particular brand of student defiance, a burden reeking of nothing short of death, the wish for it and the fear of it, a burden causing an ex-orbitant expenditure of energies merely to keep dreams of death back and out of sight. Anger has given birth to these dreams and has revital-ized, as macabre as it seems, an interest in and fascination with death. Yet in observing this anger, we outsiders tend to see little beyond waste and self-demise.

In another sense, a more precarious sense, moreover, "youth" compli-cates our own visions and impressions of death. Sometimes we feel that their age alone should prevent their comprehension or preoccupation with death; they are too young, not yet prepared for such thoughts. I wonder. Do they come from a land where death rarely travels and where a true belief in immortality and infinitude linger? The young seem to us to act as we imagine their bodies to be, either unaware of natural even-tualities or preferring to laugh aloud with youth's cunning, speed, and impulsiveness. We think the young enjoy life; we think it is their wish that all people should know freedom and not worry about death for a long, long time.

When young people inquire about death, their words almost convey a charm, not a gaiety, of course, but hardly the lugubrious grays and blues of the words directed toward death whispered and written by those who recognize that their lifelines have begun to trail out behind them. In a crazy way, youth protects or ought to protect our own stock-pile of hope and of life. "Our only hope is with them," we say, meaning in part that they must inherit our place and our errors; but meaning as well that time's uncanny flexibility allows us to transplant the rightful property and spirit of youth's future onto our past, which means that occasionally we flourish through their aspirations and their notions of what is possible. In fact, we sometimes feel high and giddy, as though on drugs, from the excitement and freedom we imagine will soon come to our young people and then, somehow, to us. Our hope, we proclaim, is that the young might be spared a repeated trampling down of their intentions and robust eagerness; but no one yet has spared anyone this.

In their early years, the very young reveal a confusion of death and sexuality, a confusion about how life starts and stops and about the fact that family members young and old may die, walk out, or vanish. These can be costly confusions and they can persist. For a long, long time it seems that despite our efforts to restrain it, something in our psychology urges us to try to comprehend absences and losses that at one level are at the root of anger, defiance, and the concept of death. Absences and losses as well as those mysterious additions through birth, marriage, and remarriage are also part of youth's experience. The young have become the grand accountants and census takers of a family and of a society that shift in population even as they tally up their members. People go and new people come to take their place or establish a special place of their own. The young will find that their concern with missing persons and the dead will remain with them forever. But the concern starts even as language itself forms.

"Daddy go to work now," the child tells his mother, defining for himself the departure of his father but, more essentially, hoping to assure himself of his father's reappearance and therefore continuing existence. Like a flag announcing the start of the race, the child's announcement begins the count of the workday hours, the count of hours of separation that contain for him the initial exposure first to desertion and aloneness and soon to the notion of simultaneity as well. For the child temporarily will lay his anxieties to rest with the recognition that death does not occur just because I am here while Daddy is there.

"Want to speak to Daddy on the phone?"

"Hello, Luke, how are you?"

"Daddy at work?"

"Yes, I'm at work, Luke."

"Daddy come home soon!"

"Yes, very soon now. Can I speak to Mommy now? . . . Give Mommy the phone now, Luke. Luke!"

But there is confusion. Child here, parent there, people coming and going, people leaving, people left. It all has something to do with life and death, or moving in and out of life and death, not in a playful way, but as a means of touching the walls and railings of reality outside, and the layers of consciousness inside. Life and death, the outside and inside, the possible and impossible, past and future, self and other, actual and ideal, all heaped together, all pulling and falling over one another. The young become our children. With fingers locked and stretched they grip at our hands, dragging us to their ends, to safety and to danger. Now, perhaps because of their rising power, we feel ourselves to be in the last movement approaching an end to something, a decade, a century, an era. The sense of the present expands and then collapses. With each breath the lungs suck in heavy molecules of time then pump them out again, tired and used up.

9

To move about the dungeons and palaces where youth is kept and where the images of youth become institutionalized as schools, clubs, or political fraternities and sororities is to recognize that the anger of youth accompanies the compassion of youth just as the hate accompanies love and the impulse to care for someone accompanies the impulse to hurt him. It is not merely, then, that some schools or teachers or administrators, that some of us, are good and some bad, or that some educational philosophies seem genuinely custodial or murderous whereas others seem more imaginative or, as they still say, "progressive." Dichotomies of this sort are usually cognitive conveniences, rarely gauges of the truth.

It is rather the antinomies and ambivalence, the intense feelings of such extraordinarily discrepant meaning and emotion and conflictual push to action and then away from action that cause us to wonder about ourselves and our institutions and then turn us into immobilized fools, distraught and humiliated right in the middle of personal and political revolutions. It is the ambivalence and confusion that attracts us to youth's expressions like "identity crisis," "copping out," and "getting it together." And if we are immobilized, struck down by two competing drives or wants, then most probably there are four, eight, sixteen drives pining us to the tracks where moments ago we glided so easily into healthy life, that is into love and work. In these times we just cannot "get it together" no matter how intense our rage, for we have been stilled by the antinomies and ambivalence.

What a profound conceptual contribution Freud made in the notion of the Oedipal configuration, not only because of the social psychological relationships it describes, but because of its inherent insistence that portions of a man's imagination simultaneously hold secret packages of feeling sometimes so discrepant, so foreign from one another it would seem that he would burst into hundreds of swollen pieces. It is the reverence for the parent and the impulse to kill him, not separated, not one in each hand, but both in one reality, both clutched in one fist, both stored in one mind. Assuming an almost religious magnitude, the respect and adoration become united with a hate and brutality supposedly known only to prehistoric monsters. Behind the ambivalence are masked demons dancing a curious and chaotic commotion in our souls.

Parents, teachers and the companions of the young breathe that life and death and dance that demonic dance. The young and the small at times wish that the old and tall might flop over dead. The old and powerful wish that the young and insignificant might recede or wander away or maybe find another country. Love it or leave it! The number of these kinds of murders committed each day must be fantastic! But at the same time, adulation and unquestioned obedience to much authority also stand high. Pride is swallowed one second, hate the next, the wish for love and the wish for death the next. So it is that we almost can see the signs of life and death flickering on and off the surfaces of authorities appointed to oversee youth's daily and nightly routines.

What complicates these matters even more is that our customs and rituals often cannot keep up with or comprehend the consequences of our changing sensations and private trials. Society seems to have no place for ambivalence and the indecision it yields. Often it is as if the social casings, the social roles into which we are obliged to fit our personal intrusiveness, our "real" selves, perhaps, cannot accommodate the presence of all of our feelings, especially the anger. And how unfair this is, not just for youth, since all these other feelings have as much right to be seen and heard as the ones for which the social customs and rituals were originally conceived.

More generally, societies and psyches have developed ingenious procedures for honing conscious and unconscious materials, patterns and processes that change and rearrange themselves as much in sleep as in action, as much in death as in life. Dangerous experiments with drugs are undertaken, flirtations with lunacy are repeated, and undeniable self-destruction is sustained partly as a reaction to the realities of our societies, partly as a reaction to anger and loss, but partly as well to find and demonstrate that these marvelous and frightening experiences exist not as bizarre extensions of our world, not as cantilevered perches, but as hunks of the same substantial structure that houses language, rudimentary perception, and pedestrian reasoning. What frightens us, I think, is that at times reality itself seems to overhang a valley entirely unsupported in a way that would make the most daring architects gasp. The young help to erect this new reality of political actions, ideologies, and lifestyles. They build it, behold it, then just as we believed we were adapting to it, they tear it all down and start in again constructing a still newer reality and a fresher definition of social order and peace.

By their hopes for the young and in their prayers that the young may liberate the world if only because they are young, the old seek a liberation of their own lives of increasing constraint and incapacities. On these prayers and the efforts they initiate glistens the love being transferred between the generations. But often, too, the old wish for the obliteration of the young, and in this curse they covet a paradoxical liberation, a liberation turned on its head with time running backward, for we just cannot be young again like the young. We must instead be young like the middle-aged, or young like the old. When care for and trust in the young are entertained, succeeding futures, also paradoxically, are preserved and the histories of prior generations finally safeguarded. But when enduring antipathies toward the young dominate the transactions between generations, a false freedom is born, a freedom conceived in the belief that if one liquidates another's future, one's own past is cured and one's own future is rendered limitless. Among so many inherited rights, aging confers the power of potential rejector on all who survive. Soon the son will become the father who leaves. Still, rejection is no new business, as the young practice it among their peers, often reaching a precision and dexterity with its weapons that make us think they have been advised of its lifelong utility. Quite possibly, they have been. It's funny and sad to think what we teach our children in the name of "preparing" them for adulthood and for the time when we are no longer here.

It's also funny and sad to think of the number of false liberation movements attempted each day as parents and children wrestle with and among themselves in the hopes of "getting together" and moving apart all at the same time. In these moments, which seem to make up so much of our present society, the faces of the rejectors and the rejected are frequently seen close together. But this is part of what "they" call maturation and ambivalence, love and hate.

It is also part of what "they" call "rapid social change." The place, resting and moving, of each person who lives or has lived has become so fragile today, so evanescent. Once we were taught to believe in the permanent sanctity of the dead. Surely *their* reputations were finalized, sealed, and delivered and their skeletons left untouched to rot deeper and deeper into the ground. But no more. Dead men have been lifted and carted away as the bare scent of their posthumous spirits have come into disfavor and their corpses made the recipients of national animus. More recently, the racially segregated status of cemeteries has been violated in ways that make churchgoers tremble in their appeals to parardisic courts. For when a black man is allowed to lie alongside a white man, the time has finally come to alter the most grotesque of written histories and to rearrange the substance of individual memory. The time has come to mature, resolve, or at least recognize ambivalence and find a place for it in society. The time has come, in other words, for social change.

To some extent, these are but a few of the demands that youth outlines, some of the supposed crimes that youth allegedly commits: the tearing down of saints, the ripping open of tradition, the denial and desecration of memory and custom, and the obliteration of authority. Our impression is that youth's many and often capricious philosophies teach that no man knows such worth that he cannot be expended and that no man maintains such control over his energies that he can be expected to embrace all of fidelity's covenants. Through their boisterous sexuality, for example, the young are said to every day chew away at the fibers not "merely" of society but of the realities it labors so hard to contain. It is said that the young rip the fibers of realities and throw them in the faces of generations they know planted them and nourished them.

But it isn't so. It just isn't so that they alone are the guilty ones. We know this by the intensity of our own urges to run to the books and movies, drawings, music, poetry and lifestyles that in their gaudy and flavorful way reenact the same fantasies we now project onto youth, rightly or wrongly, the true owners of these particular products. We know it, too, by the actions we somehow cannot help ourselves from taking that fortunately remain private and unsuspected. Yet even with our most impeccable constraints, the products of the young, or of what Philip Slater has called the "counterculture," kindle reminiscences of our own timorous advances and almost comical regrets: "When I was young and used to listen to the sixteen-year-old boys in the high school locker room," the young man recalled, "I used to dream about growing up, so that one day I too could do what these older boys did. Lie!"

To write about youth means confronting one's prior and future selves and generations and, even more, one's single self properly bound, trapped and free, in the single glowing point of now. It means confronting not just one child, one day, one dream, or one event, but all days, all dreams, all events, all the best friends, the few lovers, and the ancestors, too, and all according to the sequences and antisequences these people and these events dictate and underwrite. It means a confrontation in which no one is left out as well as an understanding that the physics governing our psychologies recognizes that an expenditure of energy is required in the movement we make toward generations and objects identical to that required in the movement made away from them. The physics, therefore, describes a logic in the sometimes violent separations from parents that occur at precisely the same instant as the sometimes violent couplings with new friends and in the same way, probably, with a new sex, the other sex. Strange how that special unit of time circumscribing psychic transactions can seem so small and yet retain so much. It seems less strange if we recall that enclosed in this unit of time are all the remains, all that so far has been constructed of a unique identity. All eternity, perhaps, as some philosophers have taught, recurs in that one unit.

The escape from home, for example, and the sniping at family values and peculiar social structures are not exactly the precursors of attachments to people and institutions outside the family. In the beginning, they are part of one single action disguised as fragments by a seemingly long extension in time. It is not, therefore, that the engine of sexuality runs only when the engine of generational obedience is turned off. More precisely, the engine of obedience runs its energy into the engine of sexuality. When everything in that first engine is seemingly flat and impotent, the other engine appears to catch. But while it may seem as though the engine of sexuality proceeds under its own power, it remains attached to its parent engine in a single system for quite a while. (Only later on does the child dare examine the possibility that these engines may be separated and thereby gain the health and wisdom that this separation yields.) In the beginning, however, the major source of attraction and attachment to people and the fundamental linkage between people and the autonomy provided by their friendships is still the family, or at least relationships defined by kinship networks and authority.

Although it is true that with each decade aspects of maturity bloom earlier and earlier, the concept of adolescence has not yet lost all its validity. Gradations of psychological and social growth persist that, ironically, seem more and more in evidence as the young increase in what we call sophistication and awareness. So like a child running away from home to claim a vital independence and a chance to choose and own, the child running into love and sexuality, protest and freedom, the child running, really, toward the border between adulthood and childhood (a border that *does* in fact exist in our minds and in our societies) must pack together and stuff into his pockets the coins, food, and mementos of his entire life. For they represent his first social psychological, and economic arrangement with the family. With little preparation and even less warning, everything in this all-or-nothing transaction is packed, as if by the act of physically moving the child might lure away the memories of those places and people with such a devastating impact and finality that he might alter the content and rationality of his future and, most especially, of the reveries that future will hold.

The child takes the currency and foodstuff and runs to those he loves, and like a despotic general burns the villages behind him, the bridges, the outposts, and the supply depots. Through this militant outburst the past presumably is pillaged and a sparkling new present and future are made to wait for him, his goals, and his greatness. And who's going to stand up and say it isn't so or it doesn't happen this way!

To write about youth and youth's lives of attachments to things and people and work implies a presence of myriad feelings, all the feelings and emotions that human beings can generate, and all at once, feelings generated in varying formulas, in varying proportions and saliences. Perhaps the metaphor of emotional debits and credits has worth, for it does seem that we run some emotional accounts into the red when we absolutely require clean and crisp capital in other accounts. Possibly, too, when we come to know emotions and feelings well, there will emerge a principle of balancing payments and monies received. But the systems of feelings now are so incomprehensible that to call any behavior, or political revolt for that matter, actions of love or hate, actions of guided or misguided purpose, actions of children or adults can be only partially correct. Too few actions will be so clear-cut that they might be assigned merely to one account or another. For there *will* be anger in love; there *will* be bitter regret in vast hope. And, regardless of what the words mean to us, there *will* be adult maturity in childlike expressions and childlike imagination in adult impressions.

To label or diagnose, observe or record, which after all constitutes the process of writing about youth, is to select images and language from realities only thinly "in touch" with the magic of one's own conscious and unconscious worlds. In some ways and in some glorious times, we are one with or feel ourselves to be united with this "other reality," this counterculture, joined, that is, with these people and their generation. But, mainly, the source of our impressions, the grist, as it's still called, is our own interiors, interiors that do more than pay homage to materials that once lived outside of us or before us. It is *our* love and hate, *our* feelings of despair and courage, plasticity and conservatism, and *our* ambivalences that haunt the pages on which we print and draw a transient, flickering youth. It is unspoken talent and shameless temerity as much as it is insight and sensitivity.

Now, in the "real" sciences we could not exonerate such blasphemously personal thrusts at the truth. But somehow, in the outlandish physics systematizing and ordering social and psychological action, whatever it is that accepts our invitation to be written on a particular morning when the night before we had all but convinced ourselves that we were, finally, written out becomes part of the reality we have chosen to study. It becomes a part here just as much as it explicates a part there, and for a moment we are young like the young. The parts must pertain, moreover, for we have chosen youth, of all things, as this reality. But the parts must also be connected to the currency, food, and souvenirs we, too, once stuffed together, hurriedly and without forewarning as we made our plans to pillage a past and thereby create a dazzling present and bountiful future.

But now, writing about youth seems impossible, since everything happens so quickly, pouring forth so rapidly that too little time is left over to catch much of anything anymore. Perhaps it wasn't this way once, in our youth, when resiliency was assured and our bodies were proud and indestructible and maybe our souls immortal. But it all happens so quickly now that no one seems to treasure even the impressions that emerge, unrefined, still dripping with the fluids of unconscious and conscious substance. Everyone demands finished products, all perfectly intelligible. Yet, even worse, it all happens so quickly that we have begun to lose people from our land. What really is happening to the poor and the sick, and those who once were strong but whom failure has made frail and scared? Because of the rushing lives of so many people it is essential that we stop absolutely still, that we stop writing and stop talking and through our simple impressions, thoughtful and impure, regain those whom we have before burned away and restore the rare collection of time they have broken and hidden from us.

There is no life that can stand our taking away its fragile estimations of worth, just as there is no life that can come away unharmed from the tensions and deprivations endemic in our contemporary patterns of training, growth, education, bureaucracy, socialization, and career. All of us suffer in our way, the rich and the poor, and no one waits out the time of the temporary well. No one manages perfectly or completely a splintered life of demands heaped on demands. No one knows youth; no one knows aging; no one can adequately speak for another, even in a democracy. But each of us guards impressions of a life space colored and swept by time, and a sense of what it means to have morsels of the world we're able to see change, and what it means to have things resist even our most forceful efforts, singular and collective, to alter them. When the bewilderment of change, of time, really, and the reconciliation of the unchangeable properties of reality come to be internalized, then everything everywhere seems to have "gotten together," and identity arises as part of that everything. Life now is fat, and death, even to the very young, a bit less terrifying.

The arc of time diminishes; youth waits its turn, then takes its sometimes foolish gambles with predestination and immortality. The rest of us work our narrow work, hoping that the markers separating the generations might move again and that when sophistication, knowledge and anger, style and unbecoming pride are for an instant laid away, each day and each person in that day might repossess a fundamental dignity.

On Studying the Young

Interviewers' Past Illuminates Young People's Present

IT IS OFTEN HARD to believe in performing studies of youth, as one travels to school with "the kids," attends their parties, talks to them about parents, about careers, girls and boys, that any general concepts can ever be formulated, or that from impressions of the young, singular and vivid as they are, sociological concepts or psychological propositions might emerge. In fact, the observations of another person's life come at us in these friendships so forcefully and in such quantity, we almost never know where we are at unless, of course, we disregard everything the other person says until he speaks directly to what we want to know. But then, one of the best ways to learn whether what we want to know matters at all to this other one is by trying to get a feel of his emotions or of his own sense of intensity and commitment to the observations we have made.

So there we are, having reached a fuzzy area of impressions, an area where our feelings and perceptions are conjoined with the feelings and perceptions of those with whom we speak—those whom we "study"—an area where normal differentiations in social and psychological contacts tend to become blurred and where something intensely human happens.

Often, for example, in trying to sort out impressions, I find myself asking questions of young people I might not dare to answer myself. But, surprisingly, those whose eyes meet my own rarely retreat from my words or the facts of my age, or my status or job. Indeed, they frequently make their stand right where I should have been, where they want me to be, and where they believe my research efforts should be directed. And often, too, they point to that convergence of our impressions: the

130

feelings, the themes of childhood and adulthood as we experience them, and as we display them simultaneously to ourselves and to one another.[1] Then occurs a sometimes staggering collision of their ideas and musings about race, sex, authority, maturity, and their looking forward, backward, and presumably, at times nowhere at all, with my own responses to these very same things and to different things that also matter greatly to me. And, finally, all of this is united with our sentiments and impressions about being young or at least younger, or being old, older, too old, or too young.

It is in this convergence of feelings and impressions, theirs and mine, that a changing, wafting method of exploration emerges and an attempt is undertaken to unite our imaginations in order to get some hold on a reality that none of us understand too well, but that all of us care very much about. And it is because of this convergence that I dare to look again at bits of my own past and to examine just how that time trespasses on what I experience as a present and what I dream of as a future.[2]

If there is a single most striking issue that returns again and again in my discussions with the young, it is the concept of ambivalence.[3] On the one hand, the concept suggests the coexistence in a single heart of ostensibly opposing sentiments or ideologies, while on the other hand, it symbolizes the complexity and richness of not only every human being, but also every human encounter. I think, for example, of the way so many of my young captives—I almost wrote *subjects*—speak of their parents, even those few who have never met their parents. There is in their language and in their responses to the questions they themselves construct when they are compelled to disregard some of my own queries, such hatred and love that I simply cannot distinguish the direction in which they are headed. Nor can they themselves on some occasions.

The ambivalence, particularly about such things as dependence and independence, caring and hurting, fighting on and giving up, destroying and preserving, is always present.[4] Indeed, little about the lives of these people seems so unequivocal or sufficiently discrete and "right" that I can actually put it in my notebook for safekeeping. The best that I can do, usually, is check it out in my own imagination. But even this is unsatisfactory, because after locating my own ambivalent yearnings and sensibilities, I then have to ask just who initiated this ambivalence imagery in the first place: Was it they or I? Or was it all of us, and is this ambivalence, therefore, the presence of our mutual convergence of impressions?

What I do know with certainty, at least for today, and I suspect for tomorrow as well, is that I can never fully know these young people I "study," that I can never speak for them, and that I can never totally articulate the impressions born from our contacts together. And yet, while it is never enough to say that you cannot fully know me, or I you, there is great worth in letting others know about you and me, particularly when our society makes one of us the more visible, the more newsworthy, or the more hurting.[5] Thus, just as we learn that no one can speak wholly for us, so do we also come to realize that others' impressions, theories, and words do speak for substantial parts of us. And because they help us to clarify that convergence of feelings and events that comprises our intellectual and social involvements, they assist us in taking a step perhaps, or overcoming error. But if this is too abstract, I learned that I didn't care for some of these young people as much as I did others, and, at times, I didn't care for any of them as much as I was fascinated by, or at least rather pleased with, the stuff that came out of my own head after long encounters on school playfields, in restaurants, hangouts, homes, and all those places where I travel to seek out that thing some of us call "youth culture."[6]

But this realization, too, is not particularly surprising: While it is not always the case in every social scientific inquiry, when one studies young people, it is essential that the self-interested nature of such investigation be recognized. And rather than be frightened by the contamination this solipsism may cause, it just might be best to take full advantage of the insights that ride those unbelievable feelings now coming back from heaven only knows where, when one meets the excessive displays, tragic lots, hopeful days, and that partly comprehensible, partly incomprehensible fabric that is, in the end, the soul of youth. Studying youth, after all, is a bit like surfing, in that we can watch the ways in which our source of fascination moves from the gush of the water, to the smooth and slippery planes of the board, to, finally, the erotic patterns that are the muscles holding us aloft amid the spray and chopping motion of natural currents that play about the boards we manufacture to ride these currents. And yet everything seems to pass by so quickly and with such devastating finality that, in the long run, some of the best time is the time we make stand still by recalling our impressions of the ride. For in the recollections and the impressions they guard we have a chance not only to replay past experiences, but also to shape them any way we want with a fluidity and boundless majesty that the ocean itself might envy.

But does this mean that our impressions of youth or of the past are untrue, or only true in their special way? Does this mean that the essence of any experience, the stress point in fact rests just slightly beyond the beat of the experience so that to capture the genuine impulse of youth, the flow of younger people through life, is just about an impossibility? Do we perhaps make young people bigger than life by writing about them and laying on them the wit and elegance as well as the blandness and foolishness of our own perceptions of them? And how does one manage best this business of maintaining what at our old high school dances the faculty chaperones determined to be "proper distance"?

Excess and Overreaction

From all sorts of varying distances and intensities, I have tried to determine for myself an "appropriate" closeness with the young people with whom I speak regularly, whose worlds I have been touched and attracted by—though at times angered and threatened by as well. As the work went on and events unfolded, I found myself moving away from the uncomfortable objective indifference I had seen come over me on trips to various high schools. I was becoming involved in politics and with people. No, it wasn't exactly that. It was the very thought of human life that I found missing in most of the political and curriculum materials, in the braggadocio, in the blasphemy, as well as in the serious programs that thoughtful people were outlining. My temptation to reminisce or my wish that I could call a "time out" and run away to the most pastoral and elitist solitude were clues, perhaps, to my fright and insecurity, as well as indicators that people's feelings were being mistreated, or that people, young and old, were being used or ignored or forgotten altogether. (Others, of course, had these same feelings and published words like, "Cops are people, too." Such an incredible cliché, but how important that some would remember to utter this admonition.)

But it is often the case, when people are being studied, that an objectification—dehumanization is the word I hear and use most every day—occurs that results in people being discredited and made insignificant. This is a danger the young, or some of them, know too well. Others do not contemplate these issues. Rather, they tend to keep alive the many expressions that represent simpleminded and thoughtless reductions of the richness of human existence to levels cheap and mundane. Often people are first misunderstood and then washed away by our refusal to recognize more than one or two dimensions of their humanity. So some of us say, "Love it or leave it!" and hope that by this brand of logic something somewhere might be settled. Ironically, however, others of us do so much analyzing that in the process we dehumanize our "subjects" much in the manner of those who quickly dismiss them. The tension, therefore, between the reduction of problems and the obsession with them remains, and both activities yield similarly dismal products.

Many have pointed out, moreover, that the rhetoric in studies of youth is excessive.[7] Often it is excessive—I know my own writing is—just as the emotions of the young seem excessive, just as their actions and demands, their trials and their boredom seem excessive. Exaggeration is, well, the way of quite a few young people, though certainly not all, and while we cannot, of course, be aware of all of youth's excesses, they become somehow ingrained in some of our own thinking and writing. Partly, of course, the excess is our imagination or youths' imagination, but mainly it may just be the natural end product of that convergence, that presence we have called an impression. Excess, perhaps, is the reason why impressions, for certain people, seem to lack a scientific validity, a certainty, and ultimately a graceful clarity. Perhaps, too, excess is the reason for children and young people generally to be treated by so many institutions not as whole human beings but as either half human or doubly human.[8] It appears, in other words, that those of us who spend time with the young tend either to crunch them under the feet of our rules and rituals and thereby render them half human, or to over-romanticize their talents and activities to such an extent, that the young themselves begin to doubt the worth of their very worthwhile beings. It is indeed a difficult tendency to overcome, but does it not seem as though we flunk too many students and award A⁺s to too many others?

Regard the products of youth, for example, and you will see that they are really very lovely, genuinely lovely; at times clear and wise, at times wonderfully outrageous, honest, and strong. But only rarely are they superb and able to withstand capricious shifts in style and taste. In this regard, they are the products of people. So schools and families are foolish not to honor these products in the same way that they are foolish to convince themselves that these products are far superior to all products in the world. More importantly, the young themselves know as well as we do that their position in society, their status really, is meant to be standing upright and proud alongside any pedestal anyone might wish to erect. Upright and proud alongside any pedestal; not crushed under its weight, not hidden by its girth, and not elevated by its height.

Maturation

More fascinating than youth's excesses is the way in which the effort of studying youth becomes a process of examining maturation.[9] We look back at ourselves and then over there at "the kids," and we find ourselves musing first about how our past and present fit together, and then how our present and youth's present might possibly connect. We watch the ways in which young people confront their own maturation as well as the inequalities and asymmetries in their society. While some would call these inequalities inequities, it is not always the case that what we might see as a pernicious strain in a person or in a community is seen in the same way by that community's children.[10] Indeed, what makes many episodes with young people so poignant is their frequent disinterest in situations we feel to be so serious and crippling.

Most striking, however, is that ambivalence of theirs toward maturation, toward parents and teachers, and the lack of clear-cut and unequivocal attitudes in this group of people whom we occasionally believe to be dogmatic, unyielding, and exaggeratedly settled in their approach to contemporary lifestyles.[11] Where all young people, so it seems, find a common source of complicated anger and attachment is with their parents, their friends, their schools, and, finally, as they mature, with the so-called established order that represents to them the symbolic re-enactment of the prior social order they have known, or a new social order many now have come to oppose, or perhaps a social order just too discrepant from their expectations, languishing wishes, and recently conceived demands.[12]

Though maturation generally is a deeply complicated process, there is at least one relatively simple aspect of it, one that, in a sense, is the overriding theme of youth studies. It is that each year requires new adaptations, for even if one stays in the same school, moving from the fifth to the sixth grade requires some delicate rearrangements with the social order, with people, and with one's self-image. Each year, in other words, requires that social, psychological, biological, and cognitive adjustments be made to tangible things, events, and human beings. Each year also means the continuation of the prior year and the preparation for the one to follow. And this implies that each of us holds to accumulating experiences that actually seem to undergo very little transformation in light of these other adjustments we simultaneously are making. The eighth year follows the seventh but it does not replace the seventh year, nor does it cover over or despoil the seventh year.[13] Past years remain and the experiences they contain peek through the present's lining in ways that as yet we do not understand. In truth, in ways we may never (want to) understand.

Maturation implies certain adaptations to newness, some maintenance of the prior, and discrete alterations in rational inference and anticipation. And, as if this were not sufficiently complex, events that we seemingly have no control over (though some argue that in fact we do have control over them) suddenly fall on us or lie in wait for us, or breathlessly catch up to us when, but moments ago, we were moving along untroubled and actually rather free. Suddenly something happens to make us feel as though the maturational processes have shifted and the elements themselves are in revolution. The past and present must now be recontextualized, and the future envisioned in totally new settings. But through it all, certain figures, certain symbols, and existential properties remain frightfully constant. And it turns out, often to the surprise of some young persons, that the foundations and inevitabilities of time and its properties, such as our pasts, presents, and futures, are still there. It turns out, too, that a society's properties, such as poverty, hunger, stratification, power, illness, and oppression, and a single person's properties, such as sadness, loneliness, or despair, as well as contentment and courage, are also still there. And these discoveries require adjustments as well.

Each of us is capable of making the very adjustments that ultimately prove the existence of maturational inequalities and asymmetries both in ourselves and in the institutions we structure and bequeath to our children. Each of us, moreover, works to comprehend the variables, the figures that go into these adaptations we call maturity. We wonder, for example, about our individuality and our need for group coherence; our interior privacy and external displays, and our loyalty to authority, demonstrated through compliance, as well as our desire to topple authority, often through rather ingenious enterprises. We wonder about success and failure, fame and anonymity, youth and old age, life and death, mothers and father, parents and children. All of us avoid the temptation to insert the word "versus" between these "options" and "properties" because we know, without professional training, without therapeutic intervention, without it being taught to us by anyone directly, that we maintain all of these urges and the images of all these people simultaneously. Not only that, we cannot accurately predict at any point of maturation what urge or image might take psychological or social precedence over another, or whether one stimulus might send all the urges and images scurrying in one or a million directions at once. It is almost laughable, in this regard, to think that some of us actually choose to study young people because processes like maturation or feelings of ambivalence are supposed to be more easily discernible among this population, and hence more available for assessment.

Human Behavior Is Unpredictable

At times, we have been especially unfair and unkind to America's children, or some of them, not only in our daily transactions but also in the arrangements we have made for them through governmental, educational, and religious institutions.[14] And they have been unfair and unkind to us.[15] They forbid us our histories just as often, probably, as we threaten their maturation, and both actions are degrading and terrifying. The expressions "murder in the classroom" and "the rape of the mind" do describe, although a bit overdramatically, the failure of education. But students can destroy the careers and joys of teachers just as school systems can harm creativity and inquisitiveness among students. The problem, of course, is far more complicated. For now that we know the damage done by schools, churches, governments, and maybe social scientists as well, and now that we have begun to try to lessen this damage and make these institutions and their personnel more humane, we might wonder about the strength and resiliency of those human beings who have come through the machines of systematized, standardized learning programs and have constructed magnificently creative lives.

This is a project for each of us, as we all possess a limited understanding of youth culture, or whatever one chooses to call it. Still, I shudder from the certainty with which some investigators speak about maturation, or about the young or the old, or just about people. Tentativeness is for some a stigmatized word, whereas certainty, both in personal action or carriage, and scientific inquiry quite often become the ideal. But we must continually remind ourselves that there is no certainty in our comprehension of human behavior as much as we might wish for it. Often I wonder how much of a young person's actions are made in response to his fear (or wish?) that because people like myself might try to understand too much, his privacy, his secret interior, his impressions of himself and of his life, those feelings he cherishes the most, might be taken away from him.[16]

Then again, most young people are resilient, and, because they are, they replenish what might have been taken away from them. Others are less so, and we must do more than wonder about them. Still others find their resiliency irrelevant when faced with an implacable reality that simply will not budge one inch to accommodate them, their styles, or their patterns of growth. But more than anything else, "studies of youth" make us question whether now is the time to be hopeful or despairing. For during these days of such extreme confusion, unsettled plans and purposes and outright danger, there just seems to be no middle ground between denial and safety and no easy passage through time and through childhood to freedom and peace.

Notes

1. T. J. Cottle, *Time's Children: Impressions of Youth*. Boston: Little, Brown and Company, 1971. T. J. Cottle, Billy Kowalski goes to college. *Change Magazine* 3, 1971: pp. 36–42.

2. T. J. Cottle, The connection of adolescence. *Daedalus* 100, 1971: pp. 1171–1219.

3. E. H. Erikson, *Identity: Youth and Crisis*. New York: W.W. Norton, 1968. E. H. Erikson, Reflections on the dissent of contemporary youth. *Daedalus* 99, 1970: pp. 154–176.

4. R. Coles, *Children of Crisis: A Study of Courage and Fear*. Boston: Atlantic–Little, Brown and Company, 1967.

5. J. A. Lucas, *Don't Shoot—We Are Your Children*. New York: Random House, 1971.

6. K. Keniston, Youth: A new stage of life. *American Scholar* 39, 1970: pp. 631–654.

7. P. Marin, The open truth and fiery vehemence of youth. *The Center Magazine* 2, 1969: pp. 61–74.

8. S. McCracken, Quackery in the classroom. *Commentary* 49, 1970: pp. 45–58.

9. E. H. Erikson, *Young Man Luther*. New York: W. W. Norton, 1958.

10. R. Coles, op. cit.

11. L. Feuer, Conflicts of generations. *Saturday Review* 52, 1969: p. 53*ff*.

12. P. E. Slater, *The Pursuit of Loneliness: American Culture at the Breaking Point*. Boston: Beacon Press, 1970. T. Roszak, Youth and the great refusal. *The Nation* 206, 1968: pp. 400–407.

13. E. H. Erikson (1958), op. cit.

14. P. E. Slater, op. cit. C. Reich, *The Greening of America*. New York: Random House, 1970. R. Poirier, The war against the young. *The Atlantic Monthly*

222, 1968: pp. 55–64. G. R. Weaver, Introduction to *The University and Revolution*, G. R. Weaver and J. H. Weaver (eds.). Englewood Cliffs, N.J.: Prentice Hall, Inc., 1969.

15. M. Mayer, The children's crusade. *The Center Magazine* 2, 1969: pp. 2–7.
16. T. J. Cottle (1971, *Time's Children*), op. cit.

Children's Secrets, Family Myths

JUST AS THERE IS no easy way to draw together the myriad themes of an individual life study, so is there no ultimately successful way to draw together the strands of the life studies taken as a whole. So many queries remain open to explore than even as we pursue one, we ignore too many others. In this essay we touch on a few familiar points and offer some new ones.

Two key words have been repeated far too often: secret and myth. In certain significant ways, moreover, these two words are intimately related. When a child is obliged to keep a piece of experience secret, he or she is automatically obliged, at a conscious level, not only to make sense of the experience as it exists externally but to make sense of the internal reaction to the secret. This means that the child must undergo the psychological twistings and untwistings in order to decode the experience, the reaction to it, and finally the nature of secrets themselves. We speak of children beginning to observe themselves as part of the process of intellectually and emotionally decoding the secrets they are meant to keep. We have not stressed fully enough, however, the notion that the twistings and untwistings, what Claude Levi-Strauss might call "thought experiments," are themselves part of the secrets children keep, and in time become part of the myths they subsequently hold about themselves, their families, and their cultures.

When children keep the sort of secret we are examining in these pages, they come to believe in the mythic nature of their own existence only partly because they know a lie must be preserved. The lie, literally the inability to tell someone the truth, not only affects the perception of the world as being corrupt or counterfeit but colors children's own sense of themselves. So, secretly, children view themselves as corrupt or counterfeit. The notion, then, that not telling others one's father, say, is a homosexual somehow preserves the myth of one's family as being straight, does not tell the complete story of mythification. For the child who keeps the secret, is himself or herself becoming "mythified." The mythification is part of an argument with oneself, part of a thought experiment or psychological twisting, the function of which is, first, to make sense, codify (public and private, that is shared and unshared) experience, as well as resolve the emotional responses to experience. Experiences must constantly be juggled in order to decodify them, or allow the person to make better intellectual and emotional sense of them. The young people discussed in the previous essays are doing just this. Like anthropologists or philosophers, they are at work attempting to make public and private sense of experience. Their work, juggling, twisting, is itself a process of perpetual intellectual and emotional transformation. First one solution or resolution is formed, then another supplants it, then another, and on and on. Each transformation reveals something about the person, the experience, myth, and secret, as well as secret keeping and myth making generally.

The work of secret keeping, moreover, as life studies reveal, retains a dramatic or dramaturgic quality. People become larger than life. Experience seems larger than life, mythic perhaps, because the child has no intellectual or emotional receptacle into which a particular experience might fit. Thus, the adolescent continues to work on the same problem and react to the temporary solutions as well as to the process of problem solving itself. Furthermore, just as the actual experience held as secret provides its structure (of and for experience) and plot, so do the mental acts of psychological twisting and untwisting provide their structure and plot for the adolescent. No myth is without structure or plot. Myths often make captivating stories partly because we are compelled by the underlying intellectual and emotional transformations we (consciously) recognize or unconsciously resonate to in the myth's transformations. Little wonder, then, that writers have grown fond of the terms psychological and social "scripts," implying as they do not only patterns for individuals to follow privately and publicly but mental and social acts for people to perform.

Now, what are some of these transformations? We cannot elucidate them in the detail they warrant, but we can note that myths often provide resolutions to the very sorts of antinomic feelings and concepts with which adolescents struggle. These include such issues as the private and public, individualism and collectivism, sanity and insanity, possibility and impossibility, finitude and infinitude, past and future, life and death. Antinomies, moreover, are not unlikely forms for myths; transformations in myths reduce the manifest conflict of antinomic concepts and attitudes. In classical myths, for example, the dead become alive, the sane insane, the future turns into the past, the private world becomes public, small becomes large, sad events become happy ones. Cowardice, furthermore, is transformed into courage, finitude into infinitude. Once again, our argument states that the normal act of secret keeping is itself akin to exploring myths, and particularly myths that deal with the sorts of issues with which adolescents work. Adolescence is a time when people commence their thought experiments on just these topics, and gain from their psychological twistings and untwistings a new understanding of the nature of personal (or private) and public (or shared) experiences. Note that when we use the term *shared* experience, we mean an experience one either *performs* with another person or *tells* another person.

We need not be self-conscious about speaking of adolescents as philosophers. Levi-Strauss refers to the cognitive processes involved in tangling and untangling myths as *scientific thought* merely expressed in another idiom. In a sense, the secret, propelling the child into the realm of myth, could be viewed as the basis of a special cognitive and emotional idiom. Few of us could articulate precisely what this idiom would be, but the relevant point remains that when adolescents become involved in secret keeping (or myth making), they recognize this involvement with their private and public worlds in terms of a new idiom or medium. The meanings to an adolescent of thought and feeling are transformed just as the myth is transformed, just as the secret is coded (or codified), decoded (or decodified), then coded all over again. And coding does seem an appropriate term. To safeguard a message others are not meant to learn requires that the adolescent put the message through some psychological scrambling device that makes it understandable only to those capable of unscrambling it. But here again, the acts of (intellectually and emotionally) scrambling and unscrambling are precisely what the mythic sense is all about. "Let me turn it around in my head," we say. The phrase is a loaded one. It means, manifestly, let me work on that idea in order to make sense of it. More significantly it implies, let me play with the various meanings, find new interconnections of the various parts of the idea, as well as new *connections* to other ideas, other aspects of reality, other aspects of myself, other aspects of my *sense* of self. These processes and dynamics, too, are part of what we mean by the intellectual and emotional transformations inherent in myth making. For the adolescent, however, each bit of myth making, each instant of secret keeping, each psychological twist or untwist will necessarily have some implication for his or her sense of self as private and public being. It will also have an implication for the script adolescents create, the language they employ, the moods they develop. The thought experiments inherent in or demanded by secret keeping represent simultaneously adolescents' (emotional) psychologizing, their scientific investigating, their ordering of social events, and their spiritual trial.

To follow the path of a secret is to learn the logic not merely of the mind of the secret keeper. It is to discern the structure of the reality, private and public, that the secret keeper transforms into myth. To do this, we may explore what secret-keeping experiences mean to individual boys and girls. Our focus, in other words, stays on the main character, the secret keeper. Yet the focus might also be placed on the myth preserved by the act of secret keeping. The meanings, therefore, of individual or family harmony, stability, the meaning of affluence and traditional sexual behavior, also could be explored by examining the child's thought transformations, the so-called thought experiments. Any psychological exploration offers the possibility of an examination of the individual involved, or the historical or sociological contexts and realities in which the person exists. Any psychological exploration provides one the opportunity to examine the mental acts of an individual and hence the mythifying enacted by that individual as he or she reacts to external or internal cues. We belong to myths in the same way that we create them. We hold them as secrets in the same way that we share them, make certain that others know of them or know the opportunity of embellishing them. The child keeps the family secret, which thereby activates an ongoing set of processes we have called mythification. The child keeps the family secret, which thereby perpetuates for the public a second myth, namely the untruth the family wishes perpetuated. Both myths, underwritten by secrets, become codified, twisted, and untwisted by the child. Little wonder that so many children would have so little time or energy to do much more than work at their myths and secrets. One might add that the normal process of adolescent development demands this sort of work. As we have already suggested, adolescence is a time for these scientific and social psychological cogitations to take place, cogitations that rarely become public or publicized. The results of adolescent thought experiments, like the thought experiments themselves, typically remain secret. It all makes for a great deal of work, it makes for a difficult time, it makes for a seemingly totally self-preoccupied soul.

Having offered these remarks about the conceptual connections between secret keeping and myth making, let me now point to the obvious linkage between these two processes, namely, the edict of silence that causes a message or communication to be called a secret. Psychological twistings and untwistings, thought experiments, psychological codifying and decodifying aside, the blatant feature of the secret is that the keeper cannot reveal the message or the experience, or even what he or she makes of the nature of secret keeping.

We have argued that the acts of secret keeping and myth making imply, indeed reveal, structures. The personality, like the secret, the myth, and life itself, has structure. Adolescence, we have suggested, is a period when people for the first time in their lives confront these structures in order to determine their form and content. The facts that we die, that the future is not limitless, that our possibilities and opportunities remain highly circumscribed, are systematically confronted for the first time during adolescence. Thought experiments are conducted on these rather troubling issues, just as thought experiments are conducted on all the antinomies striking the adolescent mind: sanity and insanity, privacy and publicness, reality and fantasy, etc. But all of these matters, irrespective of the idiosyncratic nature of their substance—for fantasy, dying, or privacy mean something slightly different to each person— teach the adolescent something about the nature of the *structure* of these matters. There *is* a structure to the future and its relationship to the past and present. This temporal structure relates, moreover, to the structure defined by (realistic) finitude and (fantasized or wished for) infinitude. So the secret-keeping adolescent learns much about the structure of language, thought, and action almost as a by-product of his or her thought experiments and psychological twistings and untwistings.

Furthermore, adolescents learn that the very things they are (thought) experimenting on, provide certain structure themselves. To determine whether or not one is sane or insane, happy or sad, optimistic or pessimistic, requires that one engage in the structure of sanity and insanity, optimism and pessimism, etc. Said differently, a person must work out definitions of sanity and insanity, but in addition, must come to see that the way these definitions are worked out, or the forms of thought leading to the (forms of) definitions at which one ultimately arrives, are themselves aspects of the structure of sanity in which one is now engaged. The adolescent asks, "I wonder whether I'm crazy? Even more, I wonder whether asking this question proves that I'm crazy or not crazy?" This observation of the self, watching oneself watching oneself, attests to the fact that people remain fully aware of the structural aspects of thought and language. It suggests, too, that people will often reach personal conclusions about themselves as much through inferences drawn from the *structure* of thought, language, myth, secret keeping, as from the *substance* of thought, language, myth, secret keeping. Furthermore, although the phrase seems tautological, one relies on the structure of thought, language, and action in order to make sense of thought, language, and action. Certainly adolescents are aware of this fact. Indeed, they regularly flirt with ways to change structure, "destructure" thought and language, as David Cooper has suggested.

Granted, destructuring often causes one to feel that he or she is going crazy, that there is nothing left to rely on, that nothing in the world remains calculable or predictable. The event the child has been asked to keep secret influences the child's fundamental perceptions of a particular structure. But again we must ask, where does secret keeping fit into this matter of structure or destructuring?

If the notion of restructuring thought, language, behavior, has merit, it suggests that people are constantly working out in their minds new and different meanings of thought, language, and action. We say, in light of what just happened, I now have to think about what that means to me, or how I feel about that thing (or myself). In light of this or that event, I must change my feelings about my mother or father, or whatever. The change they feel they must make involves intellectual and emotional as well as behavioral matters. Several children have said that *everything* now is different in their families, and in their lives. These changes, moreover, are what we are calling restructuring. We use the term to suggest that the parameters and ingredients of thought and language begin to shift as one wrestles with a particular problem, as, for example, one's mother's infidelity. When we say, "It's like my whole world fell apart," we mean that many of the structural aspects of living, thought, feeling, language, behavior, have shifted, and hence each phase or activity of my life must now be redefined. Words and feelings do not mean exactly what they did prior to the event, i.e., discovering one's mother's infidelity.

Let us be clear on the matter that restructuring and destructuring, myth making even, need not be negative or frightening actions. Quite to the contrary; they may be productive, progressive steps. People wish to change, people seek to reorder or reshape aspects of their lives, as well as those structures that allow them to think in new ways about their lives. A trying event occurs and we counsel a friend, make the best of it, perhaps there is a blessing to be found (in the restructuring that you will be forced to undertake). Similarly, we regularly discover people working to alter the state of various thought, language, emotional, and behavioral structures in order to become (in part) something different from what they were. Altering the state of consciousness through drugs is an extreme form of restructuring, a form all too many adolescents attempt. Having, then, experienced different forms of consciousness may give people insight into the varying structures of consciousness. In general, an altered form of consciousness, just as an altered form of living, requires that old structures, in part, break down, or are juggled, thereby allowing the person to reshape, re-form, restructure his or her existence. At times the need to change is societally determined; at times it is personally or psychologically determined. Adolescence, however, remains a time of an externally as well as internally motivated need to change or restructure.

Many children have been obliged to restructure their lives, as well as their thinking about themselves and their existence. Still, they cannot speak about the restructuring that their thought experiments yield, which in turn affects the quality of the restructuring. If their psychological twistings and untwistings represent an idiom of scientific thought, then their secret keeping prevents them from confirming the findings these thought experiments are meant to yield. Without confirmation, the children are encouraged to believe that their thinking or feeling is bizarre, even absurd. Put simply, the children are never quite certain what to make of their secret experiences. But note as well, that if their thinking about these matters, the myths they are constructing, seems to them absurd, then the reality in which they find themselves is equally absurd. It is not absurd to learn that one's father is psychotic, but it *is* absurd to discover that one's mother is denying this all too obvious fact. (The theme of the entire family already knowing the secret is also common to most of the children's accounts.) Thus, the act of secret keeping is often perceived as an absurd action; the absurdity of it reflects in turn on the child's assessments of himself or herself, assessments, to repeat, that go on in private as still another aspect of the secret.

If children's secrets are predicated partly on the recognition of external and internal absurdity, they are simultaneously constructed in great measure from shame. The secret, in other words, remains shameful; it symbolizes shame. It yields shame of the parent about whom the secret is being kept, shame of the family living with an absurd sense of itself, shame of self for keeping the secret in the first place, and hence shame of being. Restructuring, destructuring, thought experiments, myth making, psychological twistings and untwistings, require communication, even telegraphic, abbreviated communication. Secrets prelude communication. They require communication not because the final stage of a thought experiment is informing someone else of one's recent psychological findings, but because without expression the sense of (privately and publicly based) shame cannot be expiated, and reality cannot be confirmed. Shame festers without communication. When it festers, anger grows, but without the right to communicate, as the secret demands, the anger must turn against the self. Telling an experience, in other words, does not literally mean reliving it. A report of a holiday journey abroad hardly represents an experiential replication of that journey. Yet in telling about it, we restructure or recontextualize the experience; we make sense of it. We also make further sense of our reactions to it. The telling of the experience, therefore, serves a public as well as a private value. The experience is "better integrated" when we tell it, because the telling "proves" that it is real. Telling is not the experiment; it is the "replication" of the experiment.

When we examine a potentially traumatized person, we inquire first, whether he or she is about to speak of the traumatizing event. Indeed, we strenuously encourage people to speak of the event, for we hope to keep it from receding forever into the unconscious, where it festers, ultimately to affect perceptions, emotions, possibly even thought and behavior. We would like to think that the potentially damaging experience is one a person *prefers* not to speak about rather than one the person is *unable* to speak about. If the person can tell of the experience, the chances of it becoming the agent of trauma are significantly diminished. Turning this thought around, we may advance the following argument: Demanding that a potentially serious event, like discovering one's mother's nymphomania, be kept secret causes the event to be dealt with, by the secret keeper, as a potentially traumatic event. That is, if the experience does not cause sufficient psychological harm, then the demand for secrecy may produce it. There is no guarantee of this, naturally, but as we have seen, to demand that certain family issues be kept secret is tantamount, one might say, to traumatizing the child.

Let me present the argument in another way. In many cases, a child's entire life, entire sense of being actually, had to be recontextualized, rethought, restructured. No solution the child might have conceived could possibly have worked out satisfactorily, since the reality of the parents' and hence the family's circumstances remained intact. Indeed, almost all the solutions the children reached seemed unsatisfactory, if not utterly absurd, especially to them. No one needed to tell Peter Malone, for example, that his experiments with drugs hardly represented a productive way of "working through" (which in effect means restructuring) his problems. Similarly, no one needed to inform Chico Adrian of the futility (and absurdity) of his goal of landing himself in the mental hospital where he believed his father was incarcerated. But had anyone advised the children of the absurdity of their behavior, or for that matter of their emotional responses, the children's sense of shame would have increased that much more. Their level of anger, too, would have soared. One should not overlook this last point, for the life studies are replete with expressions of anger. Suicidal gestures, as absurd in their intent as in their content, run through the material. They emerge, however, in the expressions of the children in most pathetic tones. The children seem to be indicating that suicide or any form of self-destructive thinking or behavior would be foolish, ungratifying, absurd. The absurdity of the gestures and self-destructive reasoning only reaffirms for the child the sense of shame and the feeling of anger. Expiation of shame, like the release of some of the aggression, might be possible through the confession of the secret, but almost none of the thought experiments has yielded significant satisfaction.

To hold tightly to secrets convinces the child at some level that he or she is mad. If the shame and anger or the restructuring and psychological twistings and untwistings do not contribute to this belief, then the perceived absurdity of the external situation and one's internal thought processes must encourage a sense of madness. The inability to tell the secret only adds to the fear that one is mad. For cognitive as well as emotional reasons, the artist seems able to escape madness (during the process of making art, that is) by saying the unsayable, expressing the inexpressible. In saying the unsayable, the artist, paradoxically, recognizes, codifies, and ultimately tames or controls the madness. In the expressing of the madness lies the possibility of capturing madness, or at least containing it. Almost all radical restructuring processes, almost all cognitive and emotional jugglings, cause one to feel that madness is near. We noted how the experience of discovering some horrendous news about one's parents may cause one to believe one has been made crazy. Yet the restructuring of thought, language, feeling, and behavior made in response to the discovery can only enhance this belief, especially when one is unable to confess either the experience or the thought experiments made in response to it. Secrets, therefore, of the urgent type we have been considering remain deeply related to the sense of madness, which is itself a common theme in mythology. Through myths, people reveal their constantly changing comprehension of and response to madness and death. It is no coincidence, then, that several of the children should allude to demons possessing them or boogey people living inside them. Granted, demons may be the personification (the incubus) of impulses and emotions, just as physical symptoms may be somatic representations of impulses and emotions. But (believed) madness also may be personified by demons and boogey people. In the beginning the demons reside outside us, but then we bring them inside; or is it that they are born within us? Does the ultimate secret, therefore, have something to do with our sense of madness and normality, or at least our wonderings about madness and normality? And if it does, if secrets and madness are thus entwined, can we properly expect children not to feel the evocation of madness when their culture or family, or their very being, demands that they keep a portentous secret?

In looking back on the life studies, the reader will note many instances when the child's relationship to me seemed to suffer somewhat after a confession. Contrary to my original assumptions, telling me of the family ordeal did not bring me closer to some of the children. In several cases, the confession actually seemed to exacerbate the shame. Yet, expiation of the shame was made possible by my moving away from the child, almost as if I took a bit of the shame and anger away with me. The popular expression "Let me lay some of my burden on you" seems particularly relevant in this context. For there is a fantasy, a wish that the hearer of the confession will physically carry away the shame or burden of the secret, and bury it forever. One way to bury the secret, although hardly a satisfactory one for the researcher, is to disappear altogether. If secrets kept the children chained to their families, then telling the secrets often let them feel that if they were not liberated or released, then at least they had earned their parole. Yet even this point must be examined against the background of adolescents' normal ambivalence about being imprisoned within their families. Despite youthful belligerence and protestation, who is to say that total freedom from one's family is precisely what all adolescents covet? As we have remarked repeatedly, individual personalities, families, and cultures create and perpetuate the need for secrets; and all must bear responsibility for these secrets.

Given the themes and philosophy of this essay, it seems appropriate that a child be granted final say. Accordingly, we conclude this essay with one last life study, one last secret. In this instance, however, the secret is of a more hopeful kind. I seriously doubt that the following life study could be called typical of anything. Still, it contains a momentous secret, a secret of the type we rarely encounter. If nothing else, it is comforting to observe how one young woman overcame anger, shame, a sense of life's abject absurdity, and found the results of her thought experiments sufficiently gratifying that she would affirm nothing more, and nothing less, than her own being.

Patsy Sawyer is now twenty-six years old. She is a tall, strongly built woman with warm brown eyes and hair cut short, very short. She smiles easily, but rarely laughs. When something amuses her she merely nods, and perhaps taps her fingernails on a table. The small one-bedroom apartment she has rented for several years is crowded with books, pictures, record albums, all sorts of objects. And plants. The windows are covered with plants. They hang from the casings and ceilings. Any available space reveals a plant. Yet as crowded as the apartment surely is, it remains orderly. Objects have their place. When moved, they are put back. The orderliness is not excessive, but apparent. Patsy is all too aware of why it may be this way, why it probably has to be this way. She has told me: "It's part of my way of making the old mess feel more straightened out. I put it together nicely now, the way I want it; that helps me to keep the past from coming back and destroying everything, or most everything."

It is no secret to Patsy Sawyer's friends that her father spent a stretch in prison for attempted murder, and that her mother was convicted for prostitution and issued a suspended sentence only because her husband, though they were estranged, was serving time and nobody was around to look after their three children. In fact, there were never *any* secrets around the Sawyer home. By the age of five, Patsy, along with her older brother and younger sister, had watched their parents' marriage collapse. Arthur and Sally Sawyer were always fighting, never friendly, if Patsy's recollections are accurate. When Patsy was seven, she learned from her mother that her father had been sentenced to prison. Her mother told the news with relish; Arthur's criminal act publicly confirmed his reprehensible nature, and served to condone Sally taking in one lover after another, each of whom pranced through the Sawyer household practically advertising his illicit intentions.

At age ten, it became clear to Patsy Sawyer that her mother was a prostitute and that her older brother, Tim, was selling drugs. As it turned out, he was arrested six times for possession and sales but released from custody each time on the grounds that prison, as the judge claimed, would only serve to harden his criminal tendencies. Besides, the court-appointed lawyers always argued in his behalf, imprisonment would only add problems to an already beleaguered family. Patsy was relieved Tim was never put away, but her mother could never understand the judge's reasoning. How could a prison sentence possibly add to *her* burdens? It would mean one less person to worry about. It would rid her of the men in her family, and might just make a decent man out of a "sick mixed-up psycho," her pet description of Tim.

At thirteen, Patsy Sawyer had quit school and with one of her close friends had become a prostitute. A man named Donlevy pimped for the two girls who took in more money than Patsy ever imagined she would earn. In the beginning, she found the trade disgusting, and frightening. In a few months she felt herself to be a seasoned professional. She hustled five or six men a day and pocketed between one and two hundred dollars after Donlevy took his share. It wasn't a bad life. In fact, it was a good one if you didn't get arrested as no intelligent woman should. Only the irresponsible ones, like her mother, were arrested, and they deserved it. Getting arrested, Patsy told me, was no different from getting pregnant. If you took the precautions, there were no problems. If you lost your head, anything could happen. Her mother took chances and got caught. Patsy took no chances; the only policemen she ever met were the ones who came to her as customers.

Add one more fact to this brief view of a family's history—that Patsy's younger sister also became a prostitute—and one has what Patsy Sawyer calls her family's vital statistics. She told me once:

Some people, it takes them weeks to spin out the story of their lives. Me, I'm lucky. I can do it in a few sentences. Mother convicted for prostitution but sentence suspended. Brother arrested six times, drugs, possession and selling, no convictions. Why, I'll never figure out. Father in jail. Deserves to be, although his life wasn't so great, even before he met my mother. Sister, a prostitute, school dropout, the whole business, no chance; no, I take that back. No chance for my brother, or that I can see, still a chance for my sister. Pretty moral family, huh? Maybe we should have gone to church. That might have had an effect, though they tell me you have to pick a religion before you go. Our poor family, they couldn't even get it together enough to *think* about religion much less pick one, much less spend a Sunday in church. But what am I getting so worked up about religion? I don't have one, and don't seem to be moving toward it. So I'm no better off. Anyway, there you have the Sawyers' wonderful vital statistics.

No one, of course, could adequately summarize his or her life in such a short passage. For that matter, no one could describe her life experiences in any number of words; experiences never stop, there are always more. For convenience sake, and psychological sake, and because of the natural constraints of space and time, we offer up abbreviated life histories and hope that we have presented the flavor of our lives, as we call it. And, as much as we may decry the use of those inevitable human classifications, I come from a typical middle class, or Greek, or affluent background, we find ourselves resorting to just these categories in our shorthand self-descriptions. Patsy Sawyer did. She saw her family in the context of their criminal activities and court judgments and pronouncements. Yet, while her early descriptions of her family were truncated, and sorely incomplete, they were also compelling. One isn't accustomed to hearing, even in shorthand versions, a family story where *nothing* seems to be turning out well. But let me not sit in judgment of the young woman I met when she was eighteen. Let me say only that it was she who consistently called her family amoral or immoral—she used the terms interchangeably—and found nothing of value in their behavior. The Sawyers had always known poor conditions, Patsy would agree, but that was hardly an excuse for attempted murder, drug selling, or prostitution. There were other routes all five Sawyers could have traveled. In Patsy's own words, life didn't have to "fall out" the way it had. People aren't mere victims of their circumstances.

I have known Patsy Sawyer for eight years. I've now met all the members of her family. I have spoken with them about their lives, and have heard their perceptions of Patsy's life. Each of the Sawyers views the family as a home of immorality, a seedbed of unhappiness, dishonesty, hardship. They see nothing good coming out of families like theirs. They have recollections of experiences where children lied, parents lied, children hit one another, parents beat one another and the children, family members stole money from one another. It also seems clear that incest was practiced on more than one occasion. "Put it together," Arthur Sawyer remarked to me from his prison's visiting room, "and you get a family heading for hell because they were already living in hell." But then one learns of the last seven years of Patsy Sawyer's life, seven years of the most remarkable turning around. At twenty-six, this young woman has, well, transcended the past. She cannot shed it, she cannot forget; too many experiences and regular contact with her family keep the past very much alive within her. But her own life has changed. She returned to high school, entered college, worked jobs, and presently contemplates the idea of attending graduate school. It is a very likely outcome given her strong academic record.

It is difficult to speak about this extraordinary shift in the trajectory of Patsy Sawyer's life without sounding patronizing. She knows I marvel at her accomplishments and constantly stand on the brink of congratulating her each time another one of the pieces of what she calls her master plan falls into place. She is more than sympathetic to such a response; she knows better than anyone the magnitude of the effort, and the result. What accounts for it all, however, is her personal secret:

"It wasn't really anything I planned to do. I just started feeling, sort of all of a sudden, my life was pretty terrible, even though I was earning pretty much money. I knew if I followed along the way I was going, I'd end up right alongside my mother, so I made a change. I made it on my own, didn't tell a soul, not even my brother. I took a job in a cleaning store that paid so much less than what I was getting with Donlevy it was a laugh, took a one-room apartment, worked my way through those evening high school courses, got into college, and that was that. I had to do it on my own because I *was* on my own. I mean, there was nothing in my life that had been set up proper for me. I was like a kid trying to get out of a room with the doors and windows boarded up. See what I mean? No way to get out. So, I disappeared. I started all over again. It was like I left behind everything I had, and I was; kept only some clothes and my name, 'cause I wasn't really ashamed about who or what I was, and started again.

"My philosophy, the little it is, says that people have to start with where they are right this minute, not just from what they've always been. I mean, you don't have to be a sociologist to see the odds of my reaching anything worthwhile were a million to one. Is hitting a child bad? I was hit. Is letting your kids go hungry bad? We went hungry, lots of times. Is incest supposed to do anybody any good? We all knew a little about that, too. Nothing was good; nothing was set up the way it was supposed to be. My mother always told us my kid sister was an unwanted pregnancy. Is that good to tell your children? But it didn't matter because my brother and me, we knew we weren't wanted either. She just had us, accident or not. But when you're small, you don't know what to think, or how to think about any of this stuff. So I said to myself, look, Sawyer, the start stinks, there's not much good to take out of it, so you got three choices: Go on like you're going and your mother and father will give you a pretty good idea of how that road turns out. Or, change, become what you become on a different road. Or, kill yourself.

"I'll tell you, for a long time I did think a whole lot about that last choice. Because I could only see down the one road. All I could know was what had been; I had to assume the future wouldn't be any different. Then I decided, now hold on, girl, there are lots of things going on in the world, and I don't have to keep going in the same direction. Dammit, I'm *not* going on in the same direction. So I changed. I took fifty steps backward, it sure looked like in the beginning, but then I saw how they were really fifty steps forward. As I look at it all over again, I see they were really fifty steps neither backward *nor* forward; they were just steps to the side. See what I mean? I was moving away from childhood; not back to it, not forward to anything, not yet anyway, just to the side. I told myself, Sawyer, you have to be a little bit like the schizophrenic kid, a little of this and a little of that. A little bit of life on the low side, you might say, a little bit on the high side. But there's going to be a difference, because the schizophrenic, he's walking both sides of those two lives at the same time. It was easier for me; I only had to give up one and take on the other. I suppose I had to see the high life wasn't really the one on the top, and the low life the one on the bottom; it was just on the side of the city. So I went sideways first.

My parents were very bad with me. Maybe they couldn't do any better, maybe it was because they always needed money, maybe it was because their parents treated them lousy and they didn't have the strength or energy to turn it around for themselves. But they were bad. They didn't make mistakes with us; the whole *thing*, life, family, the works, was a mistake—okay? And maybe deep down where I love them, despite all the awfulness, I hate them, too, and *won't* or can't or won't—it was right the first time—forgive them. I don't know about this. But it struck me, looking at my life the way I was doing there, ending up in the direction where they had sent me was foolish. Talk about cutting off your nose. I thought to myself part of me is formed, part of me isn't; it's just as simple as that. Now I can believe all of me is formed, which is what a lot of people think, I'm pretty sure, but how do I know? I don't know until I work hard on another road, a really different road, and see just how formed I am. And if I fail then, well, maybe I'll give it up for lost. Because I came to believe I wasn't all formed. Part of me, but not all. How much was left of me to be formed, no one could say. If *I* couldn't say, no one else could say either, let me tell you. So that's where the schizophrenic idea came in. I told myself, I'm not going to be a different person, or a new person like all these articles tell you you should be. I was going to try to tack a couple of different-looking lives together. Where one leaves off, the other starts up. No more complicated than that!

"I don't really think I did anything that special. I just decided, hey, people can lead a couple lives, ten lives for all I know. It helps to have money, but money isn't all there is to it. You have lots of people going on and on living the same life. They could change even easier than I did, too. But I said, I'm moving myself into a different life, and the trick is not to pretend you didn't have the old one. You don't forget. Not one thing, not one day, not one minute! It's always there. It may not be calling you back or, like, in my life telling me you sure don't want to come back to this, do you! But it's there. Because lots of people are there, in this city, in this neighborhood, living that life. It's there because my parents and brother and sister are there, going on in their little rotten jungles, and they know they're rotten, too, not just my father. People don't forget those things no matter how hard they try. I cry for those people. I can be sitting in the middle of having a conversation and I'll start crying because I don't even know I've been thinking about one of them, or something that happened to one of us. You believe, I don't have one single happy memory of all my childhood. I mean, the only good days I can remember, barely, is when it was calm, when the war wasn't going on in our house between someone and someone else. I cry for them, about them, to them. But I have to live my life, not their life. I'm going to make it; I can see that now, I won't fall back. Couple of years ago I thought I would, but I won't. I honestly think I could go back to the streets, be an honest-to-God hooker, tomorrow, on the stroll, and I still wouldn't be back where I was. I'd be starting a whole new low life, I suppose, but it wouldn't be the same old one, not after all this other stuff has happened. I'd be the third me, although that's not about to happen. All I said it for was to show what I meant about stopping one thing and going on to something else. Sure, it's always me doing it; the little girl in me will never go away. But there's a lot of new experiences the little girl doesn't understand at all. It's like the big girl has to explain the new stuff to the little girl, then sort of tell her, but this new stuff isn't really for you. You see what I mean?

"There *is* a kicker in all this. I mean, I have a little sort of secret to confess. s-c-h-o-o-l. See what I'm getting to? A child grows up in what you could call two homes. Home where he's born, and home where he goes to school. One fails him, he's got the other one. It can work either way. But if both fail, he can call the music to an end. I was up to calling my own music to an end several times there myself. Family didn't do too much good, and I wouldn't have thought the schools were going to be any different. But they did their job. I didn't think so at the time, but they were grinding away, all those evil little school machines; putting all those facts in my brain.

"Why do I call it a secret? 'Cause when you're a kid growing up like I did, you don't have all that much you want to brag about. Wasn't too much I could say about all the folks I was living with. Not too much to brag about school either. Then, later on, I thought to myself, you know, Sawyer, there's a game going on here, and everybody's playing it. I'm playing it, too, 'cause there's no way nobody can't play it. Game goes like this: Tell everybody your old man and old lady is worse than their old man and old lady, and for God sakes don't tell *nobody* you like *any-thing* about school. Even if one day, by some miracle or other, they're serving some kind of pie you like for lunch, don't tell nobody. You just eat it but make all your friends think you're ready to throw up. Play it the same way with your subjects. Don't tell nobody you like what you're doing in the classes. Teacher comes up to you and says, 'Patsy, you're really smart, you look like you might be enjoying this, you could be somebody.' You just look at 'em tough and say, 'You got the wrong kid, Mrs. Thernstrum. I can't stand this work, I can't stand the work we do. Can't stand you neither.' You're playing the game, see. That's all you're doing. Playing out your life like everybody's telling you to. With the pie, with the books, with your old man and old lady, you got to make them think you're about ready to throw them all up. You certainly ain't going to let 'em think you're smart, 'cause that ain't playing fair.

"My secret was not so much liking everything we did in school—I certainly didn't like *all* the lunches-but I did like some of it, and a few of the teachers. Not a lot of them, but you don't need a lot of them. Fact is you only need a few. Maybe you don't need to like any of them if the principal is your friend, or the guidance counselor. Course, even if they are, you don't tell nobody. You play the game out till the end, which is supposed to be when you either quit school, throw the pie in their faces, or get your-self thrown out, which I guess is supposed to win you the big prize, 'cause now you've proved how horrible *everybody* in your life really is. Got to win the game now, don't I, gang? I'm the biggest failure you've seen, ain't I?

"Good teachers, they know the game. Hell, they play it, too. Some of them even teach it to us. But some of them, they have their ways of letting you know there's a couple other games you can play, and you can keep a secret, too, if you want. I mentioned Mrs. Thernstrum. She was somebody who knew another game. She told me once, I was a freshman in high school, coming in and going out, like I used to do. She told me after English—kept me after class like she was going to punish me or something—don't be afraid to like some of the books. Don't feel ashamed to be sort of smart. She didn't tell nobody else in the class, she just, like, planted a little seed. I don't remember what I said. Probably told her to go to hell. None of her business how I wanted to feel about nothing. I was still playing the game. 'Nother teacher . . . Miss Pellicote, hated her, least I thought I did. Never said two words to me. Didn't even know she knew who I was. She stops me in the hall one day, and she's treating me like I did something bad so's the other kids won't think I'm getting special attention. Woman takes my arm, almost slugged her, pulls me over to the side, tells me, Patsy, I expect you to be taking the exams for college. For college? You crazy? I want you to try, and for one lousy day, that's what she says, for one lousy day I want you to give it everything you got. But everything! Probably told her to go to hell, too, knowing the way I was, and how you had to play the game to the day you died. But I never forgot her saying that. 'Cause what they both were telling me was, okay, you want to make a secret out of it, that's cool. But we could either forget you and let you fall away like everybody else, or we can, like I say, plant a little seed in you.

"That's what both of them did, too, plant little seeds. Took a long, long time for those seeds to grow into something, but they did. . . . What they were telling me, see, was you can play the game, but we want to tell you we'll support you playing a whole 'nother game if there ever comes a time you feel you might be ready. Maybe they were daring me. And the school, see, it stunk like it always stunk. Nothing changed. Wasn't like the day after they spoke with me everything was perfect again, and my mother was all good and my father flew out of prison. No magic. But the seeds. Two funny old ladies, two funny little seeds. So school didn't fail out like everything else. Didn't teach me all that much, but how the hell could it? Teachers knew they were in a losing battle right down the line. But like, what they did was plant those time capsules of theirs, kind of like they were saying, Hey, you might like to see what's inside you one of these days. Might like to find out there's more than one way to go in this world, game or no game. Fact, they never did say, think about it. Neither woman did. They just took a chance. Probably took it with lots of kids. Damn strange, school. Damn strange somebody seeing inside you to where you keep your secrets, where they *know* you keep your secrets. I had a secret, too, going with my school. Used to say to myself; School, get me a ticket out of this life. And baby, make it one way!

"I think a lot about my mother. Maybe when I'm *really* over all that happened to me I won't think of her as much, but maybe not. I'm sure I won't think of her when I'm sixty like I do now. But I can tell myself, look, my parents didn't need me, they didn't particularly want me, I'm not even sure what they think about me now. But they see me for what I am now, and they admire me. I know they do. They see me as a good person, a sort of moral person, even though I did all the things I did. They can sort of put some of the stuff where I'm concerned behind them. They never lost sight of the good life, the high life. They knew what they were doing was immoral, amoral, nonmoral, every kind of no-way moral. Somehow they must have taught that to me, taught me not to forget there was another way, not that they did a damn thing to make it easier for me to find that damn other way. But they put the thought inside me. Tell you something else that mattered, two things really. They never got a divorce. They fought and hated each other, and split up, but they never married another person, and they could have. Funny how I keep thinking about that, isn't it? They stayed together in their sort of separate way. For some reason that's always meant something. It was like they were saying, we made our choice, and we're living with it, not happily 'cause it didn't work out, but we won't complain. And they could change certain things in their life if they wanted to.

"The second thing they did was never send me to a foster home. That might have really done me in. They told each one of us a million times how it was the worst mistake of their lives to have us, but they kept us. Course it didn't affect my brother and sister too much, but I think about that, too. I just thought, maybe the way it worked out, I might have stayed the way I was if it hadn't been for my brother. He took the lowlife road but good. So in a way, if I wanted to be special, or different, I had to take another path. It's all too complicated. But I think about those two things. I guess I think about those two people, too, more than I admit. But they won't drag me back there. But why'd I say that? They wouldn't want to. Only my thoughts would drag me back there. They want me up here. I know they do. They better. It is really complicated, isn't it? But *you're* the psychologist. *You're* the one who's supposed to know why I am like I am. Or maybe I should say, why I'm *not* like a lot of people would think I'm supposed to be."

College: Reward and Betrayal

⌐⌐⌐⌐⌐

THE LAST DECADES HAVE seen enormous transformations in
the roles of parents and children, and in the related definitions of the
male and female role in the family and the society generally. Not only
have these changes been observed by psychologists and sociologists,
but the very observations of the professionals have affected the nature
of the family and the stated and unstated expectations of young people
entering college. The cycle of change is completed when the expectations of the new generation of students results in changes within their
colleges.

An examination of several historical developments in the modern
family leads to a description of the two fundamental traditions of the
modern college: the classical tradition on the one hand, and the tradition of relevance on the other. The classical institution of learning may
be characterized by achievement along traditional forms in which
seemingly immutable standards and the legitimate authority of teachers
set the tone. The traditional education is predicated on intellectual and
cognitive growth, long-term and hard-earned professionalism. It em-
phasizes rules, decorum, and order, and results in predictable, calculable,
almost quantifiable performances. If one receives an 86 on an examination, one knows exactly where one stands.

In contrast, the tradition of relevance in the more contemporary institutions of higher learning stresses what might be called achievement
through being and communion. In place of hard-edged systems of authority stands an equalitarian ethic that, while hardly supporting anarchy, surely implies that human behavior and performance are incalculable, unpredictable, barely quantifiable. Where the classical education
deemphasizes feelings or the emotional life, if it does not openly derogate them, the tradition of relevant education affirms the emotional life

and personal experience often to the extent of derogating certain traditional intellectual endeavors. Whereas personal experience plays a minor role at best in the classical university, it may become the substance of classroom work in the tradition of relevance.

The exclusiveness of the classical institution may be compared with the spirit of inclusiveness of the more modern institution. The classical education demands constant delays in gratification, whereas the more modern academic institution allows immediate gratification from academic efforts. The classical is traditionally masculine in nature; the modern purports not to value one gender over the other. These phenomena in turn relate to the sorts of conflicts contemporary students may experience. On the one hand, the general character of modern, technological society with its heavy emphasis on mass communication makes the delay of gratification that much harder. Not surprisingly, many young people no longer wish to wait out the years required in traditional schemes to reach once coveted goals. Not so incidentally, they are encouraged in their thinking by some educators who seriously question not only existing curricula but the very idea that college *must* last four years. But conflicts of achievement are effected by one's perceptions of one's college, and the political priorities of that college. In simplest terms, many students wonder how it is that their school can exist in a community where local residents are excluded and where they, as transient members of that community, derive some special benefits. Within their school, they also question admissions policies that appear systematically to exclude certain local as well as national groups of people. And while it may seem strange to some, quite a few of these students honestly believe they cannot proceed with their own studies, their own careers, until these more fundamental issues have been resolved, or at least until they have convinced themselves that they have made a serious attempt to rectify these conditions.

In considering some of the changes in the nature of the family that eventually contributed to the reshaping of contemporary education, we note that the expectations, needs, and lifestyles of young men and woman coming from what we often unreflectively label permissive families are significantly different from the needs and expectations of the university students of twenty years ago. Predictably, many contemporary students found their colleges unable to meet their emotional needs and were surprised when a still newer tradition, that of large-scale political action, seemed to discourage people from valuing or even expressing the emotional worlds their parents had tried hard to protect and honor.

If this was not complicated enough, students of the modern period, while accustomed to debate and discrepancy, discovered disagreement within their colleges over the fundamental purposes of higher education. They found, as well, personal conflicts about achievement, some of which they shared with their colleagues and teachers. All of this made them wonder about the styles and principles of family life they had experienced as children and adolescents. They wondered about their preparation, psychological as well as intellectual, for institutions of higher learning, and where different family experiences might have led them. Some of them, moreover, wondered whether there might be some relationship between their own personal evolution on the one hand, and the evolution of their family and college on the other.

Despite messages to the contrary, the dream of achievement and success, the affirmation of personal worth through one's work—especially work that demands personal expression—and the desire to be accepted and still free to run alone is very much alive today. Notwithstanding some rather feeble attempts to disguise it, the desire to achieve remains intact. Quite a few people still yearn to "make it." We want to be somebody, have something to show for our efforts. Inevitably, the aggressive and competitive feelings that go with this yearning take many forms; some we handle well, some remain out of our control. But we are pushing just as hard now as we ever did. We are straining just as mightily under the yokes of application forms, training programs, examinations, initiations, trials, and those infamous interviews in which our lives are weighed by people we often wish to derogate, but to whom we demonstrate a courteous demeanor for the sake of enhancing our chances. I am certain that for most people this is true. And I am certain that it is true for a large majority of American college students, who, like their elders, want more, then more after that, even though they may find the gratification of work short-lasting and thereby require constant advancement and repetition.

One does not rest on one's laurels for long in this country, although one certainly contemplates them when present work seems overbearing and the future warns of an end to partial successes. Daydreams of prior glory are found to make a significant contribution to the increasing store of one's energy. We also find that the drive toward achievement or accomplishment, even success in the actual or mythical "establishment," cannot wholly pull us away from the days of our childhood when there was much good to say about dependencies on other people and the pleasure one received through a sense of fidelity. Sheer impulse seems to work better during childhood, and as scary as school was, there was a peculiar sort of peace about it. At least there was a sense that certain things could be mastered. There is a great difference now in the educational histories of young people because many students cannot avoid confronting the social and political realities prior generations ignored or slid right by. In the 1950s, student political action remained little more than an extracurricular activity, rarely occupying much time and—more important—rarely "moving inward" from its peripheral position in the personality. For a sizable number of today's students, it is no longer like this. However, it is wrong, I think, to argue that political purposes, as well meaning and significant as they often are, overcome or drive out the impetus for achievement. an impetus frequently captured by establishment language and establishment rewards.

The conflict for many contemporary students is not that political and social action have meant deserting childhood or adolescent aspirations in order to reshape their conceptions of a mature career. Rather, the two forces, politics and career, are now juxtaposed, bumped up against one another, each constantly demanding the attention and the time of the student, who, like it or not, is compelled to nourish both. The conflict for some students is exacerbated by the fact that, after they have expended substantial energy in some political cause or action, their achievement drive seems to remain untarnished, unyielding, only minutely alerted. Indeed, it often lingers on in its crudest and most primitive forms. The drive to do well and succeed in such "foolish" endeavors as mathematics, French, and sociology survives the days of political work and weeks of being away from so-called academic obligations. Sometimes the drive not only survives, it transcends political concerns only to resume its prominence in a hierarchy of academic needs and interests. The real conflict for so many students is how to admit that the school work, and the ends it affords, in fact matter greatly despite the threat of H-bombs, population explosions, pollution, racism, poverty, war, death. How can those mundane school assignments, that torture of doing badly or well, that struggle to gain admission to graduate school continue to upset a generation of students who blame themselves for letting achievement matter to them and who hope that by self-blame they may expiate the shame that derives from plowing ahead when the noise of destruction and oppression is more audible than ever before?

There are today fewer and fewer excuses for failure, fewer excuses for opting out. By calling attention to young people's behavior or mission, we contribute to the belief that, to remain honest and genuine, students must never waiver from their linear career plan established during childhood or adolescence. Partly because of a student's serious purpose and intensity of involvement in social and political action, the rest of us believe that activities performed during adolescence must lead directly to adult preoccupations and careers. The demonstrated seriousness of the students' own engagements convinces us that these students have settled on the final products of their lives. Indeed, it often seems that their own seriousness precludes the possibility that some among them are merely experimenting with alternative courses of action.

The conflict of social or political action and career remains a conflict partly because society, through its institutions and codes of action, finds these two needs discrepant and thereby resists their reconciliation except in appointed ways. The conflict reflects much of the ambivalence of many students with respect to their parents and teachers and their parents' and teachers' conceptions of education and career. For many, the confusion fails to recede because they want to be like their parents and not like them at the same time. Some students want to possess wealth equal to their parents but cannot admit to this, just as in childhood they felt embarrassed to be seen by their playmates when they were driven to school by chauffeurs or accompanied on walks by nannies. Yet these very same students, amid their plans for making what we still call a contribution, and their thoughts about the contributions their parents may never have made, dream as well of estates, inheritance bounties, and trust funds. And why shouldn't they?

Others, less well off financially, may feel just as unsettled about parents whom they long ago surpassed, perhaps not only in education but in that certain contemporary sophistication and style we recognize but cannot yet adequately define. In many ways, their lives will be far richer than their parents'. Social mobility, which for some people represents education's greatest dividend, will vault many of these students so far beyond their parents' craziest dreams of accomplishment and success that they now fear the mutual trust and recognition that held them to their parents and grandparents will explode, and they will be obliged to go it alone, unaided.

For the while, I am stuck with the notion that children identify with their parents; that they maintain an image of their parents such that they carry as part of their own self-conceptions and evaluations of theirs' and others' actions, something that makes them believe they are, in certain ways, identical to their parents. In this identification process, a process in which perhaps unconsciously the child believes he or she is at *one* with his or her parents, young persons begin to learn the tension inherent in defining personal boundaries and the boundaries set down by other people and by social institutions. Eventually, boundaries become unreasonably ambiguous, and each person must locate the shifting boundaries of his or her single self confronting another self, and then another self, and so on. Gradually recognizing these boundaries, we long to be autonomous and self-sufficient as well as dependent and almost totally unself-possessed. We want to care for others, and yet continually be cared for ourselves. We want to know ourselves and be known by the roles we assume, and yet be naked, "roleless," such that every utterance and movement is felt to be genuinely authentic and exquisitely ours.

One part of an identification with parents is to be exactly like them; another part is to be exactly not like them. There are historical cycles, moreover, in which one or another of these faces of identification seem more prominent. In one cycle we follow along diligently in unquestioned obedience of authority. Then we make our first revolutionary statements, bolting away from our parents, purposely violating their demands, and taking off in the opposite direction, or any direction. In time, we may well return to them and behave as if we never once questioned their rules and expectations. Or, in contrast, we may leave their aspirations behind, and set out on our own paths, living as though we might write our own definitions of achievement and human progress. Either way, whether we are strict obeyers of our parents and our parents' institutions, or creators of our own lifestyles and institutions, our achievement—which is our work, really—must have as part of its psychological component a resolution of the achievement strivings and definition of career as they were established in the presence of our parents.

More generally, when individuals, young or old, seek to achieve success of any sort, they face the decision of whether to define their achievements in traditional or contemporary terms. They choose their goals or rewards as these goals and rewards have been traditionally defined, or they seek newly defined rewards partly because they no longer believe in the traditional ones, partly because their sense of achievement demands that they create new rewards. In higher education we see these personal and institutionalized conflicts of achievement most clearly.

Institutions of higher education developed in part to suit the tastes of and supply the facilities for those who would remain in or near academic institutions for the rest of their lives. For a long time, apparently, this evolutionary process went unchallenged. While literally millions of students, the rich and the not-quite-so-rich, made their way through university, often with a feeling that many of their classes were boring and that much of what was in their books was irrelevant or foreign, they nonetheless stuck it out and crammed hard enough to pass. Their questioning of the utility of this "higher form" of education inevitably became another portion of that education. Then, forgetting most of the names, dates, concepts, and even some of their own reactions to school, these students moved out into the "real world" to take on "real work," their time of luxury and confusion having ended. I was part of that generation. I was a student in the days when the spontaneous expression of what might have been inside me was not appropriate classroom work. My feelings were made to seem irrelevant given what we were "doing" in class. Yet we rarely questioned the traditional ethic and approach to higher education. An educated man read Thucydides, Herodotus, and Aeschylus. He studied history and examined *Oedipus Rex* for its mythological and anthropological resources, and because Sophocles and Freud brought generations of ideas together. But a boredom, a sense of anxious isolation from content, an inability to find in myself some vessel into which I might pour all of this knowledge persisted. This much I can recall of college.

I know now that we all require special affirmation of our age, our gender, our powers great or small, our work, and our plans. Similarly, we all require compassion for our weaknesses. Wise that we are, we recognize when a particular endeavor, especially one that receives our dearest investment, fails to yield the personal and cultural affirmation we crave. We feel in these times an insufficiency, a lack, because our experiences and our knowledge teach us that all we desire from work, achievement, and career can never be fully gratified. In some moments, we all must achieve, make politics in our own way, and make sex, and be creative and ingenious. In other moments, we must be compliant, passive, and cared for. We resist the constant need to achieve and turn instead to the luxurious warmth of anything or anyone who offers to us leadership and communion.

If we shifted overwhelmingly in this latter direction, we might evolve into a society spirited and driven by love. Thus, those "revolutionaries" who have been begging for exactly this, namely, a university predicated on love, would have won out. And, funny as it is, at times it all seems an interesting proposition, and a rather worthwhile experiment.

Self-discovery through Play

I SAT FOR NEARLY three hours in the park near our home last Tuesday. It was a bright clear day and the children from the neighborhood who had been forced indoors for almost two weeks by the blizzards and freezing weather ran about on the cold ground excited to again be in touch with the outside. The patterns of play of these preschool-age children were quite similar. They would run from the swings to the slide, then to the merry-go-round apparatus that spun them about, and then on to something else. Always there were leaders, children whose behavior most of the others emulated. Always, too, there were quiet, reserved, withdrawn children who might sit in a corner of the sandbox playing with some dirt or a plastic cup or spoon.

Industry would be one of the words to characterize the children, the more physically active ones as well as those who sought solitude. But the difference between them—a difference so obvious we have all observed it—is that some children were running together while others, presumably, found a glory in aloneness and quiet individuality.

I wondered, in seeing those in the sandbox or those walking slowly about in the corners of the park, whether the schools they would attend in two or three or ten years would allow them to remain as freely independent from their comrades as they presently were. Would they be allowed to develop their own distinctive qualities?

Across from the bench on which I sat, a steep metal sheet is erected that some of the children attempted to climb. It is in the shape of a trapezoid; one edge long, the other considerably shorter. The design makes it possible for the smaller children to ascend to the top of the sheet. For, while the slope, naturally, remains constant, the distance to climb is less at one edge than at the other. It is a clever and thoughtfully designed piece of equipment, but it builds in competition too, and makes evident relative shows of strength and courage. It bids one child to dare another. It tantalizes the children's sense of comparison and sizing up, on physical and social levels that the children last Tuesday seemed to evince were part of their natural makeup. The little ones longed to climb where the bigger ones did, and reach the heights of the silver sheet. Clearly unable to manage this ascent, I could feel the feelings of the child looking up into the sun and quivering. Then he would bolt away as though either this one activity was too perplexing, or because another idea had struck him. Back to the swings he ran, and in an instant he was sailing up and back, increasing the size of the arc by pulling hard on the metal chain just as the downward motion of the swing began. All the while he yelled, "Look how I can push myself. Look at me pushing myself."

I was struck in watching these children how a sense of autonomy and competence were precious commodities for them. To be able to perform a task alongside someone else and still remain strictly on one's own—if that doesn't seem paradoxical—was the rule of the day. To master a particular action, like climbing the ladder leading to the landing perch of the highest slide, or swinging, or pushing oneself on the merry-go-round, actions that had once required the assistance of an adult, brought sensuous and hard earned gratification. The word "doing" crossed my mind. How important it was for these children to be able to *do* things with their bodies or their minds, or merely with another person.

Tempo, pacing, and self-regulation were also a part of this autonomy and competence pattern. There were some children whose natural pace or tempo seemed accelerated. Almost impetuously, they flung themselves into their work or play evidencing, it seemed to me, a contention that problems to be encountered would be resolved, as it were, on the job. The child, apparently, would do what was necessary as the exigency arose. Other children moved more slowly and more thoughtfully. I could see them studying the problem, the contours and slope of the slide, for example. They appeared as miniature engineers scrutinizing the problems and hazards of the job. In a sense, they were not only dealing with the spatial and cognitive problems of the scene, but managing the dynamics of time as well. One could actually observe them attempting to reason, infer, and anticipate. And all of this required them to call forth from memory prior experiences and what these experiences had taught them about slides and falling bodies, momentum, force, and acceleration. Maybe they were physicists rather than engineers.

There was much more to observe among these handsome two, three and four year old children. Some, for example, spent an enormous amount of time talking. Even when no one was around to listen, they jabbered on, practicing their words, learning new combinations, trying out the rules of speech that children in that miraculous happening come to learn. Even more, they were communicating with themselves. Communing with themselves might be a more exact description. Through their use of language, they were staying in touch with their private worlds, worlds they might not yet be able to speak about, but only speak to. And they were, in a fashion I continually noticed, using language and work to construct bridges between the world they saw about them and the world that has begun to form inside of them.

None of this should sound especially surprising. We have all watched children playing and told ourselves that each step we see them take is a step of self-exploration. We have seen children's impulsiveness and their growing capacity to control, their search for chaos as well as constraint, their driving temerity as well as their periodic diffidence. We have heard their squeals, their crying, their tearful or angry demands for justice and a democratic ethos, and we bear witness to their inchoate totalitarianism. Still, fairness is an important concept to them. Maybe then, they are not physicists as much as judges or politicians.

We hear children laugh too, and this is a more complicated phenomenon than we might think, for we love the sounds of children giggling among themselves and stay away from interpretations of it. But laughter at this age means so many wonderful things in addition to its presence as a sign of pure delight. It means a sense of inner happiness. A child who cannot laugh frightens us, I think. We fear that perhaps some inner light may have gone out. The children on Tuesday could make one another laugh. They made me laugh, too, those carefree entertainers and clowns.

Something else about the children's laughter. To look at the world and have things strike you funny implies cognitive maturation, and ultimately, understanding. Incongruity, foolishness, shame, audacity, comedy and ritual are but a few of the concepts that the child must comprehend, if only intuitively, if something is to strike him funny. Tickling, of course, will do it. So will certain tragic acts. But imagine what is required in the form of psychological and cognitive development for a child to laugh at the sight or sound of something. Imagine, too, what an extraordinary event it is for a child literally to amuse himself. We hear the expression so often: "The child is amusing himself." Usually it means that the child is unneeding of our attention. He is playing by himself and is able to pass the minutes without our guiding or directing or stimulating him.

Amusement, then, is also part of autonomy and industry. It is merely another fragment of that self-initiated and self-perpetuated industry that we earlier observed. But to make himself laugh, sitting there on the swing or on the large red block near the sandbox, well, that is surely special. What has he just told himself? What has suddenly come forth to so utterly delight him with the verbal and imagic products he himself has generated? I find myself looking about to see what it was the child saw that amuses him so. There is nothing. Just the tennis courts, women reading, and the other children sprinkled about the cold grounds. The amused one has communicated with himself. He has unwittingly discovered an inner capacity that will now enlarge what I can only call his sense of self, or his perspective. I hope, as I look at him, a smile forming on my own face, that his discovery will make him like himself. I suspect that it will.

Much has happened in these three hours. Walking home I attempt to sort out some of my observations. It is clear what children need and so evident how important to them are these years before they enter institutions of formal education. Social, psychological, and cognitive development are taking place, and without question, many of the supporting structures of their personalities are forming. What they presently are doing in their play and in their seriousness, in their waking hours and in their sleeping hours when they learn of the experience of dreams, is preparing themselves for all the stages of their life. Though they may not be able to make these associations, their behavior in the park tells me that all of them are dealing with that precious balance between individuality and collective organization. They are finding themselves as well as each other, and learning how they each influence one another.

I am thinking not only of the leaders and followers, but of the arrangements of friendships and the establishment of neutrality. I am thinking of the freedom to explore competitive feelings as well as cooperative ones. These children were learning about their own alternating feelings of competition and cooperation, uniqueness or "bestness," on the one hand, and conformity or just plain getting along, on the other. And that autonomy of theirs, that oscillating current that drives them to work alongside their partner one minute, sharing everything from toys to parts of their own anatomy, but urging them the next minute to work on their own and protect their bodies and possessions such that no army of bandits could capture them.

I was almost home, wondering how much I would forget of what I had seen and what of my own preschool years I might be able to recall. The word that stays with me from my childhood, and from the park, is "play." So many children use the word that it must mean more than it would appear to on the surface. Freedom to find oneself, or to be oneself when alone or with another, to determine one's pacing or comfortable tempo, one's involvement with learning and industry, underly the notion of play. No need to structure too much, for a child can turn a sandbox spoon into a chisel or a car, or, sadly enough, a gun.

Funny that I should forget such fundamental park ingredients as indignation, anger, and violence. Why do I wish to deny the fact that children know and experience anger, and at times even thrive upon it? Through their play, children have a chance to learn the sensations of anger or its social repercussions. Even more, the child must learn not to be so angered by his anger that he forfeits that delicate capacity to control his life and not feel overcome. Through play, a child develops a sense not merely of freedom and expression, but ironically, a need to be constrained, or at least to have his expressions defined. Play, therefore, is one of the first steps of personal and social evolution. It is a step of enunciation and of coming into contact with a world of seemingly endless possibility.

Play is a forerunner of work and creativity. It is more than an activity. It is a medium through which people mature and cultures are made richer, if not healthy. Through play, children come to learn their connections with the past and with the present world of their comrades and elders. Play is their own product, self-initiated and molded according to criteria children themselves establish and impose. Allow a child to play and one permits him to experience the necessity both of individual action and social control. One permits him, moreover, to experience the meaning of choice and from this the inevitable limitations set by any society, any culture, and indeed by any person for himself. Constraints and restrictions are inevitable products of any society. Right or wrong, a child ultimately will be, as we say, toned down. But the child who has never known the experience of encountering his own potential, is a child too early strangled.

Play is opportunity—the chance to have a chance. To grow up wondering about one's capabilities often leads to a sense of worthlessness. Through play, personal exploration, and an atmosphere of free choice, a person at least has the opportunity to discover what he cannot do, or do well enough to feel adequately gratified. Still, he has made his attempt and has come to know in his body as well as in his mind the feelings of that activity and that one venture. For many of us one time is sufficient. We know the activity is not for us and this fact adds to our knowledge of what it is that we are, and what it is that our biology and now our psychology and intellect has made possible for us.

Looked at from this perspective, I think, play becomes a major activity in the shaping of a philosophy. While it will not dominate the child, play will at least advise him of the existence and value of such a "thing" as a personal philosophy, as well as its relationship to social ethics and cultural values. Paradoxically, then, play brings the child into contact with himself and with the dynamics of generations, customs, and rituals. Play provides a sense of continuity in that it teaches the inevitability of repeating and accumulating experiences, as well as the inevitability of discontinuity, for change and innovation are themselves the scions of play.

One could go on summarizing the values inherent in children's play behavior. But let me mention one last point. Imagination and autonomy are what I think best capture what the children revealed in the park. Their capacity for imagination was practically limitless. Anything could be enacted in their minds. They could become anything or anyone: they could be creators of worlds that have never existed, children living free of any temporal order or spatial constraints. This means that someday, they might conceive of and bring forth notions or products or inventions that no one before them has even dreamed of. No culture survives without these products of imagination, eventually to be transformed by adult intelligence and adult need.

Personal autonomy, self-possession, and integrity were also part of the play last Tuesday. In their play they were tasting independence, self-generated activity, or work, and personal actualization. Alone, they commenced work, brought it to completion, and then stood back to see what they had achieved and what the moments of work and achievement felt like. This is, indeed, the very basis of learning, a basis that in no way precludes teachers, but, instead, prepares for the entrance into the child's life of teachers and ultimately the wisdom of other human beings.

III

EDUCATION

I mentioned in the introduction to this volume that my own life studies research began on a street in Cambridge, Massachusetts, during a conversation with a young man, experiencing, I was soon informed, "one of those Oedipal things." Significantly, our meeting took place not far from his school, a place I would in a few weeks' time visit with him.

There's no mystery about the fact that any attempt to understand the world of a young person means traveling to his or her home and school. The mystery only begins when one attempts to enter the minds of young people and learn their answers to questions like, Why do I have to go to school? How I'm supposed to know whether I'm intelligent, or competent? How do I know whether I will ever amount to anything?

Among the biases I bring to my work in education is my intense admiration for the school I attended in Chicago for fourteen years. I knew no educational institution before I entered college other than the Francis W. Parker School. I loved going there in the morning and probably would have stayed all night had they permitted it. Of course I knew that this elite private school was exceptional in a variety of ways. For one thing, it was small; thirty-six of us constituted the entire graduating class. What I didn't know early on was how dreadful were the schools many people attended, and how anti–intellectual, hurtful, and utterly oppressive they were for so many students. Coming from a privileged background, I don't think I fully understood the nature of a child's boredom in school, his or her sense of loneliness, or of regularly being shamed by fellow students or, even worse, teachers and administrators. I never understood how so many people's destinies, even decades ago, were being constructed on the basis of test results. Private school students were always being tested, every year it seemed, but I never realized that my own personal fate hinged on the results of any of those onerous chores.

When the busing crisis hit Boston—and there was a feeling of it, somehow, hitting the city, its families, schools, and children—I read many accounts, including academic studies on the positive and destructive elements of traveling to school by bus. I interviewed dozens of people involved with the busing program, eventually deciding that to learn first hand the experience of being bused it was essential that I ride the school buses with the children. I remember particularly those morning rides, sometimes huddled with the children on the floor of those large lurching vehicles as busing protesters threw rocks against the windows. The adult riders were called monitors; we were expected to protect the children and report our observations of the experience. I thought it best to offer my reports through the eyes of all the busing participants: parents, teachers, administrators, custodians, and, most especially, children, many of them utterly confused and terrified, all of them more courageous than I ever would have been, for my sister and I were driven to school each morning by our father who made the ride along a lovely route on Chicago's north side, where the only element of danger might have been a careless driver.

The busing experience put into focus a host of educational matters for me, not the least of which was the nature of America's class system, its continuing struggle with the palpable realities of race, the fact that most every public educational decision turns out to be a political one, and most especially the idea that, more often than not, the significant steps toward a genuine democracy are taken in schools. It caused me as well to look to the personal experiences of children and teachers when it came time to explore issues like competence, intelligence, testing, learning. Something magical and wondrous happens in classrooms where knowledgeable, well trained, thoughtful, and just teachers perform their art. Part of the wondrous nature of this art is the way learning seems to occur almost as if ideas and concepts were being called up and out of children as opposed to be being pushed down and into the children like food they find distasteful. The magic, or the possibly of it, continues well beyond high school, along with the intense emotional experiences that forever remain part of the student's baggage, although modern times dictate that I should properly locate these experiences in the student's backpack.

I think what excites me most about the educational piece of the research work is captured in yet one more term I cannot adequately define: creativity. All I know is that when the learning act goes well, and it does in so many remarkable classroom settings, even in schools that survive with questionable reputations, something palpable is discerned in the children, and their teacher, that wasn't there a moment ago; at least I didn't witness it a moment ago. An idea, a product, a competence, a dance, a song, a correctly read passage, a magnificent interpretation of some experience, circumstance, or passage of literature exists that was invisible before that class commenced. Moreover, and this is part of the magic and the mystery, even if all the participants cannot properly define this creative moment, their spirits appear to be uplifted by it.

Conversely, when it never occurs, when the work of the mind fields is not valued and there is no recognition shown the students, or the teacher for that matter, then just as palpable is the lack of spirit, the lowered shoulders, the perpetual unhappiness, all of it causing the student once again to wonder: "Why do I have to go to school?"

The Voices of School

I HAVE A YOUNG friend who lives in Boston. Terry Bingham is thirteen and attends what he calls an "okay" school located six blocks from his home. For the past three years he and I have been meeting, watching each other grow, I suppose, and inspecting one another's styles and plans. In that we do not see each other regularly, there is always a bit of catching up to do.

"School's pounding along," Terry will say. "I'm still hanging in there, winning some, losing some, keeping my bad eye on mischief and my good eye on college." Then he will pause. "And what you got to say for yourself?"

"Well," I will answer, as I did recently, "looks like I'll be writing a book on education."

"All those kids?"

"All those kids."

"Together in one book?" he asked incredulously.

"I'm going to try, Terry."

"Man, you got to be out of your mind thinking you can get all those kids together in one book."

"That may be, but I'm still going to try."

"Well," he said, "I want to see the way you're going to begin."

"You want to know something?" I answered. "So do I." We laughed. Then he became serious. For a moment he began to resemble some business people I know.

"Let's see now, who you going to write it for?"

I was surprised. "Students, teachers, people studying to become teachers, parents, everyone, really," I responded.

"Everyone," he mused. "Everyone. Big seller like?"

"I doubt it quite seriously." He remained deep in thought. Then, as an idea came to him, he spoke.

"All right. You tell them that school isn't really buildings or anything like that, ballparks and swings, stuff like that. You tell them school's in your mind. In your head. Everything that you are is what school is. Like, school's happy or sad 'cause you're happy or sad, or it's big 'cause you're small or small 'cause you're big. You can tell them that. Tell them school's made up of everything in the world and that's why sometimes it's real cool, and sometimes it's the worst place any person would ever have to go. Can you remember all I'm saying?"

"I'll do my best." I looked at him in amazement. He had one more thought.

"And since it's all about people, and since you aren't any television or movie man, you tell them that you're going to present them with the people who are in school, their voices like, what they're feeling, what's making them do what they do, go where they go. Stuff like that. Tell them to do what I do."

"Which is what, Terry?"

"Close my eyes every once in a while so I can hear all the voices around me. And in me." He had captivated me. "I can dig it," he went on, "'cept for one thing." He had already begun to laugh again.

"Yeah?" I wondered.

"You tell them to close their eyes to listen for the voices, you aren't going to have anybody reading your book!" He exploded with laughter, the top of his body bending forward, his hands coming to rest on his thighs.

Although the fact is disguised by contemporary technology and rhetoric, observations of schools ultimately rest on the words and deeds of the people involved with school. It is the sound of voicing a set of experiences and personal histories, that tell finally what education is all about. No doubt the experiences shared with me by teachers, students, and administrators are incomplete. No doubt, too, my background and style of inquiry at times constricted the people with whom I speak in their schools and in their homes. Yet, whatever the limitations of our conversations, one fact was always in evidence: Education is for people and about people. Buildings, facilities, regulations, philosophies, and techniques are the products of people. People's lives are awakened or dulled not exactly by educational methods but by the lives of other people. Culture, social structure, language, and personality may constitute the form of education, but its essence is found in the single life, a single human being speaking about himself or herself, about history, circumstances, knowledge, and a sense of possibility.

Not especially self-centered, the visions and self-assessments heard in conversations with those who attend school are as insightful as they are delicate. For at every moment these people are threatened by the power of politics, mass culture, and economic injustices. And still education remains the one institution they continue to regard as the connection between childhood development and adult career and social position. Vocational training as well as learning for pure enjoyment remain important ideals for more families than one might expect. Human potential, talent, opportunity, and freedom, furthermore, are more than mere words. They are at the heart of what many people hope to enhance in the lives of those attending school.

So much stands in the way of a human being maturing, learning about the world, growing with dignity and a conception of worth. To a certain extent, contemporary protest is made precisely because of these impediments. In the end, we want the dignity of people preserved, and their capacities honored. Yet, when some protest the existence of these impediments, others are frightened, and so they ask the protesters: "But you do want the best for your school and for your country? Surely you want this." But some protesters answer them, "No, that's not exactly what we want. We want the best for people. School pride is fine, though at times troublesome. But what we seek is a school and eventually a world designed for people."

Because of the politics and economics that swirl about all schools, and because of the sophistication derived in part from a knowledge of the social sciences, the task of participating in education is as difficult as it ever has been. Even the child too young to attend nursery school is implicated in the changes and resistance to these changes occurring in American education. Also implicated are students, young adults preparing for careers in education, and still older persons committed to teaching or administration. Adding to the complexity of it all is the media's often overly dramatic representation of education and the self-consciousness born from the hundreds of studies undertaken in schools everywhere, as well as the pronouncements made as a result of them.

As sensitive as we are to the issues of education, some of us continue to push notions and programs at such a pace and with such an impressive ideology seeming to support us that we often appear deaf to the voices that ultimately constitute school. Is there not time enough, I wonder, for these others to be heard? Does their status, perhaps, fail to earn them a hearing? Many people surely have touched us by what they have said about education. Yet, when I think about school, I am struck not by any special ideas, observations, philosophies, or theories, but by the sounds of human beings: their orders and pleas, their anger and obedience, their crying, their silence.

I am struck, too, by the fact that no one with whom I have spoken has described educational experiences that perfectly coincide with my own. Accordingly, we constantly teach one another what our respective educational histories have meant and someday might mean. Strangely, though, I cannot rid my mind of the expression that goes: Under the skin we are all the same. A part of me wants to believe this, but even brief conversations in schools have convinced me that quite the opposite is true. For when one enters classrooms one observes a group of young people acting very much alike. While clearly they look different, their attitudes or behavioral styles make them resemble one another. But when the class bell rings and they move in the halls, and I, with them, am flung about in a wave of energy and motion, even the traces of conversation tell of the differences, the qualities that proclaim our separate identities.

I would stress this singularity, although the perception of it is hardly new, because it relates to several issues in education. First, it reminds us that students, teachers, and administrators dread being categorized and, in this way, having their humanity stripped away. Second, it reminds us that these same people who often find comfort in standardized behavior and proper decorum feel, as well, a need to bolt from certain demands or expectations if only to prove to themselves that they are free and independent. Each of us maintains a complex balance between conformity and autonomy. Frequently we desire to be like certain others, but we also wish to initiate styles and moods that make us different and distinct. We seek alternative ways of acting or speaking, even alternative schools, and although these new developments may liberate us, we soon find ourselves rearranging the balance of a new conformity and a new autonomy.

Third, this awareness of individuality reminds us of those people who continue to want their voices heard politically. Like the rest of us, they are curious to know in what ways their schools, homes, families, and geographies are special and unique. They are curious, furthermore, about knowledge: what there is to be learned and how it feels to learn. It is only natural, therefore, that they should be especially attracted to education and the destiny of those who are committed to it.

Finally, the consciousness of individuality reminds us of the various ways one can choose to work in education. In my own case, I have spoken with students and teachers, deans and principals, over long periods of time. I come to these people with no particular questions, and, admittedly, labor hard to dissipate my prejudgments and premonitions about them and their circumstances. All sorts of private thoughts, naturally, are evoked in me during these conversations, many of which, as part of my research, I choose to make public. Perhaps my own reflections and utterances demonstrate to these people that we share a mutual reality despite the inequality in our relationship. (That I interview them and write about them surely provides me with a certain advantage.) And so we recount experiences for one another, hoping that these experiences will be affirmed and considered part of the educational enterprise.

Throughout these conversations, however, I have tried to sustain the idea that no person can fully speak for another, and that no series of discussions, or pieces of personal experience, ever constitutes a complete history. Even the most intense personal examinations yield only fragments of someone's life. The young students who sit before us and for whose attention we bid, guard experience that no school environment or method of social science inquiry can ever fully engage. More generally, the study of human behavior is endless; always there is more; another facet, another year's experiences, another person, another feeling. Still, the fragments of lives that form our images of the experience of school point to the fundamental issues of education.

Education has always meant learning and the shaping of behavior. Whatever a particular movement in education may suggest, the development of personality, social relationships, and the transmission of knowledge occupy central positions in education. Factors, therefore, that influence children's development—as, for example, native talents and capacities, social backgrounds, relationships with family and friends—necessarily assume significance in any discussion of education. In this regard, many educators use the word "socialization" to describe the major purpose of school: that is, the training and preparation of students for adult roles and careers. Those interested in student socialization may find themselves concerned with issues of authority and obedience, personal maturity, responsibility, and with techniques for evaluating all forms of student behavior. They may also choose to study the effects of culture and society on the development of personality and classroom learning. Values and rules that regulate private and public behavior, they would argue, are vital parts of education. But so, too, are the institutions of politics, the economy, religion, and the family, that influence student behavior and development.

No one involved with education, moreover, can overlook the process of learning: How does it occur? What facilitates or inhibits it? Cognitive operations and the notions of intelligence and creativity are as much a part of education as classroom dynamics, teacher-student relationships, and the meaning of schoolwork. It is not surprising, therefore, that we have developed all sorts of methods for testing these phenomena and incorporating the results of these tests in the educational process.

As everyone approaches the issues of education with his or her own perspectives and experiences, it is only natural that still more facets, more levels of richness, more limitations of education, will be identified. Presumably, ideas for change will come to mind along with plans for what one would do if it were possible to relive school experiences, or, better, assume the role of teacher or administrator. But let me hope that no one's visions or designs will totally drown out the voices that one can hear if one choose to listen for them.

The voices of school are not necessarily organized educational, political, or social movements. They are the voices of people experiencing that special balance between autonomy and conformity. At times, these people seem quick to ally themselves with their brothers and sisters: at times they seek to be alone and unencumbered by the values and ideologies of institutions and of these same brothers and sisters. At some point, each of these people has evidenced a self-consciousness about the fact that he or she may not be a good representative of a particular group. "That's how I feel," some will say. "Perhaps I'm not supposed to admit this, but honestly, this is how I feel." And then they will go on to say something personal in ways that make it seem that they are defying anyone to take away this one part of them.

The need for autonomy and privacy is particularly important now in education. It is disturbing to think that any educational or therapeutic ideology or philosophy would oblige people to believe things against their will or against their sense of what is right and truly their own. Elders bend our visions and affect our voices, but so too do contemporaries. I am continually impressed by those who express their feelings knowing full well that as an observer I may stand opposed to what they have said. By revealing enough of myself in conversations with them, we learn together of the stumbling blocks and blind spots in our friendships, and develop some sense of the reasons why we might divulge certain bits of information or emotions while keeping other bits tucked away and out of sight. And in this sharing of experiences we are able to abide by the wise counsel of a thirteen-year-old man: "Tell them to do what I do," Terry had said. "Close my eyes every once in a while so I can hear all the voices around me. And in me."

Two More Boys on the Bus

CASSIE MCDONOUGH'S MOTHER, ELLEN, got the news first unofficially by phone, then two days later officially in the mail. Cassie himself, who is eleven, barely remembers the details. He remembers walking home from school on a spring afternoon in 1974 and finding his mother fretting in a way that he had never seen. He didn't speak much with her; he merely watched her as she telephoned her friends, pacing about the small kitchen and almost pulling the phone out of the wall. That night, his father too began what Cassie calls "fretting," the same way his mother had that afternoon. They told him not to listen and sent him to his room. "You'll find out soon enough if the letter comes," they said. The letter came. It was the official announcement that Clarence Charles McDonough III had been selected one of a group of students to be transferred starting in September. Cassie McDonough, from the South Boston district of Boston, was going to be bused to school.

If Ellen McDonough was upset by the news, her husband Clarence, a tall handsome man with reddish curly hair and a long straight nose, was outraged. "They did it to me," he yelled one evening when I visited their home. "They went and did it to me, those goddam sons of bitches. I told you they would. I told you there'd be no running from 'em. You lead your life perfect as a pane of glass, go to church, work forty hours a week at the same job, year in, year out, keep your complaints to yourself, and they still do it to you. They're forcing that boy to go to school miles from here in a dangerous area, to a school no one knows a damn thing about just so they can bring these other kids in, kids who don't belong around here, don't want to be around here. Someone's got to explain it to me. I'll listen to anybody, but someone's got to tell me how this Garrity guy, this big deal judge, gets all this power to move people around, right the hell out of their neighborhood while everybody else in the world comes out of it free and equal. It's a goddam joke, busing my kid halfway around Boston so that a bunch of politicians can end up their careers with a clear conscience. You know why they're busing? Because the kindly old mayor of this city wants to be president, and if you want to be president you get yourself involved in national issues. So who does he pick on? The rich? Sure, the rich. He picks on the people right here, this street. What the hell does he care about us for? What the hell does he care about South Boston for? We don't vote for him, he ain't losing no votes by busing our kids around the city."

"You going to fight it?" I asked.

"Yeah, I'm going to fight it," Clarence McDonough replied sarcastically. "And after I win that, I'm going to run for the pope!"

During the month of August, I met regularly with Cassie McDonough. He was wearing his hair longer now than he did a year before and his voice seemed to be getting lower and more sonorous. In September, a few days before the start of school; he was confused and frightened. At times when we spoke there was anger in his voice, but mostly he was unsure how to think about this new adventure. He had lined up friends who would be going with him to the new school, and had spent time figuring out how to remain friendly with the boys who would still be at the neighborhood school. Three days before school opened, Cassie and I met at a local spa for a sandwich. He was frightened, and his appearance, for the first time in our three years of friendship, was disheveled.

"I've been fighting," he said. "Kid I know called me a nigger lover 'cause I'm going to school over there, so I punched him out."

"You win?"

"Not really. Nobody won. Maybe I won a little. I just hope that being in this new school doesn't mean I got to do a lot of fighting. I don't even know if there's going to be more of them or more of us. My mother says there will be more of them, which is weird 'cause I ain't never been with so many of 'em before. Walking around here and going to stores and stuff you see colored people, but going to school with 'em, that's different. Eating with 'em, in the cafeteria, you know, at the same tables, being on the same teams with 'em, sitting next to 'em. Like this one kid told me that, like, colored kids get talking this strange way and you can't understand 'em. I figured that could be, too, 'cause how do you know if you can talk to someone when you ain't never talked to 'em before. Then, when they dress different from you, and have their hair different from you, how you going to be friends with people like that? I don't have nothing against 'em. How could I? I don't even know 'em. But I seen them all around and they're different. All you got to do is look at 'em and you can see that.

"And another thing. They don't live over here. *We* live over here. They live where they live. My dad says it isn't so different over there but it isn't as nice. They don't have lots of money. Lot of their fathers don't work so they don't have lots of money. We don't have lots of money, either. Maybe that's how we're a little alike. But we look different to them, too, so they don't like us and we don't like them. But that's okay for two groups, you know, who don't have to see each other. But when you have to see each other, then you might get a war. And if I have to fight in a war then I'll fight over here where *my* friends are, not over there where *their* friends are. That only makes sense. You go where you have the best chance. They beat up white kids over there. So if they don't want us, and all they're going to do is beat up on us 'cause they don't want us over there, then I can't see why the government's forcing us to go there. Maybe they got kids around here who want to go there, and colored kids over there who want to come here. If they do, then the government should let 'em. But if they don't want to, then they shouldn't have to."

I spent several minutes explaining to Cassie the reasons for the forced busing program. I spoke about school desegregation, the fact that black children his age had never been given fair opportunities in school, and how the people making the busing decisions were not punishing the white children. Cassie heard me, but his thoughts were elsewhere.

"I've been thinking," he began, "ever since we found out about the busing, you know, about going to school with colored kids, everytime I think about this new school—I don't call it *my* school yet—all I think about is colored boys but never colored girls. And I also never think about what the teachers are going to be like. I thought all the teachers would be white but maybe they aren't. But I never think about learning anything over there. My mother says the whole thing is unfair. She says it's like a big experiment, and everybody's going to lose. I hope I don't lose my teeth in some fight. Some kids maybe are going to die. They got kids, littler than me, carrying knives and guns. So some people really could die. Boy, would my old man go crazy if some kid from around here dies. He's always saying the government doesn't care whose kid dies, just so it isn't one of their kids. I don't want to die. Those other kids might not care about it, but I do. I want to go to school around here and if I have to fight around here, for fun or 'cause some guy starts something, okay. But I don't want to fight just to be alive. And especially not for no experiment!"

Two of Cassie McDonough's friends were far more bitter about their assignment in an integrated school. One week before the start of the busing program, Joey Billingham insisted he would quit school before he would let anyone send him anywhere. "They can put a gun to my head," he said, "and I wouldn't go. That school is three miles from my house. I wouldn't go, wouldn't go three feet to no school on a bus. I walk to the school around here or I don't go. Nobody's busing me just so some niggers can get a better deal. I didn't set up the schools. I didn't make 'em like they are. No one I ever knew had anything to do with it. Niggers don't like their schools, let *them* change 'em, but they don't have the right to tell me what to do. Kids don't got any rights anyways. The only right we got is to go to school near where we live. If they think they're going to change that, they're out of their minds. I ain't moving a step. I ain't going no three miles on a bus just so some nigger kids get it better. Why do I have to have it worse just so's they can get it better. I don't see that nothing's fair about that. I ain't going!"

Jack Griff, who palled around as much with Cassie's brother Ken as he did with Cassie, said he would now have to carry a knife to school. "Everybody knows what's happening," Jack told me as Cassie and Joey listened. "Everybody in the city's rooting for the niggers. One minute they don't give 'em nothing, next minute they give 'em everything, including *our* schools. Maybe I'll go, maybe I won't, but if I'm going, I'm going protected. There ain't a nigger kid in this city goes to school without a knife, or a gun, too, maybe. Every one of 'em carries something. That's the truth. You ask 'em. They'll tell you. They come armed so we're coming armed. People who voted for busing, all they wanted was a war between them and us. They'll get it, too, 'specially if one of them starts something with me. Them kids have no right going to the same school with us. If they didn't learn their lesson before, we'll have to try all over again. They don't belong around here, not healthy and going to school anyway."

The day following my talk with Cassie I visited the home of Francine and Ronald Dearborn. Francie is a woman in her mid-thirties, black, the mother of three young boys, one of whom, eleven-year-old Claudell, was preparing to attend a school located in South Boston. The Dearborns, too, had been chosen to participate in the busing program. During the week prior to the start of busing, Francie's friends and relatives stopped by her cheery four-room Roxbury apartment, some of them bringing food, all of them wanting to be in touch with her, and with Claudell, too. All three sons had been especially quiet during these days, none of them wanting to talk much about what everyone in the house was calling Claudell's school trip.

Ronald Dearborn, Claudell's father, spoke little about busing. He read the morning and evening editions of both Boston newspapers, and he waited, somewhat surprised by how little the school had prepared his own child for the busing program. On several weekends, always during the day, he drove around the area of Claudell's new school, inspecting the streets and homes, and seeing the small neighborhood businesses. "It's a long way," he said, "even by car. Let's hope they keep those buses running fine. I'd hate to think what would happen if they broke down some night over there. If white folks don't look kindly to having black folks attending their schools, then they sure won't like to see a bunch of black youngsters parked outside their home all night."

Francie told me that in years past her husband might have uttered these same words and laughed at the thought of white parents up in arms over the presence of fifty stranded black children. Now, since the busing program and Claudell's participation in it, black children stranded in a white neighborhood was no longer an amusing image. "Ronald's not fearing for the boy's life," Francie explained. "He and I are just plain fearing. You have to take steps like this, it may not be the best way or the easiest way. But you start like a baby: small steps, careful easy steps, your parents watching with their arms out, ready to catch you, *if* they can reach you when you fall. Ronald's not worried about the falling. When you're black you know all about falling, and what you don't know this country teaches you mighty fast, even when you go to schools where everyone is black, like we did. Falling's easy. It's like they say, it's the bump when you hit. That's what we worry about. Busing's a fall, and you have to hope that no one, not one of ours, not one of theirs, gets their head split open.

"It's an experiment," she sighed, using the same word Ellen McDonough had used and passed on to Cassie. "They don't call it that, but everyone knows what it is. You manipulate people, bus them here, bus them there, measure how *we're* doing, measure how *they're* doing, count the casualties, maybe even find out—heaven forbid—whether any of the children are reading better or talking better or counting better than they did a year ago. When the experiment's over, folks making the experiment decide what it means. It's just as simple as that, except for one thing. Those who liked busing in the first place, are going to decide the experiment worked. Those who never did like the idea, they'll say it never was any good to begin with and it still isn't. So it's an experiment that only fools get to be a part of. I say fools not because they're dumb, but because they all know how it's going to come out. Those folks over there, they know, just like folks over here know. We all hear the same stories, read the same newspapers, listen to the same shows. We all care for the lives of our children. That part of it everybody knows. So the only part of the experiment my husband and I really care about is, will those folks in charge be careful with the children? Before they guarantee me that Claudell's going to end up in a better position, I want them to guarantee me that if I put him on that bus every morning, Monday, Tuesday, Wednesday, Thursday, Friday, some very responsible human being will make sure that he comes home safely every afternoon, Monday, Tuesday, Wednesday, Thursday, Friday. When that part's taken care of, then we'll discuss reading scores, racial desegregation, America's efforts at doing something worthwhile for its minority people. Anyway, Claudell says he wants to talk to you."

Claudell Dearborn wasn't so certain that September afternoon whether or not he did want to talk to me. Dressed in bright blue pants and matching sportshirt, and wearing a wide gold band high on his right arm, he looked at me as we sat on the front steps of his house with an expression I had never seen. I'll talk about my feelings, he seemed to be saying, but I'm just not sure any of this is doing any good for anybody.

"See over there," he said, pointing to a filling station partway down the block. "That's where the kids from here going to meet on school mornings. Parents drop us there, then they got another group of people going to walk us to the bus and ride with us. That's our protection. White folks going to do it, too, they said. Makes you think you're some famous person. When I was a kid my dad took me to this theater somewhere, you know, and somebody real important came in. I think it was Martin Luther King. Anyway, this man walked in there with a whole lot of people walking all around him, protecting him like. Now they're doing it for us. Makes me scared thinking about what we need all that protection for. I know what it is, only I get scared thinking about it. You can know all this stuff in your head, but down here," he patted his stomach, "it don't care about what you *know*. My stomach says, 'Look out, man. Keep a look out for everything that's going on, and everybody too!'

"My mom says this is the way it has to be. She says children will be all right, only they get their ideas from their mothers and fathers. She's trying to make me feel better. I know they got kids over there waiting to see us walking into their schools. They call 'em their schools, too. They got it in their heads they *own* those schools, and they aren't about to go renting them to us just 'cause a judge says you got to let them other kids come in. They're getting ready to keep us out of there."

"You know that?"

"For sure I know that, man. You think they *like* all this? They didn't *ask* for it. They're taking their orders same as us. And somebody's going to get hurt. Even the littler kids. All you got around this city now is a bunch of old folks telling young folks what's going to happen, and young folks looking at each other like to say, 'Let me out of here, man. I never asked for none of this.' That's what they're saying. 'I ain't never asked for this to happen.' Least that's what I hear."

"Don't you want to be bused over there, then, Claudell?"

"Sure I do. It's better over there, least that's what everyone keeps saying. Besides, even if it ain't, it ain't fair that one group of people get to do what they want, and another group's got to sit around and pick up the pieces nobody wants. My dad says black folks pick up the pieces. He says, their folks eat the chickens and us folks eat the pickens." Claudell looked down at his hands folded in his lap. "Busing's just got to be, man. Got to be. We got it coming to us. We got to open up ourselves, spread out. Get in to this city, man. Move in to all those places we can't go at night, you know. Go to good schools, live in good places like white folks got. *You* got all that stuff. My folks don't, so they want it for me and my brothers. That's why they're busing us. Anyway, I been scared before. This ain't no first time for me. You guess they'll have lots of police around there in the schools?"

"I imagine so."

"I guess they have to. Hope they watch out for *us* like they watch out for *them*."

During the autumn months, I visited with the McDonoughs and Dearborns almost weekly. Both the boys, Cassie and Claudell, were keeping records of their experiences, writing down some of their thoughts about this special school year. Both said writing helped them to understand things a bit better. Their parents, too, were eager to read these personal notes.

By November, Mr. and Mrs. McDonough were members of two community organizations opposing busing and attempting to pressure the existing powers to reduce the scope of the following year's busing program. If the news accounts were accurate, the next year would bring even more communities into the program. Both of the McDonoughs felt uneasy about having Cassie hear their arguments and complaints. They felt it important that he not have his school day, already trying enough, complicated further by the rantings of his parents. But it was impossible to keep their feelings and what they themselves called their prejudices from him.

"There's lots of parents who stick their noses into their children's business," Ellen McDonough told me. "People like us always thought it best to leave the teaching to the teachers. When it comes time to vote, you vote, but when the voting is done, you mind your ways and live by what the people have asked for. That's how we felt 'til the busing thing came along. But those days are gone. Now we have to keep an eye on things. I don't give up worrying about Cassie. I don't know what happens to him two seconds after he leaves that door. I don't know what the teachers are planning, or the mayor, or Judge Garrity. If the parents in this community don't look out for themselves, no one will. The days of voting and sitting back are gone. We're going political. I got a whole new way of looking at this country now, and this city, and this government. When it comes to your children you don't let politicians run your lives. We'll be looking out for ourselves, police or no police, *Boston Globe* or no *Boston Globe!*"

Indeed it was the Boston newspapers that continually received the hatred of the McDonoughs and their neighbors. The editorial stands, the cartoons, the accounts of events seemed to present a powerful case against those, like the McDonoughs, opposed to busing. Moreover, whenever I visited this one South Boston community, I was invariably reminded of the distinctions between the rich and the poor, the city families and the types in the suburbs, the shanty Irish and the lace curtain Irish. But I never once heard the McDonoughs express a desire for violence or personal injury. They wanted the forced busing program stopped; that was all. When a black man was dragged from his car and beaten in a nearby neighborhood, they were shocked. "No white person in this country," Clarence McDonough told me the day after the beating, "has one hundred percent decent feelings about the colored. Every one of us has some feelings that maybe we wish we didn't have. Maybe I'm even a bigot. Maybe I am. But I don't go for beating up an innocent man. The people that did that are animals. They have no right walking the streets!"

Cassie said he talked with some boys who had been in the crowd when the man was dragged out of his car. "All I could think of was that maybe *they'll* start doing that to *us*. All they have to do is stop one of the buses, come inside, pull us out and beat us up like they did over here. They could do it to get even. They'll have more cops in the schools now than they had before. There'll be more cops than children going to school, but otherwise it hasn't been so bad," he said, with surprise in his voice. "I'm learning some stuff. Our teachers are pretty good. Our homeroom teacher, she's all right 'cept she spends all her time taking attendance. Lots of the teachers don't care who's there and who isn't, but old lady Prisely she's got to know everything. Sometimes she'll take attendance twice in one day, once in the morning and once after lunch. She's always afraid some of the kids will skip out after lunch, you know. Lot of 'em do, too. Like we got kids in there who skip out one day and then you never see 'em again. We even had a teacher do that. But 'cause of the busing they're all counting who's there. But they teach you a lot, some of 'em. Some of 'em shouldn't be teachers. They even tell us they don't like it. They say school would be great if it wasn't for all the kids. We say it would be great if it wasn't for teachers who say things like that. I can't see why they want to teach if they don't like kids. They could get other jobs . . . or maybe they couldn't. Some of 'em could get other jobs 'cause they're *real* smart. But some of 'em couldn't get other jobs 'cause they don't know nothing about nothing. Not even how to teach. They're only in the school 'cause their brother or father or somebody's the principal.

"We got new books in the school, and a lot of those other kids aren't as dumb as everybody said they were. I thought, you know, that the teachers would be spending all their time helping *them* instead of *us*, 'cause they needed extra help. That's what I heard. But they're as smart as us. Fact, two of their girls are smarter than any of us. One of 'em," he smiled, "this big fat girl, she's smarter than everybody put together. I could really respect her, too, 'cause she's smart. She was the first one of them to speak in the class. Know what she said? She said, 'My name is Janice and I don't want nobody to call me colored. I want everybody to call me black.' She wasn't mad, she just said it like she was telling us how she wanted us to call her."

"So you'll call them black people now?"

"Sure, if that's what they want. I told them to call me Cassie, too, like the kids here call me. So you know what they call me?"

"What?"

"Cassie." He was smiling broadly. "They tell us, we tell them. It ain't so bad like I thought it would be."

"You still scared going there?"

"Sure. None of that's changed. There's fights almost every day. Sometimes everything's fine almost the whole day, then somebody starts something and man, does it get tense. Some of the time you're sitting there trying to concentrate, you know, and some of the time you're like a night watchman in this big dark place thinking you just heard some sound that ain't supposed to be there."

Francie Dearborn looked forward to my visits to her home with an eagerness that grew with each week. The television and newspaper accounts of episodes related to busing couldn't be complete, she insisted. There were far more injuries than anyone dared report, far more trouble than anyone dared confess. I always told her I knew no more than she did but she would not accept this.

"You're the one who told us of the boy in that one high school who they put in a locker and threw out the window. You know the details 'cause you can go to those places. Even when they integrate the schools, partway like they're doing, the schools still belong to you white folks. No one's going to tell *us* what's really happening. We read in the paper there's some outbreak here or some business with kids in the halls. They tell black folks nothing going on, no problems, but they tell *you* a boy is put in a locker or held in a steam shower. I can't stand not knowing, or feeling that folks are lying to you. Most days now (we were approaching the Christmas vacation) are pretty calm, at least at Claudell's school. But I don't know, last Tuesday here I was watching television while I was doing my work, and all of a sudden, on the noon news, the man's talking about something going on right near where Claudell goes. I called the school. I even called the police. Nobody knows. Nobody tells you nothing. I'm like a mother waiting for her son to come home from a war somewhere. Is he going to be all right? Is he going to come home with a limp, with a bump on his head? Will he be here when Christmas comes?"

"But, so far so good," I said quietly.

"So far, beautiful. Claudell really likes his school. I don't even think he misses the kids from around here. Have you heard the latest? He was invited by John Doherty's family to go to a movie for the Doherty boy's birthday. Two of them are going. I mean two of us," she laughed. "Mr.

Doherty's taking six boys to a movie. He called here, you know, and asked our permission. We thanked him and asked Claudell. He said yes, so we said why not. And Mr. Doherty will bring them home." Francie's eyes widened. "There are days when the sun sure shines. Saturday these kids will go to the movies together and in South Boston they'll probably have to close the high school, they got so much trouble. What in the name of the good Lord, that great colorless Lord in the sky, is wrong with people? The sun shines one minute, then the war starts up all over again."

Claudell's notes over the months of September, October, and November contained references to just about everything he was doing in school. Indeed a fascinating diary was developing. He never let me actually see the notes, but preferred to read them to me.

"I don't want you to see how bad I write," he said sheepishly on the last school day. "I'll just tell you, okay?"

"Of course."

"I think someone will be murdered in my school and I think it will be a black girl. My favorite teacher is Mrs. Levine but I don't tell anybody. Even though she's white, she's smart. I think the black children think she's smart but you feel strange saying it 'cause you want the black teachers to be better.

"Most of 'em are about the same, 'cepting that you can't always go to a white teacher and tell her your problems. You can't be sure what they'll say. And you can't always go to the black teachers 'cause they're always so busy. They ain't got but a few of 'em anyway. They're trying but they got too much work to do. We had one of 'em come to our house to talk to us before school started. He was real nice. That's Mr. Cranston. He came and told me about the school. He said he liked it and I would, too. He didn't have to come, neither. He told my father he wasn't getting paid for it or nothing. He just wanted to on his own. I went to see him once and he's all right, 'cept he's got so much to do. I thought there'd be a lot of black teachers but there ain't. They said they'd get more, but the school says a lot of things that never happen. Like they had this one teacher who you can really tell hates black kids. She can't even stand to look at 'em. I think she's taught in the school since they opened it. Fact is, she probably built it for herself. Some of the older kids told the principal she was really unfair. White kids knew it too. Everybody hates her, man. Everybody. So the principal, he said they'd get her out of there, put her in another school. But they never did. She's still there. My friend Sandy, he asked was she coming back next year. She told him it ain't none of his business but she was. She's coming back. That type always comes back.

"She ain't the stupidist, though. The stupidist person in the school is Mr. Archery, who is like an assistant something. All he thinks about is kids running in the halls, smoking in the bathrooms, talking when they ain't supposed to. So he noses around like an ugly old dog, sniffing around, you know, always hoping somebody's getting into trouble so he can arrest them. You should have seen me the other day, man. I'm running somewhere, outside the gym, you know, and out of the corner of my eye I see Archery. I couldn't stop real quick so I start running in place pretending I'm into doing these exercises. The dude walks right past me. I'm afraid to look at him, man, but I'd say he was smiling. Sylvia Backham, she saw me, she started to laugh and all, watching me making up exercises. I'm going to the movies on Saturday. John's old man, he's taking a group of us." He had changed topics without a pause. "We told him we were up to see a Bruce Lee, but they got some other flick they want us to see. Makes no difference to me, just as long as I get something to eat, I'll watch anything.

"I wrote this thing too on playing basketball and how they made some of us take off our shirts which is okay, you know, but lots of time they let the girls go walking through there. And another thing, they ought to fix that gym or open a window 'cause it's always smelling in there, man. You take a deep breath in that place, you like to blow away. Lassiter, he smells the worst, man. Everybody knows it, too. My mother talked with his mother about it. They talked about putting him in a bath with Ajax cleaner."

Claudell was beginning to giggle. I was starting to laugh, too, and thinking about how in the midst of the turmoil surrounding desegregation I was hearing old-fashioned, eleven-year-old schoolboy talk.

"My mother said, 'Put the Ajax over that boy and rub it in good.' But Lassiter's old lady, she says she's going to put him down with Drano. 'If it clears up the sink,' she says, 'it'll take out the stink.' Out of sight, man. They'll be busing me to the school and Lassiter to some laundry and dry-cleaning place." Claudell exploded with laughter. "You see some dude opening up his laundry somewhere and out pops Lassiter, all fresh and clean. Good-bye, ring around the collar. Hello smell."

There have been, in these last months, many scenes and experiences that these two boys, who do not know one another, have described. Cassie continually refers to his parents' notion of the lack of freedom, the breaking up of his neighborhood, the special treatment shown black children in his school. Yet he confesses he sees no changes in his neighborhood and has witnessed no special treatment of black children in his school. In fact, he admires their courage and feels sorry for them when he sees them entering the school in the morning through a rear door near the gymnasium. He argues frequently with his friends in the neighborhood about going to school with black children.

"I tell 'em I'm learning a lot of things that you can't read about in books. It's like, when we're not supposed to be learning we're learning anyway. That's one good thing about the school."

By his own admission, Cassie thinks less and less about busing, being reminded of it mainly when he hears discussions among people who oppose it. Also by his own admission, he has stopped using the term colored to describe black children, and has noted that he no longer speaks about "us" and "them." He prefers to think of us and them as referring to "us" students, and "them" teachers. But the feeling of being scared at school has not wholly subsided.

Claudell, too, has recognized that what he still calls the experiment is going fairly well. He sees unfairness in the treatment of black children but realizes that often white children don't understand that an injustice has just been committed. "Lots of times," he says, "I feel sorry for them. Sometimes it ain't their fault. It's some teacher's fault, but the kids don't understand." Claudell believes he's learning more in school than ever before, although he says that some teachers let some of the kids get away with things they shouldn't get away with because people are afraid that small incidents might turn into giant explosions. "Most folks walk around in that school real uptight. Everybody's afraid of everybody. Everybody thinks everybody's going to start something. You go blow your nose or ask to go to the bathroom and they look at you like you're going to start a war."

Like Cassie, Claudell's fears have never disappeared. Unlike Cassie, the bus ride to and from the school, while filled with laughter one day, boredom the next, is a time when frightening events occur. On three different occasions I have been on a school bus with Claudell that was pelted with stones. Claudell reports that his bus has been stoned eleven times. Lying on the dirty floor of the bus one afternoon, listening to rocks clanking against the metal sides and hoping the windows wouldn't be broken, I heard Claudell ask me: "You scared?"

"You better believe I am. Why, aren't you?"

"You kidding me, man? I'm scared all the time. Second I see this bus I'm scared. I don't need no rocks out there to tell me I'm scared."

"You be on the bus tomorrow morning, Claudell?" The children were still lying flat on the floor.

"Sure. Will you?"

There is so much more to say about these two boys, these two families. The richness and complexities of their lives cannot be captured in a few pages or found in descriptions and citations involving the desegregation of two schools. No one claims that these families represent anyone but themselves. No one claims that their views in fact reflect upon all the issues connected with the autumns and winters of busing. It is questionable that one can end with a feeling of hopefulness, although it would be inaccurate to say that the families I have called the McDonoughs and Dearborns are despairing and utterly pessimistic. Certainly the boys, Cassie and Claudell, are not pessimistic. If not genuinely hopeful, they are at least hoping. Cassie has spoken several times of a wish that his school would be awarded a prize for the best school in Massachusetts. The prize, furthermore, should indicate that his is the best school because black children and white children go there together. A short time ago, Claudell Dearborn dreamed that his school was given an award by the President of the United States. In the presentation of the award, the president said that Claudell's school was the best school in the world and that Claudell and his friends were the best students and the bravest students in the world. Claudell and a white boy whose name he didn't know received the award for his school.

The Garden of Children:
Education in the Suburbs

BY STRESSING BEHAVIORAL APPROPRIATENESS and career preparation, suburban high schools give the impression of suspending adolescents between what should have been the goals of childhood and what clearly can wait for adulthood. The very concept of these high schools, therefore, first symbolizes, then actualizes the timelessness or "nowheresville" of adolescence. Schools, in fact, may be a major cause of these well-known adolescent sentiments. As school activities come to be attached at both their past and future borders to such ephemeral reminiscences and anticipations, they begin to lose the identity of their own present sense or life force. The act of thinking about joyful pursuits like singing, acting, politics, journalism, and athletics (the so-called extracurricular activities), in terms of their legitimated and affirmed values on college applications, demonstrates the temporal suspension and alienation experienced by high school students and their teachers. Nonetheless, the model of too many schools remains the kindergarten, the garden of children, where students are taught to behave and to pass the time with a smidgen of fun and a mite of disciplined routine. School keeps children off the streets and provides mothers and fathers with breathing room.

Recognizing the erudite baby-sitting features of high schools, many students now seek the freedom of individual tutorials, work-study programs, ungraded seminars, and encounter groups. Whatever their choice, the significant fact is that they not only emulate strategies of politicization witnessed in their college brothers and sisters, they internalize the university or their impressions of it as a model for high school reform. In this regard, students put forth their strongest point when they ask what cognitive, social-psychological, or natural magic is performed over the summer following high school graduation that "permits" them to study sexuality, philosophy, and psychology as college freshmen but not as high school seniors? What many students seek, therefore, is a university model for high school, a model that at present most high schools seem reluctant to adopt. But who exactly is it in the high schools who disapproves of this model and continues to perpetuate custodial schools? The answer: some administrators, some teachers, some parents, and some students.

For administrators and parents, behavioral control might be seriously shaken if the so-called university model were adopted. Students would be too free to come and go, hence too great an emphasis on "premature" responsibility and autonomy would result. At present, schools are "fine," for essentially they are designed primarily for the people who professionally run and financially support them. By employing some universities' albeit limited concept of freedom, administrators and parents might lose control. In the university model, parents, after all, play a rather silent role. Moreover, they must forfeit all rights to the behavioral control feature of university socialization, even to the extent that many students treat the autumn of their freshman year as the time when parents must relinquish total rights to authority altogether, even "at home"—wherever that might be.

Where parents hold on is in the channels of career guidance and opportunity, although frequently this hold is insecure, if not invidious. It is said of elite men's colleges, for example, that getting the boy in is a minor problem, as presumably a good preparatory school can handle that. More difficult is assuring him a position in the eating club, fraternity, or secret society that offers him a direct and exclusive link (almost as an underground railway) to financial, business, even law firm positions. During high school, however, the influence of parents is made more explicit. Parents will bring their grievances to a school committee or esteemed headmaster, as one father did recently during a dispute with his school's "Dress and Appearance Committee." In attempting to protect the sanctity of his son's hair, he wrote, "I am sorry for you because I am afraid you are trapped: Meaning to teach manners, you will find you foster cynicism and hypocrisy." Rarely would this happen at the college level.

To a degree, high school represents a time of suspense as well as temporal suspension. For, given the established order of many contemporary high schools, the honoring of socialization practices normally legitimates parents' neglecting of their children's needs altogether. Or, if this is too extreme, it permits them a reasonable justification for abdicating their part in socialization and learning. As parents bequeath these question-able rights, high school teachers come to define their purposes as part-time guidance counselors, part-time nursemaids, part-time disciplinar-ians, part-time therapists, and, if a piece of time remains, teachers. Teachers, therefore, have been trapped between the instrumental chores of pedagogy, irrespective of how they might interpret them, and the so-called expressive core of their involvements with students, represented by after-class discussions and counseling.

As much as teachers might resent these obligations—although one does not know that they do—they cannot refuse them, since the social structure of many suburban high schools makes it almost impossible for students to bring their problems, much less their person or personality, to administrators, whose very purpose connotes judgment, disciplining, lawbreaking, and permission requests. Because of the school's structure, students cannot freely approach administrators with problems other than academic ones, as they feel, and maybe rightly so, that administra-tors are in collusion with their parents. Administrators represent their parents' agents in the school; hence, teachers are the potential source of genuine, although cumbersome, friendships.

Guidance counselors and high school psychologists would be the logical resource in these times, but many students complain that these people, too, tend to be influenced by the ethos of the administration (their bosses), or, if not, orient their advice too much in the direction of what is suitable and adaptable for the school, but not necessarily for that one student. What many students really wish to communicate is that guidance counseling essentially means one of two things: behavior problems in the realm of mental illness, or advice on improving records for college admissions' officers. In a real way, students cannot "afford" to engage counselors if they fear that psychological diagnoses will appear on college letters of recommendation. Thus, counselors, too, tend to embody the school's socialization functions.

More generally, in most high schools and colleges, there is not a soul with whom (not just to whom) students may speak about personal needs, difficulties, or problems, who remains free of some mental health, disciplinarian, or counseling stigma. To receive help, encourage-ment, or advice (and this is not as exaggerated as it sounds), students practically have to break a rule, flunk a course, or "crack up." Then, pre-cisely because they sit facing the dean or "shrink" or "cop," they become obliged by the situation to play the role of student in academic, psychological, or legal trouble. The definition of the situation demands that students play out the "misdemeanor" as well as the behavior and feelings publicly associated with it. What probably saves many students and provides them the strength they require to make it through the day are the prolonged bull or rap sessions, Ironically though, these sessions are discouraged both by the regulation of students' free-time socializing and, more subtly, through the architecture of buildings. So, to keep their sanity and pursue their interests, students charge furiously into after-school intimacies, and when dinner hours terminate even these, they spend the rest of the night on the telephone.

Given these exigencies and the absence of almost anything resembling an educative community, the suburban teacher remains the single school authority to whom most students may turn. Their emerging relationship is hardly free of complications, but in a genuine school way, each is all the other has. Despite this, many students veritably wince from the swishing of a chain of constraints swung at them by parents, administrators, school board members, as well as by teachers and fellow students. While their work involves straightforward and not so straightforward learning procedures, other happenings occur "on school property" that also shape their existence.

For example, students see more clearly than ever before the battles waged by teachers with their "superiors" whom the students and teachers feel are inferior to them. At times, teachers invite students to join them in their campaigns; at other times, they try to keep these campaigns from "the kids." Furthermore, in their sophisticated awareness of college programs, and in their attempts to initiate the ideals of these programs, high school students recognize that, given present conditions, administrators openly infringe upon a sacred realm when they enter classrooms. Students feel the infringement through their teachers' self-consciousness particularly when school officials reeking judgments come to "observe a class in action." To assist their teacher during these watched moments, and to demonstrate an uncanny and often unpredictable loyalty, students put on especially good performances for their silent but hardly innocuous visitors. When the visitors enter into the discussion, perhaps hoping to prepare a miniature educational community, the relief is noticeable and the experience rewarding. Authority has receded for a moment, and equality seems believable. However, when visitors refrain from communicating on the grounds that involvement is "inappropriate" and necessarily implies spoiling the "objectivity" required in teacher assessments, their silence is construed as judgmental, if not disapproving.

As if this were not enough, the educational experience is further complicated by the abdication by many parents of supposedly home-based socialization functions, the eager willingness of many teachers to take on such functions, and the pervading social class phenomena underlying these functions. To be more specific, in speaking with high school teachers, particularly those in English and history, one gets a sense that the parents with whom they meet are essentially concerned about their child's daily behavior and his future career. Parents ask such questions as: Can you get him to discipline himself? Can you get her to stop biting her fingernails? Many parents, therefore, not only abdicate much of what belongs at home, they sometimes give the impression of denying the fact that teachers have any worth, talent, or purpose beyond that of grooming adolescent personalities and then hitching these personalities to some appropriate social tramway.

In fact, very little discussion between teachers and parents of classroom philosophies, exercises, and assignments ever takes place. From the teachers' perspective, this omission may be degrading, as it implies that they are professionless employees or, more accurately, the man and woman servants of the parents, and hence of the students. Teachers (and administrators), therefore, have no alternative but to be the servants, but the more they accept this profane and harsh contract, the more schoolrooms resemble anachronistic kindergartens, if not plantation estates, and the more students and their faculties may feel alienated from anything relevant or valuable. Now, not only suspended in time, students' very lives dangle on the teeter-totters of adolescence and childhood. Just as bad, they come to see their elders teetering and tottering in the same playground.

In the suburbs, the explicit class differentiations between the local families on the one hand, and teachers *and* administrators on the other, at times render the school almost unworkable. As students seek a natural and honorable emancipation from their parents, often exhorting cries of intellectual superiority in the process, they discover that teachers do much the same thing with administrators. Each group, then, has its unique conflict with authority, its own special brand of "generational gap," and its own history of oppression.

What prevents teachers and students from allying themselves in a truly Homeric battle for freedom is more complex. It transcends the fear, however, that teachers who "get in too tight" with students or assign what students have suggested in the first place, actions seen by some as acts of unfortunate communion if not of student takeover, may be relieved of their duties. In part, it has to do with expertise, age, and experience, all natural obstacles, and probably importantly so, to a consummate teacher-student alliance. What prevents the alliance has to do with the fact that the majority of America's suburban teachers can neither socially nor economically identify with the families of their students. Their origins and lifestyles are not on the same continua, or, if they are, then too great a disparity with these families is felt. As a result, although for some it may involve intellectual and professional compromises, teachers acknowledge their sociological and psychohistorical ties with administrators.

Neither free yet from their own understandable ethnocentricity, nor sufficiently aware of these certain continuities and social continua, students do not fully comprehend the dynamics of this class phenomenon. It is but one of many cases where student sensitivity and insight fail to compensate for clearly codified, rational knowledge. In evaluating pedestrian school work and in dreaming of future achievements, students rarely grasp the sense of incompleteness so many teachers feel in their constant orientation toward protection and preparation of the young. Just the impact on a teacher of the term "preparatory" school may never be contemplated by the most brilliant and mature of students until years after their graduation.

In contrast, preoccupied with students' "behavioral adaptations" and their college and career dowries, teachers knowingly guarantee the social and economic separation among themselves, those in their charge, and the university people soon to take charge. Merely by witnessing the paucity of students who express to them aspirations to become high school teachers, contemporary suburban teachers must wonder about the worth and esteem of their profession and its still tender rank in the American prestige hierarchy, not to mention its relationship to the "betterment" of the already "bettered" classes.

Surprisingly, few students recognize the sociological divisions between themselves and their teachers. It is appreciated rather suddenly when one questions them on the degree of association between their parents and teachers. It became crystal clear to one high school junior. The edges of his eyes wrinkled slightly as he confessed, "None of my parents' best friends is a teacher." Parents, naturally, have noticed the differentiation and in some instances have attempted to ameliorate the problems it causes. In one suburban community, for example, residents organized a program in which every teacher in the high school was assigned to a local family with whom he would dine one or two nights a year. The proposal's patronizing tone was so painful, however, that teachers requested an abrupt termination. Administrators, incidentally, were omitted from this particular program.

Something else students often do not comprehend is the division of faculty members over various issues. Most understand political polarization, naturally, but often they fixate too strongly on generational and political differences, and thereby miss the substance of adult culture and the nature of differential career commitment. This point requires some elaboration

To begin, career teachers cannot afford to jeopardize their chances for tenure, or if it is already attained, the safety and sanctity they have inherited with it. Even if they secretly plan to transfer (or transform) school systems, they, like students, dare not spot their records or threaten the image of tenure with public exhibitions, classroom flamboyance, or political muckraking. A certain group of teachers, however, can afford the luxury of pedagogic daring and defiance even to the point that they may cause a scandal. By dint of their marginal position in the school's structure, this group knows it can rely on a freedom held in reserve, a freedom quite handy when, in fact, entanglements bloom as scandal. Comprised of teachers dedicated to their students but for various reasons uncommitted to a lifetime of teaching in that one school, this group remains somewhat immune to the sanctions of control actualized in future job offers and tenure. Professionally, they can afford to take risks, something that shows in their work and local reputations.

Reinforcing the marginality of the women teachers in this group are their marriages—actual or prospective—to professionals on the "way up" in other fields. While this situation and the rationales it offers exist essentially because of the inequalities of jobs and social positions between men and women, one result has been that these particular women teachers may excuse themselves from their social class affiliations with regular career teachers, and at 3:30 P.M. each weekday plug back into society at a substantially higher notch. Social and economic identifications accordingly, if they materialize, are liable to be more with local families than with the administrators and teachers who stay behind. And almost everyone in the community knows this.

The male members of this special group, usually teachers of English and history, have, after several years and often at severe personal risk, achieved such charismatic reputations and personal followings that administrators dare not impose burdensome restraints for fear of bringing "the kids" down upon them. In these cases, love literally conquers all, for parents, too, can do nothing but support those cherished teachers who may well be ideologically opposed to the ethos of the local school board. Given their age or sex, achieved charisma, associations with the upper-middle class or openly self-confident political liberalism, this group of men and women knowingly predisposes itself to open hostility. They become the frequent topic of conversation at town meetings, school cafeteria tables, and in faculty lounges. In interview after interview with all sectors of the suburban high school community, their names are among the first to be mentioned, their status among the first to be challenged.

The challenge takes several forms, one of which has to do with the occurrence of teachers spying on one another or of co-opting students to become underground sources of information about other teachers' lifestyles, attitudes, and classroom proceedings. Often teachers will report the names and actions of their colleagues to principals who then request departmental chairmen to supervise and regulate the classroom and out-of-classroom behavior of these "marked" teachers. When teachers are admonished or even fired because of sloppy dress or because hemlines are judged to be too short, administrators and fellow teachers may be meting out punishment not for these "noncrimes," but for the political and social postures represented daily by these teachers in their appearance. Nonetheless, appearance, and especially those sexual features of appearance that get people into trouble, is only part of the daily policing of values and positions undertaken by teachers and their colleagues. Still, to criticize either side of this educational matter is really to remove schools from the greater society in which they are merely members. It is, moreover, to stand above teachers and administrators, parents and students, and condescendingly refute the intellectual and emotional worlds they only naturally know and at present respect.

Yet it must be observed that much of this policing behavior violently contradicts many university interpretations of academic freedom. But this is exactly the point: Little academic freedom or adequate conception of it exists in many American high schools, suburban or inner city. Consequently, with teachers *and students* left structurally and philosophically unprotected, there can be minimal spontaneity, limited free expression, or discussion of "controversial" issues, and ultimately only the barest tracings of democracy in any classroom. When a teacher knows that his job may be jeopardized by what he might say or wear in class or outside, he comes to know very little autonomy at all. Indeed, it takes only one student to go home and report the day's classroom activities for the machinery of constraint and repression to grind. In these cases, without even a morsel of academic freedom, students have joined administrators in their unwitting sanctions of faculty. Cases of mere rumor destroying a teacher's career, or episodes of students exaggerating or even lying about schoolroom conversations to the extent that teachers must defend their jobs are not as rare as one might wish.

For career teachers, the double constraint of teacher-student surveillance is often too much to surmount. They soon learn that one lives longer by staying in the middle of the road and abiding by the social and pedagogic traditions of the school and community. This, finally, becomes the essence of their adaptation. The teachers who launched their careers in the fifties and sixties and continue to thrive today in the same school and with the same curriculum only assure their inheritors that theirs is the formula for longevity and a memorable yearbook dedication. The fact that teachers do adapt to less volatile and less politically extreme positions is well known. Because of the adaptation, or as some might choose to call it, adjustment or maturation, many young teachers are seen as the proverbial "sell-outs" by the youngest teachers just starting in the school. As always, they are accused of compromising principles and values for the sake of job security and tenure. They suffer inside from these pressures of political activism and the necessity to maintain both their job in a good school and the moonlighting employment that permits them to approach financial solvency with a ray of dignity. But occasionally they will strike back at the group younger than themselves, only to become the most severe critics and judges of behavior, appearance, and ideologies that only months before they espoused. Some naturally have "changed their minds" or "seen the light," but some undoubtedly require this derogation of their immediate past as part of the insurance that the present might flow more deliberately into a continuing future.

For that group of marginal teachers who, if they were irresponsible, might dare to flaunt their present jobs and future employment opportunities, the leverage of administrative and collegial social control is greatly reduced, and the rewards and benefits of academic freedom noticeably less relevant. So they will not get tenure. So they will not be rehired. So they will teach in the inner city. Maybe they will quit altogether! Most, probably, do not wish to quit. Very likely they value tenure, but primarily in terms of its adjudication of accomplishment and excellence, and not so much in the rhetoric of professional permanence and economic security. For this reason, they are likened by some of their colleagues to invading society matrons donating their afternoons for hospital work. In the same way, ironically, their lack of career commitment inhibits their own struggle for academic freedom. It seems to be true that one does not push so hard for freedom in one sector of his work life if he is guaranteed even a greater freedom ten or twenty miles away in the community he calls home. No one can yet be blamed, moreover, for placing his own future and the future of his family before the future of anyone else, even with those who once, in genuine intimacy and comradeship, he shared a bountiful past.

Despite the various degrees and manifestations of professional commitment, high schools, if they are to survive as educational institutions rather than as elegant child-care centers, must at least institute academic freedom in order to protect marginal and career teachers, as well as students and administrators. Everything else may best be relegated to facilitating this freedom. The arguments often raised about granting teachers liberty to choose classroom topics are, excusing the pun, academic, or, if not, highly politically oriented. Teachers continually make choices of one sort or another anyway. They choose to teach this course rather than that one, or assign this book rather than that book. To question the legitimacy of a teacher's personal opinion, therefore, is academic because they constantly offer personal opinion.

Unfortunately, however, the public opinions offered by high school teachers do not count for too much. Relative to opulent university professors and prospering high school consultants, high school teachers' persuasions merit little credence at all. One hopes but is not yet assured that their word carries more weight in classrooms where their latent status as servants is either overlooked or made invisible. But for the most part, within the tangible structures governing suburban and inner-city education, teachers possess practically no autonomous prerogatives nor a basis from which to claim absolute authority, much less wisdom. They too are among the victims of education, rarely the sources of knowledge about it. Their awareness and experiences are overlooked or dismissed by so many investigators that in some cases teachers have actually come to believe these experiences are second rate and unworthy of being recalled or communicated. In other instances, our overly zealous acceptance and romanticizing of teachers' accounts have caused some teachers to distrust as well as to question the data they have presented. But in the main, it is the drama and tension of school that we applaud and reward, and not the drudgery and pedestrian activities that constitute portions of everyone's work.

Politically and professionally, high school teachers have yet to be granted full citizenship. Their growing bargaining power and union tactics have grown to impressive proportions recently, but it is at best questionable whether or not this is the image they ideally wish to portray, and the political, social, and economic community with which they would choose to be identified. There is, after all, a noble white- and blue-collar history to high school teaching, but there is also an intellectual tradition of universities that teachers have directly known and once admired. And the fact that they may cherish this orientation means that they must sustain a certain conflict of personal identity and social definition when they take part in, or even read about, teacher union negotiations. But, as yet, the oppression of school personnel persists. Administrators still find it difficult to go against the social and political grain of the local residents, and if teachers threaten to strike, parents and much of society at large still cannot decide whether to treat them as working-class employees appropriately, and certainly legally, demanding profane rights, or as sacred healers who, like doctors, dare not place self-interest before the interest of the community's children.

On the intellectual side, the fact remains that teachers' expertise is doubted, maligned, or totally ignored. In the suburbs, where relatively low salaries and lack of occupational prestige place them "beneath" the social gazes of their bosses, their literally disenfranchised status renders them servants, or, at best, paid tutors. Against the backdrop of a culture that fundamentally values education for the possibilities it offers in occupational mobility and social opportunity, and where the "teaching of knowledge for its own sake without obstruction or diversion"[1] is reserved for an elite and insular group, high school teachers too frequently have become nursemaids or educational and social travel agents. This fact remains whether students recognize or confess to it or not. Over time and through the unrelenting strictness of educational systems normally tolerating only miniscule adjustments and refinements, teachers now have resigned themselves to performing a great many purely socialization functions. Perhaps because of this resignation, they presently seek a legitimacy in intervening in the psychological realms of their students where even with their own patients, the most arrogant psychotherapists dare not trespass. Some teaches now argue literally that the best "service" they can offer their pupils is psychoanalysis.

Administrators, too, are caught in the locks of socialization enterprises and, like it or not, they have acquiesced to becoming ruthless deputies and clean-up squads. Somewhat obliged, partly willing to be the hunters of young persons, they, by the very act of hunting, contribute to the transformation of a few adolescents into "criminals." Like certain representatives of the press, television, and social science, administrators are accused of focusing attention on the split seconds of errors, misdemeanors, or rebellions, while permitting the remaining millions of hours of law-abiding and utterly obsessive loyalty to go unobserved. They are the feared judges and censors of a microsociety that students, by law, no less, must first taste, then swallow, then digest.

Yet administrators, too, are constrained by a "community's control" and find themselves forced to prowl the grounds of inequities still unacknowledged by certain parents, teachers, and students. We must not forget that administrators' salaries originate from the same purses as do teachers' salaries. So administrators are battened down by restrictions on their freedom as well as by the "backlash" of their own dogma. What a complicated phrase it is that goes, "I'm sorry, but my hands are tied." As is true for everyone else, the restraint administrators first impose, then reify, reflects the expectations they hold or fear, or maybe even secretly wish would come to pass. Most serious is that when school situations and interactions become dominated by people living under severe social constraints and psychological impingements, each and every classroom will contain the scent of their ideology, expectations, and the secret wishes of which they may not yet be aware.

Finally, legitimated by that lavish swatch of society cut by most American suburbs, the parents, the rightful rulers, run their schools on a stage of so-called community control that must make residents of inner-city schools weep with angered envy. As it is elsewhere, the key word in the suburbs is control. Each person, each link, asks the next to behave. Inevitably, socialization factors, the behavior inspections, and career preparation tend to minimize the values of human involvement and restrict the communication of personal worth. Fantasies, jealousies, and regrets aside, the day-by-day routines of education insist that, periodically, teachers and administrators be reminded that even though as part of their job they must fulfill parental obligations and duties, they do not own the flocks of students passing through. This is the way it has come to be psychologically as well as sociologically defined: "passing through." Teachers may be admired, even treasured by some of their students, but they have not escaped from the social fact that at some level they are indentured shepherds possessing no claim to the fields and the flocks. Students pass through the lives of teachers who long ago agreed to claim no percentage of someone else's presumably opulent future.

To be sure, a small number of parents publicly demonstrate active interest in their children's education. Perhaps more do, and the low attendance at PTA meetings, parents' nights, or silence at the dinner table each evening means that they acknowledge teacher-student priorities and choose to remain discreetly prudent with their interventions into their adolescent's world. Or perhaps the social structures of high school or the essence of adolescence is such that parents cannot afford to trespass on school grounds or attempt to discover the paths where their children walk each day. Still, many parents cling to the fact that their taxes pay salaries and hence they begin to believe in some misplaced religious decree that makes their bellows and squeals the ultimate "words" on education, and their swatch, the ultimate citadel of democracy.

But parental bellows and squeals are to be expected and, as painful as it may seem to some, protected. Suburban parents want good, success, and happiness for their children. They want, in a word, exactly the same things all parents want for their children. In proclaiming their ideals, they employ the very words used by the school administrators they hire, administrators who have learned well and remain constant. Many parents have moved to suburban residences precisely to put their children on the social and educational tramway they knew departed from there, a tramway advertising a rather impressive record of safety. Accordingly, they keep a careful vigil on their tax monies, and a twenty-four-hour guard detail on the politics and politicians of their communities, until all of their brood are well-stationed in college. At that point, they pack up the old yearbooks and hockey skates, letter sweaters, and report cards, and move, perhaps back to the city, perhaps farther out in the country. Then a new family comes to take their place, and as these two sets of parents converse, younger children again swarm over the damp autumn grounds and argue the perfect spot for a hideout or a tree house. The memorabilia lie in wait for the college students or young marrieds, who, for a stolen moment, may feel again the pace and exhilarating anguish of high school. Rarely though, do these reminiscences and possibly unspoken calls for returning in time constitute a substantive interest in education, their own or their children's. Still, the poetry alive in their feelings keeps the spirit and emotion of education awake, if not alert. So all of this means that children, too, in their way, will someday come full circle.

Not so simply, the problem arising for many suburban high schools is for the constituencies, in the context of their social structure and the template of history in which this structure breathes, to articulate their respective interests, priorities, and prerogatives. This task alone would constitute education. Indeed, the school committee meetings and hearings, when students are invited, represent archetypal forms of orchestrated community education. Harvey Pressman's[2] concern for the urban school, furthermore, is equally viable for those he calls their "overprotected suburban counterparts": "[T]he schools must allow the experiences, needs, and facts of life within the community to generate much of the curriculum, and they must permit meaningful participation by high school students in governing these schools." But, as is the case in an honest poker game, the suburban players must commit themselves to action before the announcements of the final ante amounts. That is to say, parents and administrators, teachers and students, must proclaim their commitment to the value of education on a daily and nightly basis. It is not fair for any group merely to jump on a school political or social issue, then jump back again as quickly to resume the callous indifference so many people display the remainder of the time. It seems a bit unjust, moreover, that the regular, dependable players can so easily be evicted from deliberations and decisions when the ante gets high and be replaced by the ultimately powerful people who suddenly appear when it is reported that big killings can be made.

Too often, small conflicts in school systems become not the reason but the justification for all sorts of people invading school grounds to demand rights, rule adjustments, and personnel changes that might easily have been considered and argued over previously. Scandal, for example, serves to legitimate the entrance into the school of the entire suburban community and often renders insignificant the voices of certain constituencies. Parents, therefore, should be in on the regular decision-making apparatus that is itself part of the educative process. Yet their role in this apparatus must be carefully examined, for at present they very frequently bring little more to educational pursuits than their socialization and political tenets. And while these tenets presently bear rather heavily on educational institutions, they cannot yet be said to constitute the entire academic enterprise. For political reasons, there are clearly times when one does "charge" an institution essentially to highlight or emphasize a particular happening, event, or policy. In these

times, the so-called extreme or isolated behavior of an institution is attacked, heralded, or mocked. But for the most part, the kind of social
change almost all school systems sorely require in order to make them
democratic and equitable would come from the "interruption" of each
and every daily activity, and an insinuation of new sentiments and philosophies in practically every cubic foot of institutional space.

These last statements are not made in advocacy of destroying
schools. Nor are they meant to imply that no one anywhere does any
good at all. This would be absurd, undeniably condescending, and dis-
respectful of those persons who every day sustain the constant injury
and only momentary glory of educational institutions. More important,
it would be to strengthen the position of those like myself who now
enjoy the comfortable posture of social critic. It would be to exalt those
of us who need not bother to rise at six each morning so that we may
begin a gruelling school day, but rather may wait until the early evening
hours to commence writing our lists of criticisms and surefire recom-
mendations, while the objects of our vituperation themselves now enter
the last weary phase of the work day, the homework, the paper-grading,
and the endless preparation.

How easy it is to believe that if we could but hold a few certain powerful ones in our hands, spank them, or tell them a thing or two, all of
society's children everywhere would just, well, make out fine. Still, to
possess financial resources and power does advantage people enormously in a variety of ways. One way is by allowing them to stumble occasionally, often, even regularly, and still "make it," whatever that
means. Money, after all, may be employed as a medium of exchange not
only for goods and services, but for error, irresponsibility, remission, failure, even crime. With the social standing it affords, money alleviates the
potentially visible and "telltale signs" of all those nasty things poor people, black people, or foreign people are supposed to do every day in their
exotic urban jungles.

As the rich and successful, we can afford to gamble, stumble, and experiment with education. From time to time we may even want to dab-
ble in community scandals, because, like it or not, we are practically assured of a window seat on that tramway. It is this same assurance of
accomplishment or public success that Russell Baker caught in the bus-
tling but confident ambience of the Harvard Yard. And it is the same
self-assurance that Kenneth Clark, Jonathan Kozol, Nat Hentoff, Peter
Schrag, and the others just cannot discover in urban classrooms where
students are derogated and self-contempt boils.

In the end, I think that equity is the goal: all men and all women holding the identical rights and claims on the past, present, and future of their nation. All men and all women lovably profane, wondrously sacred. Hopefully, someday a society somewhere might be able to transform those political, sociological, economic, and psychodynamic features that now predispose our institutions and their members to the abuse on all sides of conflict, to instruments of receptivity and acceptance, or at least tolerance. Right at the moment, we are nowhere close to this. While our proven intellectual capacities are nothing short of fantastic, our collective psychology, in an evolutionary sense, just seems not to be up to it.

Notes

1. T. Parsons and G. M. Platt, Considerations on the American academic system, *Minerva* (summer), 1968.
2. H. Pressman, Schools to beat the system, *Psychology Today* (March), 1969.

The Felt Sense of Studentry

AS PART OF THE parent-child relationship, not of its contract exactly but of its natural arrangement, children honor their parents. It goes with knowing elders, especially those who represent the first figures of authority. Later on, some young people come to appreciate those events, values, and ideals that encouraged them to leave home and travel to college, there to experience new opportunities as well as new burdens, but they cannot leave behind them feelings for their parents. They have faults still to find, and grudges that will not be evened out, probably, until the next generation's sounds are heard, but their feelings toward their parents remain (Chickering, 1969; Erikson, 1968).

It *was* good, then, what these certain parents did for their college-bound children; it *was* worthwhile that plan of theirs, the child-rearing and socialization that they struggled with or perhaps never questioned in the first place. "Someday my kids will go to college," is perhaps all they said on the matter. And it *was* good their finding for these young people the tracks of success, as well as those seemingly corrupt packages like achievement and fame that "the establishment" holds aloft as divine and appropriate for social evolution. And it *was* good that these parents could intellectually and spiritually transcend what these students now see as somewhat limited if not impoverished lifestyles and make plans for their children that excluded themselves (cf. Mead, 1970).

A degree of ambivalence was created in certain of these college-bound children as they watched their parents' struggle with society's values and career procedures. Not only were the idealized perceptions of childhood now giving way to more realistic definitions of adults and adulthood, society itself was changing and new attitudes toward career

The author wishes to thank Sally Makacynas, Andrew Effrat, Paul Paschke, and Gerald M. Platt for their help in this essay.

and lifetime commitments were emerging. That some parents were getting divorced and shifting careers, and that many institutions were questioning their purposes and social ideals, caused these students to weigh the values and roles associated with achievement and success. Thus, while many entered college with the same career orientations as those of their parents, some were immobilized by their fight to resolve the conflicting concerns of their past and present (Cottle and Eisendrath, 1974; Eisendrath, Cottle, & Fink, 1972).

Still, many young persons going to college recognized that they left behind people to whom they owed, simply, thanks. Their debt, as some called it, could never be paid off since payment itself was precluded by the inequalities between the generations. It was expected that what the old invested in the young, the young returned, through hardly in kind, when they reached a point of social and psychological solvency. That just seemed to be the way it was.

The conflict engendered in young people by transformations in society and the development and values of their own parents is the focus of the present essay. When profound historical changes occur, institutions react to these changes, and their reactions in turn affect those people associated with the institutions. In this regard, it was commonly believed that to rid universities of harsh political protest, admissions committees in recent years carefully culled those high school students who might possibly engage in campus political activities. While such selection procedures may well have occurred, a more likely reason for the decrease in political activities is that the nature of the colleges themselves changed: Incoming populations of students adhere to the new priorities and ceremonies.

Given the interaction between personality development and social-historical evolution, a major problem for educational institutions is to determine how much emphasis must be placed on students' career preparation on the one hand and their psychological well-being on the other.

Enhancing students' psychological development is typically not in line with the stated careers or scholarly concerns of most faculty members, except perhaps for some young instructors and some extraordinary senior people. Paradoxically, the psychological well-being of students has often been assiduously avoided by faculty members, as attested to by the information collected by student health services. But campus psychiatry cannot for a moment compensate for the lack of human care that is so evident on many campuses. Many students, naturally, are not in need of any special safeguarding; they do their work, meet their commitments, and graduate. But some do not fare as well. Certain emotional resolutions have not yet happened. The students are not yet released from their "hang-ups" about the past and hence are not able to confront what they still call their destiny (King, 1973).

Explaining the problem in a slightly different way, one finds in some students a tension between present actions and prior experiences. Enormous change has taken place; the students have left home, in a sense for good. Whatever their plans, the break with the past, and especially with the people of the past, must eventually be transcended. For some students, this initial departure from home is barely resolved by the end of college when it is reawakened by the need to settle on some future course of action.

But if the discontinuity for students lies between the past and the present, the orientation in most schools is on the present with certain gestures directed toward the future. Because students' past typically interests college officials very little, students are obliged to derogate their past experiences or, conversely, package them in psychiatric terms. The examination of psychological properties, moreover, turns out to be inconsistent with the general policies and programs of most universities.

Two natural developments tend to throw students back upon their own private concerns: the lack of individual recognition at college, and the separation from home. While their high schools may have been large and impersonal, the students at least had their family life to sustain certain personal needs. At college, family life is replaced by dormitory associations, which, while often gratifying, are hardly substitutes for family involvements. Both the separation from families and the lack of recognition at college contribute to precarious feelings and attitudes, ones easily affected by campus activities and ideologies. What emerges, therefore, is a systematically determined sense of emptiness or incompleteness that students fear may never disappear. Their seemingly self-indulgent activities, of which many of their seniors disapprove, frequently turn out to be ungratifying as they fail to counteract this sense of emptiness (Goethals & Klos, 1970).

Another reason for the precarious feelings is that the autonomy presumably derived from so-called parental sacrifices is not so easily attained. A burden of guilt hangs heavy on those young persons reared by the notion that individual progress comes at the expense of parents' efforts. Unable to manage the feeling of loss, many students seem almost deliberately to make attempts that fail: They select courses they cannot handle, let their work slide until they find themselves in academic jeopardy, or push themselves to their own psychological limits. When these attempts at failure are studied, one finds that the students have acted so that their parents' own development may not be stymied; in other words, they believe that their parents' whole life has been geared toward making it possible for them, the children, to progress. Yet progress in the form of college success implies that the parents' work and reason for living are over. Failure makes life worthwhile for their parents as it again provides them with parental responsibilities. With this logic, the failure represents a gift to their parents, an almost suicidal gesture offered—in repayment perhaps, in anger perhaps—for but one of numerous intergenerational imbalances.

Failure of this sort may also imply angry retreat from parental goals and ideals, a device for regaining parental protection, or a protest against the circumstances of college turned inward in the form that college demands these acts of protest be demonstrated. We should not forget that, because idiosyncratic needs are found to have little relevance for college authorities, the only way they can be expressed is toward the self.

For some students, issues of parental sacrifice and repayment are not significant. Before they get to college, many students have thought little about their life plans or aspirations, nor have they seriously contemplated the conditions of their family or its social-psychological evolution. They moved their psychically quiet ways through grade school and high school, fully convinced of the natural logic and purpose of almost every rule they followed and almost every ritual they honored. At the point of entering college, they may well have felt that society had done well and that their parents had lived up to their end of some invisible bargain. Once at college, some of these students awaken from their complacency to begin that interminable questioning and wondering that so many adults find wasteful or "charmingly adolescent" (Feldman & Newcomb, 1969). Within a short time however, the educational and psychological discontinuities become so great that some of these young people actually believe they are in the throes of either a genuine political revolution or a mental collapse. To shift proposed career plans or even major fields of concentration proves to be psychologically overwhelming. Months go by before they right themselves and realize that these alterations in plans are permissible and not deceitful, healthy and not self-destructive.

Complicating these tensions between the past and present, and between earlier family life and present conditions at college, is the still unresolved definition of career. The personal wishes and aspirations that contributed to the determination of career early in life must now undergo transformation at college where new social structures and ideologies affect them. Students must now account for their decisions, plans, and career definitions. For some, the notions of childhood remain; they are merely accounted for in adult terms. Even the most narcissistic drives become altered and less grandiose. For other students, the plans of childhood and adolescence or, more exactly, their self-accountings undergo explicit transformations and all sorts of potential roles may be explored. For these students, an entire system of self-accounting is altered if not replaced by a new system that includes realistic possibilities, financial considerations, and, typically, a degree of social consciousness (Perry, 1968).

Underlying these forms of self-accounting and the public and private rebellions that usually accompany them is the conjoining of prior and contemporary definitions of themselves, their career, and their sense of appropriate behavior and accomplishment. The conjoining, however, produces a conflict in values experienced not only in particular families but in society as a whole. The discontinuity caused by leaving home only exacerbates the tension between these major value systems. To put their new values up against the more traditional values of their parents is, in effect, to put themselves up against their parents. The situation almost requires that students derogate old values and totally accept new ones. Either way, they stand to lose, since one set of their involvements, with family or with college, must suffer. The social structure of universities demands this commitment (Parsons & Platt, 1973). The rebellions against parents that were undertaken during adolescence were pursued in the context of an integrated family. Now, by token of leaving home and beginning anew, a fundamental integrity is broken and students are left on their own to realign their values and make peace with two generations, their own and their parents'. In working out their new role with parents, many students discover their grandparents or the society's elderly people as though for the first time. Although the need for older companionship has not lessened during development, grandparents suddenly are seen as representing value systems espousing love and warmth while deemphasizing career directives and methods for guaranteed accomplishment.

Whereas some students suffer from the recognition that theirs is a qualified autonomy because their erotic or, as they still call them, "platonic" attachments reactivate dependencies upon their parents or teachers, others believe they have successfully left behind all realms of childhood and adolescence. Bolstered by adult strengths, they believe themselves to be on their way, and so they are (Ellison & Simon, 1973).

Let me summarize some of the points raised thus far. Students leaving home to attend college confront a serious discontinuity between past and present experiences. Their career orientations as well as their personality must be reassessed in terms consistent with the university's social structure and the ideology of higher education generally. The developmental task for the student is to integrate prior experiences with present ones and then reintegrate all these with the new intellectual, political, religious, and emotional contexts of the university. At the same time, the university, recognizing the discontinuities as well as the conflicts in values and lifestyle, must determine the degree to which it wishes to intervene in the psychological considerations of its students. So far, at least in the larger schools, the intervention is minimal. Although the topic of various courses, psychological issues essentially remain under the watch of university health services, a situation that means students may come to associate normal psychological resolutions with psychiatric problems (cf. Snyder, 1971). A refusal to consult psychiatrists and psychologists may well reflect a distrust of these professionals or a resistance to psychotherapy. It may also represent students' conscious or unconscious awareness that their problem is not one of a psychiatric nature, at least as psychiatry is presently defined. Thus they turn to their friends or, more likely, inward, and university life continues as though students had resolved their developmental discontinuities, had their career activities perfectly under control, had chosen a viable value system, and were firmly committed to academic work (Eisendrath et al., 1972).

Like the students, faculty members and administrators must deny certain realities just as they renounce certain impulses in order for their own enterprises to progress. If large-scale universities are to run smoothly—a task that requires administrators to be given minimal maintenance problems to solve and professors maximum time to do work other than teaching—then the individual needs of students, faculty members, and administrators must be deemphasized if not ignored. Psychological development, therefore, cannot be a salient consideration for universities. This fact is communicated to students, who react in terms of their assessments of universities as well as of themselves. The paradoxical result has students believing they are simultaneously worthy and worthless.

A point that surprisingly receives little attention is that, for many students, a successful high school career leading to a place in university, sometimes hundreds of miles away, means separation from their family (cf. Trent & Medsker, 1968). In more abstract terms, socialization into channels of mobility involves independence, which, ironically, may be translated by students as parental desertion or rejection. There comes a time—and to many it seems a perfectly arbitrary one—when parents and schools reward their children's accomplishments by throwing them out. In reaction many students say, "It's about time. One more day in high school or with my parents and I would have lost my mind." But some of these same young people leave for college only to experience a depression and sense of loneliness, which they often call disillusionment, that may last for years. In their fantasies, they exhibit a disbelief that their parents or high school teachers could permit them to be away from home for yet a second year. While some stay at their work, others find themselves in a depressive period of inactivity and self-indulgence, which they may recognize as an indication of a longing for parental protection and the continuation of adolescent if not childhood ties.

This point relates to the earlier one regarding students' discontinuous development. Students may blame their parents for what has happened to them at college, or even for pushing the idea of college and career in the first place. But the anger, like that found in depression, is hidden. How, after all, can they blame their parents after a successful high school graduation and admission to college? And yet, the perpetual symbols of dying and death found in songs, student papers, and art forms, suggest an intensity of anger as well as the death of the past.

The dilemma, as we noted, derives from the need to renounce the past and develop psychologically and intellectually within the confines of a wholly new social structure. The realization that prior goals and attachments are no longer relevant, coupled with the constantly shifting lifestyles of students, cause young people to believe that if they are not dying, then bits of themselves surely are. It is the shedding of selves students feel to be deathlike. Not only are self-assessments changing and new forms of personal accounting taking hold, old forms are relinquished and hence one correctly states, "I'm not the person I used to be; the old one is dead!" (cf. Coopersmith, 1967).

American institutions, as Keniston (1965) and Reich (1970) among others have written, hold back the development of young people. Through their once prevalent *in loco parentis* philosophies, boarding

schools and colleges fostered student dependencies and general immaturity at costly psychic and social levels. At present, amidst the residues
of these philosophies, some students remain bewildered if not immobilized by what appears as a sudden requirement to become competent
and independent even though in high school they demanded to be left
alone and treated as autonomous human beings.

The times have changed, in other words, and many schools refuse to
act as surrogate parents. The values and goals of higher education
shifted and universities turned outward to political and social realms
and away from the personal welfare of their students. It was only a matter of time before students perceived a similarity between conditions
outside the university and their own circumstances within it. Suddenly
students were claiming that they were oppressed and that achievement
in traditional terms was fruitless if not in some way evil. The so-called
apathetic students could not be explained merely in terms of political
alienation. Some were stymied by separation from home, others by anxiety about the future, still others by the impersonality and predictability
of the new roles and gestures associated with higher education. Apathy
does not imply total disinterest and boredom. It is immobilization
caused by conflicting interests—intrapsychic tension probably—but
more importantly by the tension between students' emerging personalities, the new social structure of universities, and those parts of the
greater society touched by universities (cf. Riesman, 1973).

As the *in loco parentis* attitude came to be replaced by an uncertain
concept of permissiveness, students faced still another developmental
dilemma. College officials decided that students were adults and should
be treated accordingly. Where once students were watched after, they
now went almost totally unrecognized. They learned that independence, achievement, mobility, competence, proper maturation, motivation, and all the rest had to be played out in colleges where a philosophy
of permissiveness masked an outright disinterest in them except as they
performed their role of learner or disciple. One dislikes to conceive of
the impact of higher education in this way, but the actions of universities are often felt by students to be rejecting. The influence of much of
modern psychology and sociology on the descriptions and explanations
of these phenomena suggests, moreover, that we look at the role of authority in these institutions and the influence of the actions of authorities on students (Parsons & Platt, 1973).

It is still true that in most cases the task of integrating an institution,
be it family or school, with the outside world and ultimately with the

establishment and established order belong to the man. It is the father still who leaves home every day and by this example teaches the child to tolerate interpersonal separation as a social and economic necessity. And it is, typically, the university president who communicates to students that in the main his major functions necessitate his spending only rare hours with them, just as the high school principal, who was too busy to deal directly with them, hired assistant principals whom students reluctantly sought out in times of emergency.

In the modern sense of family, the father represents independence and autonomy: through his work and accomplishments he demonstrates the value of independent effort and achievement. The mother is still characterized by many students in terms of the social, emotional, and integrative functions she performs within the family. Given this role, it must come as somewhat of a surprise to young persons that their mothers would side with their fathers and support the plan of their going away to school and making it on their own. Surely mothers would protest the consequences of this plan, however mildly. Surely mothers would intervene in these father-child discussions and argue the merits of the local college where, even if students live on campus, they might regularly visit with their family. Of course if mothers actually dared to intervene in these decisions the children would be the first to laugh at their overprotectiveness and scorn their reluctance to grant them freedom and individuality. But for a while students may ponder their mothers' ultimate loyalties and—what they refuse to admit to themselves—deceit in favor of loyalty to the society about which they often profess such ignorance. It is expected that fathers would urge their children to follow them toward careers, autonomy, and positions of authority. But how could mothers go along with that? How, furthermore, could mothers consider leaving their children every day to take on work that matters as much to them, apparently, as their children do?

The pattern of maternal behavior becomes crucial for the psychological development of young men and women. The degree of so-called maternal oppression they have witnessed may be as important to students as the type of interaction they now enjoy with their mothers. The literature on women's experiences constantly reveals the tension between young women and their mothers: Some pity their mothers, others lament that an organized liberation movement came too late to include them, others express a brittle anger toward them. At college, all of these attitudes must be incorporated into the context of intellectual and emotional needs and in terms of the separation of children from their parents.

We seem to know less, however, about young men's responses to the behavior of their fathers toward their mothers. How this treatment of women by men affects young men's conceptions of male and female roles is most important. So too is the question of whether or not mothers pursued careers outside the home. Although this essay is not addressed directly to these issues, we might briefly consider them, again in the context of the conflict of earlier and contemporary value systems and role definitions (cf. Jencks & Riesman, 1968).

With the increasing analysis and criticism of the traditional family and its sex roles and functions, many young people seem to be unable to perceive themselves as ever having children. It is not only that they wish to postpone the time of starting a family, for this would be a natural part of establishing a career, but that they omit the possibility of having children altogether. Where once it was said that such an attitude reflected something about a student's own childhood, it can no longer be said with any assurance. The conception of family has changed; so too have the norms of sexual behavior, homosexual as well as heterosexual. Even knowing this, we continue to ignore the power of sociological forces and focus on purely psychological responses. Clearly, political and economic realities enter the conflict between traditional and modern family structures on the one hand, and family experiences and college experiences on the other, and thereby affect students' decisions about parenthood. Some students resent bringing children into a world of corruption and political oppression, but it is doubtful that these constitute their only concerns. Their own private resolutions of family dynamics, dynamics that have changed drastically since leaving home, would also make the act of child rearing difficult to contemplate while they are at college.

Just as they did as children, college students inspect their new environments in terms of men and women's treatment of each other, and older people's treatment of younger people (cf. Astin, 1968). The alleged permissiveness they find and the expressed belief in student maturity on the part of college officials are frequently construed as disinterest or rejection. In the beginning, perhaps, students feel even the limited freedom of university life to be nothing short of liberating. In one week of freshman orientation, as the styles and moods of this new life become evident to them, they feel emancipated. Some months later they start to feel a loneliness and sadness that is only exacerbated by the fleeting Thanksgiving or Christmas vacation trip. So they return to college, which they now call "home," grieving as though the objects and people of their childhoods from whom they have been separated had been pronounced dead. And, in a way, they have.

At school, these students quickly learn not only that there are few figures around to carry them through their loneliness, but that the older people on campus cannot give them sufficient time. They learn too that university personnel differentiate the task of caring for students into academic, psychiatric, or legal compartments, leading students to believe they will be dealt with only when they exhibit a prefabricated problem, like flunking, stealing, or "freaking out." While some students wake each morning praising the new-found freedom of universities, others tremble at the thought that they might not be able to muster the strength to carry them through today and tomorrow. Other students find ways of avoiding the depression or loneliness: They turn to drugs. Still others, feeling guilt as well as loneliness and fright, collapse. Announcement of their being sent to the college infirmary or back home, or the arrival of their parents on campus, angers them as it means that they have failed. But the collapse grants them a renewed sense of inclusion and acceptance, a sense they had almost forgotten or never could articulate before. It makes them feel good, although seventeen-year-old students are not about to admit this feeling to their college friends, much less to their parents. That would be to confess dependencies and a need for care when presumably they are self-possessed, strong, and at least as resilient as the routinized race of bureaucrats that conceived them. To admit relief at the moment of collapse would be to expose one of those secrets that hold entire personalities intact (Cottle, 1973a).

Again I must stress how the social structure and routines of college determine behavioral outcomes. Granted, unique personality predispositions exist in each student, but the outcomes, timing, and much of the substance of the behavior of each must be examined in terms of the cultural and social-historical features of the university environment. It is not frivolous to say that merely walking through the halls of a building may cause one to feel that one is going crazy. Similarly, the cries of lack of closeness between faculty member and students are not mindless repetitions of the noises of prior generations. Class and dorm life, cafeteria and meandering-in-the-halls life, walking about campus or in the streets of a strange city, all may have profound effects on the human psyche, particularly when an individual has reached that point in his life when severe social structure and personality discontinuities have recently been experienced.

The effect of environmental features on students is great indeed, especially because students, as they undergo the transformations of style and value that college demands, comprehend the fact that the world is changing them. Their control over events has suddenly lessened, and for the first time perhaps they bring into consciousness the power of culture and society and recognize the limits not only of psychological reasoning but of their own personal experience (Sanford, 1962). If only because they are structurally vulnerable to social and cultural change, students will be victimized. Autonomy, moreover, becomes an almost impossible ideal, not anachronistic, but structurally unviable because of the discontinuities in development and the incompleted task of reintegrating prior and present experience.

To repeat, the lack of care shown students is itself a message to them to become self-indulgent, self-preoccupied if not self-possessed. The culture of the university imposes its values on students with little regard to the unique history of each. Alone or with friends, students are obliged to internalize these new values along with the new ways of accounting for themselves that these new values imply; all of this is part of the so-called learning experience. Even if the most deeply personal issues are raised in class or become the topics of term papers or examinations, the social structure of college remains and the dilemma of psychological growth still must be addressed as a function of cognitive learning. Colleges tend to forget that the same mind that deals with cognitive and rational processes must also deal with irrational, emotional, and social-psychological issues (Cottle, 1973b).

As long as there are families, systems of authority, and age-graded capacities, there will be a need for all degrees and varieties of human contact. In the large-scale university, however, and many smaller colleges as well, there is very little teacher-student contact of the type required by young people. No doubt there remains an appreciation for its importance, but the culture of higher learning has made it almost impossible for the true psychological *and* intellectual needs of students to be met. Those who drop out, perhaps to return, and those who linger around universities well after they should have finished, testify to this special need of students and faculty members, and to the fact that human contact and genuine enjoyment have been distorted if not made an altogether implausible pursuit.

The point is easily documented. In three universities with a total enrollment of almost 40,000 students, 65 full-time teachers were sampled. The average number of students taught each semester was 250. This number represents students who attended lectures and seminars or worked with faulty members on individual projects where academic credit was awarded. Among these same 65 persons, the average number of published office-hour minutes per week came to 8.5. While students work with three, four, or five professors simultaneously in their various courses during a semester, for the men and women in this sample, 2.9 minutes per week, theoretically, would be devoted to speaking with an individual student outside of class. These would be the private minutes, those given to special concerns and personal recognition.

This little measure only indicates the different sets of needs and intentions, indeed the different definitions of work held by students and professors, but the problem has been outlined numerous times before. We know that the worlds of eighteen-year-old people are hardly the worlds of fifty-five-year-old people, or forty-three-year-old people— the average age of faculty members at a university recently advertising the youth of its faculty. More significantly, the social world and psychological attachments to this world of young people are not the world of thirty-year-old instructors who are themselves but a few years beyond their own graduate school anxieties and dependencies. It may be the world that many thirty-year-olds are working hard to avoid since it represents the adolescence they wish to transcend. Indeed, that some young instructors spend "too much" time with students is taken as a measure of immaturity by some, the shirking of adult career responsibilities. While expressive involvement with students is viewed as kindly, it is also seen as unproductive in terms of academic advancement (Cottle, 1973b; Parsons & Platt, 1973).

With all the literature and discussion on faculty-student relationships, the precise nature of this relationship remains only barely understood. As we know, the university, like the family, is one of the few institutions in which people of almost all ages interact with one another. Furthermore, because the university does not employ students, per se, the nature of the work role often becomes confused. Does one work for, with, or under a professor? What is the true basis of collegiality? Differences in role are based in part on differences in position on a career line. The needs, therefore, of undergraduates, graduate students, and junior faculty members are distinctly different although many activities would make these people appear to be logical colleagues. The competitive features among these groups usually are played down, or at least masked, especially when attacks are made on the tenure system. But many junior faculty members discover that, when their own tenure consideration is at hand, they experience a change in their relationships with students or else take the chance that those deciding their academic fate will look kindly on their closeness with students.

One of the ironies of higher education involves the assessments of older faculty members, who, throughout their lives, remain wholly accessible to students. On the one hand, students treasure these people, flock to them, and justifiably make heroes of them. On the other hand, students may wonder why these teachers have chosen them over the lofty goals of national or international fame. Their assessments of teachers are thus reminiscent of their assessments of mothers who chose children over career. The assessments also anticipate their own ambivalence toward future career achievement. Can one be successful, famous, wealthy, and still be a good and caring person in the manner of those idolized teachers? These same considerations, not so incidentally, are being made by junior faculty members, who also may be ambivalent about their present conditions and future possibilities.

Underlying this ambivalence is the familiar idealized conception of higher education. Despite the charges of elitism, isolationism, and the new conservatism, many students and young faculty members cannot rid themselves of the belief that decency and truth prevail in the university. They still look to it as the institution of honesty and equality; business and politics continue to be the derogated worlds of huckstering and corruption. Although it is not long before students realize the foolishness and childishness of these conceptions, they cling to them hoping that the competitiveness and immorality they have discovered might vanish and the links between the university and the grand establishment might weaken. In this sense, students may wish that universities were more isolated, but, then again, the connections between universities and large-scale organizations and the professions may prove useful to them later on, and so about this situation, too, students may feel ambivalent (cf. Trow, 1966).

There is another ironic situation, one that students in part create for themselves. When demanding policies of social and economic reform, students tend to clamp down on what they publicly announce as "childish psychological needs" better kept for the "shrink." Against a background of sophisticated student politics and global concerns, not too many young persons can freely admit to, much less lobby for, old-fashioned student-teacher closeness. When the poor are being oppressed and people are being slaughtered by imperialist powers, that group of students who might like to speak about closer student-teacher ties must remain silent. It is not necessarily that they are bullied by voluble political types who push them to attend meetings or to join the hordes in the streets. Rather, political tactics, along with lingering notions of elitism and priorities, restrain the expression of often deeply personal needs. As a result, many students find themselves unable to speak openly with one another and simultaneously reluctant to seek out once trusted faculty members now reallocating time from their academic work to political action.

The question may be asked whether students would react positively to a suggestion of old-fashioned student-teacher closeness. My feeling is that they would, although in an effort to avoid the responsibilities of student care, some academics refuse to hear the request. Or perhaps this is an unfair accusation and it is more accurate to say that maintaining close relationships with students is a full-time activity that university faculties can hardly assume if their major work is to continue. No one asks, however, that professors and administrators drop everything and spend their time attending to the young (or even to each other). The point is that the social structure of universities has made the activity of attending to the young so specialized and contrived that many young people in the midst of seemingly self-indulgent acts come to believe that their psychological worlds are worthless and empty.

Given the circumstances of university life, it is not surprising that students would want to become involved in the collective world of politics. By joining "the movement," a new purpose, a new set of friends, and a new brand of idealism are discovered. Students can fight oppression by demonstrating and politicking, and they can find companionship and a new style of fidelity with people whom they once may have suspected. And while politics adds to their general education, it also enhances their own belief in a growing sense of competence and worth. For here is a new task to be performed with people once viewed perhaps as strange or foolish. Furthermore, to know that they can transcend prior sentiments, prejudices, and rationales is surely gratifying and healthy.

Political investments are difficult to discuss for when one examines the psychological gratifications derived from politics, one implicitly minimizes the importance of the political activities and the political realities that originally demanded public response. One feature of the collective apparatus of political work worth mentioning, however, involves the rearrangement of work roles and sex-role distinctions generally. In political work, the traditional lines of authority often give way to more equalitarian dimensions as men and women work as partners. One may wish to interpret these political work relationships in terms of sibling associations for it is true that siblings band closely together in the face of powerful authority. But to suggest that political work is little more than an extension of familial conditions or indeed misplaced protests against family and university authority is to totally miss the genuine inequities and injustices students seek to redress. It strikes me as ironic, in this regard, that some psychoanalysts and sociologists would view campus political activities in terms of psychological origins when governmental leaders consider these same activities in terms of their political implications (Lipset, 1971; Mayhew, 1972).

Still, the social and psychological portions of political activities remain. Even after experiences "in the streets," the political work apparently continues to fail for some students, partly because long-standing career directives persist. Establishment values, reluctantly, are still upheld, and certain psychological needs have not yet been attended to. They have been silenced but not adequately met even by the investment made in political action. Clearly, there exists a magical belief that to uphold the going political banner or lifestyle means to extirpate the sins of the prior and erode the anguish of the present. The fact that long-standing career aspirations endure is demonstrated by the high percentage of students making application to medical and law schools. So-called alternative lifestyles and careers are tried but it is wrong to believe that the contemporary social revolution has done away with traditional forms of achievement.

By way of reiteration, college for some students is treated as a hiatus; it is not only a place of learning, but also an institutional affiliation intervening between adolescence and adulthood. Careers, therefore, may be redefined during college even if earlier career decisions remain unchanged. In its intellectual and sociological dimensions, the college experience allows students the opportunity to contemplate careers and lifestyles and to conceive of these decisions as though they had been arrived at autonomously. The developmental hiatus represented by college causes conflicts, particularly when students recognize that, despite the noble caveat about knowledge for knowledge's sake, university personnel are just as striving, competitive, and capitalistic as notorious business people. Thus the hypocrisy students perceive angers them even as they attempt to reconcile their own drives for personal publicity and public accomplishment.

The constant reference to the term "sell-out" reminds us that many students actively pursue lifestyles that keep them apart from what they see as the establishment's insidious elements. The role of professor, some decide, is a reasonable resolution; one can lead a pure life and still be affluent. This perception too will change, although one is generally uncertain of how carefully students examine all aspects of the academic life. Whatever their views and the limitations of their visions, established career means and ends remain very viable for contemporary students. Some may wish that alternative courses of action could be devised that would lessen their conflicts about career, but, in the meantime, applications to traditional career routes abound. In the end, the decision of career conjoins the values of college and family and weakens the image of college as a true hiatus.

The presence of earlier needs to achieve in ways consistent with the value systems of their parents and the persistent desire to be close to adults emerge in at least two forms: the content of faculty-student advisory or governance committee meetings, and the demand for relevance. Granted, radical students oppose these forums and ideals, but the people who attend meetings, weighted down as they are with liberal intentions and a genuine commitment to academic reform, seem to arrive at roughly the same crucial stopping point: how to get students and teachers closer together and make school more democratic and humane.

The inclusion of students, for example, into what formerly was solely faculty or administrative business reveals the simultaneous expression of political intention and psychological need. While I again fear that even a brief discussion of this topic tends to neutralize the political purposes of students, an avoidance of the personal needs exhibited by certain students in these sessions also seems unwarranted. Let me then recount an episode that shows the tension between the modern social and political reform aspects of education and the older and familiar demand for humane treatment of students.

A young professor was invited to visit a university to be looked over for a job. He eagerly accepted the invitation and made the rounds of visitations and interviewing normally associated with employment negotiations. During his stay he was obliged to meet with a group of students who had established the right to have a voice in academic appointments. This meeting, too, seemed to go well, and upon his return home he believed that a job offer would be forthcoming. A few weeks later, he received a copy of the student newspaper from the school with which he was negotiating. The paper contained an editorial publicly evaluating him and the two other candidates for the position. Until that time he had no knowledge of the other persons under consideration. The editorial denounced him and one other candidate because of their academic associations with "notorious liberals," and because their research interests in elites automatically rendered them "elitists." The third candidate was awarded top priority essentially because his research interest in minority groups rendered him sympathetic. On closer examination, however, what came across more strongly than the candidates' assumed political positions was their treatment of students during a question-answer period. The two men with "bad" politics evaded questions or indulged in circumlocution, whereas the man with the "good" politics dealt directly and kindly with students and thereby evinced his concern for them.

Not having witnessed these events, one cannot dispute the printed opinions and evaluations, nor would one argue with the fact that in the main, more and more professors, feeling students to be encumbrances to their own career advancement, are turning away from teaching. Let us not forget those 2.9 minutes of office "hours" or the reports of academic secretaries who quickly acknowledge the role of gatekeeper they play between their bosses and students. Still, the events of this one job interview point to a possible confusion of political and psychological intentions. Unquestionably, political issues are involved in employment considerations, but there is also a suffusion of personal welfare into the political fabric, a suffusion that some cannot identify and others refuse to recognize. Every day students and faculty members alike dismiss and applaud applicants and colleagues because of their politics and lifestyles as well as their exhibited academic competencies.

The point is not to criticize student political action or the naïveté students frequently share with their elders. The point is, rather, that, because of the political atmosphere of their campuses, some students are no longer free to openly state their psychological interests. There are few editorials demanding student-teacher closeness and almost no cries about the lack of it. But if one speaks with students, or teachers and counselors who spend time with young people, one learns how intense is the need for closeness, even when it is encouched in attacks on the psychiatric health services or the structure of governance committees. As powerful and valuable as peer relationships are, students report that they need contact with faculty members. To legitimate what they feel to be "second order" needs, they often bury these needs in political rhetoric even if this means employing unfounded syllogisms and that often illogical although not always incorrect argument of guilt by association.

Many of these students, however, find themselves trapped because they continue to fear that their feelings, lifestyles, and status are illegitimate and fragile, barely worth having, much less telling. Like it or not, they live in a world where politics is viewed as masculine (or strong) and psychotherapy or confessions of problems as feminine (or weak). Even those students who avoid therapists and investigate sensitivity training are judged as suspect by the supposed strong, and at best marginal by the supposedly committed and healthy people (Cottle, 1973b). What else can these students do but turn to committee meetings or seek programs of academic relevance, a form of personal expression shaped and legitimated by an intellectual or academic mold?

Traditionally, universities have operated in ways that intellectually and psychodynamically exclude the personal experiences of students. From one perspective, higher education has not met the needs of the society, but has responded instead to a sample of the intellectual curiosities of a small percentage of the population. In this sense, there can be no doubt of its elitist underpinnings. But it is also true that higher education developed in part to suit the tastes of, and supply the facilities for, those persons remaining in academic institutions for the rest of their lives, and this fact is not so easily explained by elitist charges.

It is reasonable and necessary that an institution gear itself to those persons occupying central roles even if that institution is not planned essentially around these roles. Hospitals must make it possible for doctors and nurses to work efficiently if adequate patient care is to be maintained. The same is true for universities where professorial facilities are among the most essential concerns. The problem arises when institutions substitute administration for vital functions like patient care and teaching. After years of looking to someone else to run institutions, one awakens to find universities in the hands of administrators who see their role as product- rather than person-oriented.

Once upon a time, the various groups inhabiting a college genuinely believed they shared equally in its traditions, existing resources, and legacies. Later, various groups of scholars, students, and administrators began to feel tensions in their organizations, and some minor and very major battles were waged over just whose interests the university should honor. At present, some of these same battles are being fought, and while those on the outside label these struggles elitist if not infantile, the fact is that the results of these struggles will determine the fate of higher education (Metzger, 1971). At the moment, on many campuses, students feel they have lost the struggle for equal representation, yet, ironically, those they feel to be in control complain of their own disenfranchisement.

For a long time in universities, the movement toward bureaucratization and a growing disinterest in students' personal lives went unchallenged. While thousands of students, the rich and the not quite as rich, made their way through school, often with the feeling that their classes were boring and much in their books seemed irrelevant, they nonetheless crammed hard enough to pass. Then, forgetting most of the content, the names, dates, concepts, and even some of their own reactions to school, they moved out into the "real world," the days of luxury and confusion having ended.

I was part of that generation. I was a student in the days when teachers asked, what do you make of *Lord Jim*? or, are you personally struck with anything in *Jane Eyre*? but where spontaneous expression of what might have been inside me was not appropriate.

In truth, the structure and politics of complex universities make it almost impossible for many of the committees on which students serve and the new curricula to accomplish a great deal. These exigencies, however, cannot hide students' desire for inclusion by or intimacy with those in authority. The rhetoric and style may have changed; the theater and costumes are not the same as before. But the need to be close to teachers and to one another, to be watched over and treated as human beings seeking affirmation and assistance in justifying past activities and sculpting present tasks and future intentions, is almost identical to the need I knew years ago and the need I am certain students will know years from now (Heath, 1965, 1971). Feelings and ideas such as these will not be dissipated even by heinous civil rights murders, assassinations, and anti-imperialist slogans and campaigns, as portentous as they may be. In the depths of a colossal psychological and sociological apparatus lies our sense of a continuity with the past, though not precisely the past of social and political traditions and protocol, rather, the past of personal, social, and intellectual evolution.

We all require that special affirmation of our age, our gender, our powers great or small, our work, and our plans, as well as compassion for our weaknesses. Wise that we are, we recognize when a particular endeavor, especially one that receives our dearest investment, fails to yield the personal and cultural recognition we crave. We feel in these times an insufficiency resulting in part from our knowledge that the sublimation of impulses can never supplant their direct gratification. At some moments, we all must make politics in our way, and be sexual, and be creative, and ingenious. At other moments we must be compliant, passive and cared for; we resist the urge to be agentic and turn instead to the luxurious warmth and sacred beauty of anyone offering to us leadership and communion.

Notes

1. A. W. Astin, *The College Environment*. Washington, D.C.: American Council on Education, 1968.
2. A. W. Chickering, *Education and Identity*. San Francisco: Jossey-Bass, 1969.
3. S. Coopersmith, *The Antecedents of Self-esteem*. San Francisco: Freeman, 1967.
4. T. J. Cottle, *The Abandoners: Portrait of Loss, Separation and Neglect*. Boston: Little, Brown and Company, 1973.
5. T. J. Cottle, Rationales for relevance in higher education. *Interchange* 4(1), 1973: pp. 64 –78.
6. T. J. Cottle and C. Eisendrath, Of Parents, children and psychology. *Educational Forum* 38, 1974: pp. 135 –143.
7. C. Eisendrath, T. J. Cottle, and L. Fink, *Out of Discontent: Visions of the Contemporary University*. Cambridge: Schenkman, 1972.
8. A. Ellison and B. Simon, Does college make a person healthy, wealthy and wise? A social-psychiatric overview of research in higher education, in L. C. Solmon and P. J. Taubman (eds.), *Does College Matter? Some Evidence on the Impacts of Higher Education*. New York: Academic Press, 1973: pp. 175 –224.
9. E. H. Erikson, *Identity, Youth and Crisis*. New York: Norton, 1968.
10. K. A. Feldman and T. M. Newcomb, *The Impact of College on Students*. San Francisco: Jossey-Bass, 1969.
11. G. W. Goethals and D. Klos, *Experiencing Youth*. Boston: Little, Brown and Company, 1970.
12. D. H. Heath, *Explorations of Maturity*. New York: Appleton-Century-Crofts, 1965.
13. D. H. Heath, *Humanizing Schools: New Directions, New Decisions*. New York: Hayden, 1971.
14. C. Jencks and D. Riesman, Feminism, masculinism, and coeducation, in *The Academic Revolution*. New York: Doubleday, 1968.
15. K. Keniston, *The Uncommitted: Alienated Youth in American Society*. New York: Harcourt, Brace & World, 1965.
16. S. King, *Personality Change During College: Lives of Harvard Men*. Cambridge: Harvard University Press, 1973.
17. S. M. Lipset, *Rebellion in the University*. Boston: Little, Brown and Company, 1971.
18. L. B. Mayhew, Dissent: A campus view. *Change* 4(5), 1972: pp. 45 –47.
19. M. Mead, *Culture and Commitment*. New York: National History Press, 1970.

20. W. P. Metzger, The academic profession and its public critics, in R. A. Altman and C. M. Byerly (eds.), *The Public Challenge and the Campus Response.* Berkeley: Center for Research and Development in Higher Education, University of California, 1971: pp. 71–87.

21. T. Parsons and G. M. Platt, *The American University.* Cambridge: Harvard University Press, 1973.

22. W. G. Perry, *Forms of Intellectual and Ethical Development in the College Years: A Scheme.* New York: Holt, Reinhart & Winston, 1968.

23. C. Reich, *The Greening of America.* New York: Random House, 1970.

24. D. Riesman, Commentary and Epilogue, in *Academic Transformation: Seventeen Institutions Under Pressure.* New York: McGraw-Hill, 1973: pp. 409–474.

25. N. Sanford (ed.), *The American College: A Psychological and Social Interpretation of the Higher Learning.* New York: Wiley, 1962.

26. B. R. Snyder, *The Hidden Curriculum.* New York: Knopf, 1971.

27. J. W. Trent and L. L. Medsker, *Beyond High School.* San Francisco: Jossey-Bass, 1968.

28. M. Troy, The undergraduate dilemma in large state universities, *Universities Quarterly* 21, 1966: pp. 17–43.

Going Up, Going Down: On IQ Testing

∽

THIS MORNING, I WALKED down the halls of a Boston area public school. The atmosphere in the school, that intangible quality that observers of education always mention, was difficult to describe. The children were in their classrooms running around or sitting at their desks. In one room there was utter chaos; in another room there was an uncanny sense of order and obedience. In still another room, a group of about ten children, perhaps eight or nine years old, huddled together on a green rug. They sat at the foot of a young man and looked up at him as though he were imparting the secrets of the world. The children obviously loved that teacher. Outside their classroom a small sign was taped to the blond oak door. It read, "Shh—we're testing in here."

It was pleasant enough in that room—unlike the atmosphere I usually find in the schoolrooms I visit. In one of Boston's city schools, where a sign also indicated that testing was going on in a classroom, I witnessed very different behavior. I watched a child sit for more than fifteen minutes—it seemed like a century—refusing to answer even one question the tester was asking. The tester, an older woman, seemed patient enough, but it was evident that this child wasn't going to speak. It was also clear that the child was terrified. She might not have been able to speak even if she had wanted to. The child stared at the tester, her eyes rarely blinking, and with each new question or request she swallowed, opened her eyes as wide as she could, and smiled—just slightly.

After fifteen minutes of this torturous routine, the tester gave in and excused the child. The girl stood up, opened her eyes wide, and walked slowly from the room. Outside in the hall she began to run, and disobeying the signs to walk at all times, she raced up the stairs at the end of the corridor and collided with a friend. She began at once to explain her testing session, and in an instant the two children were laughing hysterically and darting up the stairs together. That same day that same ten-year-old girl had the following statement entered in her official school record, "The child's IQ is so low she is not testable. Recommendation: Special class work is required, probably not in this school."

Several months later the girl was out of school. Unable to find her a special class or special school, her parents let her drop out of school for a time. After several months, the child was readmitted to the same school, and a young psychologist was brought in to test the child. It was late spring, and the psychologist took the girl and the testing equipment out-of-doors. After talking together for almost an hour about all sorts of things, the psychologist explained the testing procedure and began to work with the little girl. The psychologist's final accounting showed an IQ of 115. The child's verbal ability was outstanding. Her weaknesses were in reading comprehension and arithmetic. A tutor was provided to work with the child in those weak areas. One year later she was tested by one of the school's guidance counselors, and her IQ tested 124. In the fall of the same year, the girl was admitted to a voluntary busing program, and she now attends the suburban school that I visited this morning. Her classmates say, "She's neat, except when she talks too much!"

The great advantage of IQ tests, in the opinion of many people who debate the value of IQ tests—all tests for that matter—is that the testers never have to know the children and young adults whose lives are affected by the tests. It is true that much research work *must* be done under isolated, even sanitized conditions; personal feelings and human interactions, it is said, spoil experimental results. But when people make bold pronouncements about what education should or shouldn't be, and how tests do this or that, or even proclaim that school doesn't matter, I wonder whether these people ever talk with the children in America's schools or stay associated with schools long enough to follow the lives of any students. After observing schools for ten years—most of them in poor urban areas operating under the worst possible conditions—I have come to know a group of young people and their families, and I have watched closely what tests, and the whole testing procedure, have done to these children.

Some three or four years ago, I recall speaking with a group of four black boys in the fourth grade of a Philadelphia school. Here is something of that conversation between Bernard and his friends.

"There ain't no fair test no black kid's ever going to get from no white man or white woman," Bernard said. "They put grades on those tests. We behave good, and they give us extra points. We bad mouth 'em, like if we did something to them once they didn't like, they take the points away from us. Only reason they give us those tests is so they can make us look bad to each other.

"Law says they got to give the test, so they give them. Man told my mother I couldn't read. He said the test showed I couldn't read. Test didn't have nothin' about reading in it so how'd he know I couldn't read? So my mother says, 'Bernard says the test wasn't on reading.' So the man says, 'You want to see the test?' So she says, 'Yes.' And here's this big part on the test about reading, you know—remembering what you're reading. But they never gave me that part 'cause I'd've remembered. Just 'cause your lips move when you read don't mean you don't remember.

"My older sister took this test with this other girl," Bernard went on. "All of 'em were supposed to be getting this test, whatever it was for—individual—but they made her take it with this other girl. So while the test is going on, my sister's trying to answer the questions, but the teacher ain't giving her a chance. She keeps telling my sister, 'You're next, you're next.' So my sister waits for the other girl to be done, keeps her mouth shut, being polite, but when the other girl is done, the teacher don't come back to my sister. She says, 'We're done.' So my sister thinks they didn't have no time and that she'll have to be tested another day, which kind of makes her nervous all over again. But there ain't no other day, man. She's had it. That was it. Hell, she'll be in the bottom track of this school 'til the day she dies."

"And you're going to be with her," his buddies teased him.

"That's what *you* think," Bernard retorted. "When they test me they're going to say, man, you're a genius, you got IQ points to give away."

"The day you got too many points, man, is the day I'm going to be the principal of this school," one of his buddies replied.

In a small industrial town in the western part of Massachusetts, I heard other accounts of the effects of testing on some white, middle-class juniors who attended the town's main public high school and who met with me on several occasions. On one rainy afternoon at the front entrance of their school, a young woman told me a sad story.

"Georgia Willows," she began, "had been in my class ever since kindergarten. I never liked her too much, but I had to see her all the time 'cause our parents were friends. I remember she lived in this real large house. We used to play there. Georgia always thought she was the smartest girl in the world. God's gift, you know. By the time we were in grammar school, everybody considered her the smartest girl in the school.

"Then last year this other girl visited the school on one of these exchange programs—from Holland—and not only was she gorgeous, she was even smarter than Georgia. I think she spoke about six languages. She'd never even been in America before and she spoke better than I do. And she'd read a lot of books I hadn't even heard of, American books! So Georgia really had someone to compete with in school. She had thought she was going to be the queen all by herself, but then this Stephanie came and Georgia really got upset. One time at our house, when her parents were visiting, all of a sudden she started to cry. We were up in my room, and out of the clear blue, she began to cry. And she kept saying, 'If I'm not the smartest person in our class, if Stephanie's IQ is higher, I don't want to be alive.'

"I didn't think she was serious about it, but she was. Just before Easter she killed herself. Her mother told my mother that Georgia never got over not being the smartest. I think if IQ means that much to someone, something must be wrong. But maybe there's something wrong with testing people and making them think that how smart they are is the most important thing in their lives."

In that same school, the issue of testing was discussed by a young man who had just learned of his own performance on a set of standardized achievement tests.

"I try not to compare myself with anybody," he began, "but kids talk. Everybody says they aren't going to tell anybody what they got, but in about five minutes everybody knows. Some mystery. I was thinking about tests and all that the other day, and I decided that there's only one way to get rid of them—which they should 'cause they only make people anxious. If you eliminate money in our society, you could eliminate tests and all these test scores. See, to be American means that you have to have a lot of money. No matter what you earn you aren't satisfied until you have more than the next guy. That's the same thing with tests. Giving us our score isn't enough. They have to give us the percentile reading as well. Nobody's supposed to get 690 and think they're really special. The guidance counselor tells them right away that 690 may sound good, but it's only the eightieth percentile. You got to have money and you got to have IQ points and PSAT points and SAT points. Americans love numbers and quantities. Big's the name of the game. Produce and get bigger. Inches, pounds, dollars, points on test, that's all anybody cares about—even the minority students in our school. Nobody asks them whether they're happy. All people want to know is whether their achievement scores have gone up, or how many points they scored in a basketball game."

I have experienced many pleasant incidents in grammar schools and high schools during the last few years. I remember how proud and excited a boy was as he bolted out of an assistant principal's office after being awarded an academic prize. I also remember the concerned faces of children as they were told that the results of some test indicated a problem that the school officials needed to discuss with their parents. Those children were crushed and afraid. They could barely hide their hurt from their classmates.

One of the most vivid school scenes, which usually occurred first thing on a school morning, was the look of anxiety and anticipation on the faces of students as they waited for their teacher to hand back a test. "Abrams, Adams, Basch, Brady," the teacher calls out looking one last time at the test sheet as if memorizing the score. And Abrams, Adams, Basch, Brady—four children half sitting, half standing, waiting eagerly—bounce up or rise slowly and walk to the teacher to receive their grand accounting.

No one needs to announce their scores. Indeed, one doesn't even have to see their faces to know their scores; their bodies reveal everything. Abrams slinks away, careful not to touch anybody. Adams practically flies back to her seat and sits as if she rests on a cushion of clouds. Basch looks at the teacher and his body slouches; he actually seems to be several inches shorter than before he walked the few steps to his teacher. And Brady seems to grow several inches as the teacher walks forward to bestow the good news on the slim girl whose eyes now seem to explode with excitement. Not only does she grow, but her step changes. She dances backward, showing the paper to her friends.

When the teacher returned last week's test to the third graders in that one class, the children were literally going up and going down in response to the numbers they read in the upper right-hand corner of their papers. Going up and going down—in posture, in stature, and in spirit.

Throughout my life I have been troubled by the business of psychological and achievement testing. For years, the words *Princeton, New Jersey,* caused me to tremble with fright, for no matter how many people raved about that town and its renowned university, Princeton, New Jersey, meant the home office of school testing. I never questioned the use of testing. Few students in those days did. If adults had to reconcile themselves to death and taxes, then adolescents had to reconcile themselves to test results and acne, or something equally humiliating. It was a private and public response one had to the test-taking procedure. One might smile as if "who would care," like the girl I saw in that Boston school running out of the room and colliding with her friend. But inside, something was shattered. It is almost forty years since I graduated from high school, and the nightmares of being tested and all that went with the testing procedure persist. They are dreams of terror that never fail to awake me.

How many billions of words have been written about education? How many thousands of articles have been written about the goals of schooling and the need for testing? But how many people know the financial aspects of testing? Do we pay close enough attention to what all this multimillion dollar testing business does to people? How many people know the reasons for testing that have nothing to do with diagnostic or intellectual inquiry? Are we aware of the hundreds of thousands of children who, on the basis of some test, will stop going to school and lead a life in which this early sense of incompetence, failure, and lack of grace will never be erased from their self-concept?

Children in this country are deeply affected for all of their lives by testing and the industry that underwrites it. They are going up and going down in a pattern that ought to frighten us. Some children do just fine. Others rise so quickly that they cannot comprehend the ascent, and they often never recover from the fall when they learn that test scores represent very little when hard work and disciplined ingenuity are required.

We ought to worry, too, about the child who goes home after learning that his test scores have earned him a place in the lowest academic track of his inadequate grammar school, and with tears in his eyes tells his parents: "They told me in school that I'm stupid. I didn't know what they were talking about. They told me there was no use talking back to them because they had it in their tests—everything they wanted to know about me. I said I should be in the other group because those kids were learning more and, besides, they were getting all the best teachers in their classes. I didn't want them to put me in the class they put me in. But they said it wasn't what they *wanted* to do, it was what they *had* to do 'cause they don't decide what classes to put the student in, the tests decide that for them. People don't decide. . . ."

The Mosaic of Creativity

JULIETTE MARTINS SQUIRMED IN the uncomfortable chair. She looked about the small office and came very close to appearing satisfied when she let herself see the few Japanese prints on the wall and other little objects about the room. Then she righted herself, not at all concerned with physical appearance, and looked as though she were about to cry. "When I think what they make us do and think, that's really it, what they make us think, I could puke. And I don't care who hears this! There are so many people around here with so much energy and there's just no place for them to shunt it. It all just builds up inside of them and they seem better off when they just forget everything and go crazy."

From far across a grassy meadow and down the most gentle slope over a wide boulevard that might be the dream of students somewhere, of Paris or Brasilia, hulk the concrete towers and low, lugubrious dormitories of still another university. It's a giant plant, the factory some of them call it, worshipping it, despising it, depending on it, plotting first to own it, then kill it, then wishing, as in a children's story book, it might all fold up like an accordion and disappear between the covers of great colored shapes and objects, its words and writings trickling down the side of the shelf and off the table, then under the office door, to the granite corridors. Vanished.

"Good-bye, energy of my soul." "Good-bye, childhood." "Good-bye, anything good."

"Hey, little boy, you see anything of me just walk out of here?"

"No, sir."

"You been here long?"

"Four years, sir, although I thought of leaving once. Maybe even for good. But then I thought of the Army and I thought, well, this is bad but that Army thing, it's got to be worse. What a bummer!"

"Well, if you see me coming by, stop me. I'm wanted somewhere."

My friend Paul sat on a curb, not far from our home. He carried books by André Breton and Franz Fanon. He carried his oboe, too, in a black leather case, neat and tidy, its delicate white stitching holding it all together. Musician going on a house call, caring for ills. Maybe he carried life in that oboe case, or don't the students speak so foolishly as that now, as they used to? Are they truly more poetic than before?

Paul spoke of pulling his life together. "I've got to get it together. I'll get it together. Then I'll get back to the writing. Maybe poetry, too. I'd like to be back in school. Maybe in a year, I'll pull it together."

"I have that, too, Paul. I can't always get it together. I do the best I can. That's all I can do."

"Is there someone inside us?" Paul asked. "I wish I could tell whether to wrestle him down or just follow him right into the square."

"You still on drugs?"

"No."

"Is that good, do you think?"

"Yes. Is this your home?"

"Yes."

"Now I know where you live, I'll come by. I promise to come by."

"But come by soon. We leave in a few weeks."

"You all, they all, we all leave in a few weeks. Will you come back?"

"Yes. Soon."

I was about to ask, just then, how does one really come to speak of the spark, the energy of creativity in college students? I was about to ask how one even approaches that angry defiance, or the sullenness or lethargy, joy, and bounce, or the depressive anguish, even as one gets close to a friend, sitting, as grownups, not as children, on curbs where the drivers glare at the wasteful sight of people seeking to get close? How does one get to the long hair, the short hair, the long skirts, the short skirts, the wide pants, the thin pants, the unmarked books, the marked all over books, the posters and accoutrements, the charms and memorabilia, the childhoods on the desks on the walls on the lips of the hundreds of thousands of students, burning, exploding, oozing fire, shot like arrows, breathing death, being reborn or rekilled in classrooms by their spectres and teachers and parents? And by their history. How does one get close to that kind of creativity, whatever it might mean?

Is it their politics or drugs, or their music? Is it rather our politics or drugs, or music? Can these things, these activities that often seem to own students, that pull the young around, and that as an irony, possess true life, cause students to taste their first tastes of death? How does one come anywhere close to that sense of the creative child's total, absolutely total digestion of objects, particularly those with which he works and that simultaneously make his work and play come to life? And how should we react to the inseparable resistances to life and death and the ambivalent infatuation with the perishable and imperishable all about them and us?

Life burns within that creative casing, and the students suffer from that very same burning within whose midst they pool some magical and unknown energy, or turn utterly hollow emptiness into the forms and stilts of their being on the "outside." Their work starts, their work ends, and with their work, deep within the marrow of their work, the cells of a most ingenious, expansive, but inexorable stain make their way to the surface of our collaborations and friendships with them.

How late so many of us come to our insistence that creative students know a place of consciousness whose tracks we can never trace. Their existence is within, more on the slopes than on the concrete, more along the tissue and dripping on the brain than in the lecture hall or discussion section. They admit to the drippings and even to their tumbling under a bombardment, an armageddon of trafficking currents and cellular stimulations. They hear the sudden explosions of their impulses. They see the aftermath, the craters left as clay and words and designs from the firing of invisible nerves. Theirs is a world often of the darkness, of the turning within and the authenticity of coldness, impersonality, exhaustion and the cradled refuge of lifeless life. And they can never speak of it, nor write of it, nor even sculpt or act or scream of it. Yet they suffer the very aloneness they require and despise, and the breathless fright they've never forgotten from childhood, nor perhaps wished to forget.

My work was created only by *elimination,* and each newly acquired truth was born only at the expense of an impression which flamed up and then burned itself out, so that its particular darkness could be isolated and I could venture ever more deeply into the sensation of Darkness Absolute. Destruction was my Beatrice. I can speak of this now because yesterday I completed the first sketch of my work. It is perfectly outlined: it will be imperishable if *I* don't perish. I looked upon it without ecstasy or fear: I closed my eyes and *saw that it existed....*

I think the healthy thing for man—for reflective nature—is to think with his whole body: then you get a full harmonious thought, like violin strings vibrating in unison with the hollow wooden box. But I think that when thoughts come from the brain alone (the brain I abused so much last summer and part of last winter), they are like tunes played on the squeaky part of the first string—which isn't much comfort for the box: they come and go without ever being *created*, without leaving any trace. For example, I can't recall a single one of those sudden *ideas* I had last year. On Easter day I got a terrible headache from thinking only with my brain, after I had gotten it going with coffee: because it can't get going by itself, and my nerves were probably too tired to respond to any outside impression: I tried to stop thinking that way, and with a tremendous effort I braced the nerves in my chest so as to produce a vibration—still holding on to the thought I was then working on, which became the subject of the vibration, that is, an impression: and so that is the way I am beginning a poem I have been dreaming about for a long time. Ever since then, whenever the crucial hour of synthesis approaches, I say to myself: "I am going to work with my heart": and then I feel my heart (at those times my whole life is undoubtedly centered in it), and the rest of my body is forgotten, except for the hand that is writing and the living heart, and my poem is begun—*begins itself.* Really, I am shattered. To think I have to go through all that to have a unified vision of the Universe. But if you don't do that, then the only unity you feel is your own existence.[1]   [Mallarmé]

There is a spirit that says find in your teacher and all his or her assignments and directives the entrance to internment camps, the gates of hell, the incarceration of all goodness. There is a spirit flaked with that delicious and poisonous anger of theirs toward authority, toward demands and scripture. Curses on the academics. There cannot of course be teachers in their life, not unless their teachers would climb inside them and hold clandestine tutorials at the foot of their brain stems. For the unknown they might acknowledge has no place for teachers. (It has no place for anyone—not even themselves, they're forced to admit on stronger occasions.)

The unknown is not the incorporation of history nor combinations of contemporaneous facts, nor even anticipations of yet to be found facts. The creative unknown begins with the atavistic combination of temporal portions. It is the child with the boy, the boy with the man, the old man with the old child, and the tormented bliss of relinquishing no time, anticipating no space, and praying that childhood's energetic form might be melted down and used again and again and again in nothing but work-life. That is why teachers fail to discover even the property lines of the creative one's sources. It is because, at best, they coexist in different times, in different energy systems, and worship opposite temporal ideals. The old go forward toward the inexorables, the young diffuse backward and forward, inside and outside of time.

Nothing new happened to me. I found intact what I had acted, what I had prophesied. There was only one difference: without knowledge, without words, blindly, I *carried everything out*. Previously, I had depicted my life to myself by means of images: it was my death causing my birth, it was my birth driving me toward my death. As soon as I gave up *seeing* this reciprocity, I *became* it myself: I was strained to the breaking point between those two extremes, being born and dying with each heartbeat. My future eternity became my concrete future: it made every instant trivial, it was at the core of the deepest attention, it was an even deeper state of abstraction, it was the emptiness of all plenitude, the light unreality of reality: it killed from a distance the taste of a caramel in my mouth, the sorrows and pleasures in my heart: but it redeemed the most trifling moment by virtue of the mere fact that this moment came last and brought me closer to it: it gave me the patience to live: I never again wanted to skip twenty years and skim twenty more: I never again imagined the far-off days of my triumph: I waited. Every minute I waited for the next one because it brought the following one closer. I lived serenely in a state of extreme urgency: I was always ahead of myself, everything absorbed me, nothing held me back. What a relief! Formerly, my days had been so like each other that I sometimes wondered whether I was not condemned to experience the eternal recurrence of the same one. They had not changed much: they still had the bad habit of slipping away with a shudder: but *I* had changed: time no longer flowed back over my becalmed childhood: rather, it was I, an arrow that had been shot by order, who pierced time and went straight to the target.[2]   [Jean-Paul Sartre]

No, the creative student seeks no new combinations of that healthy and sick, insulting and penetrating reality on the outside, if he can just manage to manipulate his own senses into marvelously new, erotically new, sardonically new combinations, and best of all, noncombinations. How, he asks, can he arrange to have that certain and secure cognitive apparatus of his collide head on with that vast unknown, and then save and savor the child-man that in the colliding copulation most certainly is conceived? How can he do that? Certainly not with teachers! Maybe with poetry. And with music? Guaranteed!

So is it, as some have alleged, the expression of infantilism that finds air and life and breathing room in the creative student? Is it regression to the distant past, or resumption of what must seem as near past or the constant starting all over again as in a sketch or verse that constitutes this energy? Is it the order of a secret motive or direction of an impulse that drives the student into and unto himself and makes him seek the omnipotent turmoil of the child as lining to his manhood? Is it that sexualized demon screaming to be both released and imprisoned forever just at the time when one's very soul smacks, eyes open, against society's granite toughness? Is it the "unmakable" quality so many students feel, the immutable, the inevitable, the deaf, the soldiers, the teachers? What can they do in the face of faceless administrators, teachers, and governments crying accomplishment and achievement? What sense can they make of today's confusion and indecisiveness and utter lostness becoming tomorrow's exceptional and adventurous history? And what about us on the other side?

There remains and always will remain for these students the most precarious sense of boundary. Where, they question in their naive brilliance, can I make a mark that might for even a night proclaim the edge of me and commencement of them? When may I know that it is I with whom I commune and not with political marauders seeking to eclipse their voracious hunger for control and tradition? How, they weep, can I be permanently freed from any intervention, any incision, yet be protected by the nurturance of arms and breasts and hair that creep within those not so arbitrary boundaries of one's definitions of self and being? It is the conflict of outside and inside, the unique person and the seemingly contrived group. Then the obligation held over from grammar school to hold everyone's hand while marching to the playground, all the while cracking under the anger, the sense of injustice, the unfairness of bigger brothers, older sisters, upperclassmen, and taller adults.

They seem, these creative students, so often preoccupied with the unfairness and lack of gentleness of social orders and stresses on cohesiveness and coherence. Propelled by their mysterious motives, they slam into worlds of graded regulations and biased restrictions. To be taught law and discipline is to be fed poison, for never in their schooling are they permitted to peek at the glass cases that someday may just house their very own works. Stymied by systems within systems and that unfilled childhood that suddenly stopped, fearing an adulthood of insanity, boredom, and the certainty of an inner death, they retreat momentarily from the demons and from the motives, from the impulses and sensuous disorder and disarray inside, and take on, of all enemies, the world with all of its warring aggregates and all of its legalities and illegalities. They take on the rich and the poor, the black, the brown, the white, the yellow, and the red, the living and the dead, the possible and the impossible, and they work while their elders sigh at the first glimpses of youth's inevitable period of idealism. But their special politics give life, and like a white-hot iron it whips across that private unknown of theirs and scars more than a few passing years and what soon may be more than a few products of creative joy as well as discomfort.

Looking back through the last page or two, I see that I have made it appear as though my motives in writing were wholly public-spirited. I don't want to leave that as the final impression. All writers are vain, selfish and lazy, and at the very bottom of their motives there lies a mystery. Writing a book is a horrible, exhausting struggle, like a long bout of some painful illness. One would never undertake such a thing if one were not driven on by some demon whom one can neither resist nor understand. For all one knows that demon is simply the same instinct that makes a baby squall for attention. And yet it is also true that one can write nothing readable unless one constantly struggles to efface one's own personality. Good prose is like a window pane. I cannot say with certainty which of my motives are the strongest, but I know which of them deserve to be followed. And looking back through my work, I see that it is invariably where I lacked a *political* purpose that I wrote lifeless books and was betrayed into purple passages, sentences without meaning, decorative adjectives and humbug generally.[3] [George Orwell]

The terror of the boundary between the ringing self and the groups with whom students flirt, and from which they take away ideas, ideologies, and finally partners, comes from the conflict between the security and democracy found in possessing tolerant companions and the anarchic fear that involvements with others can mean being devoured. Loyalties, reasonableness in friendship means competition just as much as recognition. Loyalty means compliance and running away as well as running dry. Loyalty means to the students submitting to systems of evaluation, censorship, and adult persecution, maybe anonymity as well. The goal is to be recognized for worth, not by name, nor by face; by work, not by grade, nor by arbitrary number. Better by mood than performance; better by sustained effort than by common deed.

But loyalty also has something to do with one's work. For in the work is both the breathing of life into words or sculpture or colors or fabrics or food that but moments ago existed in the lush darkness of the unconsciousness. In the work is the despair of aging and the secret wish to please families and friends and, if possible, everyone who lives or who ever lived. Or, best of all, those who haven't lived yet.

In the work is childhood brought up to date with and socialized by adulthood, and the thunder of hate cleansed by and in love and kindness. So the creative student hopes his work might be loved and with it, that he might be loved. But none dares admit to this, except perhaps in recollecting, for in the exquisite instant of demonstration or production, it always seems as though the demon of anger carries the weight of productivity, leaving love first to fill the crevices between work sessions and then to spray over the people who mill about one's thoughts and blue-prints for the future. The work makes time congeal. History now becomes tomorrow, and last autumn—the first autumn of school—means forever. The creative work, the truly creative work, not only turns a man or woman deeply inside himself or herself, it allows a diffusion of feelings that no one will ever come close to describing, much less recounting, except, of course, as through reminiscence we regain the primitive sensations of our first aloneness, then our first public presentations, and finally our earliest need to be watched over.

And these reminiscences in turn, being as they genuinely are, the creative products of all people, in a funny way, place us intimately in touch with the others and their epochs. They reveal to us our favorites and our inchoate notions of a society watching over us, caring for us. Creativity then, in a most uncanny but intriguing form, seems never to separate itself from fathers, mothers, and schools, be they real, fictive, or bits of both.

In the first composition, I was last. Young feudalist that I was, I regarded teaching as a personal bond. Mlle. Marie Louise had given me her knowledge out of love: I had received it out of bounty, for love of her. I was disconcerted by the *ex cathedra* courses which were addressed to one and all, by the democratic coldness of the law. Subjected to those constant comparisons, my fancied superiority vanished. There was always someone who answered more quickly or better than I. I was too loved to have doubts about myself. I wholeheartedly admired my classmates and did not envy them. My turn would come. At the age of fifty. In short, I was ruining myself without suffering. Seized with barren panic, I would zealously turn in extremely bad work. My grandfather had begun to frown. My mother hastily asked for an appointment with M. Ollivier, my official teacher. He received us in his small, bachelor apartment. My mother put on her melodious voice. Leaning against her armchair, I listened to her as I looked at the sun through the dusty windows. She tried hard to prove that I was better than my work showed: I had learned to read by myself, I wrote novels. When she had run out of arguments, she revealed that I was a ten-month child: better baked than the others, more glazed, crispier as a result of staying in the oven longer. M. Ollivier, who was more sensitive to her charms than to my merits, listened attentively. He was a tall, lean, bald man, with a large head, sunken eyes, waxy complexion, and a few red hairs under a long hooked nose. He refused to give me private lessons, but promised to "follow up" on me. That was all I asked for. I would watch his eyes in class: he spoke only for me. I was sure of it. I thought he liked me. I liked him: a few kind words did the rest. I became, without effort, a rather good student. My grandfather grumbled when he read my report card at the end of the term, but he no longer thought of taking me out of the lycée. In the following grade, I stopped getting special treatment, but I had got used to democracy.[4]   [Jean-Paul Sartre]

Just as the individual fights to be away from the collective and fears being devoured by it, so too do his self-love and pride scream to be silenced by socialized modesty and self-effacement. Hear me and answer, one will shout. Know that I'm here in part even when I'm not here, another will shout. Let my works substitute for and thereby live for me. Let them be my living. He fights as well to know everything and become, in this way, a leader, and to know nothing at all, and to become, in this way, a follower of the strong. But the students seem at times to wish for both. And why not? School tolerates both these drives toward life and work: The drive to stay behind and the drive to lap all the runners and be seen, and then vault ahead.

There is a certain fun that comes with all that bookish knowledge. There is a certain satisfaction. It isn't creativity of course, they argue, but all of the knowledge packed so neatly away, retrievable, forgettable, retrievable again, makes a rather lovely accoutrement to or crown for adolescence, as well as something to desert entirely so that starting all over from nothing seems a bit less scary. Knowledge also means competence. But just how much of others' works they permit to enter depends on just how much of themselves they feel to be emerging out of their search.

At times the reading goes well and they feel expanded, inflated, adventurous. At times the reading keeps them from stories utterly more important and from work utterly more triumphant. Then, for months, as their teachers and prodders say "study," they retreat literally, under a sacred ground and reappear as leader, painter, writer, or just plain spirit. And in these times, no assignments or evaluations can match the outpouring from the spurts of fluids and cubes that they generate or imbibe from an apparent emptiness or depression. Creativity moans in these times, and the calls of scholars seem coarse and foolish . Only the caller himself, by himself, has the slightest hope of finding their sounds and moods, resentment and bitterness.

PRAISE OF LEARNING

Learn the simplest things. For you
whose time has already come
it is never too late!

Learn your A B C's, it is not enough,
but learn them! Do not let it discourage you,
begin! You must know everything!
You must take over the leadership!

Learn, man in the asylum!
Learn, man in prison!
Learn, wife in the kitchen!
Learn, man of sixty!
Seek out the school, you who are homeless!
Sharpen your wits, you who shiver!
Hungry man, reach for the book: it is a weapon.
You must take over the leadership.

Don't be afraid of asking, brother!
Don't be won over,
see for yourself!
What you don't know yourself,
you don't know.
Add up the reckoning.
It's you who must pay it.
Put your finger on each item,
ask: how did this get here?
You must take over the leadership.[5]
                    Bertolt Brecht

For the creative ones, all the voices on the outside seem consistent,
unequivocal. The battling theme of holding back and plunging ahead,
as redundancy, occurs and occurs again. The limitations and utter freedom of self-love and self-importance hammer away at them, and the
meaning of choice or decision gets buried somewhere or put away for a
later time. Procrastination and wastefulness seem uncontrollable.
There's so much to do, so many, many options to scan, so many careers
to pursue, so many opportunities to ponder. The potential of success
seems just about as scary as the potential of failure. So what's the point
of living? Retribution, in its often grotesque cloak, appears either way.
And somehow, in the mystery of it all, creativity seems to carry with it
the certainty of success *and* failure, retribution *and* pride.

Still the decisions remain to be made and they always say, the various
paths one might follow begin to be visible. But where does one take
comfort or guidance when the entire enterprise means throwing off the
past, publicly if not privately, and lurching into upright independence
and autonomy? Where does creativity really permit training and hearing,

advice and counsel? If to be creative means in part to accept that inner darkness, whatever it holds, and there's no assurance or promise it holds anything "valuable" at all, how could it be that the creative one might find any admissible leader, decision maker, or teacher? Does it not seem as if the whole process demands that everything, absolutely everything, must come from the inside? Otherwise it cannot be authentic or right. Otherwise it cannot be creative. Otherwise, as craftpersons say, it doesn't work. Is not this the case?

So when college portentously holds itself up as the institutionalized epoch for deciding all of the future, the creative person somehow slides backward, collects what seems to him a vanishing strength, and looks, just as the platitude prescribes, to his heart. It is this that gives him direction, though very little solace. But he can comfort himself during these momentous years of decisions in the thought that truly wise men could do no better in their humble search for some light outside and with it, a style of life and a plan for immortality and Godliness. For in the jagged times of creativity, there is no direction, no guidance, and rather little else but those platitudes about seeing what is in your own heart and accepting whatever it is that flows from your soul.

It is impossible to tell men what way they should take. For one way to service God is by the teachings, another by prayer, another way by fasting, and still another by eating. Everyone should carefully observe which way his heart draws him, and then choose that way with all his strength.[6]   [Martin Buber]

Thus, as frightening as it may seem to many, the message to teachers is clear: Even if they could do something constructive about it, they had better stay out, but not away. They must be around, close and in touch. Sufficiently close so that they may recognize the creative work, but not so close that they might smother its breath. It is a discreet and honorable role they play, for they must tolerate rebukes and harshness that the creative student, that every student, may use as a method of making certain he hasn't yet been devoured by teachers and schooling, campus architecture, and, of course, careers. It is an honorable role, for it requires the teacher to separate himself from his students in a fashion that only time would understand. It is not quite the teacher's future the student covets. It is not quite his past that the student fears may be bequeathed to him. It's not quite either of these two possibilities, but it is also not too far from both of them.

But where in the teaching present does there exist a moment for change? Where in the present does the instant of exchange or communication or teaching take place? For that matter, can anything ever be communicated or taught, or is it always the case that the creative one turns his back, and with it his past and his dissatisfactions, in the face of his teacher?

To turn away is to be left alone, which means the possibility of death. Yet at the same time turning away offers a possibility for industry. To be left overly attended, overly cared for, means competition just as much as nurturance, and who knows where either of these routes might lead? They might lead back to the secrets of the creative impulse, if it is really an impulse. They also might lead away from these secrets forever, leaving the once young mind with nothing but self-conscious and repetitive soliloquies about childhood and school.

This, then, is the magic that teachers must unravel: how to keep that energy alive. How to keep those living-dying, working-playing persons fearlessly and fearfully with and within themselves. How to keep them at one and the same time, in and out of school, in and out of themselves, in and out of their work. How to make school a playground and a nursery, a monastery and a church. How one second to make school the figure and the ground of all learning and of all knowledge, and then in the next second make it all disappear—the buildings and the teachers, the books and the trees—leaving all by herself that single creative spirit. How to do all of this and make it seem real and honest, never contrived. How to make school an edifice of the past, present, and future and hence the cord of integrity for all time, and then reverse everything, by yanking it all away: the cord, the past, the present, and the future—leaving all by herself that single creative spirit.

How does a teacher bring this about? By what he does? By what he doesn't do? By his wishes and aspirations if he can liberate them from his guilts and dissatisfactions, recriminations and regrets? By his actions, private and public? By his disclosures, intentional and unwitting? Maybe he never thinks of any of these strategies and concerns himself with the only plausible magic he knows, the calling of his own work. And maybe, too, this is precisely what the creative spirit needs: the reaffirming structure of solitary work. For with work alone comes the response to his own staging of mockery, namely the refutation of teaching altogether, from of all people, his teacher. At first glance it seems pleasurable enough, this refutation, but it cuts its way to the very spine of that darkness, and now he wonders whether it is worth the mockery, the anger, and the outrage. He wonders, too, about a war with parents and the image of the future that, good or bad, school has begun to carve.

Then there is his work, and suddenly of all things from still another portion of darkness, his unborn children and their whole generation appear before him.

Dear Miss——,

I have read about sixteen pages of your manuscript and it made me—smile. It is clever, well observed, honest, it stands on its own feet up to a point, and yet it is so typically feminine, by which I mean derivative and vitiated by personal rancour. I suffered exactly the same treatment at the hands of my teachers who disliked me for my independence and passed me over when they wanted assistants. (I must admit that I was somewhat less of a model student than you). But it would not have been worth my while to write anything about my school life, still less would I have liked to be responsible for anyone's printing or actually reading it. Besides, one always cuts a poor figure if one complains about others who are struggling for their place in the sun too after their own fashion.

Therefore pocket your temperament and keep your manuscript for your sons and daughters, in order that they may derive consolation from it and—not give a damn for what their teachers tell them or think of them.

Incidentally I am only coming to Princeton to research, not to teach. There is too much education altogether, especially in American schools. The only rational way of educating is to be an example—of what to avoid, if one can't be the other sort.

With best wishes,[7]
Albert Einstein

Surely the teacher finds himself in the student. Surely, too, the student wonders whether he too has not seen some anticipated reflection in the teacher. Will their times ever cross? Or is it perhaps not age that keeps them apart, but, instead, the essence of authority, the control of one over the other? This is the logical but hated inevitability, that one should have and the other should want, or that one dares to be there before the other and thereby earns what invariably each generation perceives as the single reward. When you look at it long enough, it seems right that most of the "information" should be passed on genetically; the hard part is just speaking together honorably, the parent and the child, the teacher and student. But here again, time has intervened and renders friendships so trying and painful.

Sometimes it seems as though the creative student treasures the tradition he shares with wise men and idols, but then he changes his mind and rejects any time he has not encountered face on. So he rejects his father's dreams, or he masks them by erecting his own realities in their place. But his attachments to the prior are always in evidence. Soon he cannot find the truth or fantasy of any authority, until, of course, that authority comes thundering back to him with the strength of a monster-God. Then, as in nothing short of a biblical flood, the words and the deeds and then, finally, the secrets of that authority just explode over the land on which the younger one walks, or someday, like it or not, will have to walk.

Poetry readings, dramatic presentations, graduation ceremonies, perhaps eulogies heard too early, and always letters—they're all words, clusters of man's words held together by iron. Words and music shackle people together, then bind them all to history. The words don't teach, really, they launch creativity, slap at it when it finally arrives, and often brutalize the soul whose fear of work, or war with it, or just plain idleness prevent the next wave, the next movement of creativity from appearing.

Sometimes the storm of words from the old and accomplished to the young and trying bounce away in meaninglessness; sometimes, too, they sting the recipient and everyone around him. The old demand effort, work, more effort, coming back from failure, resistance against the seductiveness of success, fame, wealth, and all of that. The old see the past only, so the young think; the young the future only, so the old lament. Yet both struggle and struggle some more with their respective childishness and self-love. Where the old have the upper hand, at least in the creative enterprise, is that they have begun to live with but a few rewards not of creativity necessarily, but of the work that supports all those sparks and all of that darkness. The truth they dare push on their children, their children with the fresh eye and unformed heart, is work. Work, work, the litany, work—"When I was your age . . ."—and the young run away from the adolescence of their parents and in so doing prevent their elders from regaining the unregainable.

Adolescence and childishness are not creativity; let no one think that they are. Let no one think, either, that they couldn't be if it were not for a society so ambivalent about letting its precious children grow up at all. The stuff of creativity is all there, in their bellies waiting to be ripped open. The darkness inside is there, too, glistening, waiting to be discovered. Dip into the well and see finally what's in the deepest deep of your insides, is what they ought to teach. But it's not so easy a request to make, it's not so easy a lesson to teach, for it means that the teacher, too, must accept an inside and have disclosed to himself by himself what heretofore has remained merely the secret potential of his own creativity and health.

But parents can tell their children about creativity, especially when they themselves dared to hunt for that glistening darkness. And find it or not, they still preserve a bit of love in reserve. Parents can push for the work and the solitude and the aloneness that they know for themselves have given birth to creativity right out of their marrow. Their lives practically on fire, their dreams all but fallen away, their futures practically useless and timeless, they cling to their work, the source of their every breath, and as the strictest of autocrats, they order their children to look to themselves and not the vicariousness and deception of others. Work, work alone with and in yourself, they scream in thunder and rage and with an almost primordial certainty. Turn away from the capricious and work, or make the capricious into work. Short or long, words or notes, life or death, work alone. Here is the truth. Here, here where you work or ought to work. Let them teach that and nothing more, say some.

July 7, 1938

Dearest Scottie:

I don't think I will be writing letters many more years and I wish you would read this letter twice—bitter as it may seem. You will reject it now, but at a later period some of it may come back to you as truth. When I'm talking to you, you think of me as an older person, an "authority," and when I speak of my own youth what I say becomes unreal to you—for the young can't believe in the youth of their fathers. But perhaps this little bit will be understandable if I put it in writing.

When I was your age I lived with a great dream. The dream grew and I learned how to speak of it and make people listen. Then the dream divided one day when I decided to marry your mother after all, even though I knew she was spoiled and meant no good to me. I was sorry immediately I had married her but, being patient in those days, made the best of it and got to love her in another way. You came along and for a long time we made quite a lot of happiness out of our lives. But I was a man divided—she wanted me to work too much for *her* and not enough for my dream. She realized too late that work was dignity, and the only dignity, and tried to atone for it by working herself, but it was too late and she broke and is broken forever. . . .

For a long time I hated *her* mother for giving her nothing in the line of good habit—nothing but "getting by" and conceit. I never wanted to see again in this world women who were brought up as idlers. And one of my chief desires in life was to keep you from being that kind of person, one who brings ruin to themselves and others. When you began to show disturbing signs at about fourteen, I comforted myself with the idea that you were too precocious socially and a strict school would fix things. But sometimes I think that idlers seem to be a special class for whom nothing can be planned, plead as one will with them—their only contribution to the human family is to warm a seat at the common table.

My reforming days are over, and if you are that way I don't want to change you. But I don't want to be upset by idlers inside my family or out. I want my energies and my earnings for people who talk my language.

I have begun to fear that you don't. You don't realize that what I am doing here is the last tired effort of a man who once did something finer and better. There is not enough energy, or call it money, to carry anyone who is dead weight and I am angry and resentful in my soul when I feel that I am doing this. People like——and your mother must be carried because their illness makes them useless. But it is a different story that *you* have spent two years doing no useful work at all, improving neither your body nor your mind, but only writing reams and reams of dreary letters to dreary people, with no possible object except obtaining invitations which you could not accept. Those letters go on, even in your sleep, so that I know your whole trip now is one long waiting for the post. It is like an old gossip who cannot still her tongue.

You have reached the age when one is of interest to an adult only insofar as one seems to have a future. The mind of a little child is fascinating, for it looks on old things with new eyes—but at about twelve this changes. The adolescent offers nothing, can do nothing, say nothing that the adult cannot do better. Living with you in Baltimore (and you have told Harold that I alternated between strictness and neglect, by which I suppose you mean the times I was so inconsiderate as to have T.B., or to retire into myself to write, for I had little social life apart from you) represented a rather too domestic duty forced on me by your mother's illness. But I endured your Top Hats and Telephones until the day you snubbed me at dancing school, less willingly after that. . . .

To sum up: What you have done to please me or make me proud is practically negligible since the time you made yourself a good diver at camp (and now you are softer than you have ever been). In your career as a "wild society girl," vintage of 1925, I'm not interested. I don't want any of it—it would bore me, like dining with the Ritz Brothers. When I do not feel you are "going somewhere," your company tends to depress me for the silly waste and triviality involved. On the other hand, when occasionally I see signs of life and intention in you, there is no company in the world I prefer. For there is no doubt that you have something in your belly, some real gusto for life—a real dream of your own—and my idea was to wed it to something solid before it was too late—as it was too late for your mother to learn anything when she got around to it. Once when you spoke French as a child it was enchanting with your odd bits of knowledge—now your conversation is as commonplace as if you'd spent the last two years in the Corn Hollow High School—what you saw in *Life* and read in *Sexy Romances*.

I shall come East in September to meet your boat—but this letter is a declaration that I am no longer interested in your promissory notes but only in what I see. I love you always but I am only interested by people who think and work as I do and it isn't likely that *I* shall change at my age. Whether you will—or want to—remains to be seen.

Daddy

P.S. If you keep the diary, please don't let it be the dry stuff I could buy in a ten-franc guide book. I'm not interested in dates and places, even the Battle of New Orleans, unless you have some unusual reaction to them. Don't try to be witty in the writing, unless it's natural—just true and real.

P.P.S. Will you please read this letter a second time? I wrote it over twice.[8]

F. Scott Fitzgerald

The irony of the creative spirit is that sooner or later it seems to brush up against, perhaps even collide with, school, and, even more, with education. Here lies life for some, here too lies poison for others. They all crash together here for a short time, all of those mysterious furies: intelligence, ingenuity, innovation, creativity, learning. They crash head on producing the roar of grades to be sure, but merely the whisper of newness and the bare wisp of art. The very halls and floors of the school, painted as they are with politics, verbiage, and aggrandisement, exude the poisonous oils that spread over creativity's pores. Yet somehow the fresh words and notes, models and movements, push their way up, up to the outside and freedom.

School plays a funny trick, it seems, on all of those creative ones. It holds them back, we all know that. But in that holding back, in that attempt to make them all comply and conform, some just have to break their necks and, like colts, gallop away. But their attachments to the prior are always in evidence. They fight the ropes and the tethers, they fight them right down to the very end, and even beyond the end. But maybe it is precisely the knowledge of it all and the feeling of being constrained, of being hemmed in, pinned down, that at first drives them inward and thereby far away from all the ropes and tethers, and then launches those secrets of theirs into the molds of action and production that light a sleeping darkness. Could it really be true that school protects the creative spirit by at least providing a ground, a foundation from which to erect a dream or vision or a gate from which to run away as fast as one can? Somewhere in the ground of learning after all, are the seeds of ethics and goodness, even among all that poison. Somewhere in the ground too is the scent of freedom—freedom with restraint, but freedom, even among all of that conformity and obsession with respect.

Let's be honest. There are times when total individuality and aloneness, aloneness with work especially, is scary, and we run to the side of anyone who may be walking there. Just to talk.

All of this, of course, has more to do with people than with creativity. School is good, truly good, when they all run away. If it's only hard work, it's incomplete. If they only think it, it's incomplete. Whatever it is, that creative thing, it required pacing and moving, moving away, coming back, moving away again. Not only the dancers dance; not only the sculptors sculpt. There must be movement, enormous, wonderful, swirling movement in colored and colorless space, all at the same time. And the space on the outside must pour like white hot iron into the space on the inside, and then be able to pour out again so quickly one can see the steam. School ought to be that, too! The outer space, the inner space, the movement of arms and legs and bodies along with ideas and plans, anticipations and reworkings, groups and singles, movies and stills. There has to be pacing room, running room, room to run away.

But there has to be as well a tower, or a person, right in the middle of the school, a beacon, a glow, a something that offers a return to the run-aways and to the idlers, the knowers, and the seers. There has to be a base, a root, a setting, a constancy, a ground, a whole. This the creative spirit and the creative darkness in each and every one of us needs from the world. Without them, the thoughts of perishing, transiency, imper-manency, temporariness would simply overwhelm, and there would be no energy left over for pure and unrelenting work, much less surprise.

In that beacon or that person, and again ironically in school, is just enough of what they call "religion" to justify, probably, the concept of— or the words—*creative soul* or *spirit*. The religion need not contain the ritualization that for many gives it purpose, but it fits nonetheless alongside the mysterious and the incomprehensible out of which the multilanguages of expression and expressiveness breathe creativity. Where after all does a poem or sketch, a recipe or design, a joke or play or altogether new sensation come from? Does anyone know? More im-portantly, will some of us who seek creativity destroy it by finding it, or is that the same old unwarranted fear that always precedes exploration and discovery? It seems now as though the creative spirit and those who work with it and abide by it have a way—not intentionally, of course— of covering up the tracks of their work, the footprints that might make the experience of their innovations and industry fathomable, even com-patible with our own ingenuous lifestyles. "I don't know where it comes from," they say. "I change my mind every ten minutes." "I turn mistakes into purposeful alterations." "I don't think about what will happen to it when I finish it. I just want people to like it when it's done." "What are you trying to do," they ask, "psychoanalyze me?"

A lot of "I's" in all those descriptions. A lot of narcissism, egocentrism, some would say. What are you going to make of the statement, "I can't bear to part with the pieces I've made"? Wouldn't you say that's kind of infantile, holding on to everything, believing every note, every word, every gesture should be finalized and made immortal? "Hey, Mom ... Mom ... Mom," I screamed. "Watch me swim under water." And then, "Did you see me?" Remember those times? "I drew these pictures in school today and I'm going to hang them here in the living room. The ones I made last week aren't good now and they're coming down. I don't like them anymore. O.K.? But you won't throw them away, will you?" Surely that's infantilism. Or is it, rather, the beginning of work and recognition, genuine industry and public honor that know no particular age or starting point, only changes in the form they ultimately find and agree to over time? Even at death, our freshest pictures still go up, and the old ones of a week before come down to join the batch in a withered portfolio. Still more of the attachments to the prior.

What then of school and the single child, the single spirit and the single creative darkness it dares to embrace? Are there better schools and lesser schools? Lighter schools and darker schools? And what of the sadness and fear that the very buildings proclaim? Does a school have anything to do with education or with learning or, for that matter, with creativity? Do they correlate in some complicated human statistic? And does it matter if they do or if they don't?

Let us be certain of one thing. Creativity comes out of a core of dimness and miraculous human mystery. We touch only its shadow, only its reflections, only its production. It comes out of a core of dimness with the suppressed fury of anger and love, sexuality and hate, poison and blood. (The antinomies again.) And it lasts but moments, not only in its own life force, but in the life cycle of those who urge its birth or watch its growth and demise. More serious than its evanescence is its impermanence. More sad than its unintelligibility is its swift passage and suddenly resumed indivisibleness. Work holds it all aloft, triumphantly aloft for some hours or for some lifetimes and then it's gone. But it has left life in its wake and the chance for others to be born, and this after all is realistically more important than rebirth, which belongs properly to mythology and literature.

If there is a sadness or grief at the passing of even a few creative spirits, it is most certainly that human beings prevent one another from reaching the ground, maybe even the school ground, where creative work often is, well, played out. This is the sadness. Because all of these perfectly human constraints continue to keep us from knowing just what about creativity comes from genes and what from God, what is really there and what exists only in our descriptions.

What then of school and the single child, Juliette and Paul? Simply this. If there is to be a sacred earth under learning and therefore under creativity, it is made so by the single child who walks upon that earth. Education, then, some would say, is little more than a prayer. But even as that, it would be enough.

Notes

1. From The Poet, in *Mallarmé: Selected Prose Poems, Essays & Letters,* translated by Bradford Cook, © 1956, the Johns Hopkins Press, pp. 95–96, with two paragraphs deleted.

2. From *Words* by Jean-Paul Sartre, translated from the French by Bernard Frechtman; reprinted with permission of the publisher. English translation copyright ©1964 by George Braziller, Inc., and Copyright © 1964 by Editions Gallimard.

3. From Why I Write, in *Orwell: A Collection of Essays.* New York: Doubleday Anchor, 1954.

4. Jean-Paul Sartre, op. cit.

5. From *Selected Poems of Bertolt Brecht,* translated by H. R. Hays, copyright 1947, by Bertolt Brecht and H. R. Hays. Reprinted by permission of Harcourt, Brace & World, Inc., and Ann Elmo Agency, Inc., New York.

6. From The Way, in *Ten Runes: Hasidic Sayings.* New York: Schocken Books, 1947.

7. From *The World as I See It,* by Albert Einstein. The Philosophical Library, New York, 1949. Reprinted by permission.

8. Reprinted with the permission of The Bodley Head Ltd., London, and Charles Scribner's Sons, New York, from *The Letters of F. Scott Fitzgerald,* pp. 32–34, edited by Andrew Turnbull. Copyright © 1963 Frances Scott Fitzgerald Lanahan.

IV
SOCIAL ISSUES

Now, finally, a few of my own takes on society, or, more precisely, a few scenes that have struck me as being particularly significant. The reader recalls my childhood encounters with justice and so is now prepared to hear a bit more of this second skin, this second family that society, in my eyes, is meant to be. So, from my own special chair, wherein I assure myself a lovely view of America, I offer, in this section, these few takes.

It is by now evident that in the minds of many social scientists, making a differentiation of the self and society is accomplished merely by distinguishing between social constructs of self and society; each encounters the other, each lives within the other. What gives them their unique definitions is precisely our own perceptions, visions, histories, circumstances, and probably, too, if we wish to be completely honest, our illusions. To be more precise, many of our takes on society actually represent our respective ideologies, which themselves provide an overarching social orientation.

Ideologies are remarkable phenomena inasmuch as they provide perspectives on the most personal of our past, present, and imagined events and experiences, in the same way that they structure the social and political realities that guide our individual actions as well as large-scale social movements. Ideologies help us to formulate and probably, too, tolerate the rational and the irrational facets of our lives. How we even conceive of something like the experience of a school or family, how we place value on something or articulate a personal or social grievance is rooted in ideological considerations, for, inevitably, norms and values constitute ideologies. Even the way we choose to investigate the world as disciplined social scientists or merely as responsible, thoughtful citizens is determined in great measure by our ideological leanings. Ultimately our versions and visions of a particular phenomenon, our reactions to a law or a particular ethic, find their origins in our ideologies, some of them shared with others, some of them not.

Like most everyone else presumably, I, too, watch human events unfold, most especially those events that, for one reason or another, touch something inside me, like that abiding childhood connection with emotion and justice, and particularly when they are contextualized within someone's reading and/or rendering of a personal story or narrative. I suppose one could say that there are certain accounts that just get under one's skin where they encounter that second skin, society's skin. Or is it that certain events and experiences that grab our complete attention for even an instant are the ones that smack us right at that point where the skins of self and society merge, a point of immediate sensation from which, among other things, ideologies and hence idiosyncratic takes on self and society are generated?

It is also the point, I have concluded, where nature locates a goodly number of nerve endings, a point prompting us to find some meaning, to make some sense of what it is we have encountered and then render our own intimate appraisals. Look at this, I often joke with myself, moving my metaphorical chair slightly to gain a better (internal and external) vantage point, I now play what I claim to be a pernicious and utterly unhelpful role in the culture, a role spawned by television news itself driven by the requirement to entertain: I have become a spin doctor.

modesty and loyalty. I guess that's all the two of them have in common. I'm not even certain she likes the name Kent.

Most children dislike the fact that some baseball players do drugs. Similarly, children would dislike the idea of my wife smoking. Unlike a lot of baseball players, she doesn't smoke or drink because she has to stay in shape, even if she isn't an American role model. Only three children that we know of want to grow up and be like her, and she gave birth to all of them. Therein lies another dissimilarity. The public would say that Jeter, Langston, and McGuire keep the fantasies of childhood alive, but that my wife keeps alive one of the necessary realities of childhood.

Ball players are big on stats; my wife is fond of ideas. All sorts of people crowd around baseball players in the parking lots when they leave the ball park. They order special license plates that read ROCKET and HOMER. A few people say good-bye to my wife when she leaves work. Nobody presses their face against the windshield to get one last look at her. Nobody shouts her name or feels the magic when they touch her car. Many students drive more expensive cars than my wife. The only magic is that her car starts on cold days. Neither my wife nor I can remember our license number. Most baseball players leave the park empty-handed. My wife drags home books and the written assignments of her students. And she goes shopping for food before she arrives home. She's twenty-five years older than most of the baseball players.

My wife says she is lucky to be a teacher. She doesn't risk the physical harm inherent in athletics, or face the constant possibility that she may be sent to another city. She has, however, known the reality of unemployment. Unlike baseball players, she realizes that a second income is required. Unlike baseball players, her world is filled with clamor, not glamour, and when she fails she can never use the expression, "It's only a game." When it's all over, a few people will secretly remember her, perhaps mention her, possibly even love her. A few will recognize her last name. But it won't be with the same nostalgia that people remember the Babe, Hank, Willy, Mickey, Whitey, Wade, and Orel.

Over the course of the year, my wife and others will talk about the state of American education, the priorities and values that Americans have chosen to perpetuate, differential incomes of various professions, the role and outcome of academic programs, magnet schools, drop-out rates, public and private education, school drug and alcohol programs, teenage pregnancies and suicide, academic standards and testing, education councils and school boards, teachers' strikes, guns and knives in classrooms, illiteracy, curriculum reform, universities administering community schools. In this way, too, my wife is sort of different. For most people will talk about how the Red Sox could have lost both Clemens and Vaughn, why the Yankees signed Clemens, how the Expos lost an entire pitching staff, and wonder if, with $12 million a year, Brown will be happy in Los Angeles.

My wife still believes that learning can be joyous and that education ultimately is more important for an individual and their culture than entertainment. She doesn't give up hope. She may wish that the Japanese would study our public schools as assiduously as they hunt for American real estate and over-the-hill ball players, but she holds to her faith. And when I'm not watching the game of the week, I support her. Yesterday I showed her an article in which some infielder, who will make millions of dollars because he had one good year somewhere, said that a major reason for choosing to play in Atlanta was that he didn't want his children to change schools.

On Thomas:
Clarence, Peeping, and Doubting

⟨~⟩

FOR THOSE OF US who party in Cambridge, Massachusetts, where no one forgets, we either block or repress, where no one blames, we project or displace, and where no one ever feels ecstatic but only hypomanic, Washington's lost weekend with the Senate Judicial Committee years ago was a psychologically tantalizing affair. For, along with the unforgivable treatment of sexual harassment and the daggers of racism, including Judge Clarence Thomas's noticeable self-hatred, a veritable panoply of psychological jargon and concepts were proffered, most of them with almost impeccable inappropriateness.

In most states, those of us in the mental health professions are obliged to accumulate continuing education credits in order to maintain licensure. For a while there, given the ingenuous references to concepts like personality disorder, hallucinations, fantasy, transference, and martyr complex, it appeared as though many of us might actually be able to propose that weekend experience as our continuing education requirement. While few of the concepts were treated with much sophistication, it was nonetheless extraordinary to note that psychoanalytic language now is part of the Congressional Record. The mention of a martyr complex brought forth chuckles, but transference was considered in the same respectful tone as P.M.S.

In the end, however, the lost weekend barely added up to a good intake interview. God only knows it went on long enough, but it failed in the same way America often fails; it failed because too many of us, not just our senators, choose not to look dead-on at human truths. If psychology does one thing well, it is not that it comes up occasionally with intriguing theories, jazzy concepts, or even nifty insights. Psychologists don't read minds or know any human soul better than that soul himself or herself. What psychology does, often in glorious fashion most never get to witness, is assist a person in groping toward the truth of his or her being. The process is commonly caricatured by that phrase, "How does that make you feel?" It is mimicked, albeit respectfully but nonetheless superficially, on national talk shows, but it remains a sacred process, one that barely was revealed during the lost weekend, where at least one lawyer, anyway, seemed willing to let herself be seen.

Most of us tend to resist the truths of our individual and social lives. Even those of us committing fortunes on psychotherapy spend inordinate amounts of time resisting the very thing we sought in the first place: our personal truths. And why do we do this? Because we sense that these truths somehow will displease us, and that the groping toward them will rank among the most terrifying and painful experiences of our lives. Presumably to protect ourselves, we resist the truths as well as the search, and justify this resistance on the grounds that no one in his right mind (though many in his left) purposefully seeks pain.

As a nation, we regularly do the same thing; we force ourselves to live in an "as if" state of mind. In time, our resistance has become institutionalized in the form of national distractions; we claim to want the truth. We watch *Sixty Minutes* and *20/20* in droves, but news investigations must be packaged as theater, otherwise we turn away from them even when they are served up to us free of charge. Enhancing our own distractive states, we ingeniously look dead-off rather than dead-on, as if turning on our night-vision apparatus when in fact the day is still bright. We seek entertainment and diversion rather than enlightenment and immersion. As Saul Bellow once remarked, we confuse information with knowledge, and, I would add, gossip with inner vision. We confuse legal with justice, and demand that scientific principles underwrite psychological insights and patterns of human behavior.

In our hunt for motives and explanations, we turn aside the essence of human beings: namely, their capacity to narrate experiences, or simply tell their stories. We're normally so quick to find the reasons behind human action we barely listen to the words of those brave enough to bear witness to experience. Too many of us interpret the dream before it is even fully recounted. In the same way, we depend on reviewers rather than novels, on critics rather than music and painting. We don't trust, apparently, our own intuitions and insights, hunches, feelings, and experiences. Psychologists are encouraged to undergo therapy themselves for a host of reasons. Mainly, in my eyes, so that they may know the exquisite pleasures and pains of inching toward the truth, as well as the seductively tantalizing sounds and sights that one inevitably creates in order to keep one off course, and hence resist truth.

Senator Arlen Specter of Pennsylvania brought wrath down upon himself by declaring Professor Anita Hill's testimony to be perjury. It is the only word lawyers know for narrative inconsistency. The psychologist, in contrast, eschews words like perjury, and wonders instead about the fabric of the story that, in its inevitable inconsistencies, reveals its richness and usually, too, its emotional intensity. The psychologist's mission, in other words, is to accompany the storyteller on her trip, on her road less traveled, in Robert Frost's words; it is not to trip her up. No life story emerges without inconsistencies; they are not necessarily the confirmation of falsehood, which is something else one learns in psychotherapy, but rarely in law school. The fact is a mother can love and abuse us, support and mock us. Her actions may leave us hurt, confused, and filled with recrimination and guilt, yet somehow we remain loyal. We return to her, telephone her, and love her even as we recall with humiliation and rage certain childhood experiences. No inconsistencies here; merely human complexities, antinomies, and contradictions. If one cannot abide by this complexity, one better stand clear of the postmodern art form known as the human personality.

Conversely, where psychologists claim to hear the barely audible sounds of truth is when bits of the unconscious—a concept, incidentally, wholly accepted during the hearings—pop through as they do in dreams and, yes, fantasies and hallucinations as well. In slips of the tongue and pen, it is alleged, manifestly unintended material pops through, as it does as well in a flashback, thereby revealing a truth about oneself, if one is able to snare and honor it as authentic data.

With all the psychological stuff flying around the Senate Judiciary Committee that one weekend years ago, with all those smarty-pants types from prestigious eastern schools who delighted in singing arias from their curricula vitae on national television, it is interesting that no one picked up on one such slip of the tongue. Clearly it won't be found in the Congressional Record along side Senator Orin Hatch's tasteless reference to Senator Edward Kennedy and a certain Massachusetts bridge. It was uttered by Judge Thomas. Intending to say "fact finding," the judge uttered instead "fact *fighting*." Make of it what you will, but it is rather delicious, isn't it?

Distraction occurs in the human mind just as it occurred in the Senate chambers and in the country's most powerful institutions. The rush to alter the mechanics of Supreme Court confirmations is but one of a million daily distractions. When President Bush suggested shortening the confirmation period to six weeks, it was merely distraction. Focusing on whether a six-week period would have avoided the problems of the Thomas hearings put me in mind of Alexis de Toquville's observation that rarely in America do the best people enter (or come to be chosen to enter) politics. Distraction by proposed changes in the process allows one to overlook the fact that the best may not be nominated to the bench, and that even Supreme Court justices, like unsupreme psychologists, are loaded with personal and ideological biases—as if counter-transference wasn't sufficiently disruptive—which, if not assiduously controlled, play significant roles in decision making and interpretation.

As a child, I believed with all my heart that judges made objective, truthful decisions. They were always right, just as they always determined *what* was right. The proof of this? They wore robes. In fact, without their robes they weren't judges; they were merely people. I held a similar belief about God who I also imagined wore a robe, only He wore white.

The child's mind, we have learned, moves beyond distraction into the wondrous realms of imagination and magic. That I imagined justices always told the truth, or created it in the first place, was part of the social order I had come to internalize and employ to assure myself that there was order in the outside world, and sanity in the inside world. To learn that a judge, a president, or a member of the Chicago Cubs was corrupt not only would have destroyed my outside world, it might have meant—and here is where psychology is eminently fascinating—that I was insane. A piece of my mind still holds to the notion that just as judges always tell the truth, so would my parents protect me from everything, even death. That I would believe that senators would do the right thing is not evidence of naïveté or misguidedness; more likely it is transference.

That America sank to all time lows during the lost weekend of the Justice Thomas confirmation hearings is the headline of a far more complicated and personally distressing drama. What hit us hard and evoked in us something instinctual and frightening was our recognition of just how paper thin is the line between control and the loss of it, sanity and insanity, beauty and degradation, rationality and irrationality, health and illness, civilization and anarchy. We had to talk with friends about the hearings not merely to share perspectives, but to broach the subject of national insanity. We asked each other, "Am I the only one . . . ?"

As happened during periods of assassinations, Watergate, and Contragate, the Cuban missile crisis, and the savings and loan scandal, we saw a knife cut through society's scrim, and for an instant witnessed the wild and helpless organism we fear, or even know ourselves to be. We saw instincts barely disguised, emotions barely constrained, and we lived for several days—abetted by commercial-less observation—as if in a hallucination or drug induced state we experienced as irreal. We saw just how close to the edge we can get, individually and collectively. Even worse, we saw—and when you see it on television it has to be true— how often ineffectual are the people we have selected to safeguard us and prevent from happening exactly what happened.

The Thomas hearings, America figured early on, would take the usual time and assume their usual pattern. Dirt would be hunted for, ideology, however masked, debated, and leaks and gossip would play their familiar roles in the advice and consent ordeal. Even the best dirt, however, is usually unable to effect a penetration of Washington's allegedly thick political skin.

Viewing the hearings, like the Kennedy, Bork, Souter, and Scalia hearings before it, was a bit like watching a dermatologist scan the surface of the body's largest organ. We discovered moles, scars, warts, even cancers. Importantly, the good dermatologist's reading of skin tells us much about what is to be found inside the organism it safeguards. The notorious political pundits remain the grand Washingtonian dermatologists. Their observations of the surface fascinate, their conjectures and analyses connect that surface to something deeper, and at times more foreboding.

Still, as they say, politics is just skin deep. It rarely goes deeper in Washington, at least publicly, except on those rare occasions when, without warning or anesthesia, an invisible surgeon makes a ripping incision. A president is killed, we stand on the brink of nuclear war, our banks are shown to be robbing us blind, a president's gang breaks into an office building or negotiates with the enemy, the Oval Office is used for trysts. Or perhaps a minister or teacher is found molesting a child, a doctor is discovered raping a patient. Or maybe our boss is speaking to us in ways that seem inappropriate and terrifying.

These are the instances of lacerations and compound fractures. Painfully, traumatically, we get a glimpse of the body's (and body politic's) interior. To the trained ones, the sight is magnificent, but most of us, like children, recoil; we are disgusted and mortified. We look as long as we can, almost as if we wished to see how many seconds we can stare without feeling nausea, but then we look away begging for someone to clean up the body or take it away. The next time we look it should appear good again, sound and whole, as always it was and always was meant to be.

Anyone who witnessed that Washington lost weekend felt the rupture and saw the fissures within. They saw the oozing out of what they felt to be disgusting, insidious, and ugly, the blood and gore, and they saw no one able to clean it up or even take charge of the cleanup. In psychotherapy, the process often works this same way. The client and therapist together push back the cobwebs and boulders of memory hoping (and dreading) to create interior fissures through which human truths may be born. While some of the rubble is merely brushed away, some remains immovable. Inevitably the effort produces pain along with the cleansing, anguish with the purifying.

In the most humanistic fashion, these moments of horror and dread, these moments when life appears out of control and one encounters the fragile threads of sanity and order, constitute quintessential moments of truth. Appropriately, some of us refer to it as the "sickening truth." Few of us can withstand these moments, for they carry such pain. So, within moments, only naturally needing to defend ourselves, we rush to distraction. Predictably, for days following the hearings, America's newspapers, magazines, and television news broadcasts were filled with stories and information on sexual harassment. Also predictably, the stories disappeared as quickly as they had appeared. It was good and valuable information, but it was not the truth that for a few heartbeats was there for the viewing, if not for the taking, during the lost weekend.

The slip of the tongue, the incision, the compound fracture have all disappeared now. Justice Thomas has his life, job, and name back. One assumes he has found the joy he claimed hadn't been his for the 103 days preceding the confirmation. Anita Hill has resumed her life, her mysteries and motives once again, appropriately, her own business. In the aftermath of the hearings, the president signed a token civil rights bill he had vetoed months before. Then Governor Clinton of Arkansas, at the time coveting the presidency, urged us to forge a new bond with politics, a surprisingly outworn idiom for a supposedly vibrant first-time candidate. Both actions missed the mark by miles, and symbolized the best and worst of political distraction.

Some believed the Thomas hearings to be a sham if only because each senator already had committed himself and was doing little more in his interrogations than documenting his preconceptions. For psychologists, it was hardly a sham; a shame perhaps, but not a sham, unless one equates sham with distraction, digression, and resistance. The answers senators begged to hear from Professor Hill regarding why she stayed with Mr. Thomas, telephoned him, and never before reported the harassment, in fact were contained within her narrative, but the senators were unable to search for truth because they were too busy fashioning it with their questions. A witness shares one thing with her interrogator: Both hold to their stories and story line, thereby making it impossible for the other person to budge. Not surprisingly, the senators found precisely what they wanted to find and believed they knew in the first place.

On the crest of Yale University, whose law school received ten billion dollars of free advertising—advertising the school would gladly have refused—are the Latin words, *lux* and *veritas*, light and truth. Indeed, there was light and truth that one weekend in Washington, the same light and truth the anatomist, pathologist, and psychologist discover during those very moments the rest of us find sickening and inhuman. The rest is all darkness and untruth.

Most of us don't even examine our own skin, much less wonder about the clamor and action of the great inside that remains to be deciphered. Not merely symbolically, we cover our skin, our private and public parts. As for the tiny fraction necessarily left exposed if we are to touch, see, smell, hear, and speak, we paint it with chemicals appropriately called makeup and blush. In the biblical sense, ashamed by what we witnessed during the lost weekend, we now rush to cover it over with rhetorical makeup and the distractive excitement of yet another presidential election. We'll go poll shopping, mall shopping, food shopping, and fun shopping. Some of us may even get involved in urging the Washington Redskins football team to change its name to something less offensive to Native Americans.

However mangled and ugly it may have seemed, we nonetheless caught a glimpse of the truth. The part of me still angry about the fact that judges do lie, professionals with advanced degrees do betray, and parents die, wishes to take America's head in my hands and force it to look at the truths of our collective and individual lives. The image reminds me of the proverbial movie scene in which the once stoic hero suddenly loses his mind and grabs some poor soul and forces him to look at the face of death, misery, or evil.

Like the surgeon, I find myself content to leave the wound open a moment longer so that I may continue to work inside. I am the psychologist not yet easing the person away from a painful remembrance. Look at that ripped-open body, I want to call out, for you will find truth in it, the same truth that is found in death and dying, something else from which Americans continually seek to distract themselves.

Everything now has receded. The hearings are long past; they're old news. Americans have abbreviated attention spans, made even shorter by television. For a moment, however, this country cracked open affording us a chance to see the inside, the bowels and sinews, and we recoiled, ironically latching on to a safer raft, harassment. The rest, the instinctual, the hate inherent in sexism and racism, the heinous and ugly, the despicable and pathetic and yet all utterly human, have been closed up, and thankfully so, we add. The hearings were like a comet; we'll just have to wait for another opportunity to witness the likes of it again, and next time perhaps, grab hold of its tail.

I am no different from anyone else who stayed to the bitter end of the lost weekend. With all my cynicism and anger, not to mention desperate pleas to engage the truth no matter what the cost and pain, I found myself those last few evenings utterly transported not by the truths of Mahler or Schubert, Bellow, Fanon or Sartre, but by extra inning World Series baseball games.

I lay awake late into the night, the games, as they say, making me forget all the cares of the world. Having no particular allegiance to either team, I found myself in these early hours serene and at peace, enjoying the good play, forgiving the bad, reflecting only rarely on the madness of athletes' salaries, and thinking of Justice, something wholly absent during the lost weekend, as nothing but a sweet swinging Atlanta outfielder.

Director's Call

⌒

THE NEWS FROM CALIFORNIA is tragic. A famed Hollywood actor and director has revealed that his seven-year-old daughter has died of AIDS. What is more, his wife and five-year-old son also carry the dreaded virus. Quite possibly, he, too, is a carrier.

Once again we shake with fright. Indeed, it is a plague, we say, wondering how we would react if the tragedy hit us. We wonder too, whether one of the blood transfusions we have received over the years has ignited the same physical havoc as when the director's wife received her ill-fated pints during a complicated pregnancy.

The news reminds us that AIDS travels in all circles and neighborhoods. Gays and drug users, contrary to popular conception, own no monopoly on this one death notice. These facts, presumably, we know by now. It is pure denial to believe that only those certain types remain susceptible to the disease.

There is, however, another story to this announcement of one family's heartache. For the director, albeit courageous in the act of going public with his account, has been obliged to reveal his pain. In truth, if the press accounts are accurate, he only went public after learning that one of those ubiquitous tabloids had gotten wind of his daughter's death and was planning to publish its findings. To make the story more dignified, he told it to a more dignified branch of the press. Thus we learn from him directly the outlines of what he and his family have been going through as they bury a little girl and wait to see what other horrendous fate may await them.

Surely the director's announcement serves to humanize AIDS. Surely, too, there must be no tampering with the freedoms of the press. It remains democracy's voice as well as our most trustworthy watchdog of democracy's progress and miscreants. As we perhaps spread a disease by keeping silent, so do we destroy our freedom by limiting the right of the press to make its inquiries and report its findings and opinions.

Enter now the elements of sensitivity, discretion, and taste. The director's choice, obviously, was to remain silent. He was not forced out of hiding exactly, but out of a perfectly justifiable family privacy. So what we get in the end is gossip, pure and simple, a form of gossip, moreover, many of us have come to adore. A well-known man with this sort of story looms as great copy. The interviews will commence and we will watch him tread his way through interrogatives like: How do you feel about what happened? How do you cope with such difficulties? Do you believe in God, and if so, then how do you explain this happening? Maybe, too, someone will nab the exclusive interview with his wife.

To repeat, the essence of democracy quite possibly teeters on the right to make these inquiries, no matter how smarmy, in some instances, they appear. In the end, however, what exactly do we learn from it all? That the man is in pain? That he lives with anger, guilt, confusion? That he can't enter his daughter's bedroom without feeling physically ill? That he now will donate money for AIDS research?

More to the point, one wonders what it is about our lives that makes celebrity gossip part of our very blood. Some claim we have no heroes, others claim that heroes are people who, upon reaching larger-than-life proportions, are brought to ruin through self-imposed or externally caused tragedy. Is this why we often secretly delight in the tragic news of celebrities? An announcement by this same director that his wife gave birth to a child would mean little to us. The child's death through AIDS warrants headlines. Celebrities weeping are more appealing—we say human—than celebrities laughing. We dwell on their lavish ways, their ostentatious houses, boats, and parties, but, best of all, apparently, is their sadness, their scandals, and ultimate downfalls. So while we claim to worship celebrities, they very well may have become the symbols of our own ambivalence about capitalism, or at least the most conspicuous and lavish successes of capitalism.

The celebrity's tragedy remains the grand leavener. We say it makes him or her human, but actually tragedy does more; it transforms the have into the have not. In turn, our own family, free of AIDS, at this moment anyway, becomes the have. For a while we're content, but only until the next celebrity reveals his own rich and famous lifestyle.

In some important respect, civility rests on constraint, and constraint, as Goethe observed, is an art. In all of our significant relationships, we are forever capable of hurting if not destroying people by divulging what we know about them. The social psychologist Georg Simmel remarked that relationships are predicated on what I know about you that you don't know I know, and vise versa. His words could launch a vaudeville routine, but they speak a truth. For there are lines demarcating the boundaries that permit relationships to flourish. Demarcations of the private from the public, the intimate from the sexual, the discrete from the indiscreet, help to sustain friendship, civility, and probably, too, civilization.

Our lives are not meant to be open books. It is not incumbent upon us, furthermore, to open them to anyone. Nor is it proper for others to pry us open. Psychoanalysis reveals the extent to which people resist opening their lives even as they realize this to be the purpose of their analytic undertaking. Ironically, some of the most unsuccessful books are the ones in which people tell all. They are rivaled only by those works in which ersatz biographers pry open the unopenable. Either genre gains its power from gossip and runs the risk of mass appeal. The frequently proffered justification that gossip offers us insight into the human condition rings false. The human condition is revealed to us through an examination of the *inner* life and its confrontations with history and circumstance. The *private* life, conversely, offers us insight mainly into one of the most profitable commodities our culture has unearthed: gossip. As a husband crosses a line of fidelity when unbeknownst to his wife he commits adultery, so does his wife transgress when she reveals his vulnerabilities and frailties at a dinner party.

The healthy person takes charge of his or her life; the healthy society need not invade the citizen's privacy for mere pleasure or profit, or just plain news. The social good must be at stake when we make the decision to cross the line of decency, or retreat from it. Granted, it's frustrating to be close to some intriguing or titillating territory only to stop oneself at an invisible border. Self-imposed constraint always is in order when human insights, freedoms, and life itself lie in the balance.

Given the rules of our marketplace, no foul can be called when a newspaper publishes an article in the hope that it will draw readership, recognition, and hence profit. Given the intent of democracy, moreover, no curbs ought be placed on the work of reporters and editors, but that's the easy part. The more difficult moments arise when those invisible lines defining constraint, sensitivity, and taste enter our deliberations.

No one facing the dreadful drama known to one Hollywood director must feel obliged to tell his story. The human heart must be as carefully protected by society as it is by anatomy. In this case, the director should have been allowed to stage the scene, not we the audience, and especially not gossips masquerading as journalists.

The Right to Silence

IT WAS HARDLY SURPRISING that the hospitalization of Kitty Dukakis years ago would be of such interest to the media. Anything untoward occurring behind the closed doors of public figures signals the rush of reporters and photographers. And when the news is sketchy or just plain withheld, the rush becomes a stampede.

In the absence of facts, the press clearly struggled in their inability to dig out information. One television reporter actually prefaced her broadcast with the words, "Rumor has it . . ." Indeed, rumor was about all anyone had to go on. Accordingly, the media turned to the experts for discussions of seasonal depression, alcoholism, and the psychological effects of living in a fishbowl. For once, however, the public didn't buy it. Normally hungry for gossip packaged in any form, accounts of Mrs. Dukakis's hospitalization were rejected. There just are times, the public seemed to say, on talk shows and through letters to the editors of newspapers, when people should be left alone, and this is one of those times. The act of withholding information about Mrs. Dukakis, which so irritated and frustrated journalists, notified the public (and, interestingly, many members of the media) that the family was saying back off, respect our privacy. This one time, apparently, the public argued for the right *not* to know. How strange the sounds of people demanding silence.

Ironically, amid the debates on personal privacy and the need for public information, it was the public that demanded a standard of ethical conduct in personal investigations that the authors of this standard were unable to uphold. Years ago, Dr. Dana Farnsworth, a Harvard psychiatrist, urged his colleagues to be especially prudent when speaking to members of the media. He wrote of the necessity of studying well the diagnosis of a patient before reporting publicly about that person. He warned of the need to maintain confidentiality, which of course in this case was absent from the beginning. In addition, he offered two admonitions that, in the days following Mrs. Dukakis's hospitalization, were utterly ignored: first, that we speak with the patient, and second, that we receive permission to violate promises of confidentiality. The mental health professionals who leapt forward with their interpretations, explanations, and treatment plans, thereby eschewing these ethical standards, only irritated the public that much more.

Surely it is disheartening to hear a television reporter rely on rumor. Surely, too, it borders on the preposterous to hear a television host ask a mental health professional, What is Kitty Dukakis thinking at this moment? Still, the ethical standards of the mental health professional are never weakened by ignorant inquiries. They are weakened by conjecture, ideology, hunch, and the articulation of unconfirmed preconceptions being passed off as psychiatric truths.

In the aftermath of the infamous hospitalization, we listened to professionals tell us that Mrs. Dukakis was overloaded with all the emotions of her family; that Mr. Dukakis, still disturbed by childhood experiences with his older brother, had no outlet for his emotions, which he furthermore considers dangerous. We learned that as Mrs. Dukakis grew depressed by her husband's loss of the White House, Mr. Dukakis turned away from her. We learned that women carry the weight of their husband's problems and that she in particular was in psychological trouble because of her caring nature. Finally, we learned that both Mr. and Mrs. Dukakis had turned away from emotionally supportive people.

It all made for such provocative reading and listening that we quickly forgot the qualifiers like "speculation" or "based on public persona." We forgot the fact the most of the experts never had met a member of the Dukakis family, but "knew" them strictly through appearances in the media. In short, while the ideas may have fascinated us, we were left with little more than gossip and the ingredients of myth, which brings us to yet another irony.

Unwilling to meet Dr. Farnsworth's standards, or become aware of them in the first place, the myths put forth by the mental health professionals may have caused the public an anguish whose sources they never acknowledged. Ours is not a culture that honors mental illness and health as it does organic illness and health. We maintain a more childish, frightened, unenlightened approach to matters of the mind than we do to any organ of the body. Too many of us still attribute the cause of mental problems to weakness or lack of will. We continue to stigmatize those who suffer with mental illness as well as their families, and withhold admiration for those who treat them. Myth, ignorance, and distrust still enshroud the mentally ill and their doctors. Indeed, too many in our society still see the practitioner in the context of insubstantial feminine caregiver, which means slightly less than rock-solid substantial masculine doctor.

There is a very discrete fear, at once primitive and complex, that we maintain: If I should consult one of these emotional healers, will my most valuable secrets remain safe, or will I be revealed? Will others learn what I choose to keep private, even from myself? Will others know me intimately after I utter but a few words, and in so doing will they strip me of my mysteries, allusions, and art? Where are my own boundaries of the private and public, and who but I may draw them?

Unfortunately, when the healers speculate without data, confirmation, diagnosis, or permission, they arouse more than suspicion in the public's mind; they arouse resentment and fright in the public's heart. We ask the physician for confidentiality, for it assuages our feelings of weakness, vulnerability, and fright. We stand in awe of the person who knows our body better than we ourselves. Still, we know in some mystical way that no one understands our minds better than we ourselves. It is our last human boundary, our last refuge from the abyss we barely can articulate.

For we all contemplate going crazy, losing control, committing suicide, ending up in that place that carries the appellations "funny farm," "loony bin," "booby hatch." We may be comforted knowing that fellow citizens study the mind and its frequent misadventures, but we beg nonetheless for the sanctuary of private offices and confession booths. We may recognize that women more often than men take the pledge to safeguard human relationships, but woman or man, we request professional discretion and respectful constraint.

"There but for the grace of God" turned into something all too real when Kitty Dukakis was hospitalized. Many of us felt ourselves observing her from inside and outside as well. We heard, somehow, her private torment and her family's consternation. That her mother-in-law was hospitalized at the same time only brought us closer to her and her family. Yet we heard as well the gossip chorus of the media and the healers, the well-intentioned invaders and storytellers. We watched as though we were being drawn on to the stage of a Greek drama until suddenly we, the audience, claimed a say in its authorship, and hence its outcome. In this final act we voted for confidentiality, closed files, and the end to incursions into a family's private realms.

At no time in recent memory have Dr. Farnsworth's admonitions seemed more relevant. They offer tangible guidelines not only to the professional, but to all of us seeking respectful and moral ways of dealing with one another. For it is to this that living beings, irrespective of the texture of their emotional worlds, ultimately are entitled.

The Voice of Harassment

ON READING AN ARTICLE on sexual harassment by Gloria Steinem, I was moved to write a letter to an editor proffering an ironic thanks to her for clarifying the laws pertaining to sexual harassment as well as placing them in proper perspective. As Ms. Steinem reads the laws, a man can do anything he wishes with a woman as long as he stops when she says "No." What could be clearer and cleaner, and how clever of her to avoid that perpetually messy matter of morality. It reminds one of Harvard Professor Carol Gilligan's distinction between (masculine) morality as abstract justice, and (feminine) morality as human care. It reminds one as well of an old story, one that long predates Clinton, Packwood, et al., of the man standing on the corner asking every passing woman to have sex with him. "Goodness," a friend reacts, "you must have millions of women slapping you in the face." "True enough," the man replies, "but I also get a lot of sex!"

Unfortunately, something profound gets lost in even careful readings and interpretations of the law, something that cannot be overlooked. Sexual harassment involves legal definitions surely, as well as ideological adumbration, but most importantly it refers to human action that hurts girls and women in ways, even years later, they cannot always adequately articulate or explain. The nature of the hurt and humiliation of sexual harassment may render behavior following the harassment seem peculiar, illogical, unpredictable, inexplicable. Psychologists, psychiatrists, teachers, and social workers frequently encounter this sort of hurt and the psychological if not always logical repercussions of it.

In her book *Reviving Ophelia,* Mary Pipher alleges that America is a "girl poisoning culture," "a girl killing place." Strident remarks, hyperbole even, but Pipher has in mind the human cost of sexism, which includes matters of glass ceilings, inequitable power arrangements, and sexual harassment and rape. It is not a poison easy to assay, and the aftermath of years of poisoning, alas, is impossible to quantify. In fact, as Professor Gilligan has taught us, the best we can do, often, in listening to girls who have been poisoned, is just learn from them.

And herein another problem Gilligan once noted about girls, a problem that becomes an ingredient of the poison. Girls learn early on to mask their feelings and act in ways that are different from the ways they actually are thinking. It was Simone de Beauvoir who suggested that at some point in childhood, girls begin to stop *being* and start *seeming*. Boys traditionally, after all, are not taught to be as selfless, caring, and giving. As Pipher remarks, they are not told to smile, as girls are, when they feel down. Girls, in contrast, are rarely encouraged to be authentic, but instead are taught the "value" of pleasing just about everyone.

One might do well to think of these notions as one reflects on any woman's account of sexual harassment. It is not enough to ask whether the woman *seemed* credible, truthful, or exploitative. To judge the woman claiming harassment on how she seemed is to perpetuate the same old pernicious assessments we have always made of girls and women, the very same assessments we teach girls to make of themselves: Everything is in the appearance, the looks.

One of the great ironies of Western culture is that while girls and women are given almost total license to appear any way they wish and employ almost any device or accouterment they imagine will enhance their appearance, thereby making themselves more appealing to others, they are at the same time asked to quiet their inner world, their inner voice. Surely this demand is part of what Professor Pipher deems the degrading poison.

In a final irony, I sense that many of us, like well-brought-up girls, never revealed our truest feelings about the White House scandals. Would we be so forgiving of our spouses and lovers if they pulled off what the president pulled off? What a man does in his private life has no relationship whatsoever to his conduct in the public sector? Is the matter of morality so messy that we don't consider it at all in making judgments about human action? Upon discovering that our partner has been unfaithful we don't utter phrases like, "And what precisely am I supposed to tell the children?"

Oh, yes, the children. In conversation after conversation, the issue that brought everyone to silence was the one involving the president's daughter and what she might have been thinking and feeling. Ultimately, this was the painful and saddening place where none of us wished to go. Here was the lingering hurt no less easy to put into words than the feelings of having been harassed. It is, however, the piece that gets us closer to knowing what it might be like to have people we love and want so much to love us, do things that hurt and humiliate us, and then seem incredulous that we would even mention these things.

So how about that story of the guy asking all those women for sex? Pretty great, no? I wonder whether my family would find it funny. In fact, I wonder how they would feel about my even telling it.

Miss Spoke

⁓

LETTE POGEBRIN, THE FEMINIST author, sits on the stage of the *Oprah Winfrey Show*. She is celebrating women speaking openly to one another. You see, Oprah, she proclaims triumphantly. Men can't do this. They can't be intimate. That's why they don't appear on your show. Oprah doesn't challenge the generalization but instead turns to an audience member: "You say what?"

A radio commercial reminds people that greeting cards for all occasions may be purchased at a particular pharmacy. The commercial reveals a group of men being trained to say, "I love you." They are urged, cajoled, pleaded with, but they cannot stammer past "I lo . . . I lo . . ." Alas, they must remain content to buy a greeting card.

Somewhere near the end of an Academy Awards ceremony, Martin Short and Carrie Fisher conclude an especially inane routine wherein they appear on stage wearing identical dresses. When Mr. Short departs, Ms. Fisher announces to millions of people: "Men. You can't live with them, you can't kill them!"

Three isolated examples selected from a host of media "events," all celebrating the alleged sport of male bashing. Absurd, erroneous, offensive, no one questions Ms. Fisher's remark, no one reminds us of how serious the repercussions would be if any group other than men were the object of such humiliation and venom. Blacks: You can't live with them, you can't kill them! Gays: You can't live with them, you can't kill them!

There are other more sophisticated versions of this antimale bigotry. Pretentious tomes "demonstrate" that all men unconsciously despise women and through the act of love making seek physically to rip them open. Other works "show" that men are incapable of sensitivity or intimacy, unable to identify their feelings, much less express them, have no understanding of or appreciation for women and children. One commercial years ago even instructed us that men have fewer emotions than women. Men are said to be left brained, women right—and therefore, presumably, correct—brained. Men are said to be instinctively drawn to science, technology, and business, rarely to the caring professions. Men are charged with living incessantly with the desire to rape. Furthermore, they must acknowledge a primitive and neurological apparatus that makes them simultaneously homophobic and unable to inhibit an instinct for infidelity.

Pathetically, the sport of male bashing even invokes men's words spoken by women. The movie theater audience watching *Dangerous Liaisons* was stirred by Glenn Close's analysis of male-female differences. She wins the audience, or some of it, with stinging attacks on men and succinct observations of women's natural prowess. One felt men squirm, women sitting up taller. Few people, apparently, were troubled by the fact that it was a man who had adopted another man's play and written the words for Ms. Close to speak. The same could be said for hundreds of television and theatrical scripts where men draw magnificent portraits of women and brutal ones of men, only to hear the audience cheer for the women as if, somehow, "the game" finally has been decided. Landford Wilson's *Fences* offers a perfect example. Poor James Earl Jones had to wait to utter his lines as women in the audience screamed their approval of his wife's speeches.

In an age when we battle the exclusion and belittling of women, as well as their objectification and dehumanization, we find ourselves in an intellectual kindergarten in which culture heroes urge us to join some primordial battle of the sexes. Magazine articles seem to adore putting men down for the sake of readership. How to get your man to do this, speak up, be loving, understanding, or something else fundamentally human that only women have mastered. On the national television talk shows, where Americans have received much of their psychological education, we see male and female hosts, sycophants to women audiences, espousing nonsensical and offensive positions. The generalizations rain down like hailstones. Men are always ... ? Why can't men ... ? Wouldn't it be great if just once men ... ? Everyday more authors emerge with how-to books helping women to wade through dense, inane, ignorant, insensitive, invulnerable, inarticulate men.

In television programs and commercials, when they aren't being absurdly macho or foolishly opaque, men often are portrayed as helpless, inept, illiterate, indelicate, thoughtless, moronic, mindless, uncoordi-

nated, power crazy, money-crazy, sex-starved boors. There is hardly a
male character in any sitcom that acts kindly, intelligently, sensitively,
modestly. Howard Hesseman in the long vanished *Head of the Class* was
one exception, except like many characters of its ilk, there was no place
in his life for a permanent woman partner. More generally, all the
"good" guys remain the same cool unemotional blokes—well, they're
capable of anger, but aren't all men?—we came to love and presumably
dismissed in the 1950s. If one runs through the file of male television
characters, likable or insipid, all essentially are one dimensional and
about as representative of American men as White House residents are
representative of the electorate. Bill Cosby, likable, clearly helpful, and
style setting, became the national symbol of fatherhood, no less. Better
him than most, but still a fraudulent image. Even the genial Dr. Hux-
table was unable to repulse the prejudicial claptrap about men emanat-
ing mainly from New York and Los Angeles media mills.

We have forgotten Flannery O'Connor's words: "Life is a human
drama." It belongs neither to men nor women, but to all the males and
females of the world, as well as the maleness and femaleness in each of
us. For the purpose of gaining rating points and commercial revenues,
Ms. Lake, Ms. Raphael, and Mr. Springer continue to reduce complex
psychological fare not only to elemental levels, but often to positions
where women are encouraged to "triumph" over men. In these moments, presumably, and there are many of them, women feel a release
from the oppression of their lives, an oppression to which men, surely,
contribute. Unhappy women in unhappy relationships and unhappy careers want to know that women everywhere live with or work for some
incorrigible, uneducable, immutable lout. Sisterhood looms as the only
salvation, and Sister Ricki, Sister Sally, and Brother Jerry will lead us to
the promised land.

While it is the loudest and most pervasive voice, it still is only one
voice, one meager level of observation and analysis. One voice carried
more by outrage than intellectual substance. There are other voices,
however unknown to millions of Americans: Men and women alike
whose stories and experiences told in a variety of forms, allow us to see
the truths of ourselves, our histories, and our circumstances. Because
their visions and expressions are so profound, they preclude us from in-
dulging in prelatency sexual envies and competitiveness. They not only
take us in their art beyond bankrupt rhetoric and cant, they hold out to
us the power of O'Connor's human drama. By definition, these seers of
the human experience do not belong to popular culture, but instead to

what is still called, alas, high or elite culture. And surely no one wants to belong to *that* group, except for a few college students who ultimately will see the light and apply to law or business school.

Granted, men rape and murder and molest and drink and drug. That is, some men do. Granted, men never come up with the "right" emotion at the "right" time for women. That is, some men don't. Granted, men confuse sexuality with sensuality, and care little about the magic of the mind and heart. That is, some men do. Yet aside from the glorious worlds created by millions of men in this and other countries, worlds that dispel the angry bigotry and misogyny associated with male bashing, popular culture has access to a host of public—or is it public television?—voices that do the same thing.

A truly democratic society supporting not only specific rights but the right to safeguard rights, invariably watches its freedoms edge toward absurd extensions and exaggerations. Free to say whatever they wish, and with all their good intentions and deeds, television's talking heads can proffer the most bigoted observations. Unfortunately, it takes the intellectual discipline of a Barbara Tuchman or Joseph Campbell, a Hannah Arendt or a Malcolm Cowley to budge us beyond anti–intellectual, singularly emotional and fundamentally undisciplined thinking about the sexes. We haven't even got the language right: We still speak of the "opposite" rather than the other sex.

Male bashing is little more than my package whacking your package. Substance often proves to be irrelevant to these "discussions"; in the name of image, anything goes, and loyalty to the truth seems to have become off limits. Importantly, in a democratic society, anybody can play, any voice heard, any image etched, any package sold, any truth created, or concealed. In short, anybody can become a celebrity; all it takes is a smidgen of outrage. The only problem is that advancing intellectually or emotionally by stomping on some hated object and through the use of outrageously false icons, language, concepts, and (fantasized) observations is a bit like repairing a burst water pipe by wall papering over it.

In the end, most of the generalizations made about men in an unthinking, acrimonious popular culture require no rejoinder, in the same way that allegations about minority group's sex drives or work capacities no longer require comment. That men won't feel, don't feel, can't feel is right up there scientifically with African-American people's lack of buoyancy. However, to the pharmacy advertisers: Be it known that many men unhaltingly pledge their love to a variety of people everyday, and mean it, and not as the moguls do when they babble, "Love ya, baby. Let's do lunch." To Ms. Pogebrin usually so filled with sensible insights and purposeful rhetoric: You're right. Some men refuse to appear on talk shows, though probably not *Oprah,* because the exceptions of their behavior and mentality are ill conceived; the show's the thing, the stereotypes offensively confining, or because the notions they might wish to proffer are a trifle too complicated to be reduced to easy how-to slogans and pop psych bromides (and tranquilizers) in a matter of milliseconds. In brief, masochism hurts. Besides, too many Americans have announced through their viewing habits that watching people think and speak hardly makes for good television.

Finally to Ms. Fisher, who one hopes had neither her father nor ex-husband Paul Simon in mind during the Academy Awards: When some of us are asked to award an Oscar, you will see us eschew the twin gown routine and hear us say something like, Women: How utterly rich our lives are with them; how utterly inconceivable is life without them. Or us, for that matter.

Graduation Speech

〜

IT IS SAID THAT graduation speeches normally rank highest on our list of least memorable events. I suppose this is because they typically contain the predictable messages about pursuing one's dreams, standing up for one's rights, thanking one's parents, speaking out in the face of injustice. So it may be true that that we dismiss them within days of hearing them. Yet one has continued to stay with me.

It was a truly magnificent morning in Boston when the Reverend Juan Julio Wicht Rossel spoke to the throngs assembled for the university graduation ceremonies. It is important to know that literally four weeks before the graduation, Reverend Wicht Rossel had been held hostage at his own request in the embassy in Peru. He had actually volunteered to remain with the hostages as long as they felt he was needed. He refused an invitation from the guerrillas to leave the embassy building, even when they warned him that he might not get out alive. He even offered his services to them. Four weeks to the day before the graduation, a reverend had completed performing his theological and, one might add, moral duty to minister to congregants, and now he was free.

After examining a host of political, sociological, and economic variables that may well have seemed irrelevant to some in the audience, Reverend Wicht Rossel told of a Japanese computer game, at that very moment coming on to the market. The game was designed on the military release of the hostages in Peru, an inspired strike that nonetheless resulted in the deaths of several soldiers. It was then the speech became memorable. That a tragic event, a quintessential human moment had been transformed overnight into a moneymaking scheme, a game no less, made one feel disgust. How clear-cut the connections between capitalism and the most basic, banal, and often selfish motives and personalities.

I thought of an American sports company slogan: "Just do it." Just do whatever you feel, just do whatever moves you. Why use your brain, your knowledge, your reasoning capacity, when you can go with your gut! Forget issues of fortune, compassion, ministering, thoughtfulness; just do it! Forget, too, Goethe's extraordinary remark that constraint is an art.

I thought, if military strikes, guerrilla attacks, murder, killing are all grist for the capitalist mill—somehow legitimized by becoming fodder for the glorious computer—then how can anyone be surprised that children in this country can't—how should I put it?—learn to control themselves, hold their violent impulses in check, honor authority, maintain touch with what is human in all of us, see the reasons for choosing to work for minimum wage when criminal activities in a month will earn them a king's ransom.

I thought, how utterly complicated are the tendrils that link the most delicate parts of the mind, human intelligence and sensibility, to almost incomprehensible political and economic structures and cultural puzzles. It's not only that the world is small; that is something technology has pressed home often enough. More precisely, it is that historical events and contemporary structures and movements everywhere continually shape not only the substance of our minds, but the very structure of them as well.

The Swiss psychologist Jean Piaget was right. Assimilation of new knowledge and the accommodation to it, which in turn prepares for future learning and hence the constant restructuring of the mind, occurs with every new moment of historical unraveling and cultural happening. In one regard, it is extraordinary that the human mind could transform tragedy into profit, and so quickly. In another regard, at times it feels disgusting, although popular culture admonishes me that I am not to find anything disgusting. Whatever humans create, promote, feel, is to be understood in some appropriate context and then, if not accepted, at least condoned. God forbid that I should ever think seriously of censorship or defy the First Amendment.

Yet I do think of censorship; not of the press, not of television programming, not of movies, and most assuredly not of artists. A civilized soul, it seems, has censorship built into the cells that nourish reasoning and thoughtfulness. In fact, censorship appears to be an ingredient of freedom, for it molds those currents that ultimately yield taste, respect, honor, morality. Censorship lives, perhaps, at the center of the responsibility of which graduation speakers typically remind us when they list the requirements of freedom. Alas, maybe these messages, too, become quickly forgettable.

Reverend Juan Julio Wicht Rossel did indeed give those of us who attended the graduation ceremony a lesson in politics, history, and economics. But without this lesson there is, I believe, no genuine understanding of the human personality, social behavior, or cultural identity. Without this lesson, words like diversity, equality, and opportunity lose their power. For, aware of them or not, political, economic, and cultural influences live in our biological endowments, our definitions of ourselves, and shape our capacity to contemplate as well as achieve genuine freedom.

Pointing

❧

THERE WERE ONLY FIVE of us in the little Central Oregon park that afternoon. I had accompanied my grandson who loves to play on the shiplike structure in the corner of the play area, while another man watched over his son and daughter. My eyes went back and forth between my own golden-haired Luke and the blond father who was assisting his daughter on what was to be her maiden voyage on the slide, her first descent ever.

I turned to check on my grandson who was playing with the little girl's brother, when squeals of pleasure brought my attention back to the girl on the slide. She made it. And she loved it. Then suddenly I saw her father, his triumphant daughter cradled in his left arm, point his right arm to the sky, the limb as stiff as iron and the one finger practically extending to the clouds.

It couldn't be. What has happened in this country that religion has become yet another ad campaign? What has happened in this overly commercialized, faux-heroic, entertainment-hyped-up world that every minuscule moment of success or good fortune has to be punctuated with that body erect posturing, and that pointing as if a person knew God's precise location. Here's the pitch, strike three. *Yes!* Sink slowly to knees, and point. There's a long pass into the end zone it's . . . *Intercepted!* Run around the field, clutch the ball, and don't forget to point. He's at the fifteen, the ten, five, *Touchdown!* Celebration. Whoops. Not yet. He's kneeling, the head in the helmet is bowed, the man's praying. Give him space. Man praying here.

Sitting on my couch, barely able to discern the game given the obstructions of the network's logo in the screen's bottom right and the corporate scoreboard in the upper left, I'm grousing. What is this, a church or a stadium! Who's up there? Narcissus? What's all this sudden interest in air rights? Didn't your mother ever teach you it wasn't polite to point! Hey, how come when you drop the pass you don't point? And how do you explain The Man wanting your team to lose? You ever think of *that*?

My anger, of course, is mere bravado, I have begun to worry. Something troubles me about all the road signs and billboards that read, I'VE NEVER QUESTIONED *YOUR* EXISTENCE. Call me paranoid, but I'm growing frightened by the omnipresence of that beautiful Irish woman and the fabulous Della Reese. This *Touched by an Angel* business is making me nervous, because those aren't the sort of angels that go poking around in my religion. Bad enough that at 35,000 feet I have to listen to advertisements for the very airlines I'm flying. But what is happening that someone has decided we should all be watching reruns of *Touched by an Angel* up there? You don't have to be an intellectual to be disappointed that a president names his Lord as the most significant philosopher; something makes me nervous about that response.

Years ago, my friend Freddy told me there's two kinds of people in the world: People who get shoved into box cars, and people who shove them. Everybody gets the reference, everybody detects the cynicism, most recognize the sounds of a Marxist paradigm describing the powerful owners and those they govern. Freddy, however, was only two-thirds right, and 66 percent doesn't pass the test. There's another group, the group that makes certain people don't get shoved into box cars. The powerful memorial to the holocaust victims in Jerusalem is reached only after the visitor traverses an alley of trees dedicated to the righteous Gentiles. Everyone must recognize that third group who hid people, nurtured people, saved people.

A couple of years ago, my wife and I sat in the sweltering heat of a central Philadelphia church witnessing the ordination of an African-American woman as priest of the episcopal church. Technically, there may not have been any of "my kind" in the sanctuary that Saturday morning, but, in the end, they were all my kind, and it was a minion. This magnificent woman walked up the aisle as minister and strode back an hour later transformed. This was a ceremony of transcendence that made one weep. I couldn't even speak to her as she greeted the congregation on our way out. That woman will die, Freddy, before she lets people get shoved into box cars on her watch. And you can bet she doesn't go around pointing. And neither do the other genuinely religious figures. They invite the spiritual, ultimately causing us to look upward, perhaps, but only metaphorically.

I am advised there are now three Jewish men playing in the major leagues. I have no idea who they are, but, based on their names, I figure they could well be David Cone, Sammy Sosa and Maurice Vaughn, who they call Mo, like in Moses.

So picture this Mo Vaughn blasting one off the right-field wall and coming to rest with a standup double. No celebrating, no pointing. Just a gesture to the dugout from which springs the batboy carrying not a warm-up jacket, but a prayer shawl, skullcap, a section from the Torah that has been carefully removed from an arc, and a delicate antique silver pointer with colorful stones embedded in the handle. And now, for an hour or so, this Mo Vaughn, in celebration of his blast off the right field wall, proceeds to *doven,* pray. Rocking back and forth from the waist, he lovingly touches the words on the sacred scroll with the silver pointer, while the bleacher fans can barely make out his lips moving quickly over the ancient words. Then, when he's finished, the bat boy returns, bundles up the artifacts, and runs to the dugout while Mo Vaughn takes his lead off second. And out in right field, Sammy is mouthing the words right along with him since he went to Hebrew school with Mo when they were kids.

I couldn't resist. I fought my psyche and my entire muscular system to not look up into that Oregon sky to where the man with the blond hair was pointing. Couldn't do it. I glanced at Luke and his new friend who were playing so happily, and then, ineluctably, I followed the man's finger. There it was, the object of his attention: a magnificent hawk circling the playground as if delighted by the beauty of these children, and then swooping away, disappearing across the pond behind the towering Douglas firs.

Now *that,* I told myself, *that* could be God. That hawk, that sky, those trees, that pond, these children, the man with the blond hair, even me.

"You okay, Luke?"

I heard his precious little voice: "Yeah."

And may you stay safe that way forever.

A Neglected Resource

ᕗ

[1]

ACCORDING TO COLUMNIST STEVEN Stark,[1] some of the most
telling aspects of America's attitudes toward children are captured in
the way movies and television have depicted families over the last few
decades.

Once upon a time, Stark notes, it was loyal, hardworking, generous
parents raising self-absorbed brats. "Viewers saw parenthood largely
through the eyes of self-absorbed children; adults were often the butt of
jokes." Now, however, the tables have turned, and movies like *Home
Alone* reveal the self-absorbed parent and the child, well, home alone.
The cultural reality Stark wants us to take away, is that "children, generally, are treated worse today than they were a generation ago." A statistic that might support this claim goes this way: The average child of
modern day *Bill Cosby–Roseanne* America spends forty percent less time
with his or her parents than the child of a quarter of a century ago,
when Donna Reed and Beaver dominated the television landscape.

Something else: Every occupation dealing with both child and adult
clienteles reveals a higher payment schedule for those who choose to
work with adults. Pediatricians earn less than internists; practitioners of
child law earn less than practitioners of adult law. Similarly, teachers of
children eighteen years and younger earn less than people who teach
children eighteen years and older, the latter group being properly called
professors. All of these facts constitute what sociologists call unobtru-
sive measures of the low status if not outright devaluing of children.

In contrast, a so-called obtrusive measure of the minimal status of
America's children is the typical urban public school.[2] Granted, we find
pockets of public education in this country that are nothing short of

remarkable. Spectacular men and women in cities everywhere do extraordinary things in their classrooms, and their students respond magnificently. Pockets, alas, do not a pair of trousers make. Expanding the metaphor, it is disgraceful that America would let this pair of pants be worn in public. The condition of many of our educational institutions speaks volumes about our lack of concern for intellectual aptitudes, endeavors, and, most importantly, teachers and children.

Years ago, it may be recalled, a small group of vocal women got practically nowhere advancing the idea that housewives should be paid for their work. Much of the culture responded to these allegedly "strident" women as misguided feminists. Nobody, many argued, should be paid for housework. But, why not? As it is more significant than the work many of the rest of us perform, why not pay for it? Because we have decided that a woman should *wish* to do that work for *free*! She should do it out of love, commitment, and loyalty. Given the history of western cultures and economies, one wonders whether men, finding themselves as the keepers of the house and children, would accept these same terms?

The argument offered by those certain housewives may provide us insight into why it is that teachers are so ill paid. Beside the matter of America's abiding anti–intellectualism, we secretly imagine that teachers, too, should be working for free. They, too, should be doing it out of love, magnanimity, generosity, charity. One hesitates calling them babysitters; more appropriately, they're parent figures, and parents aren't meant to be paid for parenting. Professors surely aren't parents; they're *in loco parenti*, even though they engage in far less contact with students than grade school and high school teachers.

In describing the situation found on many modern college campuses, anthropologist Michael Moffatt actually captured life in all too many American families as well:

[A]lmost everything in the college lives of students in the 1980's is less a product of the collegiate past than a projection of contemporary late adolescent mass culture into the particular institutions of youth which colleges now represent—places where everyone else is fairly intelligent, places where students are on their own with large numbers of their age-mates and with considerable amounts of free time, and places where adult authorities have *minimal knowledge of and real impact on their private lives*[3] [emphasis added].

One more thought about the inferior status of children in this country. Despite the increasing presence of men in the teaching profession, children still are considered to be the responsibility, if not the wards, of women. A man will accompany his child of twenty-five to the internist, but women typically take small children to the pediatrician. Far more women will go to parent-teacher conferences than men. Granted, men's work schedules may not allow free hours for this activity, but even in households where a woman's work schedule is as filled as her husband's, she is far more likely to attend school meetings. It is women who take care of children, and because women are not fully honored in the culture, the work they do also is not honored (or is it the other way around?), and hence those they educate and protect also are not honored.

The problem grows even more complex. Women, generally, are assigned the task of care taking *all* people, irrespective of the ages of these people or how they may or may not be related to these women. Studies indicate that following a divorce, women are more likely to care for the aging parents of their *ex*-spouse than the sons of these aging people. Social work still is viewed as a woman's profession, psychology and psychiatry are thought of as slightly more masculine. Some people, furthermore, continue to believe that a male in the mental health or helping professions is either openly feminine or not quite a "real" man.

Years ago, psychiatrist Jean Baker Miller wrote that, unlike men, women derive their sense of identity from constantly interacting with people.[4] One implication of this form of ego development is that women ultimately come to be trained as the culture's caretakers. Another development, and a direct result of the way the culture operates, is the permanent linkage in our consciousness of women and caretaking. The culture traditionally allocates its "real" jobs to "real" men; what "real" women do they do "naturally," and "out of love." It's as if we believe that it is in women's genes to be caretakers and, again, one need not pay people on the basis of genetic endowment (unless, of course, they're very tall men who can dunk a basketball). Sadly, women and children, the first to be offered passage on lifeboats and protection by masculine strengths and chivalries, normally assume the lower positions on the human hierarchy.

A host of statistics testify to the inferior conditions of children in the United States. Many social scientists watch these numbers closely, and, along with certain philosophers, judge the entire culture by what these numbers say about our (ill) treatment of children.

Over the last years, for example, the Fordham Institute for Innovation in Social Policy has been compiling figures on six major aspects of children's social health. Specifically, the Institute has tracked mainly federal-government-collected data on infant mortality, child abuse, children living in poverty, teenage drug abuse, teenage suicide, and high school drop-out rates. From these six individual categories, an overall social health index is computed ranging from 0 to 100.

Setting aside the mathematical details of the computation, consider that in 1970 the children's social health index stood at 68. In 1987 it had fallen to 37. Based on these six measures of behavior, therefore, the social health of children in 1987 was half as good (or twice as bad) as it was in 1970. And the trend continues to the present.

Inspecting the data more closely, one finds that America has done worse in five of the six categories. Only teenage drug abuse seems to have leveled off during these years. In the other five categories, children (or more appropriately, *we*) have done worse. Despite increases in indices of upper-middle-class and upper-class prosperity, as for example, employment and income, 1987 America witnessed a far greater percentage of children dying in childbirth, living in poverty (one out of every five) and dropping out of school. The number of teenagers committing suicide in 1987 was twice the number recorded in 1970. But the most significant factor reducing the index of social health is the frequency of child abuse cases. The numbers constituting this increase are astronomical, and cannot be accounted for merely by improved reporting procedures. For every child abused in 1970, *three* were abused in 1987!

America actually had begun to show some progress over the two decades in infant mortality and high school drop-out rates. Yet by the end of the 1980s, the numbers dropped. Equally discouraging, another study indicated that America, once number one (i.e., lowest), now ranks nineteenth on infant mortality rates among industrialized nations. The knowledge of prenatal and postnatal care surely is expanding, and delivery techniques improving, but a growing number of Americans fail to benefit from these advancements.

Not so incidentally, the Fordham Institute researchers also reported that for the second consecutive year the social health of the nation as a whole was the lowest it had been since the first such calculations were undertaken in 1970. Black and white, male and female, America's children are not being cared for, and in too many instances neither are their elders.

A publication from the Children's Defense Fund confirms this discouraging picture.[5] According to CDF, "a black baby born in Boston in 1988 had less chance of surviving its first year than a baby born in Panama, North or South Korea, or Uruguay." In addition, American children rank fifteenth in childhood immunization against polio (forty-ninth if America's black children one year old and younger are examined individually). Furthermore, for those valuing teacher-student closeness, America ranks nineteenth in teacher-student ratios, placing us behind countries like Libya, Lebanon, and Cuba.

Especially shocking are the figures put forth by the Children's Defense Fund for one day in the lives of American children. Consider, for example, that *every day* almost 2,800 teenagers get pregnant, 105 babies less than one year old will die, 67 will perish before their first month of life, 155,000 will bring a gun to school, 30 will be wounded by guns and 10 will die from gun shots, 1,500 teenagers will drop out of school (the national yearly average presently stands at slightly over 30 percent), 1,850 children will be abused or neglected, nearly 3,300 will run away from home, 6 will commit suicide, and almost 3,000 will watch their parents get divorced. That's every day!

Now comes a breath of bittersweet irony. From the Nickelodeon/Yankelovich Youth Monitor, we learn that 61 percent of America's children believe their family is like most other families and want it to remain this way. (The number is lower for children of divorced parents.) Eighty percent of America's children think it is better to have a sibling than to be an only child, and 76 percent report they wish they could spend more time with their parents.

If that's not sufficiently bittersweet, a study of middle and high school students published a few years ago indicated that of all the concerns facing American children, and with all the talk about jobs, money, music, sex, esteem, school, homework, sneakers, girls, boys, brothers, sisters, the most important matter to these young people was the physical well being of their parents. For those who may be interested, the number one concern for children of Russia that same year was world peace.

[2]

To say that the nature of the American family has changed over the last decades is a bit like saying children sort of do better in life with loving mothers and fathers. Recent census data tell the story succinctly.[6] In 1990, 26 percent of the country's almost 100 million households revealed a married couple with children under the age of eighteen. In contrast, in 1970, 40 percent of households showed this traditional nuclear family constellation.

1990 census data also indicated almost 10 million single-parent households in America, most of them headed by women. This represents an
increase of 41 percent over 1980, and 82 *percent* over 1970. (Nowadays we
speak of the single-parent family. No longer do we use the term "broken" family since many of the families encompassed by this now-
offensive word may be our own.)

Recent family statistics may be put in perspective by noting some additional facts: Twenty-five years ago, one in two families had mom, dad,
and children living together, with dad working outside the house and
mom working inside the house. By 1988, this scene was found in one of
three families. Today, more than 60 percent of mothers work outside
the family. As this trend has continued, this number is expected to reach
one in four in the very near future.

While one readily quotes statistics of this sort, one is never certain
just how accurate they are. Significantly, the poorer the families, the
more inaccurate our information about them. Far more divorces, for example, are recorded among the rich. As many poor people cannot afford
to go through legal channels, they simply split up and remarry. Numbers, generally, in social science demonstrate nothing, they merely indicate something. One such indication is the constant divorce rate that
everyone in this country knows by heart: namely, one out of two marriages. Yet even this number is misleading, since it is the people getting
divorces who increase the divorce statistics. Let me explain this seemingly redundant statement.

To remarry implies that one already has been widowed or divorced if
one does it legally. When you marry, get a divorce, and then remarry,
and let's make your case more extreme, get another divorce and remarry
a second time (your third marriage), you, and not I, who never have
been divorced, account for the rise in the divorce rates. You've been to
the altar three times; I've been there once, so the final statistic reads:
two out of four (or one out of two) marriages end in divorce. But notice,
you're the one who essentially has accounted for the statistics, and that's
the point. It's multiple marriages and divorces by the same people that
raise the divorce rate. In fact, a constant number of first marriages,
around 65 percent, will last forever.

Whatever the statistics, divorce patterns hardly exist in social isolation; rather, they reflect major currents in the culture. Professors Jan E.
Dizard and Howard Gadlin address this point in their examination of a
series of unstable American lifestyle patterns into which divorce rates
fall. People moving from one community to another, children moving

away from home, significant changes in the nature of a community or neighborhood, and a wholesale restructuring of our sense of friendship bonds and kinship ties all play roles in shaping the foundation and definition of marriage. If nothing in the society remains constant, why should marriage?

If, moreover, in our overriding disposable mentality, we teach people to throw things out when they break, it is only natural that people will transfer this consumer prescription to their marriages and seriously consider throwing out their spouse when the marriage stops working, in the same manner they would dump their broken VCRs and toasters. As psychoanalyst Joel Kovel remarked, America tends to "thingify" people,[7] and hence Americans treat one another as they do things, and heaven knows we tend not to preserve things all too well. Old means bad, new means good. Why else would a television studio audience applaud a couple announcing they have been married twenty years? In our culture, apparently, twenty years seems a veritable eternity.

In some people's minds, *the* issue of the last decade has been divorce. For too long, truthfully, many of us in the psychological community remained silent about the impact of divorce on children Perhaps we grew quiet about this matter because some of our *own* children were the objects of our concern. Or perhaps we grew quiet in deference to certain feminist ideologies that sprang up around the matter of protecting and honoring women generally, and single mothers in particular. For male psychologists to announce that divorce inevitably scars children might have been perceived by some as criticism of single women raising children. Who were *men*, after all, to comment on, much less evaluate, single women's child-rearing practices!

Presently, however, the mood has changed, and the culture seems to accept professionals, particularly women, writing about the dangers of divorce on children. Psychologist Judith Wallerstein has reported, for example, that ten years after their parents' divorces, 50 percent of her sample of California children continued to wish their parents might remarry, despite the fact that many of these parents already were married to someone else.[8] Parental couplings and uncouplings, we learn from her research, become internalized by children, and begin to reorganize the structure of their minds, personalities, and outlooks.

Divorce, however, may not be as critical a factor as the manner in which a particular divorce is conducted. A mom and dad may divorce, for example, and remain the wonderful (or woeful) parents they always were. Or a dad or mom may physically or emotionally drift away from the children. Or both may become so involved in their own distractions, the child feels the reverberations of two uncouplings: mom from dad, parents from child.

More likely, the grand uncoupling remains that of parent from child, and that is why divorce need not totally cripple a child's emotional world. Most of us knew this as we developed our thoughts about the profound changes occurring in the American family. In accordance with our observations, we developed two highly recognizable albeit laughable phrases. First, we began speaking of "working mothers" (as if there were another brand). Only mothers, we decided, who make money working outside the home may earn this title. Women who stay home with their children, presumably, are on permanent vacation.

The second term is the infamous "quality time." We might smirk at the sound of these words, but for almost a decade we actually had ourselves convinced that a few good minutes here and there were as valuable to the child as regular, ongoing "meaningful relationships," that popular term of the 1960s. Parents, apparently, had bigger fish to fry, bigger that is, than the little fish they dropped on the earth or were willing to nourish.

I trust we now know better about this quality-time business, although I also know that sometimes I don't act on what I know to be beneficial. For that matter, in my dealings with children, I still don't act often enough on those instincts I believe to hold the deepest truths about my relationships with them. I know that I sometimes find myself, metaphorically speaking, rushing to see what the experts would do, when I know that all the child needs is to have me there with her, holding or talking to her, or just sitting on her bed while she draws. Granted, ten good minutes with a child is far superior to five hours of yelling and hitting, but this comparison too often is advanced as the alternative to so-called quality time.

Children clearly need to be coupled with their parents, and then have these couplings sanctified. They need constant assurance that all bonds are safe and secure. They require, moreover, what psychoanalyst Anna Freud called an average, expectable environment. Whatever the patterns established by parents, children need to know, without trepidation, that these patterns will be maintained.

Major fluctuations and change often take their toll on children. The arrival of a baby in the home can put the child in a tail spin, although children are rather adept at revealing their despair and disapproval in clever ways, like hitting a baby sister or torturing the cat. Moving a child from one room to another, or even rearranging his or her furniture may prove seriously upsetting. Mom or dad changing job schedules, not even changing jobs, and certainly moving from one city to another, have profound effects on the child. Interestingly, research has shown that moving is one of the greatest stress inducers for adults. It literally causes people to feel that they are not only being separated from significant objects and people, but that they are coming apart, internally unraveling. (A prize, therefore, to the moving company that hit on the name, *Allied*, but what does one say about the Massachusetts company calling itself *Mom's Moving?*)

In simplest terms—and frequently children only deal in simplest terms—average to the child means the way it usually is around here. Expectable means I can await events without fear for I have lived through them before and know (how) they usually come out all right.

Few children ever take this matter of an average and predictable home life for granted, thereby confirming Ms. Freud's observation. Irrespective of their protestations, even teenagers are rattled by seemingly insignificant shifts in mood or behavior. Children know when dad is upset or mom is disturbed (why shouldn't they; neonate research indicates that they were able to sense at ten days of age when something was not right), and when these upsets are not being caused by work and career setbacks. In their way, when children aren't doing their "own thing" (an expression that derives, incidentally, from the drug culture), they often act as miniature social workers on perpetual home-care visitation.

All too often in my research on families, I will hear a child bemoan the boring quality of his or her home life. "Dad's always the same," a boy grumbles. "He comes home from work and puts down his coat in the same place and calls to my mother, 'Hi, honey, how was your day?' She has just come home from work, too, and is in the kitchen, like always, listening to public radio, *All Things Considered*, of course, and she smiles at him and drops the cucumbers on the counter and they kiss and hug and she says, 'Fine, darling, and how was *your* day?' And he says 'Not that bad, all things considered,' and they glance at the radio and giggle and he says, 'Well, something in here smells awfully good.' And it goes on like this, week after boring week after boring week."

In these moments, out of a desire to empirically test the child's observations, along with a soupçon of sadism, I am tempted to reply, "You know, you're absolutely right; your parents sound boring as hell. But you can change it. Why not advise your mother that instead of the usual routine, she should have a little romantic music playing on the radio and meet your father in the kitchen wearing nothing but an apron!"

We may smile at these thoughts, but a serious point lingers: Parents need to be an ongoing and regular presence in the lives of their children; quality time cannot suffice if the child perceives that, as we say, parents have bigger fish to fry. Many Americans nonetheless continue to manipulate parental strategies and philosophies in order, seemingly, to excuse themselves from the responsibility of child rearing. They continue to dicker with child rearing realities, strategies, and philosophies, as if the lives of their children could be played with or moved around as easily as tossing about characters on a word processor screen. Contrived techniques, we continue to imagine, can win out over simple everyday nurturance and love. It is the same misguidedness that leads many of us to believe that powerful technologies can win out in competition with natural events and human and physical evolution.

American business seems all too ready to accept and reward our manipulations of child rearing strategies and feed us still more distracting ideas. With a child crying for his or her parents, teenagers claiming there is no one in the world for them, students demanding that they be treated as people, not numbers, and that if they died it would be so long before they were discovered their decomposed bodies no longer would be recognizable even to their own parents (this sentiment from an interview with a college student), it begins to seem that the whole world is out of joint. Child psychoanalyst John Bowlby apparently felt much the same thing: "We have created a topsy turvy world in which the production of material goods counts as a plus in our economic indices whereas men and women power devoted to raising *happy, healthy* and *self reliant* children . . . does not count at all"[9] (emphasis added).

We note again this physician's simple message and the almost homey words I have italicized. Another psychoanalyst, Bruno Bettelheim, wrote that one needn't be a great or, heaven forbid, perfect parent; good enough was good enough. One doesn't need to be a child-rearing expert, researcher, or psychologist. In fact, there is some evidence that the children of therapists often experience a rather difficult time of it, precisely because of the nature of their parent's professional views and corresponding strategies.[10] One always may take one's clues from watching other children raise their brothers and sisters, or from Fred Rogers. We may scoff at Mr. Rogers, and giggle uncomfortably at his gentle manner, but all we're doing is seeking to neutralize the strong feelings we once held for him, as well as the importance he played in our lives.

Ask mothers who turn to Mr. Rogers at the miserable hour, five o'clock in the afternoon, what they think of him and his neighborhood. Trying to come down from an exhausting day that has hours still remaining in it, caring for agitated and inconsolable children, preparing dinner and sustaining that one last remnant of sanity, many women would give a Nobel Peace Prize to the man who not only engages her children for thirty uninterrupted minutes, but who, in addition, hit upon the generation's one healthy phrase that every child (and adult) needs to hear: "I like you just the way you are."

The distracted child who turns to the celebrity or material product for sustenance, happiness, and basic life foods, as so many children presently do, may well become the child who misses out on happiness, health, and self-reliance. If Bowlby was correct, then only strong attachments, and not merely to Mr. Rogers, can yield these ingredients. The distracted consumer, looking to material goods that economic index purveyors so adore, as well as contrived and unworkable philosophies and outlooks, is left with unhappiness, illness, and total dependence on other people and things to guide him or her along life's inauthentic paths.

False gods, these people and products have been called, for the true gods are to be found among those who raise and care for us, and who, in their enduring attachments to us and to one another, teach us how to genuinely know ourselves, love ourselves and others, and eventually introduce this same curriculum to subsequent generations.

Today, tomorrow, or sometime next week, surely, I will watch some young celebrity being interviewed on television. If history proves me correct, I will hear him or her say, in response to some question, "Well, you know, in order to love others, you have to, like, love yourself." Then he or she will go on with this grandiose philosophical tenet that justifies him or her loving only himself or herself for the next five decades.

Millions will take from the message, nay, the *advice*, to go home and treat yourself, bathe yourself, pamper, kiss, worship, massage and, above all, love yourself. It's not a bad idea, surely, to love yourself. Still, a profound distraction nonetheless hides among this notion, and comes at us from two directions.

First, we somehow have learned that self-love is the highest philosophical and psychological ideal. The mean, learning to love yourself, suddenly becomes the end in itself. Narcissism triumphs, and the only face and soul we ever need glorify and nourish is our own.[11] Simultaneously, we learn that you can teach yourself to love yourself, which certainly is true, but we may be distracted here, for we miss a fundamental truth:

namely, that children come to love themselves by having been loved by their parents, *and* watching their parents love each other. In a sense, loving parents do much of the early loving work for their child. Children are meant to emerge full blown, someday, as self-loving, self-approving adults. They ought to obtain these qualities, furthermore, not because honor grades were achieved in the infamous childhood curriculum, but merely because they were enrolled in the childhood curriculum. It is intended to be a part of the unwritten and laughably lopsided contract entered into by parents and children.

Some children, however, are not exposed to the love curriculum. Some children never know about unconditional love; some children never receive their copy of the contract. Instead, they receive the "how to survive childhood curriculum," and the *Home Alone* contract. These are the psychological if not literally latch key children, the ones *always* home alone, even when all sorts of people are around. These are the children asking to know the time, eager for the hours to pass so they can hear Mr. Rogers say directly to them: "I like you just the way you are."

[3]

For the venerable grammarian we recite: I love, you love, he, she, or it loves. For the venerable psychologist we recite: I am loved, I love myself, I love another. Love and trust help in my search for self-reliance, which I value, not begrudge. I can even get angry with my parents and not fear that they will hurt or abandon me; I can rely on their presence and their love. This, too, is part of what Anna Freud meant when she spoke of an average, predictable environment.

Let us just be loving and lovable, the child in me keeps repeating. Fame and wealth, the goals of all to many of us, are but props meant to fill an emptiness that each of us feels from time to time. The search for fame and wealth well may be the quintessential pursuits of distraction. Surely they bring momentary power and ego affirmation, but they are also the grand compensations. They look to be real, but they are mere falsehood and illusion. Children who are genuinely loved "merely" on that average and predictable basis, need neither stardom nor wealth for one obvious reason: They already have achieved them, and they haven't even cut a tooth, much less an album.

Fame provides us only the first three letters of the word, family; we're still three letters short. And while most of us never will experience the fifteen minutes of notoriety Andy Warhol promised, too many of us will be unable to remember even fifteen minutes of genuine family. But let me amend this observation.

Millions of people called, simply, parents, never will receive public attention or prominent roles in movies or television shows. Their lives in the context of America's public relations-entertainment mentality would be deemed boring. Produce a show with these couples whose marriages have worked and whose children are confident, secure, enlightened, happy people, and you have thirty minutes of unadulterated blandness and ennui. Most of us only become interested in people when they do something untoward or unseemly. Lured by the titillating, we apparently prefer to watch "unusual" folks paraded out on television talk shows rather than so-called usual parents doing a nice job raising nice children. Unthinkingly, we label this latter group "the silent majority," unaware, perhaps, that Homer, the author of the term, was referring to the dead.

I have met many of these parents and their sons and daughters, who, truthfully, made it tough on children like mine to get into college. I've seen these well-mannered, intelligent, healthy, pleasant young men and women in university admissions offices and college classrooms across this country, and they appear nothing short of terrific. I try to think of them not as the children of the silent majority or even the children of average, expectable environments. Rather, I prefer to imagine that regularly in their lives, in their homes, schools, and communities—three institutions presently requiring considerable refurbishing—they heard and internalized Mr. Rogers' deceptively simple message: "There is only one person like you in the world," and, "I like you just the way you are."

Notes

1. See Steven Stark, "A Look at Children that Reflects a Changing Picture." *The Boston Globe,* January 14, 1991.

2. See Jonathan Kozol, *Savage Inequalities.* New York: Crown Publishers, 1991.

3. Michael Moffatt, "Undergraduate Culture and Higher Education," *The Journal of Higher Education,* January/February, 1991, Vol. 62, No. 1, p. 57.

4. See her *Toward a New Psychology of Women.* Boston: Beacon Press, 1986.

5. See Children's Defense Fund, *Reports,* February/March, 1990.

6. These numbers are taken from a study of 57,400 households conducted by the Census Bureau in March of 1990 and reported in *The Boston Globe,* January 30, 1991.

7. Joel Kovel, *White Racism: A Psychohistory.* New York: Columbia University Press, 1984.

8. See Judith Wallerstein, *Second Chances: Men, Women and Children a Decade After Divorce.* New York: Ticknor and Fields, 1989.

9. In *Readings,* December, 1991, p. 5.

10. See *Children of Psychiatrists and Other Psychotherapists,* by Thomas Maeder. New York: Harper and Row, 1989.

11. On these and related points see Christopher Lasch, *The Culture of Narcissism.* New York: Norton, 1978.

Simpson, Systems, and Sociology

⌒

NOW THAT SEEMINGLY EVERY lawyer in America has commented on the O.J. Simpson criminal trial, might we consider several
sociological observations that seemingly never made their way into the
post-trial dialogue? Sociologists, after all, are accustomed to examining
America's cards, as they've been called, like the race one, the sex one, the
domestic-violence one, the interracial-marriage one, the social-class
one, the power one, the public-relations one, and the celebrity one.
They are also trained to keep an eye on society, which means in part
keeping an eye on the roles assigned citizens in a democracy, as, for example, the role of juror in a celebrated trial.

Two significant decisions made even before the case commenced
would not be lost on the sociologist. First, District Attorney Gil Garcetti chose Los Angeles rather than Santa Monica as his trial venue.
Presumably trying to counter the fiasco of the Simi Valley venue in the
Rodney King case, it may also be that Mr. Garcetti was attempting to
send a message, as the saying goes in the public-relations-oriented
country like our own, ingenuous or political, that Mr. Simpson could be
tried by middle- and working-class people who would assess the case on
facts alone. In this regard he may also have sought to confirm—beyond
a reasonable doubt—democracy's credo that all people can properly
judge their peers. Many would argue that while Mr. Simpson's original
peers may well reside in South Central Los Angeles, his present peers
live miles from there.

Then, in a second appeal to some democratic ethos and constitutional
provision, Judge Lance Ito made a decision that in effect may have destroyed the prosecution's case weeks before the appearance of Detective
Mark Furman. Bowing to the seemingly irrefutable concept of the
public's right to know, Judge Ito allowed television in the courtroom.

Perhaps the judge's ego won out, albeit a modest one at the time, inasmuch as his first and only television interview was granted to a local Los Angeles station. One cannot blame the judge alone; ego, after all, were it electricity, found a wattage in that one ninth-floor courtroom years ago, that could have lit (though not enlightened) the homes of Hollywood for a century. But perhaps Judge Ito, too, thought of democracy and some peculiar interpretation of freedom, and hence he allowed the camera.

During the camera debate, few people made the point that if the public maintains a right to know, it can always read. When, after all, did knowing something become tantamount to viewing that something on television? Perhaps at the same time Americans decided that information, that is, "factoids," are tantamount to thoughtfulness and knowledge. Ironically, the old adage, "seeing is believing," has been destroyed in the culture by of all things the visual medium, television. We ought to know by now that seeing and believing may have little to do with one another; and neither leads directly to knowing. Seeing predicts neither what people will believe nor ultimately know. Consider in this regard, the Rodney King case where seeing, perceiving, believing and knowing yielded truths, dare I say, of all shapes and colors.

Seeing involves perception as well as conception and cognition. We might recall in this regard, Immanuel Kant's notion that there is not percept without concept. We perceive, in other words, as a function of that which we conceive. Equally shocking, things exist that cannot be seen, like ideas, concepts, reasoning, morality. That something, a person or idea, appears believable, credible, or incredible, says little about the genuine truth and fundamental substance of that something. Equally significant, we too often overlook the fact that television shapes even as it records; it is an architect of behavior as much as technological witness of it.

When that single camera was placed in the courtroom, hundreds of millions of people became the thirteenth jurist, and ironically, the only unseen, that is, untelevised people in the entire case became scrutinized more assiduously than anyone else, even those men and women who became household names and household visitors. With Big Brother and Big Sister watching over the seen and unseen, did we really need sociologists to tell us what jurors were thinking?

Twelve men and women sat in their chairs, taking very seriously, one imagines, the sociological requirements and dictates of their task. People in and out of juries almost always rise above their idiosyncratic origins and life experiences, which means prejudices as well; sociological research shows this to be the case. Sadly, many school administrators often don't remember this, but good teachers always do. In this regard, the constitution does work.

But democracy has implanted another issue in our minds: Not at all abstract, it has to do with liberty and personal freedom. Sit in a jury and one dilemma inevitably crosses your mind. What would be worse, setting the guilty man free or sending the innocent man to prison? Attempting to be dispassionate, objective, rational, unemotional, judicious, most everyone comes to the same conclusion: If I send a guilty man to freedom I cannot sleep at night, but if I strip the freedom from an innocent man I can neither sleep at night nor nap during the day.

Democracy and freedom, the best we offer in this country, along with unlimited wealth, celebrity, oppression, racism, and lack of liberty, not the best we offer in this country, conspired to send one message to those twelve jurors. Forget the admonition of "beyond reasonable doubt"; consider only beyond any doubt whatsoever! You simply cannot make a mistake with this one; too much and too many people are at stake.

Of course race played a role, sometimes with an overly thick "cut"—Furman equals fuhrer?—and sometimes appropriately, like the inexorable biases carved into bigotry. Of course fame, too, played a role. Alas, in a television-dominated culture where recognizability alone makes one famous—Roger Clinton, after all, maintained a musical career—where people reveal an unquenchable appetite for new (recognizable) faces, sheer recognizability rather than morality or performance becomes the measure of nothing short of heroism. And of course wealth plays a role. Everyone on the Simpson criminal case earned more for this one venture than the average American earns in a lifetime. Some made even more after the case by becoming talk show hosts.

Yet it is democracy and freedom that one still can find hidden among so many of the motives and decisions, actions and final outcome of a case that would never in a million years have attained this level of interest had it not been for television. "Simpson" is a television-produced commodity. Like others, he is properly called, if not diagnosed as, a "television personality." Television itself, ostensibly a pure instrument of technology, draws its definition, too, from sociological factors, not merely scientific ones. You can use the same computer, after all, to locate people that might have a lifesaving blood factor, or people that you wish to harass because of their political ideology.

A few more sociological points. Among the justification for the present system of jurisprudence, albeit an imperfect system, is the notion that potential tyrannical methods and proceedings of a state must at all times be opposed. That means that on occasion the guilty go free. Conversely, some of my own heroes—alas, none of them pop artists or athletes—spent years in prison for crimes whose definition can only be traced to tyrannical rationales, premises, and ideologies. Solzhenitsyn, King, Ghandi and Mandela were not the wide receiving corps of the Buffalo Bills in the late 1970s. In fact many of the historical personages we genuinely glorify are the very people choked by tyranny.

That young men and women in our culture know neither the names of these choked people, nor the infamous chokers but do recognize the names of pop artists, spokespeople, cartoon characters, video game heroes, movie stars, and athletes is something we might reflect on when, if ever again, we discuss the role of racism, sexism, and social class differentiations in the Simpson case.

We also might reflect on the role of good old-fashioned public-relations-driven hyperbole in a product-oriented personality-but-not-person-oriented America. Stars, superstars, megastars, those terms "great," "special," and the English teacher's nightmare "extremely unique" are omnipresent. That O.J. Simpson was a great football player hardly renders him a great man; the syllogism collapses. He has been a famous man, never a great man; and he can't be one now. No, strike that. He couldn't be one after the first report years before, the one dismissed by many, of wife battering.

A final word. Of all the characters in this permanently closed yet uniquely American theater production, I personally shall never forget Mr. Goldman. What really are people thinking about when they speak, even plaintively, of a time for healing to begin? Pain and rage, hurt and loss not only stay with us to the end of our days, they live beyond our time in the lives and spirits of our children. Holocaust survivors and war veterans know this, families of murdered people, battered women, and citizens harassed by police know this. So do their children and grandchildren. But have not some of us, in not ironical tones, remarked that if we were Mr. Goldman we might purchase a weapon and, temporarily buoyed by some perverse reading of justice, do something utterly heinous?

What then held him back? What kept him from deliberating about revenge and allowing his instincts to explode in murderous rage? And what for that matter fails to work in others such that they grant full reign to their animal instincts or outright evil?

The sociologist Émile Durkheim, we recall, sought to answer these

SELECTED BIBLIOGRAPHY OF WORKS
BY THOMAS J. COTTLE

BOOKS

Confrontation: Psychology and the Problems of Today (co-editor and contributor), Michael Wertheimer (general editor). Glenview, Ill.: Scott, Foresman and Company, 1970.

Time's Children: Impressions of Youth. Boston: Little, Brown and Company, 1971.

(with Craig R. Eisendrath and Laurence Fink), *Out of Discontent: Visions of the Contemporary University*. Cambridge: Schenkman Publishing, 1972.

The Pains of Permanence. In *The Tenure Debate* (Bardwell Smith, ed.). San Francisco: Jossey-Bass, 1972.

The Prospect of Youth: Contexts for Sociological Inquiry. Boston: Little, Brown and Company, 1972.

The Abandoners: Portraits of Loss, Separation, and Neglect. Boston: Little, Brown and Company, 1973.

The Voices of School: Educational Issues through Personal Accounts. Boston: Little, Brown and Company, 1973.

The Present of Things Future: Explorations of Time in Human Experience (with Stephen L. Klineberg). New York: The Free Press, 1974.

A Family Album: Portraits of Intimacy and Kinship. New York: Harper and Row, 1974.

Black Children, White Dreams. Boston: Houghton Mifflin Company, 1974.

Barred From School. Washington, D.C.: The New Republic Book Company, 1976.

Busing. Boston: Beacon Press, 1976.

Perceiving Time: An Investigation with Men and Women. New York: Wiley, 1976.

Adolescent Psychology: Contemporary Perspectives. New York: Harper and Row, 1977.

Children in Jail. Boston: Beacon Press, 1977.

College: Reward and Betrayal. Chicago: The University of Chicago Press, 1977.

Human Adjustment (with Phillip Whitten). San Francisco: Canfield Press, 1977.

Private Lives and Public Accounts. Amherst: University of Massachusetts Press, 1977.

Psychotherapy: Current Perspectives (with Phillip Whitten). New York: Franklin Watts, 1979.

Hidden Survivors: Portraits of Poor Jews in America. Englewood Cliffs, N.J.: Prentice Hall, 1980.

Black Testimony. London: Wildwood House, 1978; Philadelphia: Temple University Press, 1980.

Getting Married: A New Look at an Old Tradition (with Cathy Stein Greenblat). New York: McGraw-Hill, 1980.

Children's Secrets. New York: Doubleday, 1980; paperback edition, Reading, Mass.: Addison Wesley, 1990.

Like Fathers, Like Sons. Norwood, N.J.: Ablex, 1981.

At Peril: Stories of Injustice. Amherst: University of Massachusetts Press, 2001.

Hardest Times: The Trauma of Long Term Unemployment. Westport, Conn.: Praeger, 2001.

Mind Fields: Adolescent Consciousness in a Culture of Distraction. New York: Peter Lang Publishing, 2001.

A Sense of Self. Amherst: University of Massachusetts Press, in press.

ARTICLES

Self Concept, Ego Ideal and the Response to Action. *Sociology and Social Research,* October, 1965, 50, 78 –88.

Social Class and Social Dancing. *Sociological Quarterly* 7, Spring, 1966, 179 –196.

Revolt and Repair: A Comparative Study of Two University Tutorial Movements. *Sociological Quarterly* 8, Winter, 1967, 21–36.

Comparative Evaluation of Occupations by English Speaking, Refugee and Local Hong Kong Adolescents. *Sociological Review* 15, March, 1967, 21–31.

The Circles Test: An Investigation of Temporal Relatedness and Dominance. *Journal of Projective Techniques and Personality Assessment* 31, October, 1967, 58 –71.

Encounter in Color. *Psychology Today,* December, 1967, 22ff.

Facing the Patients: Notes on Group Therapy Observation. *Psychotherapy* 4, December, 1968, 254–61.

Family Perceptions, Sex Role Identity and the Prediction of School Performance. *Educational and Psychological Measurement* 28, 1968, 861–86.

The Location of Experience: A Manifest Time Orientation. *Acta Psychologica* 28, 1968, 129 –49.

The Time and Content of Significant Life Experiences (with Joseph Pleck and Sudhir Kakar). *Journal of Perceptual and Motor Skills* 27, 1968, 155 –71.

Bringing Groups Back into Group Psychotherapy: A Rejoinder. *Psychotherapy* 5, 1968, 195 –97.

The Money Game: Notes on Fantasies of Temporal Recovery and Preknowledge. *Diogenes* 65, January–March 1969, 116 –39.

Of Youth and the Time of Generations. *Saturday Review,* February 1, 1969, 16*ff.*

Linear Estimates of Temporal Extensions: The Effect of Age, Sex and Social Class (with Joseph Pleck). *Journal of Projective Techniques and Personality Assessment* 33, 1969, 81–93.

Slaves in the Suburb: An Account of the Wellesley Affair. *Saturday Review,* March 15, 1969, 67*ff.*

Strategy for Change: Bristol Township. *Saturday Review,* September 20, 1969, 70*ff.*

Temporal Extension and Time Zone Bracketing in Indian Adolescents (with Peter Howard). *Journal of Perceptual and Motor Skills* 28, 1969, 599–612.

Adolescent Perceptions of Time: The Effects of Age, Sex and Social Class (with Peter Howard and Joseph Pleck). *Journal of Personality* 37, 1969, 636–50.

Preliminary Notes for a Model of System Change (with John F. Marsh, Jr.). *Cahiers Internationaux de Sociologie,* XLVI, January–June 1969, 67–82.

In Protection But Not in Defense of Social Relations. *Harvard Alumni Bulletin* 71, February 24, 1969, 26–29.

Notes on the "Appropriateness" of Censorship. *The Leaflet, Journal of New England Association of Teachers of English,* May 1969, 24–27.

The Duration Inventory: Subjective Extensions of Temporal Zones. *Acta Psychologica* 29, 1969, 333–52.

The Voices in Harvard Yard. *Change* 1, July/August 1969, 25–33.

The Politics of Pronouncement: Notes on Publishing in the Social Sciences. *Harvard Educational Review* 39, 1969, 558–70.

The Politics of Retrieval. *Harvard Alumni Bulletin,* June 9, 1969, 30*ff.*

Temporal Correlates of the Achievement Value and Manifest Anxiety. *Journal of Consulting and Clinical Psychology* 33, 1969, 541–50.

Future Orientations and Avoidance: Speculations on the Time of Achievement and Social Roles. *Sociological Quarterly* 10, 1969, 419–37.

College and Career Night in Bristol Township. *Saturday Review,* January 24, 1970, 6*ff.*

Prospect Street Moon. *Saturday Review,* February 14, 1970, 21*ff.*

Strike Week in Chicago. *Change,* July/August 1970, 19–28.

In Search of Creativity: Thoughts on a Sociological Education. *Kansas Journal of Sociology* VI, Spring 1970, 4.

The Relationship of Sex Role Identity and Social and Political Attitudes (with Carl N. Edwards and Joseph Pleck). *Journal of Personality* 38, No. 3, 1970, 435–52.

Simple Words, Simple Deeds. *Urban Education* 5, October 1970, 295–304.

The Children of Nine Lives. *Sociological Inquiry* 41, Spring 1971, 139–47.

The Time of Youth. *Journal of Human Relations* 19, Fall 1971, 536–49.

The Connections of Adolescence. *Daedalus,* 100, No. 4, 1971, 1177–219.

Temporal Correlates of Dogmatism. *Journal of Consulting and Clinical Psychology* 36, No. 1, 1971, 7–81.

Chicago's Columbia College: Education for Survival. *Change* 3, Summer 1971, 60–67.

Dialogue with a "Disadvantaged." *Change* 3, No. 2, March/April 1971, 36–42.

Car Shop in Philadelphia. *Saturday Review,* June 19, 1971, 49*ff.*

Otis Wagner and the MIT Man. Education Research Center *Newsletter,* Massachusetts Institute of Technology, Cambridge, October, 1971.

On Field Work. *Journal of Human Relations* 19, Fall 1971, 536–49.

Conversations with Parents and Children. *Episcopal Theological Bulletin,* Symposium No. II, October 1971, 20–32.

A Learning Place Called Earlham. *Change* 3, January/February 1971, 52–59.

The White House Conference on Children. *Saturday Review,* February 20, 1971, 56*ff.*

A Simple Change in Creativity. *Life Magazine,* December 17, 1971, 52–53.

Matilda Rutherford—She's What You Would Call a Whore. *Antioch Review* XXXI, 4, Winter 1971–1972, 519–43.

Generations. *Social Policy* 3, July/August 1972, 50–53.

Big City Busing and the Golden Opportunity. *Urban Review* 6, No. 1, September/October 1972, 26–30.

Individualizing the College Curriculum (with Craig R. Eisendrath). *Urban Education* 7, October 1972, 281–91.

The Sexual Revolution and the Young. *New York Times Magazine,* November 26, 1972, 36*ff.*

The Edge of the IQ Storm, *Saturday Review,* April 15, 1972, 50–53.

The Integration of Harry Benjamin. *New York Times Magazine,* April 23, 1972, 15*ff.*

A Phalanx of Children. *Appalachian Journal,* No. 1, Autumn 1972, 27–34.

City Teacher. *Saturday Review-Education,* December 1972, 41–44.

The Dynamics of Institutional Change. *Prometheus* 4, May 1972, 61–72.

Temporal Differentiation and Undifferentiation: A Study of the Structure of Indian Adolescents' Perceptions of Time (with Peter Howard). *Genetic Psychology Monograph* 121, 1972, 215–33.

The Other World of Baby Eyes Ellison. *Boston Globe Magazine,* September 17, 1972, 32–33.

Run to Freedom: Chicanos in Higher Education. *Change* 4, February 1972, 34–41.

College at Middle Age. *Change* 4, No. 6, Summer 1972, 47–53.

Zero Man: Anatomy of a Failure. *Change* 4, November 1972, 49–55.

On Studying the Young. *Journal of Youth and Adolescence* 1, No. 1, March 1972, 3–11.

No Way to Look but Back. *Inequality in Education* 12, July 1972, 4–9.

The Garden of Children: Education in the Suburbs. *Urban Education,* January 1972, 373–92.

Schools and the Movie of the Mind. In *Education Today,* Del Mar, Calif.: CRM Books, 1972.

Notes on Leader Disclosure in Self Analytic Groups. *Sociological Inquiry* 43, No. 1, 1973, 51-65.

The Place Between Living and Dying. *American Review* 17, May 1973, 151–66.

Marcus Nathanial Simpson—If the Lord Has Patience I've Got a Future. *Antioch Review* 32, No. 4, 1973, 607–30.

The Toughness of Education (with Craig R. Eisendrath). *Journal of Higher Education* XLIV, No. 4, April 1973, 272–79.

Wind. *Social Policy* 4, No. 3, November/December 1973, 60–64.

A Middle American Marriage. *Harpers* 246, February 1973, 56–68.

A View of the Couch. *Harpers* 247, September 1973, 90–95.

Rationales for Relevance in Higher Education. *Interchange* 4, No. 1, 1973, 64–78.

Self Discovery through Play. In *The Neglected Years,* International Volume published by UNICEF, 1973, 86–94.

We're All Prisoners. *Urban Review* 6, No. 3, 1973, 26–30.

On the Holy Ground of the Institute. *Worldview* 19, March 1976, 26*ff.*

Yale Woman. *Urban Education,* July 1973, 123–32.

The Voices of School. *School Review* 81, August 1973, 603–09.

The Survival Business. *Christianity and Crisis* 33, October 1, 1973, 182–88.

Memories of Half Life Ago. *Journal of Youth and Adolescence* 2, No. 3, 1973, 201–12.

The Man Who Sought Education. In Lewis Solmon and Paul Taubman (eds.) *The Impact of Higher Education,* Academic Press, 1973.

The Goals of Adolescence. *Physician's World* 5, August 1973, 16–19.

On the Road to Find Out. Television Script for ABC-TV, Boston, January 1973.

A Father and His Sons. *Boston Globe Magazine,* July 8, 1973, 6*ff.*

The Life Study: On Mutual Recognition and the Subjective Inquiry. *Urban Life and Culture* 2, October 1973, 344–60.

The Policeman as Middleman. *Boston Globe Magazine,* October 28, 1973, 48–56.

An Exploration of Inner Space. *Urban Review* 6, 1973, 28–30.

Pot Party. *Children's House,* Fall 1974, 11–15.

Men's Consciousness Raising Groups. *Win Magazine* 10, November 21, 1974, 4–9.

The Parents and Children of Higher Education (with Craig R. Eisendrath). *Educational Forum* 38, No. 2, January 1974, 135–43.

One Man's Confession. *Boston Globe Magazine,* March 3, 1974, 24–25.

Profiles of Children. In Report on *Children Excluded from School.* Prepared by the Children's Defense Fund, 1974.

What Tracking Did to Ollie Taylor. *Social Policy* 5, July/August 1974, 21–24.

The Equally Good Off and the Equally Bad Off. *Inequality in Education,* June 1974, 46–50.

Adrien Keller's Dream. *Urban Review* 7, April 1974, 163–69.

A Small War in Boston. *Soundings* LVII, Fall 1974, 345–53.

Growing Up Fast in Roxbury. Publishers Hall Syndicate. *Boston Globe Magazine,* February 24, 1974, 14–16.

The Surviving Family. *Boston University Journal* 22, Winter 1974, 58–68.

If B.J. Harris' IQ Score Was Faked. *Learning,* November 1974, 36–40.

College Woman. *Liberal Education* LX, December 1974, 514–20.

Dying a Different Death: The Exclusion of Children from School. *School Review* 83, November 1974, 145–49.

A Shameful Moment. *Christianity and Crisis* 34, November 11, 1974, 247, 253.

French Speaker. *Bulletin of the National Association of Elementary School Principals* 54, November/December 1974, 12–16.

And All the Rest of Us Children Voting Every Four Years. *Bulletin of the National Association of Elementary School Principals* 54, November/December 1974, 6–12.

Is That My Child Crying? *Chicago Review* 26, No. 1, 1974, 139–157.

The Modern Family Goes to College (with Craig R. Eisendrath). *Journal of Higher Education* XLV, December 1974, 706–716.

Growing Up in Roxbury. *The Los Angeles Times,* October 17, 1974.

A Child's Election. *Massachusetts Review* 15, Autumn 1974, 707–16.

The Ghetto Scientists. *Science Digest* 77, January 1975, 54–59.

The Words of Those Other People. In *Therapy as a Way of Life,* Dennis T. Jaffe (ed.), New York: Harper & Row, 1975, 17–31.

Poor Youth. In NSSE Yearbook on Youth in the 70s, Philip H. Dreyer and Robert J. Havinghurst (eds.), 1975, 390–418.

Mixed Signals from the Progressive Home (with Craig R. Eisendrath). *Journal of Human Relations,* 1975.

A March of Desegregation. *Urban Education* 10, July 1975, 115–30.

Speaking of Busing. *The New Republic,* January 25, 1975, 14–15.

Out of Work, Out of School. *Urban Education,* January 1975, 400–13.

Tasting Scared: Robert Martin Gumpert. *The Boston Phoenix,* March 4, 1975, 12–13.

A Case of Suspension. *Principal,* November/December 1975, 5–9.

A Woman Named Sarah Clarke Keller. *South Atlantic Quarterly* 74, Spring 1975, 164–77.

Ain't No Mamma Going to School. *Win* XI, February 13, 1975, 10–12.

Look What They've Done to My Score. In *The IQ Controversy: Critical Readings,* Jerry Dworkin and Ned Black (eds.). New York: Pantheon, 1975.

Show Me a Scientist Who's Helped Poor Folks and I'll Kiss Her Hand. *Science and Society,* Ann Arbor: University of Michigan Press, 1975, 216–27.

A Child's Evolution. *America* 132, March 29, 1975, 236–38.

The Experience of Kinship. *America* 132, February 22, 1975, 131–32.

On People Getting the Wrong Idea. *America* 133, September 27, 1975, 168–69.

Maturity: A Biomedical or Political Concept. *Urban Review* 8, Fall 1975, 176–80.

A Child's Voice. *Social Policy,* May/June 1975, 42–46.

Going Up and Going Down: On IQ Testing. *Bulletin of the National Association of Elementary School Principals* 54, March/April 1975, 59–62.

The Affect of Sex Role Learning on Symbolic Representations of Time. *International Journal of Symbology* 6, March 1975, 10–19.

A Note on School Suspension. *National Catholic Reporter,* June 6, 1975.

Baseball Fan. *Moment* 1, July/August 1975, 42–44.

Exposing Ourselves in Public. *The New Republic* 172, March 8, 1975, 18–21.

Rich Kids Got Their Problems Too. *The New York Times,* July 7, 1975.

On Finding a School and the Realm of Depersonalized Humanism. *Principal* 55, January/February 1976, 97–99.

Science Atrocities. *The New Republic,* September 13, 1975, 5–6.

The Strange Child. *America,* November 1975, 318–22.

Bus Start. *The New York Times,* March 9, 1975, 16–24.

Dropping Out of the Bottom. *This Magazine Is About Schools*, March/April 9, 1975, 10 –11.

Matthew Washington Who Had Death in His Eyes. *Antioch Review* 34, Spring 1976, 265 –80.

Our Country's Neglected Children (with Marian Wright Edelman). *Parents Magazine*, December 1976, 36ff.

Angela: A Child-Woman. *Social Problems* 23, April 1976, 516 –23.

A Child out of School. *Colorado Quarterly* 24, Winter 1976, 289 –99.

An Analysis of the Phases of Development in Self Analytic Groups. In *Explorations in General Theory in Social Science; Essays in Honor of Talcott Parsons*, edited by Jan J. Loubser, Rainer Baum, Andrew Effrat, and Victor Lidz, New York: The Free Press, 1976, 328 –53.

Friday Afternoon Jew. *Moment* 1, January 1976, 45 –48.

Tennis, Bagels and the Melting Pot. *Moment* 1, April 1976, 49 –52.

The Battle for Progress in Islington. *Principal* 55, March/April 1976, 68 –70.

Seeing Fate With One's Own Eyes: School Leave Taking in Brixton. *Principal* 55, May/June 1976, 78 –80.

Oh, to Be in England. *The Boston Globe*, June 27, 1976.

Working Out Nice in Appalachia. *The Appalachian Journal* 4, Autumn 1976, 6 –9.

On Pubs, Browning Versions and Corporeal Punishment. *Principal* 55, July/August 1976, 70 –72.

The Politics of Maturity. *Aim* 3, May/June 1976, 33 –35.

On Familiarity, Classrooms and a Man from Stratford. *Principal* 56, September/October 1976, 69 –72.

In Exchange for Wine and Flowers. *Moment* 2, November 1976, 35 –40.

A Time Against Race. *Principal* 56, November/December 1976, 65 –68.

Teenagers in Jail. *The Los Angeles Times*, July 21, 1976, 7.

Busing, Seen from a Unique Perspective. *The Los Angeles Times*, September 10, 1976, 7.

The Voices of Agony. *Psychology Today* 10, June 1976, 101 –7.

School Suspension in America. *New Society* 37, September 30, 1976, 699 –701.

The Case of Wilson Diver. *Health Handbook*, Children's Defense Fund of the Washington Research Project, 1976, 5 –8.

Issues Wreck a Family's Beautiful Life. *The Washington Star*, October 3, 1976, B1ff.

Deprivation and American Character. In *The American Character: Essays in Honor of David Riesman*, Martin Kilson and Orlando Patterson (eds.), New Haven: Yale University Press, 1976.

The Return of the Bat Lady. *New Society* 40, May 5, 1977, 222 –24.

At 13, He's Out to Teach Britain History. *The Los Angeles Times* Part II, January 11, 1977, 5.

The Insurance Fire. *Moment* 2, October 1977, 52ff.

Nobody's Special When They're Poor. *The Yale Review* LXVI, Spring 1977, 388 –98.

One of Those Special Student Types. *Principal* 56, May/June 1977, 55 –60.

The Cost of Hope. *America* 136, February 12, 1977, 125 –27.

Jamie Horace Pinkerton. *America* 136, April 23, 1977, 370 –73.

A Slave to No One. *New Review* 4, May 1977, 45 –47.

SELECTED BIBLIOGRAPHY

The National Center for Art and Culture. *The Boston Globe,* May 22, 1977, A2.
A Wasted Death. *New Society* 41, September 29, 1977, 656 –57.
Sporting Assets. *The Boston Globe,* June 5, 1977, A3.
We're Either Dumb or Ugly. *The New York Times,* July 23, 1977.
The Feeling of Time. *Worldview,* September 1977.
The Case of Bobbie Dijon: Children in the Slammer. *The Washington Star,* October 30, 1977.
Children Can Die Too. *Youth in Society* No. 26, December 1977, 9 –12.
The Fault of Polly Davies. *The Progressive,* October 1977, 34 –36.
One Job and They Would Have Had Smooth Sailing. *The Boston Globe,* November 6, 1977, A2.
A Deadly Despair Stalks the Unemployed. *The Los Angeles Times,* October 30, 1977, Section 4.
The Fires of Eddie Harrington. *The New Leader,* January 16, 1978, 12 –15.
A Man Named Christmas. *The South Atlantic Quarterly* 77, Summer 1978, 307 –19.
The Politics of Maturity. *Youth in Society* 30, August 1978, 44 –45.
The Bedroom of Sheila Cooperton. *British Journal of Social Work,* 1978.
And We Have So Much to Teach. *New Society* 43, March 2, 1978, 483 –85.
The Cemetery Dweller. *America* 138, April 1, 1978, 260 –62.
A Woman Named Georgia Pointer. *Aim* 5, March/April 1978, 8 –11.
The Separatist. *Integrated Education* XVI, January/February 1978, 9 –12.
The Smell of Time: Portraits of the Aging. *Moment* 3, March 1978, 29 –38.
Room at the Top: Nowhere To Go But Up. *The Los Angeles Times,* January 27, 1978, Part II, 7.
Jack the Bomb Blum. *The New York Times,* April 8, 1978.
Probing the Perils of Inner and Outer Space. *The Los Angeles Times,* February 8, 1978.
Working for the Man. *Urban Education* 12, No. 2, July, 1978.
The Hero Is Time. *Perspectives* 6, Spring 1978, 2ff.
Mr. Housewife, USA, *The Progressive* 42, October 1978, 48 –50.
The Holy Trinity. *The Boston Globe Magazine,* July 23, 1978, 2.
Urbanism as a Way of Life. *The New Republic,* June 17, 1978, 44 –47.
The Slide of Menachem Kanter. *The Los Angeles Times,* May 7, 1978.
Race Prejudice in Britain. *The Boston Globe,* May 28, 1978, A2.
A Certain Number of No's. *America* 139, October 1978, 218 –21.
The Causes of Juvenile Crime. *Aim* 5, June 1978, 29 –32.
I Do. I Do? *Moment* 3, June 1978, 24 –28.
I Do. I Do? Part II. *Moment* 3, July/August 1978, 50 –57.
The Move of Jacob Portman. *Moment* 4, November 1978, 51 –54.
It's City Life That Killed Him. Really. *The Washington Star,* May 28, 1978 D1.
Dying of the City Disease. *The Los Angeles Times,* June 27, 1978.
Enough of a Souvenir. *Worldview* 21, December 1978, 37 –40.
A Lonely Man's Decision to Die. *The Boston Globe,* July 23, 1978.
The Hardest Years. *Win Magazine,* July 27, 1978.
Cranepool the Janitor. *Psychology Today* 12, December 1978, 122 –27.
A Piece Chocolate. *Moment* 3, October 1978, 56 –57.

In Today's America Nobody Loves a Loser. *The Los Angeles Times,* November 5, 1978.

A Handful of Bullets. *New Society* 44, May 25, 1978, 418–20.

Private Lives and Public Accounts. *Biography* 1, No. 1, Winter 1978, 23–39.

The Props of Success. *Los Angeles Herald Examiner,* December 3, 1978.

The Act of Success. *Los Angeles Herald Examiner,* December 31, 1978.

Impotence as Success. *Los Angeles Herald Examiner,* December 24, 1978.

Doing It Successfully. *Los Angeles Herald Examiner,* December 10, 1978.

The Pretense of Success. *Los Angeles Herald Examiner,* December 17, 1978.

For Jewish Children 'Tis the Season for Confusion. *The Los Angeles Times,* December 24, 1978.

New School Maker. *Testing Digest,* Spring 1979, 6.

Count Every Single Child. *New Society* 48, May 24, 1979, 445–47.

Crime in Schools. *Crime and Delinquency* 25, July 1979, 318–34.

Immigration to England. *Urban Education* 14, No. 1, April 1979, 5–17.

The Mechanical Man. *Psychology Today* 13, July 1979, 94–95.

An American Family. In *On The Making of Americans: Essays in Honor of David Riesman,* Herbert Gans and Nathan Glazer (eds.), Philadelphia: University of Pennsylvania Press, 1979.

The Boundaries of Prejudice. *Integrated Education* 17, January–April 1979, 51–57.

Just a Memory. *Moment* 4, July/August 1979, 48–52.

An Unusual Gift. *Working Mother* 2, November 1979, 81*ff.*

The Trouble at School. *Working Mother* 2, September 1979, 69*ff.*

Pregnant with What? *Psychology Today* 13, September 1979, 89–91.

The Growing Racial Ugliness in the Once Majestic England. *Los Angeles Herald Examiner,* April 29, 1979.

Foreword to *Cedarview Caretakers* by David R. Buckholdt and Jaber F. Gubrium. Sage Publications, 1979.

A Job for Ollie Sindon. *The Progressive* 43, October 1979, 52–54.

A Correct Life, A Single Regret. *Psychology Today* 13, November 1979, 138–40.

The Trial of Elaine Harrington. *Commonweal,* July 6, 1979.

Playing with the Souls of Your Children. *Learning Today* 12, Winter 1979, 18–21.

Profiles of Adolescents. *Psychology Today,* February 1979, 40*ff.*

Failure of a Mother's Son. *The New Leader* LXII, September 24, 1979, 11–17.

Judy Kreston and the Magnificent Seven. *Moment,* November 1979, 52–53.

A Familiar Problem. *Los Angeles Herald Examiner,* November 11, 1979.

The Price of Growing Up Poor. *The Washington Post,* December 2, 1979, D5.

Impoverishing the Poor. *The New Leader,* February 26, 1979, 10–12.

A Very Special Mother. *Working Mother* II, July 1979, 60*ff.*

The Sex Machine. *A Review,* Amherst College, 8, 1980.

Mama's Boy. *Psychology Today* 14, June 1980, 110.

The Secret Self at 83. *Psychology Today* 13, May 1980, 98.

To Success and Good Friends. *Worldview* 23, September 1980, 8–10.

A Special Place to Go. *Working Mother,* January 1980, 110*ff.*

The Same Old Me, Only Slightly Different. *Working Mother,* March 1980, 74*ff.*

Overcoming an Invisible Handicap. *Psychology Today* 13, January 1980, 89.

Family Secrets. *McCalls,* February 1980, 104*ff.*

A Gentleman Caller. *The Antioch Review* 38, Summer 1980, 365–70.

Getting Children out of Jail. *Aim* 7 No. 1, Winter 1979/1980, 5–8.

Invitation to a Teenager. *Working Mother* 3, May 1980, 98*ff.*

The Happy Malones. *The Boston Globe Magazine,* January 6, 1980, 9*ff.*

A Special Salesperson. *Moment* 5, June 1980, 55–57.

The Young Watch Television. *Panorama* 1, September 1980, 78–81.

Mother, Am I Pretty? *Working Mother* III, July 1980, 80*ff.*

Morning of the Dead Life. *Christianity and Crisis* 40, March 17, 1980, 50*ff.*

A Father Dead or Alive. *Christianity and Crisis* 40, June 9, 1980, 180–82.

Good-bye, Kids, Mother's Leaving Home. *The Atlantic,* March 1980, 43–48.

A Mother, a Father, a Santa Claus, a Woody Allen. *Moment* 5, January/February 1980, 48–49.

Two Against the Tide. *Psychology Today* 15, January 1980, 18*ff.*

The Last Cranky Man. *Psychology Today* 14. October 1980, 108.

The Boogie People. *Learning Today* 13, Spring 1980, 18–21.

The Whiz Kid's Sister. *Working Mother,* January 1981, 79–80.

A Dirty Joke. *Youth in Society* 54, May 1981, 18–19.

Teaching Children Right from Wrong. *Family Weekly,* September 20, 1981, 4*ff.*

The Moment of Truth: Breaking the News of Divorce. *Working Mother,* November 1981, 68*ff.*

Keeping Secrets. *Youth in Society* 53, April 1981, 214–15.

The Strange Child. *Children's World* 12, Winter 1981, 11*ff.*

Curtains of the Past. *Moment* 7, March 1982, 55*ff.*

Mikko Delano: A Case Study in Moral Development. In *The Development of Social Maturity,* edited by David C. McClelland. New York: Irvington Publishers, 1982, 36–54.

The Life Study: On Mutual Recognition and the Subjective Inquiry. In *Field Research: A Sourcebook and Field Manual,* edited by Robert G. Burgess. London: George Allen & Unwin, 1982, 123–30.

When Cohabitation Isn't Good Enough (with Cathy Stein Greenblat). *New England Bride,* May 1982, 32*ff.*

A Father's Death. *Youth in Society* 63, February 1982, 9*ff.*

The Last Angry Men, Part I. *Moment* 7, May 1982, 29*ff.*

The Last Angry Men, Part II. *Moment* 7, July–August 1982, 35*ff.*

Getting Married (with Cathy Stein Greenblat). *New England Bride* 10, January 1982, 28*ff.*

February: The Month's Scandals in Review. *The Tab,* April 11, 1989, 29.

Male-Bashing: The Favorite Sport of American Popular Culture. *The Hartford Courant,* June 19, 1989, C7.

Ode to College Recruiters. *The Los Angeles Times,* March 11, 1989, 8.

Making State Government Foot the Bill. *The Boston Globe,* August 20, 1989, A17*ff.*

Heart Medicine. *Salt,* Vol. 10, No. 7, July/August 1989, 21–22.

The Right to Silence. *The Boston Herald,* November 26, 1989.

A Son Dies of AIDS. *The New Leader* 13, November 13, 1989, 15–17.

If Ads Follow Kids to School One Day. *The Hartford Courant,* April 25, 1989, B9.

The Cult of Personality. *The Tab*, July 25, 1989.

Esther Crighton Has Respect. *The Los Angeles Times*, September 10, 1989.

A Fan of Lucy's. *Television Quarterly*, Volume XXIV, No. 11, 1989, 81–82.

A Retirement Account. *Antioch Review*, Volume 48, Fall 1990, 430–38.

Men, Women and Crime. *The Tab*, February 13, 1990, 16.

School Closing. *Urban Education* 25, Number 1, April 1990, 37–42.

Press 9 If You're Losing Your Mind. *The Boston Phoenix*, January 12, 1990, 22.

Throwing a Curve at Our Teachers. *The Boston Globe*, January 7, 1990.

For Patriotic Reasons. *Read Me*, Vol. 3, Number 2, Fall 1990, 19.

Free Fall: An Atomic Veteran Speaks. *Christianity and Crisis*, February 19, 1990, 39–42.

When the Mighty Fall, and We Delight. *St. Louis Post Dispatch*, January 14, 1990, 3B.

Bostonians Confronted Their Shadows. *The Hartford Courant*, February 1, 1990.

On Recognizing Recognition and Distraction. *Quality Living* No. 13, Spring 1990, 16–18.

Big Earthquakes, Little Children. *Children Today*, September–October 1990, 13.

My Brother's Keeper. *Urban Education* 25, No. 32, October 1990, 289–96.

A Clean but Dull White House. *The Tab*, April 3, 1990.

Stretching the Truth. *Boston Herald*, April 14, 1990.

The Ache of Middle Age. *Boston Globe Magazine*, September 9, 1990, 24–30.

A Need For Reading. *The Chicago Tribune*, November 11, 1990, Section 14.

I've Got a Problem but I Can't, Uh, Remember What It Was. *Newsday*, November 4, 1990.

Don't Fret if Your Child Is Shy. *The Hartford Courant*, December 25, 1990.

Manchild in the Classroom. *Newsday*, November 28, 1990, 64.

The Invisible Causes of Illness. *The Tab*, November 27, 1990, 19*ff.*

A Family Prepares for College. *The Journal of Higher Education*, Vol. 62, No. 1, January/February 1991, 79–86.

Uncle Sam Let Bernie Durkin, Nuke Vet, Down. *The Sacramento Bee*, March 23, 1991, B7.

Muscles and Misogyny. *Newsday*, April 12, 1991.

Trapped by Scholastic Testing. *The Sacramento Bee*, May 15, 1991, B9.

When Poetry's Metaphors Are Children's Dreams. *The Sacramento Bee*, July 6, 1991.

Dr. Paulie's Snowstorm. *The New Leader*, August 12, 1991, 12–14.

(with Edward M. Gillis) Surviving the College Admissions Maze. *Private Colleges and Universities Magazine*, 1992.

Child Murder. *Social Justice Review*, January/February 1992, 15–17.

Anything Good in the Mail Today? *Salt*, Volume 12, February 1992, 21.

Fault Lines. *Quality Living*, Summer 1992, 12–14.

Kids Shouldn't Have to Reach for the Stars. *Salt*, April 1992, 21.

The Secret of Tessie Blake. *The Sacramento Bee*, February 14, 1992.

Researching the Hard Core Unemployed. *America*, December 19, 1992, 492–93.

When You Stop, You Die. *Commonweal*, June 19, 1992, 15–18.

Kids Stir Memories of Father. *Boston Sunday Herald*, June 21, 1992.

Alfred Syre Doesn't Work Here Anymore. *Salt,* October, 1992, 16.

A Universal Salary for Teachers. *The Tab,* July 14, 1992.

Unemployment Is a Killer Disease. *USA Today,* August 6, 1992, 13A.

The Terrible Human Toll of Unemployment. *The Sacramento Bee,* August 26, 1992.

An American Nightmare. *Boston Business Journal,* September 28, 1992, 15.

The Subtlety of Racism. *The Tab,* October 13, 1992, 55.

Voters Decided to Take a Risk Despite Fear of Change. *The Hartford Courant,* November 8, 1992.

The Art of Distraction. *Antioch Review,* Vol. 51, No. 2, Spring 1993, 283–93.

Witness of Joy. *Daedalus,* Vol. 122, No. 1, Winter, 1993, 123–50.

On Truth and Distraction. *Jewish Spectator,* Vol. 58, No. 2, Fall 1993, 5–7.

Trauma of Sex Abuse Can Last a Lifetime. *The Hartford Courant,* August 15, 1993.

Life Among the Unemployed. *The New Leader,* Vol. LXXVI, No. 10, August 9–23, 1993, 10–12.

Changing Family, Enduring Child. *Children's World,* Summer, July 1993, 4–11.

Reflecting on the Face on the TV Screen. *The Chicago Tribune,* October 6, 1993.

Women Who Kill. *North American Review,* May/June 1994, 4–9.

The Spirit of Work. *The Way,* Vol. 34, No. 2, April 1994, 95–105.

Playing Cerebral Catch. *University of Chicago Magazine,* June 1995, 5–6.

Conditional Love Comes from Precocious Insurance Agents. *The Sacramento Bee,* February 25, 1996, Forum, 3.

Final Destination. *Massachusetts Psychological Quarterly* 40, October 1996, 3.

When a Child Is Murdered (with Alvin F. Poussaint). *The Los Angeles Times,* January 23, 1997.

Graduation Speech. *Massachusetts Psychology Quarterly* 41, July 1997, 3ff.

Medicare Fraud and the Role of Morality. *Massachusetts Psychological Quarterly* 41, October 1997, 3.

The Child at Risk: The Case for the Youthful Offender. *Boston University Journal of Education,* Vol. 180, No. 2, 1998, 95–113.

The Voice of Harassment. *Massachusetts Psychological Quarterly,* Vol. 42, No. 2, July 1998, 3ff.

Special Education: A Test of Liberal Democracy with Gerald S. Fain. *Journal of Education, Boston University Journal of Education,* Vol. 180, No. 2, 1998.

Adolescent Criminals: Where Do They Come From? Where Do They Go? *The Brown University Child and Adolescent Behavior Letter,* Vol. 14, No. 11, November 1998, 8.

Turf-Related Violence Has Deep Psychological Roots. *Boston Herald,* November 14, 1998.

It's All in the Words. *Massachusetts Psychological Association Quarterly* 42, October 1998.

The Cost (Effectiveness) of Children. *The ATA Magazine,* Vol. 79, No. 3, 1999, 12–16.

The Boundaries of Murder. *Massachusetts Psychological Association Quarterly* 42, No. 1, January 1999, 17ff.

Offering Expressions of Turpitude to the Next Generation. *The Hartford Courant,* January 8, 1999.

The Passing of a Mother. *Massachusetts Psychological Association Quarterly,* Vol. 42, Summer 1999, 23*ff.*

Introducing the Violence Added Tax. *Massachusetts Psychological Quarterly,* Vol. 42, April 1999, 17–18.

Brain Dead. *Education Week,* Vol. XIX, September 22, 1999, 30*ff.*

Am I Worthy of Those Sacrifices? *The Los Angeles Times,* Metro Section, May 31, 1999.

Too Much Self Reflection Yields Too Little Insight. *The Brown University Child and Adolescent Behavior Letter,* Vol. 15, August 1999, 8.

The Value of Stories: Applications for Research and Healing. *Journal of Applied Sociology,* Vol. 16, No. 1, 1999, 14–37.

Getting Back on Track. *Massachusetts Psychological Association Quarterly* 42, Fall 1999, 29–30.

Mind Shadows: A Suicide in the Family. *Journal of Contemporary Ethnography,* Vol. 29, No. 2, April 2000, 222–55.

Television as Intelligence. *Television Quarterly,* Vol. 31, Summer/Fall 2000, 63–67.

The Value of Family Values. *Massachusetts Psychological Association Quarterly,* Vol. 44, No. 1, Winter 2000, 29*ff.*

Elian Is Giving Psychologists Fame. *The Pulse.* ABCNews.com. April 26, 2000.

Strive to Eliminate Student Shame, Exclusionary Culture from Schools (with Daniel B. Frank). *Brown University Child and Adolescent Behavior Letter* 16, July 2000, 1*ff.*

True Teaching Is Helping Students Find Their Hearts. *The Baltimore Sun,* June 21, 2000, 19A.

Let's Play Discourse. *Massachusetts Psychological Association Quarterly* 44, Spring–Summer 2000, 49.

Beware the Result of a Child Shamed (with Daniel B. Frank). *The Baltimore Sun,* September 14, 2000.

The Prize of Reflection. *The McNeese Review,* Vol. 38, 2000, 81–92.

Teachers Do Deserve Apples. *The Baltimore Sun,* December 12, 2000, 33A.

Booth Story. *Antioch Review* 59, No. 1, Winter 2001, 58–66.

School Peril. *Education Week,* May 30, 2001, 34.

The Reflection of Values: A Response to Toni Morrison. *Michigan Quarterly Review,* Vol. XL, Spring 2001, 279–87.

Book Review of *Glued to the Tube: The Threat of Television Addiction to Today's Family* by Cheryl Pawlowski, *Television Quarterly,* Vol. 36, No. 4, Winter 2001, 79–82.

A Plea for Thinking Heads. *Liberal Education,* in press.

A Point Needs to Be Made About Slighting the Spiritual. *The Boston Herald,* March 24, 2001, 14.

The Story of Elian and the Healers. *Massachusetts Psychological Association Quarterly,* Vol. 45, No. 1, April 2001, 26*ff.*

Money Doesn't Buy Everything (with Samantha Stuart). *Children First,* Vol. 5, June/July 2001, 22–23.

Going to Israel with the Goldsteins. *The Jewish Spectator,* Vol. 65, Winter 2001, 31–32.

Adolescent as Story Teller: The Case of Anorexia Nervosa. *Journal of Child and Youth Care,* Vol. 15–16, 2001, 313–24.

Treasure Those Who Can Teach. *The Baltimore Sun,* July 22, 2001, 3C.

Former Houseguest Recalls Stern Lessons in Life, Friendship, Courage. *The Baltimore Sun,* October 2, 2001; reprinted as Godfather Isaac Stern Showed How to Live. *The Hartford Courant,* October 5, 2001, A13.

Never Read Kafka! *The ATA Magazine,* Vol. 82, no. 1, Fall 2001, 16–19.

On Narratives and the Sense of Self. *Qualitative Inquiry,* in press.

A Thought on Premeditated Violence. *Massachusetts Psychological Quarterly,* Vol. 45, no. 3, November 2001, 34.

The Affirming Ritual of Bedtime Reading. *The Family Digest,* in press.

The Beginning, Middle and In Between of Adolescence. *Midwest Quarterly,* in press.

Foreword to *A Different Drummer: The History of Columbia College Chicago,* by Mike Alexandroff. Chicago: Columbia College Press, in press.

The Injury of Shame. *McNeese Review,* in press.

The Perils Outside Us. *Massachusetts Psychological Quarterly,* Vol. 45, June 2001, 24*ff.*

Screen Speak. *Small Press Review,* in press.

Societal Peril. *Child and Youth Care Forum,* in press.

Book review of *Social Class, Poverty, and Education.* Bruce Biddle, ed. *Columbia Teachers College Record,* in press.